Here are your

1997 SCIENCE YEAR Cross-Reference Tabs

For insertion in your WORLD BOOK

Each year, SCIENCE YEAR, THE WORLD BOOK ANNUAL SCIENCE SUPPLEMENT, adds a valuable dimension to your WORLD BOOK set. The Cross-Reference Tab System is designed especially to help you link SCIENCE YEAR'S major articles to the related WORLD BOOK articles that they update.

How to use these Tabs:

First, remove this page from SCIENCE YEAR.

Begin with the first Tab, **Archaeology**. Take the A volume of your WORLD BOOK set and find the **Archaeology** article. Moisten the **Archaeology** Tab and affix it to that page.

Glue all the other Tabs in the appropriate WORLD BOOK volumes. Your set's M volume does not have an article on **Motor oil**. Put the **Motor oil** Tab in its correct alphabetical location in that volume—near the **Motorboat racing** article.

SCIENCE
YEAR
1997

The World Book Annual Science Supplement

A review of Science and Technology
During the 1996 School Year

World Book, Inc.

a Scott Fetzer company

Chicago • London • Sydney • Toronto

The Year's Major Science Stories

From the discovery of planets orbiting other suns to an important advance in the development of microscopic machines, it was an eventful year in science and technology. On these two pages are the stories *Science Year* editors chose as the most memorable or important of the year, along with details on where to find information about them in the book.　　*The Editors*

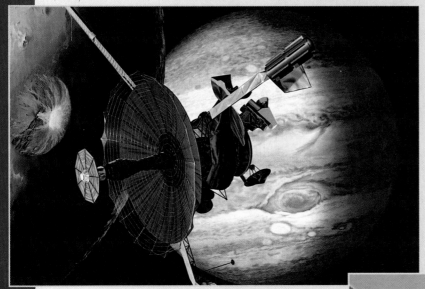

◀ **Galileo reaches Jupiter**
After a six-year journey, the Galileo spacecraft went into orbit around Jupiter in December 1995. A probe that Galileo had released in July 1995 descended toward Jupiter's surface and sent back data on the planet's atmosphere. In the Science News Update section, see ASTRONOMY, SPACE TECHNOLOGY.

A micromotor with muscle ▶
The first micromotor fabricated with the same silicon-etching methods used to make computer chips and able to drive a system of gears was announced in September 1995 by researchers at Sandia National Laboratories in Albuquerque, New Mexico. In the Science News Update section, see ENGINEERING.

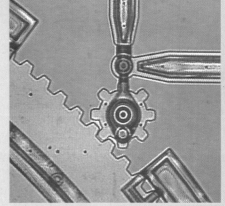

Alzheimer's disease genes found
Two faulty genes that may cause virtually all cases of a deadly brain disorder called familial Alzheimer's disease were discovered in 1995 by researchers in Canada and the United States. In the Science News Update section, see GENETICS.

World Book, Inc.
525 W. Monroe
Chicago, IL 60661

ISBN: 0-7166-0597-X
ISSN: 0080-7621
Library of Congress Catalog Number: 65-21776
Printed in the United States of America.

Largest predatory dinosaur
The remains of a previously unknown species of dinosaur, which may have been the largest meat-eating dinosaur that ever lived, were found in Argentina in 1995. The dinosaur, named *Giganotosaurus carolinii*, lived about 100 million years ago. In the Science News Update section see FOSSIL STUDIES (Close-Up)

Spectacular comet

A bright comet, named Hyakutake for its Japanese discoverer, amateur astronomer Yuki Hyakutake, glowed in the night sky during part of March and April 1996. In the Science News Update section, see ASTRONOMY.

Andean "Ice Maiden" ▶

The mummified body of a 12- to 14-year-old Inca girl was discovered in the Andes Mountains of Peru in September 1995. The girl, who died about 500 years ago, was probably a sacrificial victim. Two more Inca mummies were found the next month. In the Science News Update section, see ARCHAEOLOGY.

Advances in physics

Low-temperature physicists in Boulder, Colorado, in July 1995 reported creating a new state of matter called a Bose-Einstein condensate. In January 1996, European researchers announced that they had made atoms of a rare form of matter called antimatter. In the Science News Update section see PHYSICS; PHYSICS (Close-Up).

New planets discovered

Astronomers in the United States and Europe announced in 1995 and 1996 that they had found evidence for stars orbiting several other suns in the Milky Way galaxy. In the Science News Update section, see ASTRONOMY (CLOSE-UP).

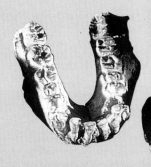

◀ Our oldest ancestor?

Fossils some 4 million years old, found in Kenya in 1995, are from the earliest known species in the human line. In the Science News Update section, see ANTHROPOLOGY.

Contents

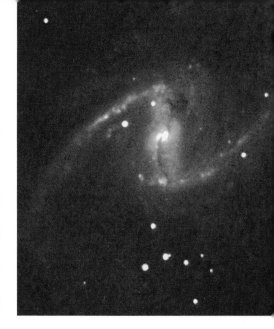

Page 40

Page 142

Science News Update ···················· 162

Twenty-eight articles, arranged alphabetically, report on the year's most important developments in all major areas of science and technology, from *Agriculture* to *Space Technology*. In addition, five Close-Up articles focus on especially noteworthy developments:

Page 241

Science You Can Use ·············· 275

Five articles present various topics in science and technology as they apply to the consumer.

World Book Supplement ·············· 299

Nine new and revised articles from the 1996 edition of *The World Book Encyclopedia:* **Immune System; Ice Age; Uranium; Uranus; Internet; Element, Chemcial; Radiation; Electricity;** and **Seven Natural Wonders of the World.**

Index ··············· 337

A cumulative index of topics covered in the 1997, 1996, and 1995 editions of Science Year.

Cross-Reference Tabs

A tear-out page of cross-reference tabs for insertion in *The World Book Encyclopedia* appears before page 1.

Staff

Editorial Advisory Board

Contributors

Asker, James R., B.A.
Washington Bureau Chief,
Aviation Week & Space Technology
magazine.
[*Space Technology*]

Bahn, Paul G., M.A., Ph.D.
Free-Lance Archaeologist,
United Kingdom.
[Special Report, *The First Artists*]

Bolen, Eric G., B.S., M.S., Ph.D.
Professor,
Department of Biological Sciences,
University of North Carolina at
Wilmington.
[*Conservation*]

Brett, Carlton E., Ph.D.
Professor,
Department of Geological Sciences,
University of Rochester.
[*Fossil Studies; Fossil Studies* (Close-Up)]

Cain, Steven A., B.S.
Communication Specialist,
Purdue University School of
Agriculture.
[*Agriculture*]

Chiras, Dan, B.A., Ph.D.
Adjunct Professor,
Environmental Policy and
Management Program,
University of Denver.
[*Environmental Pollution*]

Cosgrove, Daniel J., Ph.D.
Professor of Biology,
Pennsylvania State University.
[*Biology*]

Ferrell, Keith
Author and Former Editor-in-Chief,
OMNI magazine.
[Science Studies, *The Computer
Comes of Age*; Computers and
Electronics]

Goodman, Richard A., M.D., M.P.H.
Adjunct Professor,
Division of Epidemiology,
Emory University.
[*Public Health*]

Graff, Gordon, B.S., Ph.D.
Free-Lance Science Writer.
[*Chemistry*; Science You Can Use,
*Lessening the Hazards of Home
Pesticides*]

Hay, William W., B.A., M.S., Ph.D.
Professor of Geological Sciences,
University of Colorado at Boulder.
[*Geology*]

Haymer, David S., M.S., Ph.D.
Professor,
Department of Genetics,
University of Hawaii.
[*Genetics*]

Hermann, Richard C., M.D.
Fellow,
Department of Psychiatry,
Harvard University Medical School.
[*Psychology*]

Hester, Thomas R., B.A., Ph.D.
Professor of Anthropology and
Director,
Texas Archeological Research
Laboratory,
University of Texas at Austin.
[*Archaeology*]

Klein, Richard G., Ph.D.
Professor of Human Biology,
Stanford University.
[*Anthropology*]

Kolberg, Rebecca, B.S., M.A.
Managing Editor,
The NIH Catalyst.
[Science You Can Use, *Bad Hair Days:
A Case of Bad Chemistry*]

Kowal, Deborah, M.A.
Adjunct Assistant Professor,
Emory University School of Public
Health.
[*Public Health*]

Limburg, Peter R., B.A., M.A.
Free-Lance Writer.
[Science You Can Use, *Recycling
Used Motor Oil*]

Linhardt, Robert J., Ph.D.
Professor of Medicinal and Natural
Products Chemistry,
College of Pharmacy,
University of Iowa.
[*Drugs* (Close-Up)]

Lunine, Jonathan I., B.S., M.S.,
Ph.D.
Professor of Planetary Science,
University of Arizona.
[*Astronomy*]

Luoma, Jon R., B.A.
Writer.
[Special Report, *A Comeback for Lake
Erie*]

Maran, Stephen P., B.S., M.A., Ph.D.
Press Officer,
American Astronomical Society.
[*Astronomy* (Close-Up)]

March, Robert H., A.B., M.S., Ph.D.
Professor of Physics and Liberal
Studies,
University of Wisconsin at Madison.
[*Physics; Physics* (Close-Up)]

Marschall, Laurence A., B.S., Ph.D.
Professor of Physics,
Gettysburg College.
[Special Report, *How Old is the
Universe?; Books About Science*]

Moser-Veillon, Phylis B., B.S., M.S.,
Ph.D.
Professor,
Department of Nutrition and Food
Science,
University of Maryland.
[*Nutrition;* Science You Can Use,
*Bottled Water vs. Tap: Is It Any
Tastier or Safer?*]

Peterson, Ray G., B.S., Ph.D.
Research Oceanographer,
Scripps Institute of Oceanography,
University of California at San Diego.
[*Oceanography*]

Phillips, Edward H., B.A.
Air Transport Editor,
Aviation Week & Space Technology
magazine.
[Special Report, *Learning Why
Airplanes Crash*]

Riley, Thomas N., Ph.D.
Professor,
Auburn University School of
Pharmacy.
[*Drugs*]

Sforza, Pasquale M., B.Ae.E., M.S.,
Ph.D.
Professor of Mechanical and
Aerospace Engineering,
Polytechnic University.
[*Energy*]

Snow, John T., Ph.D.
Dean,
College of Geosciences,
University of Oklahoma.
[*Atmospheric Sciences*]

Snow, Theodore P., B.A., M.S.,
Ph.D.
Professor of Astrophysics and
Director,
Center for Astrophysics and Space
Astronomy,
University of Colorado at Boulder.
[*Astronomy*]

Stephenson, Joan, B.S., Ph.D.
Associate Editor, Medical News,
Journal of the American Medical
Association.
[Science You Can Use, *Loud Music's Assault on Your Hearing*]

Tamarin, Robert H., B.S., Ph.D.
Professor and Chairman,
Biology Department,
Boston University.
[*Ecology*]

Teich, Albert H., B.S., Ph.D.
Director,
Science and Policy Programs,
American Association for the
Advancement of Science.
[*Science and Society*]

Trefil, James, Ph.D.
Clarence J. Robinson Professor of
Physics,
George Mason University.
[Special Report, *The Search for the First Cell*]

Trubo, Richard, B.A., M.A.
Free-Lance Medical Writer.
[*Medical Research; Medical Research (Close-Up)*]

Walter, Eugene J., Jr., B.A.
Free-Lance Writer.
[Special Report, *Wildlife in Our Cities*]

Woods, Michael, B.S.
Science Editor,
The Toledo Blade.
[Special Report, *Science in Antarctica;* Science Studies, *The Computer Comes of Age; Engineering*]

Feature articles take an in-depth look at significant and timely subjects in science and technology.
● ●

The First Artists

Ice Age art found in a cave in southeast France is challenging archaeologists' assumptions about the development of prehistoric art.

BY PAUL G. BAHN

Jean-Marie Chauvet, a French archaeological official, was inspecting caves in southeast France when a breeze coming from a pile of rocks indicated the presence of an underground cave. Chauvet and his colleagues removed enough rocks to clear a narrow passageway into the cave and squeezed through the opening. Using a rope ladder, they descended to the cave floor, about 10 meters (30 feet) below, and found themselves in a huge network of passages, stretching for hundreds of meters, and decorated with some 300 paintings and engravings of animals. Images of mammoths, reindeer, bison, rhinoceroses, lions, and other creatures that roamed Europe thousands of years ago were engraved into the rock walls or painted in tones of red and black. Many of these images were remarkable for their beauty and sophisticated technique. But they were noteworthy for another reason: They were made by artists who lived during the last Ice Age and proved to be the oldest known cave art in the world.

This discovery of prehistoric cave art was made in December 1994. The art in the cave—named Chauvet for its main discoverer—called into question many theories and assump-

Christian Hillaire, a codiscoverer of Chauvet Cave, inspects its remarkable paintings, *left*. Toward the bottom of the wall is an image of two rhinoceroses fighting head-to-head. Rhinoceros images are rare in Ice Age cave art.

tions about the world's first artists. The artworks in the cave and what they tell us about the early development of art are certain to be discussed by archaeologists for years to come.

Beginning about 40,000 years ago, during the last Ice Age, cave artists created thousands of striking images of animals and human beings, as well as mysterious drawings whose meaning may be lost forever. Many of Chauvet Cave's figures display great skill and a mastery of several painting techniques. Such sophisticated cave art was generally thought to have been created toward the end of the Ice Age—from about 20,000 to 12,000 years ago. But when scientists examined charcoal samples taken from three figures at Chauvet Cave using a technique called radiocarbon analysis, they determined that the art had been created 30,000 to 32,000 years ago. (See HOW ARCHAEOLOGISTS DATE ICE AGE ART.)

Archaeologists had previously assumed that figures that appear similar in style or technique were made at roughly the same time. Most specialists imagined that there had been an overall progression from simple, crude-looking images to complex, detailed, accurate figures of animals. The sophisticated art of Chauvet Cave challenged archaeologists to look at Ice Age art in a new way, and to recognize that it did not have a single beginning and a single climax. A number of styles and techniques probably coexisted, as well as a wide range of talent and ability among the artists.

New discoveries of decorated Ice Age caves often lead archaeologists to reevaluate what they know about cave art, the techniques used to produce it, and its function in the lives of the people who created it. Researchers today believe that cave art may have played a major part in rituals or ceremonies that were important to Ice Age people. Further study may reveal whether Chauvet Cave was the site of such rituals.

Chauvet Cave has unique features that make it an important archaeological find. The cave's artwork includes images of the animals that are normally most frequent in European cave art—horses, bison, wild oxen, and deer. But the cave is dominated by figures of rhinoceroses and big cats, animals that Ice Age artists rarely depicted in other caves. And unlike many other decorated Ice Age caves, Chauvet appears to be completely intact, its original entrance blocked during the Ice Age. Because the cave had long been sealed, its floor was just as the artists left it, enabling archaeologists to study any footprints, tools, animal bones, and painting materials left by the ancient artists. Chauvet Cave will provide new evidence to help archaeologists understand how and why Ice Age art developed.

The author:
Paul G. Bahn is a freelance writer, translator, and broadcaster who specializes in archaeology and prehistoric art.

The first discoveries of Ice Age art

The existence of Ice Age art was first established in the early 1860's through the discovery of small decorated objects in a number of caves and rock shelters in southwest France. These objects—which archaeologists call *portable art*—comprise a wide variety of materials and forms, including shells or bones that were cut to form beads, engravings on

Discovery of Ice Age art

Ice Age art has been found in several regions of the world, including Australia, southern Africa, Europe, and Russia. The majority of known Ice Age decorated caves are located in southern France and northern Spain, and cave art has been studied most extensively in that region.

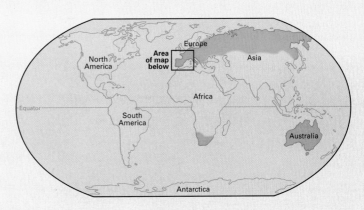

Lascaux, a world-famous decorated Ice Age cave, was discovered in 1940 by four teenagers who entered the cave to look for their dog. Lascaux contains numerous images of bulls, deer, and horses. The animals often appear grouped together in *friezes,* horizontal bands of decoration around the cave.

Pech Merle, discovered in 1922 by two teenage boys, contains a famous image of two spotted horses standing "back to back," with overlapping hind quarters. One of the horses was painted on a horse-shaped section of rock. The horses are marked with spots, hand stencils, and an image identified as a fish.

Chauvet, found in 1994 by French archaeological official Jean-Marie Chauvet, contains about 300 paintings, including rarely seen images of rhinoceroses and large cats. The Chauvet paintings are the oldest dated cave art in the world.

Altamira contains cave art that was found in 1879 by a Spanish land-owner, Marcelino Sanz de Sautuola, and his young daughter. It features striking images of bison and deer on the walls and ceiling. For many years, the Altamira paintings were considered a hoax. But in 1902, after Sautuola's death, they were recognized as Ice Age art.

Le Tuc d'Audoubert and Les Trois Frères both contain cave art that was discovered in the early 1900's by three brothers. Le Tuc d'Audoubert includes two clay sculptures of bison, each about 60 centimeters (24 inches) long. Les Trois Frères (The Three Brothers), contains engravings of horses, reindeer, bison, and other animals.

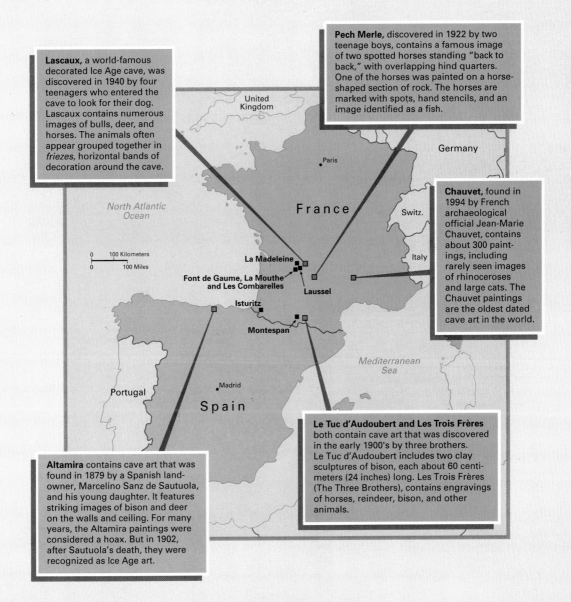

Ice Age paintings

Artists of the Ice Age used natural minerals and charcoal to paint animal images in tones of black, brown, red, and yellow. They also painted hand stencils and many mysterious symbols.

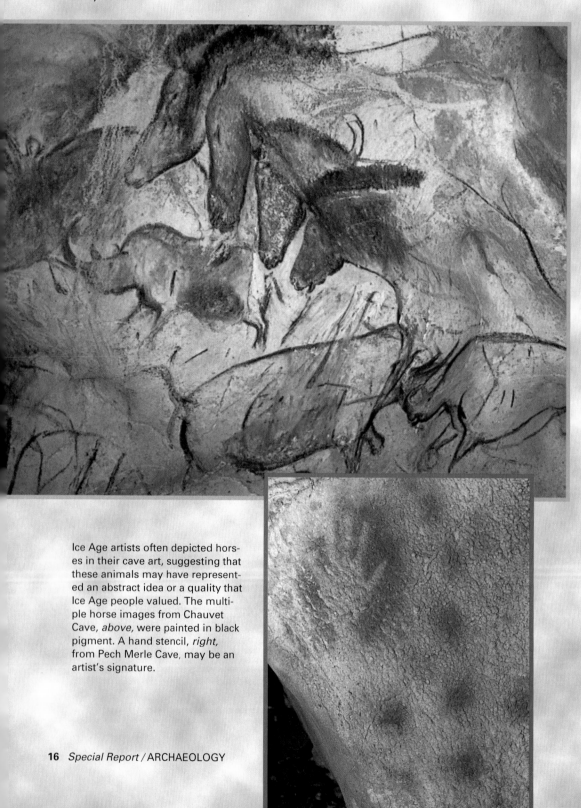

Ice Age artists often depicted horses in their cave art, suggesting that these animals may have represented an abstract idea or a quality that Ice Age people valued. The multiple horse images from Chauvet Cave, *above,* were painted in black pigment. A hand stencil, *right,* from Pech Merle Cave, may be an artist's signature.

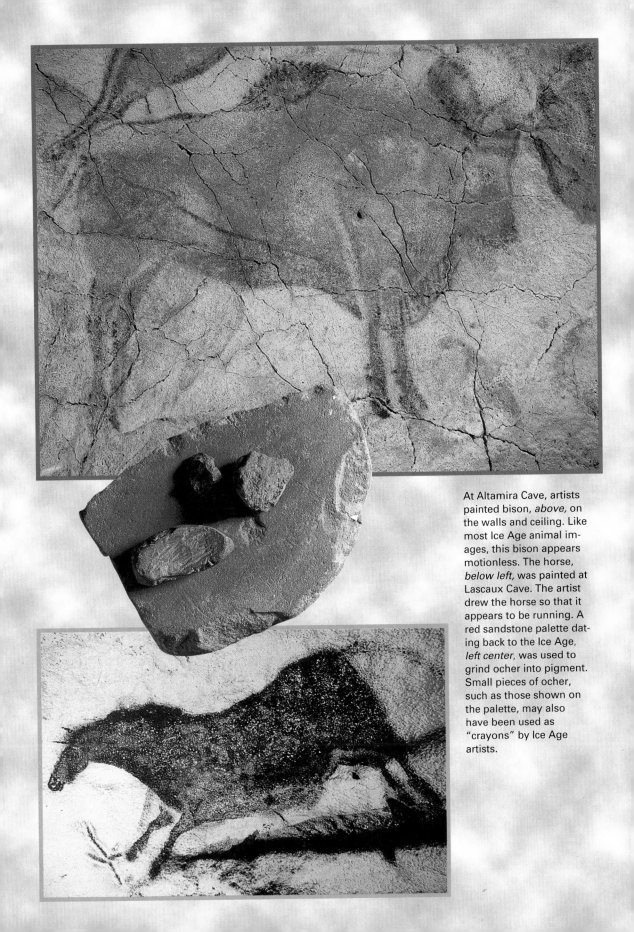

At Altamira Cave, artists painted bison, *above,* on the walls and ceiling. Like most Ice Age animal images, this bison appears motionless. The horse, *below left,* was painted at Lascaux Cave. The artist drew the horse so that it appears to be running. A red sandstone palette dating back to the Ice Age, *left center,* was used to grind ocher into pigment. Small pieces of ocher, such as those shown on the palette, may also have been used as "crayons" by Ice Age artists.

Techniques of Ice Age artists

By studying the paintings and carvings left by Ice Age artists, archaeologists have identified some of the methods the artists used to create art.

Ice Age artists made paintings of animals, people, and mysterious symbols on cave walls using pigments made from charcoal or colorful minerals. The artists applied the paint with their fingers or with brushes made of natural materials, such as animal hair or twigs. To paint on high ceilings, they sometimes built wood platforms.

To make hand stencils, the ancient artists pressed a hand against the cave wall and sprayed paint over it, probably by spitting it from their mouth or blowing it through a small tube made of bone.

Engraving, done with crude picks or sharp flakes of rock, was the technique most commonly used to create cave art. The artists engraved some figures with fine, barely visible lines, while for others they made wide, deep grooves in the wall.

pieces of bone or antler, and female figurines. The most important discoveries of portable art were made by Edouard Lartet, a French scholar, and Henry Christy, a London industrialist. Their finds included an antler with an engraving of a bear's head and a fragment of mammoth tusk engraved with a picture of a mammoth. Such objects were clearly ancient, since they were found alongside early tools of stone and bone and with the bones of Ice Age animals. Moreover, the engraved images often depicted creatures that are now extinct, such as the mammoth, or animals that had long ago deserted that part of the world, such as the reindeer.

Ancient cave art

These first discoveries triggered a kind of "gold rush." People began to dig in caves and rock shelters throughout Europe in search of ancient art treasures. One or two treasure hunters noticed drawings on the walls of some caves but thought nothing of them. The first real claim for the existence of Ice Age cave art was made in 1880 by a Spanish landowner, Marcelino Sanz de Sautuola, who discovered beautiful paintings of bison and other animals on the walls and ceiling of a cave called Altamira. But Sautuola was not an established scholar, so archaeologists of the time treated his views with great skepticism and even contempt.

The Altamira cave art was ignored for 15 years. Then, in 1895, there was a breakthrough. At the cave of La Mouthe in the Dordogne region of France, named for the Dordogne River, the removal of some earth exposed an unknown gallery with engravings on its walls, including the figure of a bison. The presence of Ice Age tools in the earth blocking the gallery made it clear that the pictures were ancient. Finally, in 1901, people exploring elsewhere in the Dordogne region found Ice Age engravings in the cave called Les Combarelles and discovered paintings in the nearby cave of Font de Gaume. In 1902, the world of archaeology officially accepted the existence of cave art.

Another rush of interest followed, and explorers found many new sites. The geographic distribution of cave art is patchy, but sites are most abundant in areas that are also rich in portable art objects: southwest France, the French Pyrenees mountains, and northern Spain. But decorated caves have also been found in Portugal, southern Spain, and northern France. Other countries with decorated Ice Age caves include Germany, Italy, Yugoslavia, Romania, and Russia. About 300 European caves had been discovered by 1996, but the number continues to climb as new sites are found at the rate of about one a year. Some caves contain only one or a few figures on the walls, while others, like the famous Lascaux Cave in southwest France or Les Trois Frères (The Three Brothers) in the French Pyrenees, have many hundreds.

Since 1981, wall art has also been discovered on rocks in the open air. Six sites have so far been found in Spain, Portugal, and the French Pyrenees. They contain animal engravings that are almost certainly Ice Age art, judging by their style.

The origin of art

Europe is not the only place where Ice Age art has been found. In the past few decades, art of similar age has been discovered in many other parts of the world, most notably in southern Africa. In a cave called Apollo 11 in Namibia, animals painted on small slabs date to about 27,500 years ago. And in Australia, scientists determined that some engravings on rock were made more than 40,000 years ago.

Archaeologists have also discovered evidence of artistic efforts from even earlier than 40,000 years ago. For example, an American researcher, Alexander Marshack, claims that a small, shaped piece of volcanic rock with grooves carved into it, found at a site in Israel called Berekhat Ram, qualifies as art. The rock, which appears to be a female figurine, dates to between 200,000 and 800,000 years ago. But some archaeologists refute such assertions, and insist that true art began about 40,000 years ago with the more sophisticated paintings and engravings of the last Ice Age. This controversy is ongoing, and archaeologists continue to search for art that predates the Ice Age. Despite heated debate about which people deserve to be called the world's first artists, there is little doubt that the inhabitants of Ice Age Europe produced art more refined than anything from earlier epochs that might qualify as art.

A female figure that archaeologists call "Venus with a horn" was carved into the rock at Laussel, a decorated Ice Age rock shelter in France. The woman's head is turned toward a horn that she holds in her right hand. Some researchers claim that Ice Age carvings and sculptures of women were related to fertility rites. But the figures, which include images of women of various ages and body types, may have had other meanings or functions that elude modern scholars.

The cave artists

The people of Ice Age Europe were hunter-gatherers who moved from place to place in search of food. Although Ice Age Europeans spent time in caves, they did not live in them. Caves were dark and damp, so Ice Age people lived only in cave entrances or rock shelters. They also erected huts or tents in the open air.

But Ice Age artists often ventured into caves to decorate the walls with images. Usually the artists depicted animals and abstract designs. In most caves, abstract markings, which may consist of dots, lines, or more complex shapes, are two or three times more abundant than recognizable figures. Although less interesting to our eyes than the pictures of animals, these mysterious designs may have held great importance for the artists. The more complex abstract markings vary according to their location and the period in which they were made, suggesting that the markings may have represented specific social groups.

Ice Age artists also created images of human beings, but those are relatively rare. Even less common are *composites*, figures that have both human and animal characteristics. Some archaeologists have interpreted composites as "sorcerers," assuming them to be images of humans in animal costumes or masks. But the figures could just as easily be imaginary creatures, humans with animal heads.

There are many obstacles to our understanding the meaning of these Ice Age images. In Ice Age art, small figures are often found with large ones, and scenes are very hard to identify. It is often impossible to prove that figures are associated, rather than simply drawn next to each other. Early artists never drew the ground or any landscapes. Most figures seem motionless, and many may depict creatures that are wounded, dying, or dead. Some drawings of animals in motion appeared toward the end of the Ice Age.

A unique environment for creating art

To modern observers viewing such images, it seems clear that the caves themselves exerted an influence on the artists and their techniques. In wall art, for example, there was no limit on size, and figures range from the tiny to the enormous. Great painted bulls at Lascaux Cave are more than 5 meters (16 feet) long. In countless examples of cave art, artists made use of natural rock formations, including projections on cave walls and *stalagmites* (conelike formations of limestone that build up on the floor of a cave), to emphasize or represent parts of figures.

Images have also been found on ceilings and very high up on cave walls. Some ceilings, like the one at Altamira, were within easy reach, but others required a ladder or scaffolding. At Lascaux, holes cut into the wall of one decorated section of the cave give some idea of how scaffolding may have been constructed. Archaeologists theorize that Ice Age people fitted branches into the holes, and then placed a platform on top of the network of branches. In this way, an artist could reach the ceiling. In most caves, artists probably leaned roughly trimmed tree trunks against the cave walls and used them as ladders to reach upper walls and ceilings.

The artists also needed to bring light to the dark caves. Light was provided by fireplaces in some caves, but in most cases the artists needed portable light. Since only a few dozen definite stone lamps are known from the whole period, it is likely that burning wood torches were generally used, which left little or no trace other than a few fragments of charcoal or black soot marks on the walls. We can imagine the dramatic effect the torchlight may have had for Ice Age people as they viewed the paintings, transforming art created by human hands

Ornately carved pieces of antler were found at Isturitz, a French cave. The function of such objects, known as batons, has not been determined. Ice Age people often decorated the tools they made with designs or animal images.

How Archaeologists Date Ice Age Art

Archaeologists use various techniques to estimate the age of Ice Age art. Dating portable art objects is relatively easy. Their position in the layers of earth at a site, in association with stone and bone tools of a known age, gives a fairly clear idea of the period to which they belong. But dating art on cave walls can be far more difficult.

At caves whose entrances have been blocked since the Ice Age, leaving the cave interiors undisturbed, scientists can establish a minimum age for wall art. The art must be older than the deposits blocking the cave entrance. Also, archaeologists have discovered a few caves where a fragment of decorated wall has fallen and lies in a layer of earth. By determining when that layer was deposited they can make a rough estimate of the age of the art fragment and thus of the wall painting it came from. This technique, however, tells only when the art fragment fell into the layer of earth, not when the art was made.

Some caves also contain *occupation deposits* (discarded matter), in which archaeologists have found things, such as coloring materials, that may be linked with art production. And if a site with art on the walls also contains portable art, there are sometimes clear similarities between the two art forms in technique and style that provide a fairly reliable date for the wall decoration.

These methods of dating are called *relative dating*. Relative dating provides information about the age of an object only in relation to other objects. It yields only approximate ages.

Scientists obtain more precise dates for Ice Age art using *radiocarbon dating*. Radiocarbon dating is a process used to determine the age of ancient artifacts by measuring their content of radiocarbon—radioactive carbon 14. It is the most widely used dating method in prehistoric archaeology. It can be used on any *organic* material (material that was once alive), such as charcoal deposits, wood, or bone. Cave paintings made with charcoal, for example, can be dated in this way.

Radiocarbon dating is possible because all living tissues are composed of molecules containing atoms of the element carbon. Plants obtain carbon when they absorb carbon dioxide from the air. Animals get carbon by eating plants or other animals that have eaten plants. Almost all carbon atoms in the air are in the form of an *isotope* called carbon 12. Isotopes of an element are atoms that contain the same number of protons but a different number of neutrons. The nucleus of an atom of carbon 12 contains six protons and six neu-

trons. About one out of every trillion carbon atoms is the isotope carbon 14, which contains six protons and eight neutrons.

Carbon 14 is produced when high-energy particles called cosmic rays strike the atmosphere, causing atoms in the atmosphere to break down into electrons, neutrons, protons, and other particles. Some neutrons collide with the nuclei of nitrogen atoms in the atmosphere, causing the nitrogen atoms—with seven protons and an equal number of neutrons—to gain a neutron and lose a proton. In this way, a nitrogen atom becomes an atom of carbon 14. The extra neutrons make the carbon 14 atom unstable and thus radioactive.

Radiocarbon atoms, like all radioactive elements, *decay* (break down) at an exact and uniform rate into more stable atoms. Half of the carbon 14 in an object decays into nitrogen after about 5,700 years. Therefore, radiocarbon is said to have a half-life of 5,700 years. After about 11,400 years, a fourth of the original amount of carbon 14 remains in the object. After another 5,700 years, only an eighth remains, and so on.

The radiocarbon in the tissues of a living organism is renewed continuously. But after the organism dies, it no longer takes in air or food, so it no longer absorbs radiocarbon. The carbon 14 already in the tissues then decays at the rate governed by its half-life. Using instruments that measure the amount of radiocarbon that remains in a sample of organic matter, scientists can determine how long it has been dead.

A difficulty with this method is that a fairly large piece of an object has to be destroyed to use in the process of dating the object. It would be impossible to remove a large enough sample from a cave painting without damaging it. But this problem has been solved with a newer method of radiocarbon dating involving the use of a particle accelerator, a sophisticated piece of machinery that accelerates electrically charged atoms or subatomic particles. This system, in which atoms from the sample are fired by the accelerator into a magnetic field and counted, requires only a tiny amount of material from an artwork.

Radiocarbon dating is most accurate when a specimen is between 500 and 40,000 years old. In a specimen less than 500 years old, too little carbon 14 has decayed to get an accurate reading. After 40,000 years, not enough remains for a precise measurement. But that span of time encompasses almost the entire history and prehistory of fully modern humans.   [P.G.B.]

into something with a more dramatic, perhaps even spiritual, effect.

The most common technique used by cave artists was engraving. Using sharp tools fashioned from pieces of *chert* (a flintlike stone), the artists engraved cave walls with figures composed of lines, some fine and barely visible, others broad and deep. They scratched and scraped walls where surfaces were too rough for fine incisions or to create a difference in color between a light scraped area and darker surroundings. Ice Age artists also carved sculptures out of sections of rock shelter walls. Almost all such sculptures, often referred to as *bas-relief*, contain faint traces of red pigment, indicating that they were originally painted.

Not all Ice Age sculpture was made from stone, however. In the Pyrenees, artists worked in clay that formed a natural coating on many cave walls. The simplest technique the artists used with clay was to run their fingers over it, leaving traces. This method was probably used throughout the Ice Age and may have been inspired by the many claw marks left on cave walls by bears and other animals.

Artists in the Pyrenees also sculpted figures on banks of clay that they mounded up on cave floors. The finest Ice Age clay figures are two famous statues of bison in Le Tuc d'Audoubert Cave and a headless bear, made of about 680 kilograms (1,500 pounds) of clay, that crouches in Montespan Cave.

Dramatic painted images

Although engravings are the most common type of cave art, perhaps the most striking to modern eyes are the paintings. Cave artists painted with *pigment* (powdered coloring material) made of natural materials, usually minerals. Iron oxide, in the form of ocher and hematite, was used to create red, yellow, and brown pigment, while charcoal or the mineral manganese were used as black pigment. These coloring materials were readily available, either collected as fragments or mined. Cave artists also mixed pigment with water, animal fats, or plant oils to make the paint go further or to help bind it to the cave walls.

Artists painted cave walls using various techniques. The simplest way to apply paint was with the fingers, and this was certainly done in some caves. But normally paint was applied with some kind of tool, though no such tools are known to have survived. Experiments suggest that the artists painted with animal-hair brushes or crushed twigs. In some cases, paint was clearly sprayed onto walls, either directly from the mouth or through a tube, to produce dots and hand prints.

The vast majority of painted figures are simple outlines, although some drawings are partially filled in. Some images of animals, such as the most refined work at Chauvet Cave, display a sophisticated use of shading. And toward the end of the Ice Age, artists sometimes used two or more colors in depicting animals, making them look more lifelike.

Such realistic depictions can be admired by modern viewers for their artistic value alone, but we could appreciate Ice Age art even more if we could learn its purpose. Archaeologists are trying to delve into the minds of the artists who created these extraordinary images in an effort to discover the motives behind the art.

The meaning of Ice Age art

The first and simplest theory put forward to explain Ice Age art was that it was just idle decoration by hunters with time on their hands. This "art for art's sake" view arose from the first discoveries of portable art, but once cave art was discovered, it became clear that something more was involved. In the early 1900's, scholars began to speculate that Ice Age art had a definite function in the lives of its creators. The limited range of species depicted, the often hidden location of the art in caves, the mysterious signs, the many figures that were purposely left incomplete or cannot be identified—all of these elements combined to suggest a complex meaning behind Ice Age art.

Some early cave art theories were based largely on published accounts about Australian Aborigines. When first encountered by Europeans in the 1700's, the Aborigines, like the

people of the Ice Age, were hunter-gatherers and users of stone tools. Anthropologists reported that the Aborigines created rock paintings of animals as part of ceremonies intended to cause animals to multiply. Because of the similarities between the Aborigines and Ice Age people, researchers assumed that similar purposes lay behind the art of both cultures.

One theory inspired by this comparison was that Ice Age art was a form of hunting magic, which is based on the belief that depictions of animals can control or influence real animals. Experts who viewed Ice Age art as having this purpose interpreted many of the figures on cave walls as representations of hunting. They concentrated on the images of animals with spears drawn on or near them or images of animals being wounded or killed. But there were problems with this theory. For one thing, many caves have no such images, and it is difficult to determine whether any Ice Age images actually depict hunting. Moreover, the animal bones found in many decorated caves bear little relation to the species shown on the walls, indicating that the artists were not, by and large, drawing the animals they hunted.

One aspect of hunting societies that could be reflected in some of

the art, however, is *shamanism.* A shaman is a person whose role is to communicate between the earthly world and the spirit world, usually by means of trances and hallucinations. Ice Age images might therefore represent spirit animals rather than real ones. The animal figures might have been used in rituals that enabled the shaman to communicate with the spirit world.

Another popular explanation of Ice Age art is that it involves fertility magic, in which artists depicted animals they hoped would reproduce and flourish to provide food. Researchers who took this view stressed the sexual or reproductive element in the art, pointing out images they thought were animals or humans engaged in mating activities. But there are very few images that can be clearly identified in this way.

Other ways of looking at cave art

In the 1950's, two French researchers, Annette Laming-Emperaire and André Leroi-Gourhan, introduced the theory that Ice Age caves had been decorated systematically. Looking at all the figures in a cave

Archaeologists have explored various theories about the purpose of Ice Age art. Some think cave art may have been used in ceremonies or initiation rituals. This theory is supported by the discovery of simple musical instruments, such as flutes, in some caves. In what may have been a typical ceremony, above, a youth is initiated into adult society. Adults watch or play music as the young person is guided by torchlight to glimpse the mystical images on the cave walls.

together, rather than just a selected few, they treated Ice Age art as a carefully laid-out composition within each cave.

Leroi-Gourhan investigated how many animals of each species were depicted in each cave, which animals were grouped together, and the location of the images on the walls. He then developed the concept of an ideal or standard layout to which each cave was adapted. He saw the caves as organized sanctuaries with repeated compositions that were separated by zones, each zone marked with particular animal images or signs. Noting that Ice Age caves were decorated with the same fairly restricted range of animals in profile, which seemed to represent variations on a theme, Leroi-Gourhan theorized that Ice Age cave art remained much the same for a period of about 20,000 years.

But this was another theory that did not hold up under examination. There are many exceptions to Leroi-Gourhan's rules, including the unusually prominent cats and rhinos in Chauvet Cave. Recent studies, both of individual caves and of regional groups of caves, show that each site is unique and has its own symbolic construction, adapted to its own shape and size.

Leroi-Gourhan also put forward the idea of a symbolic sexual element in Ice Age cave art. He developed this idea from the observation that horses and bison were the numerically dominant animals in cave art. Leroi-Gourhan claimed that this represented a basic *dualism* (division into two parts). He believed the dualism was sexual, with the horse representing the male and the bison the female. For Laming-Emperaire, the symbolism was the other way around. Leroi-Gourhan also discovered that while some animal figures are often grouped together in Ice Age art, others are never associated. For example, one never finds depictions of bison with wild cattle, or bison with stags. But why these animals were never shown together has yet to be learned. While Leroi-Gourhan may not have found a universally applicable formula for the meaning of cave art, he did discover the important concepts of order and repeated associations.

Laming-Emperaire eventually pursued a different approach, adopting a theory called *totemism*. She saw a decorated cave as a model of a group's social organization, with animals of various sizes and ages representing either different generations or the mythical ancestors of different clans. This view was more flexible than that of Leroi-Gourhan. It did not assume that the art remained unchanged over time and location but rather left room for the possibility that the art could be different in each cave.

The search for answers continues

The work of Leroi-Gourhan and Laming-Emperaire completely changed the way in which Ice Age art was studied. Archaeologists no longer saw the images on cave walls as simple representations of reality with an obvious and direct meaning. Instead, they came to view them as images symbolizing abstract ideas.

Many archaeologists now believe that there was a connection between Ice Age cave art and the social lives of the people who created it. Some theorize that art on cave walls may have been used in ceremonies or rituals, such as initiation rites in which younger members of a group were inducted into adult society. Although we do not know for certain what such rituals may have been like, further study and new discoveries, like Chauvet Cave, will open up new avenues of research.

The most recent research on Ice Age art is splintering in many directions. For example, an archaeologist investigating the shape of the wall surfaces used by the artists has found that in some caves a high proportion of horses, deer, and hand stencils are on *concave* (curved in) surfaces, while an equally high percentage of bison and cattle are on *convex* (curved out) surfaces. Another researcher is seeking methods by which to recognize the work of individual artists. At this point we do not know whether Ice Age artists were predominantly men or women.

Researchers are also investigating the *acoustics* (sound transmission) in different parts of caves and finding a clear correspondence between the richest sections of wall art and the best acoustics. This discovery suggests that sound was important in whatever ceremonies cave art may have played a part in.

No single explanation can account for the whole of Ice Age art. It comprises at least two-thirds of known art history, covering 25,000 years and a vast area of the world. Ice Age art ranges from beads to decorated weapons to statuettes, from figures on rocks in the open air to complex signs hidden in the nearly inaccessible crannies of deep caverns. The art on cave walls does not all necessarily have a mysterious or religious meaning, though some cave art was almost certainly linked to ritual and ceremony. Archaeologists generally agree that Ice Age art contains messages, no doubt of many kinds, but we may never know how to read them. Nevertheless, there is much to be learned from the art created by Ice Age people.

For further reading:

Bahn, Paul G. and Vertut, Jean. *Images of the Ice Age*. Facts on File, 1988.
Jean-Marie Chauvet, Eliette Brunel-Deschamps, and Christian Hillaire, translated by Paul G. Bahn. *Dawn of Art: The Chauvet Cave*. Abrams, 1996.
Leroi-Gourhan, André. *The Dawn of European Art*. Cambridge University Press, 1982.
Marshack, Alexander. *The Roots of Civilization*. 2nd ed. Moyer-Bell, 1991.
Ucko, Peter J. and Rosenfeld, Andrée. *Palaeolithic Cave Art*. Weidenfeld & Nicolson, 1967.

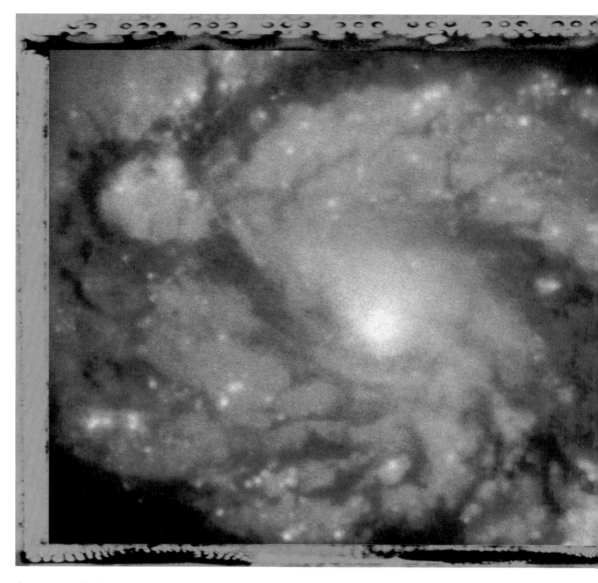

Astronomers in late 1994 measured the distance to the M100 galaxy, *above*. Using this measurement, they calculated that the universe is about 10 billion years old— significantly younger than the commonly accepted age of 15 to 20 billion years.

Would you be surprised to learn that the universe is only 10 billion years old? That was the approximate age that astronomers calculated for the universe in late 1994 using data from the Hubble Space Telescope (HST), and their finding created a dilemma in the astronomy world. Although a universe 10 billion years old is undeniably ancient, previous studies had put the universe's age at up to 20 billion years. More significantly, 10 billion years is only about two-thirds the age many researchers had long accepted for the oldest stars in our own Milky Way galaxy. How could the universe be younger than the stars it contains?

This contradiction spurred scientists to reexamine their earlier research on the age of the universe. But popular news stories exclaiming that the new findings were "turning theories of the cosmos upside

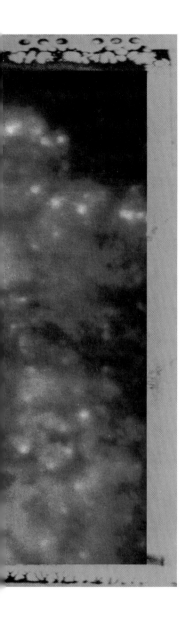

Recent research suggests that the universe may be much younger than astronomers had thought. But investigators predict that further studies will resolve the controversy.

How Old is the Universe?

BY LAURENCE A. MARSCHALL

down" exaggerated the seriousness of the problem. Contrary to the headlines, astronomers are far from ready to discard their previous work. They are now carrying out further observations that most astronomers believe will clarify our knowledge of how the universe began, narrowing the present uncertainty about its age. In 1996, in fact, other data from the HST indicated an older universe.

It is understandable that a problem as fundamental as the age of the universe would spark vigorous debate. No one was present at the birth of the universe to take note of the time and date. Nor do we have birth certificates or court records for the universe to tell us how and when things began. We can only rely on the record left to us in nature itself, and that information can be difficult to read.

Part of the record of the universe's history is written in the faint light

The author:
Laurence A. Marschall is professor of physics at Gettysburg College in Pennsylvania.

that comes to us from galaxies. Galaxies are huge groupings of stars, like our Milky Way. They are scattered throughout the universe, at distances ranging from about a million to billions of light-years. (A light-year is the distance light travels in one year, about 9.5 trillion kilometers [5.9 trillion miles].) Galaxies were first noted by astronomers in the early 1700's as faint, fuzzy blobs seen through their telescopes. But the great size of the galaxies and their distances from Earth were realized only in the 1920's, when astronomer Edwin P. Hubble of the Mount Wilson Observatory in California (for whom the Hubble Space Telescope is named) first determined the distance to several of the closer galaxies.

Edwin Hubble makes an important discovery

Hubble's research built on the work of astronomer Vesto M. Slipher of the Lowell Observatory in Arizona. Slipher in 1912 made the first measurements of a galaxy's velocity. By the late 1920's he had measured the velocities of over 40 galaxies, and a trend had emerged: Most of the galaxies appeared to be moving away from the Milky Way. At about the same time, Hubble had made rough measurements of the distances to several galaxies. When he compared his distance measurements with Slipher's velocity measurements, Hubble discovered a remarkable fact: There is a direct ratio between a galaxy's distance from us and the speed at which it is receding. For example, a galaxy twice as far away from Earth as another galaxy is receding from us twice as fast. This distance-velocity relationship, called the Hubble relation, is of overwhelming importance to our understanding of the age of the universe.

Astronomers quickly realized that the Hubble relation implied that the universe is expanding—that the space between all the galaxies is getting larger with time. If we could run a video of the history of the universe backward, we would see that all the matter in the universe was once packed together much more densely than it is today. Go back far enough in time, and one reaches a beginning. In that first moment, the universe was in its earliest recognizable form, infinitely dense and hot.

From that beginning, an explosion astronomers call the big bang, the structure of space expanded rapidly, carrying matter with it. Eventually it evolved into the universe we see today, vast expanses of empty space sprinkled with billions of outrushing galaxies. It is important to realize, however, that even though we observe from Earth that galaxies are rushing away from us, Earth is not the center of the universe's expansion— there is no center. If we could transport ourselves to another galaxy, we would observe from there that all galaxies appear to be receding from that galaxy instead. This is because space has been expanding uniformly since the moment of the big bang.

The Hubble relation, with its simple statement that the speed of a galaxy is proportional to its distance from Earth, provides a way of measuring when the big bang took place. Astronomers express the Hubble relation in the form of an equation, $v = H_0 d$. In this equation, v stands for velocity and d stands for distance. H_0 is a number called the Hubble constant, which expresses the rate at which the universe is expanding; the lower the value for the Hubble constant, the older the universe. Once astronomers have found a value for H_0, they can calculate the age of the universe.

The way astronomers use the Hubble relation equation is similar to a calculation made in everyday life. A simple way to find how long it takes for an object traveling at a constant speed to cover a certain distance is to divide its distance by its speed. For instance, if a car has traveled 175 kilometers (110 miles) at a speed of 90 kilometers (55 miles) per hour, then it has been traveling for 2 hours. Similarly, astronomers divide a galaxy's velocity by its distance from Earth to find H_0. The *reciprocal* (inverse) of H_0, or 1 divided by H_0, gives the universe's age.

Measuring galaxy velocities and distances

In order to use the Hubble relation equation, astronomers must first obtain accurate measurements for the velocities at which galaxies are moving and the distances of galaxies from Earth. Measuring the speed of a galaxy reliably is not much of a problem. Astronomers use a technique based on the *Doppler effect,* which is simply a change in the frequency or wavelength of waves we receive from a moving object. If you've heard the sound of a police car siren decreasing in pitch as it speeds away, you have noticed the Doppler effect. The sound waves have become stretched out—that is, they have increased in wavelength. Astronomers observe this same effect in light waves emitted by a swiftly receding galaxy.

Astronomers study the light waves received from distant galaxies using a device called a *spectrograph,* which collects the light and spreads it out in a spectrum. As the light waves emitted by a rapidly receding source become stretched out, they fall closer to the red end of the spectrum than they would if the source were stationary relative to Earth. This form of the Doppler effect is thus called the *red shift.* In contrast, light waves from a source moving rapidly toward an observer are *blue shifted,* or compressed and shifted toward the blue end of the spectrum. Almost all galaxies, however, are red shifted. This phenomenon is what led Slipher and Hubble to conclude that the great majority of galaxies were receding from Earth.

Although we now have much more sophisticated telescopes and spectrographs than Slipher and Hubble did 75 years ago, this is essentially how we measure galaxy velocities today. It is relatively easy to measure velocities with an uncertainty of no more than a few percent, and there is little debate among astronomers over how fast the galaxies are moving.

Measuring the distances to galaxies, however, is a very tricky business. There are many competing measurement methods, which can yield a wide range of distances to the same object, and the most ferocious debates these days are over which results are to be trusted. Just looking at a galaxy does not tell us a lot about its distance from us. While it is true that more distant galaxies usually appear smaller and fainter than closer ones, there is so much variation among galaxies

An ever-expanding universe

Astronomers have learned that we live in an expanding universe that had a definite beginning in time. But they have not been able to establish with certainty how long the expansion has been going on—that is, the age of the universe. That is a question that researchers are now trying to answer.

The universe began with a tremendous explosion of matter and energy called the big bang.

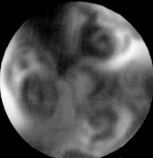

Space itself came into being with the big bang and expanded like an inflating balloon, carrying matter with it. There were denser concentrations of matter in some regions of space than in others.

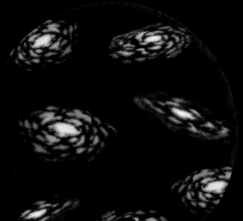

The high-density regions began to attract increasing amounts of matter. Large clumps of matter began to form galaxies and clusters of galaxies. The developing galaxies continued to be carried farther away from each other as the universe expanded.

Today, the galaxies and clusters of galaxies continue to rush away from one another as space expands.

that it's possible for a small, relatively nearby galaxy to appear the same as a large, distant one.

To measure distances to galaxies, astronomers search galaxies for objects they call *standard candles*. The idea behind standard candles is that we can estimate the distance of a candle at night because all candles give off roughly the same amount of light—the fainter a candle appears, the farther away it is from us. In the same way, if we can recognize in a galaxy an object that has a known *luminosity* (energy output), we can calculate its distance from us by measuring its *brightness,* the amount of light we receive from it on Earth. Comparing an object's brightness to its luminosity gives its distance, because light diminishes by a precise amount as it spreads through space.

Celestial candles: Cepheid variable stars

Edwin Hubble used standard candles in his measurement of the distances of galaxies in the 1920's. The standard candles Hubble used are *Cepheid (SEPH ee id) variable stars,* very luminous giant stars, somewhat hotter and several dozen times larger than our sun. Because of their high luminosity, they can be seen over vast distances.

The most useful property of Cepheids, however, is that their luminosity (and thus their brightness) varies in a distinctive way, increasing rapidly and then declining slowly. The Cepheids repeat this cycle over and over again with *periods* (the duration of one complete cycle) of a few days to a few months.

In the early 1900's, Henrietta Swan Leavitt, an astronomer at Harvard University in Cambridge, Massachusetts, demonstrated that the average luminosity of a Cepheid variable star is related to its period. The more light a Cepheid gives off, the longer its period. Thus, simply by timing how long it takes a Cepheid to brighten and dim, astronomers can determine its luminosity. Then, by comparing the star's luminosity with its brightness, they can determine its distance.

Hubble used this technique to determine the distance to several nearby galaxies, notably the Andromeda galaxy, one of our Milky Way's closest neighbors. Hubble found that Andromeda was about a million light-years away, which was considered an amazing distance in those days. But Hubble had difficulty measuring the distance precisely—his initial estimate of the luminosity of Cepheids was too low. When astronomers later found that Cepheids were more luminous than Hubble had thought, the distances to the galaxies had to be revised upward. Andromeda, for instance, was found to be about 2 million light-years away.

Cepheids are still one of the prime standard candles for measuring the distances to galaxies. Over the years, our knowledge of Cepheid luminosities has become more and more precise, so there isn't a great deal of uncertainty as to how much light they give off. The problem is that, despite their extraordinary size and luminosity, they don't give off enough light to be visible in any galaxies except those nearest to us. Using Cepheids, astronomers have measured the distance to a

The Hubble constant: key to the age of the universe

Astronomers express the age of the universe with a single number: the Hubble constant, proposed in the 1920's by American astronomer Edwin Hubble. The number is a measure of how fast the universe is expanding and thus of how long it has taken since the big bang to reach its present size. But astronomers have not been able to agree on a value for the Hubble constant. Establishing a value for the constant is dependent on making accurate measurements of the distances to faraway galaxies, and that has not been an easy task.

Galaxy B

Galaxy A

Earth

Milky Way

Galaxies are carried away from us by the expansion of space. Hubble discovered that the velocity at which a galaxy (usually located within a cluster of galaxies) is receding from the Earth is directly proportional to its distance. That is, if galaxy B, *above*, is found to be moving away from us twice as fast as galaxy A, it is twice as far away. This linkage is known as the Hubble relation and is expressed as an equation, $v = H_0 d$, in which v is velocity, d is distance, and H_0 is the Hubble constant. If astronomers could establish the exact velocities and distances of a number of distant galaxies, they could derive the value of H_0.

small number of galaxies within a few million light-years of Earth.

These distances, however, are minuscule in the overall scale of the universe. Andromeda and other nearby galaxies simply aren't far enough away to give us a good measure of the expansion rate of the universe. That is because the speeds at which our neighboring galaxies are moving away from us are influenced by the gravitational attraction between them and the Milky Way. Andromeda is actually moving *toward* us at about 300 kilometers (200 miles) per second.

The galaxies whose distances astronomers need to measure to find the universe's age must be so far from us that their attraction to the Milky Way is small compared with the effects of the universal expansion. That means galaxies more than just a few million light-years away. One group of galaxies that meets this condition is located in a large cluster of galaxies in the constellation of Virgo, roughly 60 million light-years away. Measuring the distance to the Virgo Cluster, therefore, is a step toward getting a reliable value for the Hubble constant.

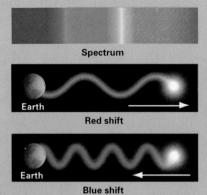

Spectrum

Earth

Red shift

Earth

Blue shift

Measuring the velocities of galaxies is relatively easy. It is done with the help of phenomena called red shift and blue shift. The spectrum of visible light is made up of the colors of the rainbow, *left, top*. As a galaxy (or any other light-emitting object) moves away from us, the light rays coming from it are stretched out and shifted toward the red end of the spectrum, *left, center*. The light of a galaxy moving toward us would be compressed and shifted toward the blue end of the spectrum, *left, bottom*. Both red shift and blue shift increase in proportion to increased velocity. By measuring a galaxy's red shift, astronomers can tell how fast the galaxy is moving away from us.

Finding the distances to galaxies is more difficult. Astronomers measure these distances using *standard candles*—stars or other celestial objects of known *luminosity* (energy output). Knowing the luminosity of an object enables astronomers to calculate how far away it is, because light diminishes by a precise amount as it spreads out in space. Standard candle A has the same luminosity as standard candle B, *right, top*. But A has four times B's *brightness*—the amount of light we receive on Earth, *right, bottom*. That means that standard candle B is twice as far away from Earth. Researchers are now trying to find standard candles that will enable them to establish the distances to a number of galaxies. Once they do that, they will be able to find the value of H_0.

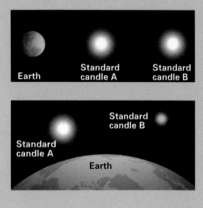

Earth   **Standard candle A**   **Standard candle B**

Standard candle A   **Standard candle B**   **Earth**

Making this measurement, however, has not been easy. Until recently, astronomers using a variety of celestial objects as standard candles calculated distances to the Virgo galaxies that differed by tens of millions of light-years. The problem was that none of the objects that astronomers could see and use as standard candles in the Virgo galaxies had luminosities that were precisely known, except for Cepheid variable stars. But it is virtually impossible for telescopes on Earth to detect individual Cepheids in the Virgo Cluster. Earth's atmosphere blurs the Cepheids' images, making them indistinguishable from the fuzzy glow of the other stars in the Virgo galaxies.

The blurring effect of the earth's atmosphere is a familiar effect. If you've ever seen shimmering images on a hot playground or highway, you know how warm currents of air can make distant objects look as if they are painted on fluttering silk. Atmospheric blurring (astronomers call it atmospheric seeing) is caused by currents of heated air that bend light rays from celestial objects. Because Earth's atmosphere is al-

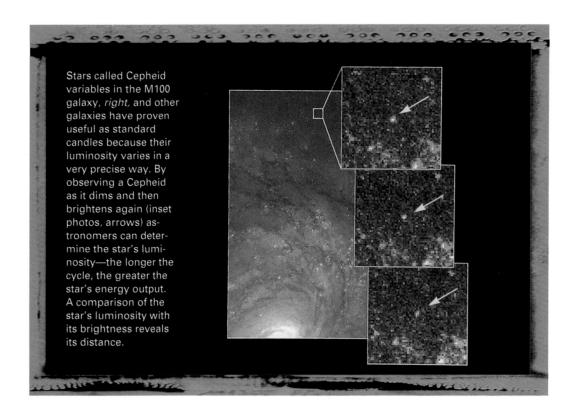

Stars called Cepheid variables in the M100 galaxy, *right,* and other galaxies have proven useful as standard candles because their luminosity varies in a very precise way. By observing a Cepheid as it dims and then brightens again (inset photos, arrows) astronomers can determine the star's luminosity—the longer the cycle, the greater the star's energy output. A comparison of the star's luminosity with its brightness reveals its distance.

ways in motion, the air currents that cause these distortions are present even on clear, still nights.

Astronomers have tried to solve the problem of atmospheric blurring by using a technique called adaptive optics. Special electronic devices attached to a telescope sense how light rays coming into the telescope are bent by the atmosphere. Computers then adjust the shape of the lenses and mirrors of the telescope to "unbend" the incoming rays, producing a sharper image. In 1994, astronomer Michael Pierce and his colleagues at the Canada-France-Hawaii Telescope in Hawaii used adaptive optics to observe a Virgo Cluster galaxy named NGC 4571. They were just able to distinguish three Cepheid variable stars, and they calculated a distance to the galaxy of 49 million light-years. This was shorter than previous distance measurements to Virgo galaxies. When astronomers plugged this figure into the Hubble relation equation, it implied a young age for the universe—between 7 billion and 11 billion years. However, astronomers needed more measurements to make a convincing case, and for that they needed even clearer observations.

The best way to avoid the blurring effect of Earth's atmosphere is to eliminate it entirely by putting a telescope in space, and that's where the Hubble Space Telescope came in. One of the HST's key projects, from the start, was to detect Cepheids in Virgo and narrow down the uncertainty in the age of the universe. After the telescope was put into orbit in 1990, however, astronomers found its optics were flawed. It

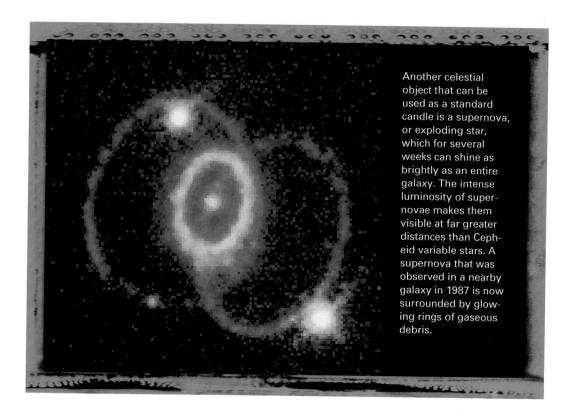

Another celestial object that can be used as a standard candle is a supernova, or exploding star, which for several weeks can shine as brightly as an entire galaxy. The intense luminosity of supernovae makes them visible at far greater distances than Cepheid variable stars. A supernova that was observed in a nearby galaxy in 1987 is now surrounded by glowing rings of gaseous debris.

was unable to produce the sharp images needed to search for distant Cepheids. In December 1993, astronauts in the space shuttle Endeavour repaired the telescope optics. Astronomers were finally able to investigate the Virgo Cepheids.

In October 1994, a group of astronomers led by Wendy L. Freedman of the Carnegie Observatories in Pasadena, California, announced that from Hubble Telescope observations of 20 Virgo Cepheids, they had derived a distance of 56 million light-years to the cluster. Using this measurement, Freedman's group calculated an age of the universe of about 12 billion years. But there is still some uncertainty in interpreting the measurement, because an age of 12 billion years assumes that the universe has been expanding at the same rate since the big bang. Actually, it's likely that the galaxies were moving faster in the past, because astronomers believe that the gravitational force that the galaxies exert on one another should slow them with time. Taking this factor into account, the universe may be even younger than Freedman's group calculated. We could thus say that the universe might be as young as 8 billion years old.

But again, astronomers needed more measurements. One of the basic rules of science is not to base a conclusion on just one line of evidence. Although astronomers have a great deal of trust in the use of Cepheids as standard candles, they want to cross-check the Virgo findings using as many different techniques as possible. That means looking for other celestial objects that can be used as standard candles.

The ages of globular clusters, spherical groups of up to a million stars, *above,* are a complicating factor for investigators who claim that the universe might be no more than 8 to 10 billion years old. Astronomers who study the life cycles of stars have calculated that the most ancient stars in clusters are 13 to 18 billion years old. Either the universe is at least that old or astronomers have a faulty understanding of the physics of stars.

Using supernovae to measure distances

Astronomers have found that *supernovae,* giant explosions in which stars rip themselves apart, make good standard candles. For several weeks, a supernova can be as bright as an entire galaxy. Because they are so bright, supernovae can be easily seen at far greater distances than Cepheid stars.

The kind of supernova that is most useful as a standard candle is one called a Type Ia supernova. The luminosity of these supernovae is a million times greater than that of Cepheids, so Type Ia supernovae can be observed at distances 1,000 times greater. The problem with using any kind of supernova for distance measurements, however, is that astronomers have had difficulty determining their luminosity.

Several groups of astrophysicists at the University of Oklahoma, Harvard University, and the University of Texas at Austin have used computers to calculate the amount of light that the laws of physics predict should be produced by a Type Ia supernova explosion. They were then able to determine more accurate luminosities of these supernovae. Other astronomers in Chile, the United States, and Australia have measured the variations in brightness of Type Ia supernovae in galaxies near enough to have had their distances measured by other reliable means, like Cepheids. These researchers found that the way in which a supernova brightens and then dims can be used to determine its luminosity. The computer calculations and the observations of nearby supernovae give results that agree fairly well with each other.

The Hubble Telescope offers another way of using supernovae as standard candles. The telescope allows astronomers to look for relatively nearby galaxies containing both Cepheid variables and Type Ia supernovae. Astronomers can use the Cepheids in a particular galaxy to measure the distance to that galaxy. That measurement also gives them the distance to a supernova in the same galaxy. They can then compare the brightness of the Cepheids, whose luminosities are well known, with that of the much brighter supernova. From there, it is a simple matter to calculate how much energy the supernova must be emitting to be that much brighter than the equally distant Cepheids. In this way, researchers use Cepheids to calibrate the luminosity of Type Ia supernovae.

This technique was used in 1996 by astronomer Allan Sandage of the Carnegie Observatories in Pasadena, California, one of the most influential researchers in this field. Sandage calculated that the universe is at least 15 billion years old, and he continued making distance measurements to Virgo in an effort to confirm his calculations.

Ancient stars present another challenge

Astronomers seeking to determine the age of the universe must come to terms with the findings of researchers who study *globular clusters,* spherical groups of up to a million stars. These clusters are scattered around the Milky Way, a few tens of thousands of light-years away from Earth, and they contain the oldest stars in the galaxy.

Stars shine because of nuclear reactions in their core that convert hydrogen, their most abundant element, to helium and other heavier elements. As a star's inner store of hydrogen is depleted, its chemical and physical composition changes, and as a result the star undergoes changes in luminosity and temperature. It takes from a few million to hundreds of billions of years for these changes to occur, depending on how much material there was in the star to start with. (The more massive a star is, the faster it uses up its hydrogen fuel.) Astronomers, using high-speed computers to solve the equations of nuclear physics, calculate how the brightness and color of stars should change during the aging process. They then compare these calculations with observations of the stars in globular clusters to determine the ages of the stars.

The ages of many globular clusters have been determined in this fashion, and the ages agree remarkably well with one another. The oldest stars seem to be between 13 billion and 18 billion years old. This age range overlaps somewhat with the traditionally accepted age for the universe of 15 billion to 20 billion years, and with Sandage's results, but is at odds with findings such as Freedman's, which indicate a universe 8 billion to 12 billion years old. Since the universe cannot be younger than the objects it contains, this contradiction must be resolved.

Although astronomers have a great deal of confidence in their knowledge of how stars operate, their knowledge may not be perfect. Future improvements in our understanding of nuclear physics and better computer models of stars may give us a lower estimate of the age of stars in globular clusters. Most researchers expect, however, that the change would probably be only a billion years or so.

By refining their measurements of galaxy distances, astronomers expect to narrow the uncertainty about the universe's age. One group of investigators was planning to study galaxies—including one known as NGC 1365, *above*—in a group called the Fornax Cluster. Observations of Cepheids in those galaxies may enable the researchers to determine the cluster's distance.

A process of refinement

A more likely possibility is that as astronomers refine their measurements of galaxy distances, the uncertainty about the age of the universe will narrow. Researchers are continuing to make observations of Cepheids in Virgo with the HST. Freedman's team plans to use the HST to make similar observations in Fornax, another galaxy cluster. Unlike Virgo, Fornax is a compact cluster, so determining the distance to one galaxy within Fornax would yield a good estimate of the entire cluster's distance from Earth. Several groups of astronomers are observing Type Ia supernovae in galaxies even more distant than Virgo. Others are using a different kind of supernova, called a Type II supernova, as a standard candle.

Some scientists are exploring methods that do not require the use of standard candles. One of these techniques is to calculate the amount by which the gravity of a distant galaxy bends the light of a bright object behind it, thereby shifting and amplifying its image, an effect called *gravitational lensing*. A galaxy that acts as a gravitational lens produces multiple "mirror images" in space of an object that cannot be seen directly by Earth telescopes because it lies behind the galaxy, though at a much greater distance. Using geometrical calculations, scientists are trying to measure the lengths of the several paths of light producing such images in gravitational-lens systems. Those measurements would give them the distances to the actual objects. Through fine-tuning and cross-checking, this and other methods of measuring distance are expected to begin yielding consistent results.

But what if further distance measurements lead only to more controversy? In that case, astronomers may have to consider the possibility that they are misinterpreting the Hubble relation or perhaps that the laws of physics need to be changed. Dividing the distance of a galaxy by its speed gives at best a high estimate of the age of the universe. This method does not account for the fact that galaxies were probably traveling faster in the past. If they were, then the universe is even younger than we calculate from a simple division, and the value of the Hubble constant will continually decrease.

But could it be that the universe was expanding not more rapidly in the past but more slowly? If so, the age we calculate from the velocity-distance relationship would be too low an estimate of the universe's age. And if this is the case, it would get rid of the apparent discrepancy between the ages of the universe and the oldest stars. At first glance, this proposition seems absurd. How could the galaxies, all exerting a gravitational attraction on one another, speed up rather than slow down?

The answer to that question may come from the work of the German-American physicist Albert Einstein. Einstein, whose general theory of relativity predicted the expansion of the universe even before Hubble observed it, considered the possibility that there might be a gravitational repulsion between galaxies as well as a gravitational attraction. He called this repulsive force the cosmological constant. But since there was no evidence that gravity could behave in this manner, he discarded the idea. Might Einstein have been correct? Could it be that a discrepancy between the ages of stars and the age of the universe is evidence that the galaxies have been speeding up, or at least not slowing down as fast as a purely attractive force of gravity would imply? Some astronomers say yes and suggest that we include the cosmological constant in our calculations of the age of the universe to bring things back into agreement.

Until astronomers are more certain of their observations, especially the distances to galaxies, it is too early to decide whether a drastic change in the laws of physics is necessary. If better observations and more experience do not resolve the uncertainty of many billions of years in the age of the universe, then the cosmological constant or perhaps entirely new theories may help solve the problem. However, if astronomers come together in their estimates, we will finally have a short and simple answer to a short and simple question: How old is the universe?

For further reading:

Goldsmith, Donald W. *Einstein's Greatest Blunder*. Harvard University Press, 1995.
Marschall, Laurence A. *The Supernova Story*. Princeton University Press, 1994.
Roth, Joshua, and Primack, Joel R. "Cosmology: All Sewn Up or Coming Apart at the Seams?" *Sky and Telescope*, January 1996, pp. 20-27.

The Search for the First Cell

Scientists are learning how the
basic components of life may have
formed on the early Earth.

BY JAMES TREFIL

A reminder of one of the most perplexing questions facing science is very likely right outside your window. A look outside reveals dozens, perhaps even hundreds, of different life forms. Grasses, trees, birds, insects, and human beings are so common that it is easy to take their existence for granted. But how did life on Earth originate?

Today's Earth is vastly different from what it was eons ago. In fact, our planet was once a very inhospitable place. Scientists believe Earth and the other planets of the solar system formed 4.5 billion years ago from gases and dust left over from the formation of the sun. In Earth's infancy, asteroids and meteors rained upon it. Each new impact raised the planet's temperature, until finally it turned to molten rock. As the bombardment tapered off, the planet cooled. Heavy materials such as iron and nickel then sank to the center, and lighter material that later formed the continents rose toward the surface. At the same time, an intense stream of particles emitted from the young sun swept away any atmosphere that the Earth might have had when it formed. In the be-

The spark of life?
Lightning flashes snake
into the sea, *opposite*.
Many scientists believe
that lightning may have
provided the energy for
many of the chemical
reactions that led to the
first molecules associat-
ed with life.

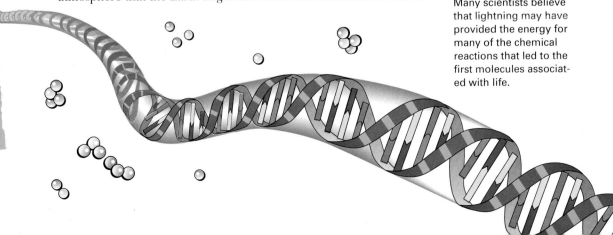

ginning, then, the Earth was a featureless ball of rock without oceans or atmosphere.

These harsh conditions persisted for at least 500 million years, making the emergence of life all but impossible. Then slowly, things changed. Gases from within the planet vented to the surface to form an atmosphere heavy with water vapor. Over millions of years, rain fell upon the Earth, and the water filled up the deepest depressions, forming the oceans.

Still, for perhaps another 500 million years, meteorites and comets continued to strike the Earth. Some of these impacts were probably big enough to vaporize the oceans, creating scalding steam that spread across the planet. Such an event would have destroyed any life that had developed before the impact. The early atmosphere also probably lacked today's protective ozone layer, which shields life on the surface from the sun's damaging ultraviolet radiation. Moreover, frequent volcanic eruptions must have raised Earth's surface temperature to perhaps 260 °C (500 °F).

This churning, explosive scenario is far different than the calm environment in which many scientists long thought life started. In 1871, for instance, the English biologist Charles Darwin envisioned life emerging among the right mix of chemicals in a "warm little pond." A caldron may have been closer to the truth.

How old is life?

And yet, life took hold. In 1993, paleobiologist J. William Schopf of the University of California at Los Angeles reported finding an unusually diverse set of fossils of 3.5-billion-year-old primitive organisms in western Australia. The fossils resembled modern bacteria. They were simple in design but had a fairly complicated structure that researchers agree could not have occurred spontaneously. Scientists believe that life arose long before Schopf's fossils lived, though they do not know exactly when. But most biologists think that life probably arose sometime between 3.8 billion and 4.0 billion years ago, soon after the oceans reformed after the last really big comet or meteorite impact. What's more, they think they have a fairly good idea how it happened. After thousands of years of speculation and more than 40 years of laboratory study, scientists may finally be closing in on the secrets of life's beginnings.

Trying to coax life from nonlife

The author:
James Trefil is a professor of physics at George Mason University in Fairfax, Virginia.

In searching for evidence of life's beginnings, scientists have focused on how simple chemical reactions transformed nonliving *organic* (carbon-containing) molecules into living ones—able to *replicate* (reproduce) themselves and evolve into ever more complex forms. And a number of researchers are trying to take this knowledge a step further. They hope to re-create the molecular origins of life in the laboratory.

The problem of creating something alive from nonliving materials—

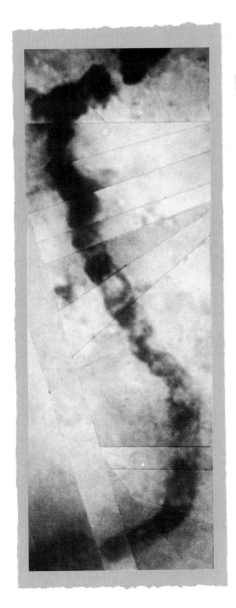

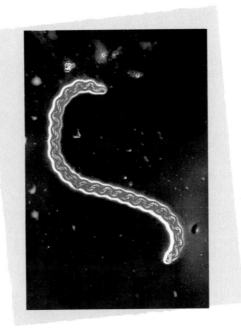

The beginning of life on Earth

A fossil of the earliest known type of organism, *left*, was discovered in Australia in 1993. The primitive organisms, resembling modern bacteria, *above*, lived about 3.5 billion years ago, when the Earth was only about 1 billion years old. Life emerged on a planet that had just settled down from a violent birth that included a 500-million-year rain of meteors, asteroids, and comets, *below*. By 4 billion years ago, the oceans and first atmosphere had formed, and complex organic (carbon-containing) molecules—the precursors of life—developed soon thereafter.

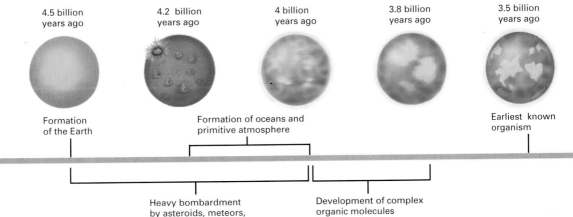

| 4.5 billion years ago | 4.2 billion years ago | 4 billion years ago | 3.8 billion years ago | 3.5 billion years ago |

Formation of the Earth

Formation of oceans and primitive atmosphere

Earliest known organism

Heavy bombardment by asteroids, meteors, and comets

Development of complex organic molecules

The building blocks of life

The basic unit of all living things is the cell. The parts of a cell are enclosed within a membrane, or outer boundary. At the heart of the cell is the nucleus, a structure containing the cell's genes.

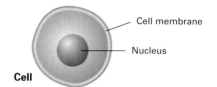

Cell

The genes, which control both the cell's functioning and its replication (reproduction), are made of a double-stranded molecule called DNA (deoxyribonucleic acid). DNA and its single-stranded chemical cousin, RNA (ribonucleic acid), are constructed from molecular units called nucleotides. DNA carries coded instructions for the production of proteins, molecules that carry out the work of the cell and make up most of its structures.

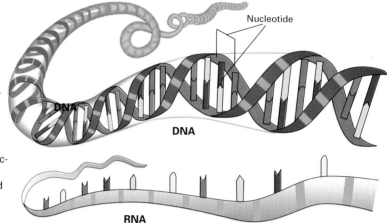

DNA

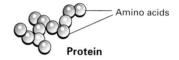

RNA

Proteins are composed of long strings of building blocks called amino acids.

Protein

Chicken or egg?

The way these molecules function in modern cells has presented a "chicken-or-egg" dilemma to researchers trying to learn how life emerged on Earth. The coded instructions in DNA are transcribed into RNA, which then directs the production of the specified protein. But none of this can be done without the help of other proteins, called *enzymes* (molecules that speed up biochemical reactions). Enzymes are also required for DNA replication. But if DNA cannot produce proteins or replicate without the help of enzymes, and if those proteins cannot be made without DNA's coded instructions, how did either DNA or proteins originate?

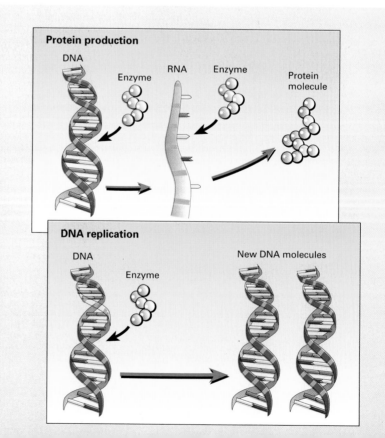

whether in the laboratory or on the infant Earth—can be broken down into two separate steps: (1) making the molecules that serve as the fundamental building blocks of living systems, and (2) putting those building blocks together to make a cell. It is the first step that scientists believe they now understand reasonably well. On the other hand, the second part of the problem, how an actual cell can be assembled from those building blocks, remains one of the great gaps in our knowledge of how life on Earth originated.

The building blocks of a cell

A cell is an amazingly complex entity in which thousands of molecules are continually being manufactured to carry out the functions of life. The most important of those molecules are proteins and nucleic acids.

Proteins are large, complex molecules made up of smaller units called amino acids. Proteins exist in every cell and are essential to plant and animal life. Some proteins, for instance, act as *enzymes* (substances that speed up biochemical reactions), and without them, cells could not function.

Proteins are intimately related to nucleic acids. There are two types of nucleic acids— deoxyribonucleic acid (DNA) and ribonucleic acid (RNA). DNA, the molecule of which genes are made, is a long, two-stranded chain—the famous double helix—made up of building blocks called nucleotides. DNA carries coded instructions for the production of proteins. Those instructions are executed by RNA, a single-stranded molecule similar in structure to DNA. But proteins are not just the end product of this process; they are involved every step of the way. The information in DNA cannot be "read" and translated into proteins without the aid of protein enzymes. Enzymes are also required for the replication of DNA.

This molecular interdependence created a dilemma for origin-of- life researchers because it raised a key question: Which molecule came first—DNA or protein? It is a classic chicken-or-egg paradox. DNA cannot make proteins and reproduce without the help of protein enzymes, but enzymes could not have formed without the existence of DNA—the enzyme is required for the functioning of the molecule that makes the enzyme. Biologists have sought an answer to this question for years as they researched prelife molecules.

In a 1953 experiment, chemist Stanley Miller of the Univesity of Chicago showed that some complex molecules necessary for life could form from simpler compounds under certain laboratory conditions. The experiment opened the door for much of modern origin-of-life studies.

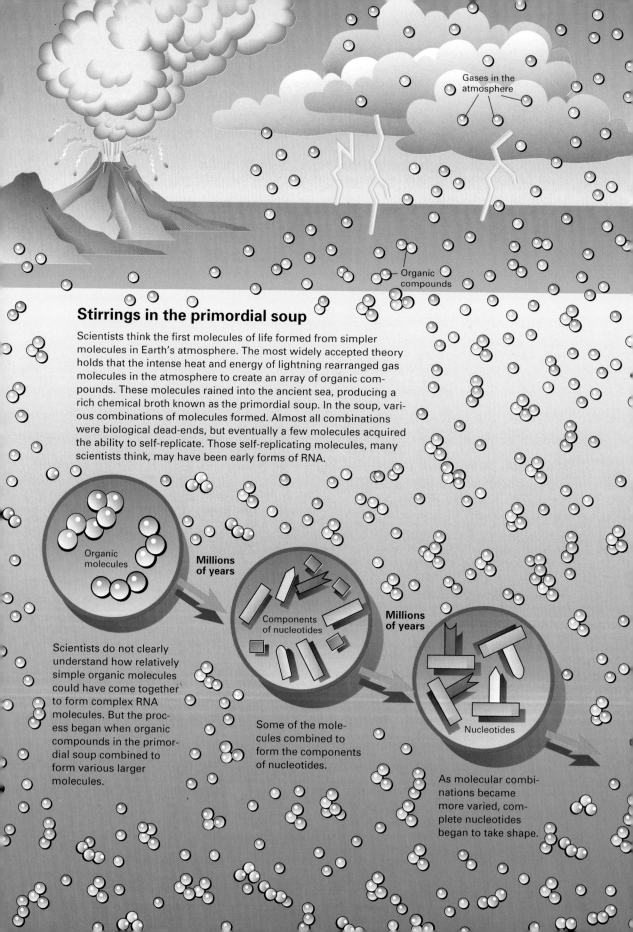

Gases in the atmosphere

Organic compounds

Stirrings in the primordial soup

Scientists think the first molecules of life formed from simpler molecules in Earth's atmosphere. The most widely accepted theory holds that the intense heat and energy of lightning rearranged gas molecules in the atmosphere to create an array of organic compounds. These molecules rained into the ancient sea, producing a rich chemical broth known as the primordial soup. In the soup, various combinations of molecules formed. Almost all combinations were biological dead-ends, but eventually a few molecules acquired the ability to self-replicate. Those self-replicating molecules, many scientists think, may have been early forms of RNA.

Organic molecules

Millions of years

Components of nucleotides

Millions of years

Nucleotides

Scientists do not clearly understand how relatively simple organic molecules could have come together to form complex RNA molecules. But the process began when organic compounds in the primordial soup combined to form various larger molecules.

Some of the molecules combined to form the components of nucleotides.

As molecular combinations became more varied, complete nucleotides began to take shape.

A groundbreaking experiment

Most researchers seeking the origins of life believe that the basic building blocks of life formed in the oceans as Earth evolved from its violent beginnings. A groundbreaking experiment in 1953 demonstrated how that might have occurred. That year, two chemists at the University of Chicago—Stanley Miller, then a graduate student, and Harold Urey, who had already received the 1934 Nobel Prize in chemistry—set out to reproduce those initial events in their laboratory. The basic idea of their experiment was simple: to see whether a mixture of gases simulating Earth's first atmosphere would, if exposed to an energy source, combine to make the kind of molecules that exist in living organisms.

Miller and Urey assembled methane (natural gas), ammonia, hydrogen, and water in a glass bulb. These gases simulated the primitive atmosphere, and water served as the primitive ocean. The researchers heated the bottom of the bulb to simulate the effects of the sun's rays on the ocean. The water that evaporated, along with the other gases, went up through a tube that passed between two electrodes. Sparks jumping between the electrodes imitated the effects of lightning. After being exposed to the spark, the gases cooled and returned to the bottom of the bulb.

After the experiment had been running for a couple of weeks, the two scientists noticed that the water in the bulb had started to turn dark brown. When they analyzed the water, they found that the color had been caused by a buildup of amino acids.

The impact of the Miller-Urey experiment was enormous. For the first time, scientists had shown how ordinary nonliving materials might have combined to form molecules essential to living organisms.

Many investigators questioned the validity of the experiment because they claimed Earth's early atmosphere was composed mostly of carbon dioxide and nitrogen and contained much less ammonia and

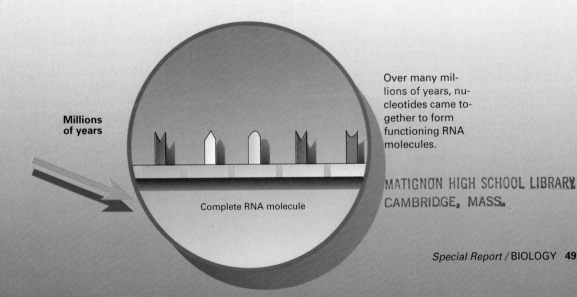

Millions of years

Over many millions of years, nucleotides came together to form functioning RNA molecules.

Complete RNA molecule

RNA, the versatile molecule

The reason many researchers think RNA may have been the first self-replicating molecule is that they have learned that certain RNA molecules can act as enzymes. This finding may hold the answer to the question of whether DNA or proteins came first in the emergence of life. RNA may have preceded both of them and then, with the help of RNA enzymes, manufactured proteins and evolved into DNA, *below*. Scientists call this scenario the "RNA world" theory.

The theory holds that several kinds of RNA developed in the primordial soup. Some RNA molecules could act as enzymes.

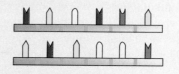

RNA

RNA with ability to act as an enzyme

With the help of RNA enzymes, RNA molecules made copies of themselves.

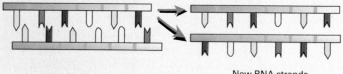

New RNA strands

Some copies of RNA, again with the aid of RNA enzymes, learned to manufacture proteins. Many new proteins were enzymes, which began to replace RNA enzymes.

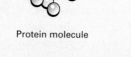

Protein molecule

Eventually, RNA made two-stranded copies of itself, and these double-stranded molecules later evolved into DNA. DNA, a stabler molecule than RNA, became the master molecule for the production of proteins.

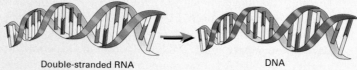

Double-stranded RNA

DNA

methane than Miller and Urey used. Despite these criticisms, however, the experiment showed that complex molecules associated with life could arise from simpler molecules without too much difficulty.

Since the 1950's, other scientists have performed many experiments of the Miller-Urey type with varying gas mixtures. Some of these experiments replaced the electrical discharge with ultraviolet radiation to simulate the effects of unfiltered sunlight reaching Earth's surface, or even with intense heat to mimic the influence of widespread volcanic eruptions. In many cases, the experiments produced not only amino acids but also compounds such as adenine, a component of nucleic acids; proteins, some larger than those actually found in cells today; and fatty molecules called lipids, which make up the *membrane* (outer boundary) of cells. These experiments suggest a scenario in which

Life from space?

Scientists discovered *amino acids* (the building blocks of proteins) in the core of this meteorite that struck the Earth near Murchison, Australia, in 1969. The discovery raised the possibility that the complex molecules necessary for life may have originated in space.

Earth's atmosphere abounded in organic materials, which rained into the oceans and formed a rich broth of potentially life-forming molecules. Scientists commonly call this watery mix of molecules the primordial soup.

Outer space as the possible origin of life

Earth's early atmosphere may not have been the only source of life's first chemicals. In what was perhaps one of the most astonishing findings of modern science, investigators in 1969 found amino acids in the core of a meteorite that landed near Murchison, Australia, after drifting in space for 4.5 billion years. After examining the rock, the scientists determined that the amino acids had been in the meteorite before it hit the Earth. Astronomers have also found evidence of complex molecules, including ones known as aldehydes, in gas clouds in the depths of space. Aldehydes can be combined to make sugars such as ribose and deoxyribose, components of RNA and DNA, respectively.

Thus, while it may seem that molecules in earthly organisms are special, they appear to be common throughout the universe. This finding has led some scientists to suggest that the building blocks of life actually fell to Earth in meteorites and comets, rather than forming here originally. Scientists have not yet determined how organic molecules in outer space were originally created, however.

Whether extraterrestrial molecules contributed to the development of life on Earth may never be known. What seems clear from the experimental evidence is that they were not required. If the early atmosphere contained a mixture rich enough in organic molecules and a source of water in which they could combine, scientists believe, the forces of nature would have constructed the building blocks of life on Earth. An intriguing possibility is that meteor and asteroid strikes created explosions of new compounds that lingered long enough in the atmosphere to be transformed into complex organic molecules.

Leaving aside the question of where the first building blocks of living cells came from, the next question is whether those building blocks could have spontaneously assembled into molecules such as DNA and RNA. Under certain laboratory conditions, including the use of particular mixtures of chemicals, scientists have produced nucleotides in simulated ancient-ocean conditions. Most biologists believe that, given enough time, nucleotides and nucleic acids would eventually form in a primitive sea. But there is debate about the makeup of the ancient ocean, and many experiments, using different chemicals to simulate the primordial sea, have not been as successful at creating nucleotides.

But even if DNA molecules arose in the primordial soup, they would have had to replicate to be truly alive, and for that they needed enzymes. Which brings us back to the chicken-or-egg dilemma.

RNA: the first living molecule?

One possible solution to this problem would be a scenario in which a molecule was able to carry genetic information and act as an enzyme at the same time, and many scientists now think that's exactly how things began. In the early 1980's, chemists Thomas Cech at the University of Colorado in Boulder and Sidney Altman of Yale University in New Haven, Connecticut, independently reported such a phenomenon in a kind of RNA molecule Cech called a ribozyme. Until then, scientists had believed that RNA was merely a molecular messenger that carried genetic information from DNA in the cell's nucleus to protein factories elsewhere in the cell. But Cech and Altman reported that ribozymes can act as enzymes. This finding raised the possibility that the first stirrings of life centered around RNA molecules able to replicate themselves and to carry out all the necessary chemical reactions of the first cellular structures. Presumably, RNA eventually made double-stranded copies of itself, and one of those molecules evolved into DNA. DNA, a more stable molecule, then became the master molecule for the production of proteins.

There were problems with this so-called RNA-world hypothesis, however. By the mid-1990's, though it had been shown that ribozymes could promote the linking of small numbers of nucleotides, no one had identified a ribozyme that could serve as an enzyme for the replication of a complete RNA molecule. Furthermore, the number of chemical reactions known to be helped along by RNA remained relatively small. These snags suggest that RNA may not be as versatile an enzyme as the RNA-world hypothesis requires. Scientists have also had trouble explaining how, precisely, RNA molecules might have arisen in the first place.

Other theories

Another solution to the problem of whether nucleic acids or proteins existed first would be to have them evolve together. In this way, a ready source of enzymes would be available to speed up the cellular re-

Getting it together: the first cells

A key question in origin-of-life studies is how DNA, RNA, and proteins came together to form complete cells. Scientists think the first cells began to take shape when the molecules of life were enveloped by globules of fatlike substances called lipids.

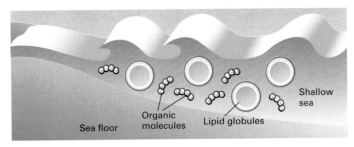

According to one leading theory, the primordial soup abounded with spherical lipid globules as well as complex organic molecules.

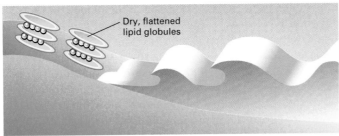

When ocean levels fell, lipid globules and organic molecules in shallow areas were often left on the dry sea floor. As they lost moisture, the lipids flattened out. Some times, organic molecules were sandwiched between layers of lipids.

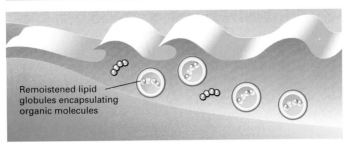

When the water returned, the remoistened lipids curled back into spheres, encapsulating the organic molecules and forming the first primitive cells.

actions necessary for DNA reproduction and the manufacture of more proteins. But most origin-of-life researchers agree that, due to the complexity of proteins and nucleic acid molecules, it is unlikely that the two molecules developed at the same time in the same place.

Some investigators side-step the problem of which molecule came first in favor of a theory stressing the evolution of chemical reactions underlying the biochemistry of all living things. These researchers believe that neither proteins nor RNA and DNA were necessary for the first life forms to emerge. Instead of assuming the existence of complex chemical interactions driven by enzymes, this theory holds that simpler chemical reactions in the primordial soup began the life-forming process.

In the simpler view, the first chemical reactions probably involved molecules containing only a few basic elements. The interactions of these compounds, according to the theory, were so elementary that they didn't need enzymes or other complex molecular machinery to make them work. According to Harold Morowitz, a biologist at George Mason University in Fairfax, Virginia, and a leading proponent of this simple scenario, the reactions gradually became faster and more complex. After millions of years, the reactions had become sophisticated enough to support the functioning of simple cells. Later on, when those first cells had established themselves, the more complex DNA-governed system evolved. Proponents of this view have pointed to a set of simple reactions involving *oxidation* (a process in which a molecule loses electrons) that still go on in living cells as candidates for the original reactions. Researchers are trying to make those reactions happen spontaneously in the laboratory.

Another idea of how life began comes from research into so-called complex systems. These systems, which range from the functioning of the brain to the stock market, involve the interactions of many components and often display unexpected behavior as the number of those components increases.

Some researchers theorize that the complex mixture of compounds in the primordial soup could have produced a series of chemical reactions in which one molecule acted like an enzyme to spur the creation of a wholly new molecule. That molecule then helped produce other molecules, which in turn spurred the creation of more molecules, and so on. According to one leading proponent of this theory, biologist Stuart Kauffman of the Santa Fe Institute in New Mexico, a sufficient diversity of compounds in the primordial soup would have virtually guaranteed the emergence of a set of self-replicating molecules. This scenario offers an alternative answer to the question of how early biochemical reactions could have proceeded in the absence of enzymes.

A possible role for clay and sea bubbles

Other investigators are studying the possibility that inorganic substances might have functioned like enzymes to allow strands of nucleotides to arrange themselves into RNA or to replicate themselves. According to British chemist Alexander Graham Cairns-Smith of the University of Glasgow and his colleagues, mineral crystals in clay can spur chemical reactions. The arrangement of electrons within the atomic structure of certain mineral crystals in clay creates a positive charge that can attract organic compounds with a negative charge.

According to this idea, particular molecules in the primordial soup were attracted to the surface of clays on the ocean floor, and the clay held the molecules close to one another so they could interact easily. Variations in the electrical pattern of the clay would have led to changes in the structure of the attached molecules. Such changes might eventually have produced enough variety in the organic compounds for lifelike processes to begin. Cairns-Smith believes that the first self-replicating molecule formed inside a clay crevice and was an ancestor of RNA.

Another view of life's origin credits bubbles on the ocean surface with helping produce the organic compounds necessary for life. According to geophysicist Louis Lerman of the University of California at Berkeley, a prominent advocate of this view, minerals in seawater, such as phosphates and certain metals, could have combined with airborne vapors inside the bubbles. As the bubbles burst, they would have expelled the solution into the air to mix with organic material ejected into the atmosphere from volcanoes or delivered by comets. Ultraviolet radiation and lightning may have helped transform components of this atmospheric mixture into more complex molecules.

The first cells

Clearly there is no shortage of explanations for how the building blocks of life originated. But what about the other major issue—how self-replicating molecules assembled themselves into fully functioning cells? That is a tougher question to answer.

A key step in the creation of cells was the formation of cell membranes. The complex machinery of cellular chemistry requires an outer membrane as a protective shield against the outside environment. Another function of the membrane is to regulate the passage of substances into and out of the cell. The membrane of modern cells consists of a double layer of fat in the form of lipid molecules.

One theory of membrane formation centers on the role of lipids in the primordial soup. Scientists believe that the soup may have looked a lot like a soup made on a stove today, with little globules of fat floating around on its surface. Each fat globule probably contained a sample of materials from the primordial soup, and the globules may have acted as test tubes to mix the molecules in different combinations.

Chemist Gerald F. Joyce of the Scripps Research Institute in La Jolla, California, is a leader in efforts to find *ribozymes* (RNA molecules that can act as enymes that can spur the replication of complete RNA molecules.

According to zoologist David W. Deamer at the University of California at Davis, who has researched this theory since the mid-1970's, certain lipid molecules, known as amphiphiles, naturally curl into tiny spheres called vesicles after losing and then regaining moisture. Deamer thinks organic molecules may have become encased between layers of amphiphiles as they dried out in tidal pools. Rising water levels rewetted the amphiphiles, causing them to curl into vesicles around the organic molecules to form the first cellular membranes. In some vesicles, chemical reactions, fed by material drawn into the vesicle through the lipid membrane, may have produced more of the original molecules. Those vesicles would have grown and, eventually, one of them would have split in two, thus replicating itself. Although that vesicle was undoubtedly extremely primitive, it would have been the first living cell.

Regardless of how it formed, the first life on Earth must have had a difficult time coping with the planet's hostile environment. To survive, the first cells may have required a protected environment. The most likely refuge, according to many researchers, was in deep-sea vents. Such vents form where cracks in Earth's crust allow seawater to filter down to meet rocks heated by *magma* (molten rock). The heated water then shoots upward, mixing minerals and organic compounds. Since 1977, scientists have found many life forms around deep-sea vents, including worms and bacteria that live on sulfur in the oxygenless water. The first primitive one-celled organisms might have originated in surface waters and then migrated to the vents. There, they would have been sheltered from meteorite strikes, volcanic eruptions, and ultraviolet radiation.

Scientists can make a pretty good guess about what happened once the first cell appeared. For a while, the cell and its descendants would have had plentiful energy sources and no competitors. Eventually, however, competition must have set in as the cells used up the energy-rich molecules that served as food in their immediate neighborhood. If one cell, just by chance, happened to have a slightly different set of molecules that allowed it to gather and use its food more efficiently than its neighbors, it would have divided faster. Eventually, populations of this cell dominated.

Over time, this process, which goes by the name of natural selection, would have guaranteed that the first cell would have many different kinds of descendants. Although the first cell would have appeared in a specific place, it probably multiplied enough to fill its local habitat in a few hundred years. Storms probably spread those first cells around the oceans rapidly, and natural selection guaranteed that cells in different locations began to look and behave differently.

Current research

The uncertainty of whether life on Earth began in a deep-sea clay crevice, a shallow sea brimming with nucleotides, or a shower of comets and asteroids laden with organic matter has generated increasing interest among researchers. Many key questions remain to be solved, but most research in the 1990's into the origin of life has focused on creating RNA molecules that can replicate themselves.

In 1993, investigators at the Scripps Research Institute in La Jolla, California, created a synthetic RNA molecule that reproduced itself repeatedly as long as it was fed the right mixture of enzymes. The experiment, led by chemist Gerald F. Joyce, produced a lifelike molecule, but it lacked a crucial requirement—the ability to replicate itself without an outside supply of enzymes.

In later research, scientists reported evidence suggesting that RNA molecules may be more versatile enzymes than scientists had previously thought. One problem with the RNA-world theory is that investigators had identified only a small variety of ribozymes, and those molecules had limited abilities as enzymes. But in April 1995, molecular biologist Jack W. Szostak of Massachusetts General Hospital in Boston and his colleague Charles Wilson of the University of California at Santa Cruz created a ribozyme that helped form bonds between *peptides* (fragments of proteins), as well as between carbon and nitrogen, a process basic to life. And in July 1995, Szostak reported making a ribozyme that was capable of joining pieces of other RNA molecules together 1 billion times faster than they would normally join—a rate approaching that achieved by protein enzymes. Such findings that expand the known capabilities of ribozymes add credence to the RNA-world hypothesis, which is presently the most widely debated theory of how life on Earth began.

Origin-of-life studies received a boost in the 1990's when the National Aeronautics and Space Administration (NASA) began a project to study whether life exists elsewhere in the universe. As part of that study, the space agency agreed to organize and fund an institute, the NASA Specialized Center of Research and Training exobiology program in La Jolla, California, to study how life began on Earth or on any suitable planet. Researchers at the institute, which began operation in 1992, are studying varying theories of the origin of life, including the formation and growth of molecules that can give rise to RNA, the possible role of clay in promoting the formation of nucleic acids, and RNA's role in the evolution of protein synthesis.

Perhaps the most compelling question that underlies origin-of-life studies is whether life on Earth was inevitable. If so, and life sprang up easily and quickly from organic compounds that are apparently common throughout the universe, then life may well exist on countless other planets. On the other hand, if life resulted from a difficult and lengthy process of development—if it was an accident, a triumph against overwhelming odds—life may be unique to Earth. One thing is certain, however: The mystery of how life began is sure to arouse intense speculation, curiosity, and debate as scientists continue their efforts to create life in their laboratories.

For further reading:

De Duve, Christian. *Vital Dust: Life as a Cosmic Imperative.* Basic Books, 1995.
Horgan, John. "In the Beginning." *Scientific American*, February, 1991, pp. 116-125.
Nash, Madeline. "How Did Life Begin?" *Time*, October 11, 1993, pp. 68-74.
Orgel, Leslie E. "The Origin of Life on Earth." *Scientific American*, October, 1994, pp. 77-83.

Wildlife in Our Cities

Abundant food, water, and habitation sites
make American cities and suburbs irresistible
to many wild animals.

BY EUGENE J. WALTER, JR.

In October 1994, visitors at Woodlawn Cemetery in the Bronx, one of
New York City's five boroughs, spotted what appeared to be a large,
mangy dog prowling among the headstones. The animal proved to
be a coyote. By early 1995, people had spotted several other coyotes
near the cemetery, some—traffic victims—dead in the street.

Most New Yorkers were surprised to learn that there were wild animals living in their midst. But it really wasn't so unusual. Despite their
reputation as wilderness creatures, coyotes have become common in
cities and suburbs across North America. And they have lots of company. Black bears are regular visitors to backyards in densely populated
suburbs of cities in New York, New Jersey, and Colorado. Peregrine falcons swoop from high-rise buildings in Baltimore, Chicago, and Los
Angeles. And deer and wild turkeys find food on the grounds of the
White House in Washington, D.C.

Although wildlife has existed in urban communities since the first
cities were built, most people are amazed to learn how extensive and
varied the populations of wild animals have become in American cities.
The growing presence of wild animals among us testifies to their intelligence and adaptability to the human environment.

Parks, backyards, cemeteries, and golf courses are among the places

wild animals have chosen to call home. Central Park, surrounded by tall apartment buildings in the heart of New York City, has nearly 300 bird species. Less obvious places where wildlife has taken up residence are grassy parkway medians, railroad rights of way, and flood-control channels. And few people would consider concrete ledges, window sills, air vents, chimneys, and storm sewers as suitable habitats, but many urban species find that such places are similar to the sites in a natural landscape where they might have established dens or nests.

For urban animals, cities imitate nature

Like animals in the wild, urban creatures require habitats that will satisfy their need for food and water, a place to rest and sleep, cover for rearing young, and protection from predators. Wildlife ecologist Larry W. VanDruff of the State University of New York's College of Environmental Science and Forestry in Syracuse has found that metropolitan areas contain three categories of habitat. He describes them as the central city core, the mainly residential suburbs radiating out from the core, and, farthest out, a fringe area that is relatively free of development. VanDruff emphasizes that these zones have no sharply defined borders. The landscape changes gradually from the built-up inner city out to the outlying areas where farm fields and forests prevail.

All three habitat areas provide rich food resources. In addition to finding their natural foods, animals can supplement their diet with pickings from a variety of sources, ranging from garbage cans to garbage dumps and landfills. Metropolitan areas have plenty of water as well, in reservoirs, park lakes, birdbaths, fountains, gutters, and reflecting pools. In fact, the food and water resources of urban communities offer animals a greater variety of habitats than was available there prior to human habitation.

Cities also alter the local climate. Heat produced by houses, apartment and office buildings, factories, and automobiles makes the city warmer than outlying areas. Suburbs are cooler than the central city core, but even there, heat generated by homes and automobiles makes them significantly warmer than wild places. The warmth of these so-called microclimates improves the survival rate of many urban species.

Urban animals share several common characteristics. First, they are adaptable. As their natural habitat disappeared, they changed their behavior to fit the new conditions of the urban environment. Second, urban species tend to be opportunists and *omnivores*—that is, they are willing to eat a variety of foods, both animal and plant. In addition, they are intelligent, some extremely so. And finally, urban species have adjusted to the presence of people. They have learned to recognize which kinds of human behavior pose a threat and which do not.

Some urban animals live in such close proximity to people that they share food, a characteristic biologists call *commensal behavior*. The common rat (also called the Norway or brown rat) heads the list of commensal species. From their homes in basements, sewers, and trash piles, they go after anything people eat. Rats rarely starve.

The author:
Eugene J. Walter, Jr., is a free-lance writer.

Some Canada geese, no longer migratory, stay year-round across the Northern states on golf courses and in suburban parks and office complexes, where grass and water are plentiful.

Deer are abundant in wooded suburban communities across the United States, often entering homeowners' yards to feed on ornamental plants and vegetable gardens.

Fringe

Suburbs

Central city core

Squirrels live in all three urban zones. They require only a few trees to provide food, nesting sites, and safe shelter year-round.

Pigeons and rats, among the oldest urban species, do well in the central city core nationwide, eating from open or overturned trash cans and drinking from gutters and sewers.

House sparrows and starlings thrive in the city core, nesting beneath roofs and feeding from streetside trash bins and bird feeders.

Cougars like the forests, canyons, and gullies of fringe areas in Western states such as California and Colorado.

Raccoons thrive in the suburbs, where they live in trees or the attics of houses and often eat from garbage cans.

Bears venture into the urban fringe from nearby forests, attracted by pet food, garbage cans, and other sources of food.

Eastern coyotes roam fringe areas of the Upper Midwest and the East, eating whatever is easy to get, from grasshoppers to domestic cats that live outdoors.

Urban habitats

An urban area contains three general habitat zones where wild animals make their homes. In the middle is the central city core, and surrounding that are the mainly residential suburbs. Farthest out is the fringe, an area relatively free of development. Each zone contains many habitats, such as parks and residential lots, that provide many different species with food and water and places to live and raise young. Some animals thrive in all three zones, and most animals use several habitats.

For as long as history has been recorded, rats have lived in cities. Biologists believe these animals originated in the wilds of northern China. They stowed away on ships traveling from Asia to Europe in the Middle Ages and hitchhiked to the Americas with European colonists. Burrowers by nature, rats can gnaw through brick, concrete, wood, and metal, and they can squeeze through small spaces. Female rats breed all year long, except during periods of severely cold weather, producing litters of six in less than a month. In a year's time, a female and her offspring can produce 1,500 rats. Dogs, large cats, and human exterminators kill some of them, but no natural predator has evolved in cities to control the rat population. The best defense is to keep alleys and basements clean.

Like rats, three bird species introduced to America—starlings, house sparrows, and pigeons—soared in number because they encountered

Finding life's essentials

Urban species require the same necessities of life—food, water, and shelter—as their wild cousins. But the urban animals usually have an easier time finding what they need.

An oppossum finds a feast in a trash can, *above,* and a squirrel quenches its thirst at a birdbath, *right,* a convenient and reliable source of water thanks to many bird-loving homeowners.

no natural predators or parasites and an abundance of resources in their new home. Central-city-core animals outnumber wildlife in the suburban and fringe habitats because of the huge numbers of these three species in the central areas. However, the suburbs and fringe areas support a greater diversity of species.

House sparrows and starlings originated in Eurasia and northern Africa and lived in European cities for centuries before coming to America. The sparrow (also called the English sparrow) arrived in the United States in 1852, when a sparrow fancier released 50 of the birds in a Brooklyn, New York, cemetery. They thrived on the grain used to feed draft horses. When automobiles replaced horses, sparrows dwindled somewhat, but soon the birds switched to trash bins and bird feeders for food, and their numbers once again soared. Researchers estimate the current U.S. sparrow population at more than 140 million.

Starlings got their start in America in 1890 and 1891, when a misguided philanthropist released about 100 in New York's Central Park. Starlings eat almost anything, from seeds and insects to garbage. They like to nest in holes, and they find abundant nesting sites beneath the roofs of buildings and in air vents. They also take over bird houses intended for more desirable species. Extremely aggressive, starlings drive

Raccoons, more sociable in the city than in the forest, squeeze together into their chimney home, *left.* But the solitude of a high ledge on a Baltimore skyscraper is more to the liking of a Peregrine falcon. The ledge substitutes for lofty cliffs as a place to raise chicks, *below.*

off native birds and sometimes destroy the other birds' eggs or kill their chicks. Scientists have found that the U.S. starling population has soared to nearly 1 billion.

Pigeons are another introduced species that flock all over American cities. Pigeons are descended from rock doves, a Middle Eastern wild species that moved into cities thousands of years ago. European colonists brought domesticated pigeons to America for food, to use as messengers, and to keep as decorative pets. Many subsequently escaped from captivity, and some were released. With their year-round breeding habits, these liberated pigeons quickly soared to millions.

City pigeons have learned that trash baskets afford easy pickings, and they are so tolerant of people that they will eat handheld birdseed, popcorn, and stale bread. Rock doves roost and nest on tall cliffs and rocky ledges, so their domestic descendants are right at home on window ledges, eaves, lofts, and under window air conditioners. They deposit large amounts of droppings on buildings, streets, and sidewalks. In addition to being a nuisance and expensive to clean up, the droppings may also accelerate erosion of stone and concrete in buildings.

Since the 1970's, federal and state wildlife agencies have been releasing peregrine falcons in urban areas to help restore the species after it had been decimated by pesticide poisoning. Peregrines naturally nest on cliffs and mountain ledges, so they were preadapted for city living. One of their favorite foods is pigeon. A peregrine will hurtle from its perch on a high-rise ledge or bridge tower at speeds sometimes exceeding 320 kilometers (200 miles) per hour. It kills its prey on the wing, and returns to the nest to feed. In terms of pigeon control, peregrine reintroduction had only modest success because the falcons fiercely defend territories of up to 8 kilometers (5 miles) around their nests. Thus, even the largest cities have space for only a few pairs of falcons—hardly enough to make a serious dent in the local pigeon population. Nevertheless, the program has boosted the peregrine population, and they now swoop around major cities all over North America.

Many bird species native to America have embraced cityscapes as readily as introduced species. One example is the nighthawk. An insect eater, the nighthawk has learned that the city's heat creates rising columns of air that send hordes of insects spiraling upward. Emitting a nasally "peent" that sounds like an electronic pager, it dives and swerves to catch insects on the wing on dark summer nights. The species also has adapted its nesting behavior to city life. Whereas in the wild, nighthawks nest on the ground in open fields, city birds nest on flat rooftops, which provide security from predators.

Bold squirrels, clever raccoons

Probably the most commonly seen animal in cities is the squirrel. Squirrels abound in parks from the central city core to the fringe. They also nest in buildings when they find a suitable niche high off the ground. The gray squirrel is the most numerous species. It is native to the eastern half of the United States from Canada to Florida. Red squirrels and fox squirrels predominate elsewhere, though they may overlap with the gray. Flying squirrels are also common in cities and suburbs, but being *nocturnal* (active at night), people rarely see them.

Gray squirrels moved into urban communities early in the 1900's, as logging cleared large areas of hardwood forest. These squirrels find everything they need where a few tall trees stand. They build nests of twigs and leaves in forked branches, and in winter they curl up in tree hollows. Trees also provide them with acorns, nuts, and bark to eat. But gray squirrels also help themselves at bird feeders, and whenever they can find them, they eat bird eggs and even chicks.

The main difference between the squirrels' native and adopted habitat is people. Although forest squirrels are extremely shy, those in the city have learned to be quite bold, coming close to people and begging for food. Begging helps urban squirrels survive, but junk-food handouts and fights at bird feeders make their fur scruffy-looking.

Raccoons are among the most prevalent and interesting of the small, furry animals populating the urban landscape. With highly sensitive forepaws that rival the human hand for dexterity, raccoons can open

Thriving in plain sight

Species that thrive in urban habitats share an important characteristic—they adjust to the presence of people. Deer quickly learn it is safe to enter suburban yards to feed when dogs and people are absent, *left,* and pigeons can temporarily escape crowds at a California zoo by roosting on a roof, *below,* then fluttering down to snack on spilled popcorn.

Canada geese flock on the grounds of a suburban home, *below.* The geese lost their migratory instinct in just a few generations, in part because they found water and grass in plentiful supply in the suburbs.

garbage cans with tightly fitting lids and even unlatch doors. In the 1980's, John Hadidian, an urban-wildlife biologist with the National Park Service, spent four years tracking 30 radio-collared raccoons in Washington, D.C. He found that the animals ate anything they got their paws on. About the only thing they would not eat is raw onions.

Hadidian also learned that city raccoons are unusually sociable. Several of the ones he studied lived in the same tree. And the animals clearly did not feel threatened by people. Nearly a fourth of the raccoons established dens in and around houses, though they avoided homes with dogs.

Recent arrivals to the urban scene

Compared with squirrels and raccoons, the beaver is a relative latecomer to populated areas. But the beaver population has been surging in the 1990's, mainly in fringe and suburban habitats.

Fairly typical is the situation across central Maine. There, beavers are gnawing down trees and damming streams in residential suburbs and occasionally even in downtown Augusta, the state capital. The beaver population explosion in Maine stems from two causes, according to biologist Gene Dumont of the state's Department of Inland Fisheries and Wildlife. First, from the 1930's onward, many farmers abandoned the land, and their farms reverted to forests crisscrossed by streams— the perfect habitat for beavers. Then, in the 1980's, the demand for beaver pelts in the clothing industry started to decline, pelt prices dropped, and the number of trappers fell by half. By 1996, Maine's beavers numbered in the tens of thousands.

Known as the engineers of the animal kingdom, beavers build dams to create ponds, and within the ponds they erect cone-shaped lodges out of logs, stones, and mud where they live and raise their young. But beavers do not restrict their dam-building to streams in forests. Beavers have found it far easier to plug a drainage culvert 1 meter (3 feet) wide under a road than to build a dam 90 meters (100 yards) wide across a stream. Water backs up behind the plugged drains, flooding the landscape and washing out roads.

Wildlife officials have tried relocating beavers, but the animals return or others move in. Moreover, once caught and released, a beaver learns to avoid traps. A new strategy calls for clearing the debris from a culvert, fencing it off, and building a half-moon-shaped structure of metal posts and fencing upstream from the drain. Once the beavers build their dam against the barrier, officials insert drainage pipes to allow water to flow through the dam to the drain.

Another relative newcomer to the urban habitat is the eastern coyote. It commonly roams the suburbs of cities in the East and the upper Midwest. Scott Smith, a state wildlife biologist, has studied coyotes living in the northern suburbs of New York City. He has found they are not only adaptable to people but are also lazy, eating whatever is easy to get, from garbage and grasshoppers to pet food and even pet cats. They have thrived where farmlands reverted to forest.

The eastern and western coyote are subspecies. In the early 1900's, the western species began to migrate eastward across Canada, eventually dispersing through the Northeastern United States and as far south as Florida. Genetic evidence indicates that eastern coyotes interbred with wolves, evolving into a larger animal than its western counterpart. Easterners average 16 to 18 kilograms (35 to 40 pounds), but they can reach 23 kilograms (50 pounds) or more, whereas westerners average 11 to 14 kilograms (25 to 30 pounds).

Western coyotes became suburbanites earlier than their eastern cousins. They had moved into the suburbs of Denver, Los Angeles, San Diego, and other Western cities by the 1960's, possibly earlier. The westerners are even less wary of people. Residents of the suburbs around Los Angeles, for instance, regularly see coyotes trotting down neighborhood streets, drinking at lawn sprinklers, and eating from dog dishes. Coyotes occasionally attack small dogs, but according to Scott Smith, such confrontations stem from the coyotes' territorial instincts, not because the dog represents food.

Surging populations of deer and Canada geese

Some wildlife species have become urban dwellers mainly through human interference with their natural behavior. Such is the case with flocks of Canada geese that nest in suburban areas of the United States and stay put year round instead of migrating to Canada, as they normally would. This behavior change can be traced to the 1930's. Up to that time, hunters who shot wild geese and sold them to food stores kept large flocks of geese to use as decoys. They clipped the birds' primary flight feathers to prevent them from flying off and tethered them by lakes and ponds to lure migrating birds within shooting range.

But in 1935, the U.S. Congress outlawed live decoys, and within a few years, thousands of semidomesticated geese were turned loose. They joined flocks of captive-bred geese that federal and state game agencies had released on ponds for public enjoyment. By the 1950's, large flocks of nesting geese were spreading throughout the Northern states. Once they select a breeding site, they are faithful to it. Thus, within several generations, the geese lost whatever migratory instinct they still had. Today, young birds in these flocks travel only a few kilometers from their birth nests to set up breeding sites with lifelong mates. Coyotes and foxes sometimes kill nesting geese but not in sufficient numbers to slow their population growth.

Deer are not far behind geese in overrunning American suburbs. White-tailed deer range everywhere in the United States and Canada except parts of the Southwest. Mule deer dominate from the Rocky Mountains to the Pacific Coast. When settlers arrived in North America, the two species had an estimated population of 50 million. Because of land-clearing and intense hunting, white-tails numbered only about 500,000 by 1900, and mule deer even fewer. But by 1996, populations had risen to more than 15 million white-tails and about 6 million mule deer.

Animals we welcome

A squirrel begging at the back door is a close encounter of a fun kind, *above*. The Peregrine falcon, an endangered species, has been brought back from the brink of extinction by being introduced to many U.S. cities, including Los Angeles, *right*.

The major reason for their resurgence is a lack of natural predators—mainly wolves, which were virtually exterminated in the early 1900's, and a decrease in hunting. In the mid-1990's, several states launched programs to increase deer hunting, but cars probably "harvest" more deer than hunters do.

Deer like the forest edge, and suburban environments mimic this habitat. They relish nibbling on fruit trees and many other popular plants in the suburban landscape. And they consider the produce in suburbanites' vegetable gardens gourmet fare. They quickly learn to avoid feeding when dogs and people are around to harass them.

Cougars in the West

The abundance of deer is at least partially responsible for the arrival of cougars in many large Western cities. At least 100 sightings of cougars—also called pumas or mountain lions—occur every year in the Denver metropolitan area, according to Todd Malmsbury of the Colorado Division of Wildlife. Residents of other Colorado cities, including Boulder, Colorado Springs, Fort Collins, and Pueblo, also report seeing cougars. The cities lie along the eastern edge of a string of peaks known as the Front Range of the Rocky Mountains.

Development around all the cities has pushed deeper into the

Newcomers we fear

Large animals are being drawn to urban habitats in greater numbers because food is so plentiful and easy to get and because human development has moved into their home ranges. Cougars are commonly seen in suburbs of Western cities, *left,* and bears, *below,* are seen outside New Jersey towns that are within commuting distance of New York City.

Coyotes roam suburbs from the Western states to the East and south to Florida. A coyote commonly eats garbage, *below,* but when times are tough, it will take anything from grasshoppers to pet food left outside.

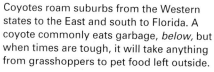

foothills of the Front Range. The big cats rarely attack people, but they often kill pet dogs and cats for food. Even dogs as large and strong as Doberman pinschers and German shepherds are easy prey for cougars.

In the 1940's and 1950's, both cougars and deer were uncommon in the foothills of the Rockies. But since then, Colorado's wildlife management practices have protected the land and animals, turning the area into prime mule deer habitat. And Malmsbury credits the booming deer population for attracting the lions.

Some scientists have additional explanations. For example, wildlife biologist Allen E. Anderson, now retired from Colorado's Division of Wildlife, thinks the cougars around Colorado cities are mostly young animals seeking their own space. During 14 years of research, Anderson found that the cats are extremely territorial, defending home ranges that for males can extend for a radius of more than 160 kilometers (100 miles), slightly less for females. His studies showed that after being weaned and driven off by their mothers, young cats may travel up to 325 kilometers (200 miles) before finding a place to settle where they will not be killed as "trespassers" by resident cougars. Anderson also found that the ideal habitat for cougars has forests, canyons, and gullies—features common to Colorado's Front Range.

In contrast to Colorado's wandering cougars, those sighted in California around Los Angeles, Sacramento, and San Diego appear to be established residents. The increased frequency of cougar sightings may be due to creeping urban sprawl that brings people into established mountain lion habitat in unprecedented numbers. The state also banned cougar hunting in 1972, allowing the population to increase. With no threat from hunting, the cats no longer seem to fear people. They regularly turn up in backyards to prey on pets or other animals.

Suburban Orange County, southeast of Los Angeles, is fairly typical. There, residential developments have crept out from Mission Viejo, San Juan Capistrano, and other towns into the foothills of the Santa Ana Mountains. The canyons, forests, and *chaparral* (dense growth of thorny shrubs or small trees) of the foothills are home to deer and elk as well as the cougars that prey on them. A study found that this habitat supports over half the lions in the region even though the foothills are included in only about a third of the animals' home ranges.

Wolves and bears in the East

Cities in the East and Midwest are also getting their share of large predators. The eastern timber wolf, a species that goes out of its way to avoid human contact, has moved into the upper Midwest. Driven nearly to extinction in the region in the early 1900's, the wolves began returning to Minnesota, Wisconsin, and Michigan in the mid-1970's. Since then, the population has ballooned. Minnesota wolves now number about 2,200, nearly double the number of the first census in 1978.

Biologist Michael Doncarlos of Minnesota's Department of Natural Resources said the wolf's protected status under federal and state laws was at least partially responsible for the animal's resurgence. Protection led to an explosion of the wolf population in Minnesota's northern wilderness areas, forcing some wolves southward in search of territory and food. Wolves now occupy the urban fringe and suburban areas only 90 kilometers (56 miles) from Minneapolis and St. Paul, an area of more than 2.5 million people. Doncarlos believes the wolves will continue to expand their range because their prey, white-tail deer, are at record high numbers throughout the Great Lakes region.

The largest animal moving into America's urban habitats is the black bear. Remarkably, people in New Jersey, the nation's most densely populated state, are sighting bears in the Highlands, which border on the state's most crowded section. This region, roughly 64 kilometers (40 miles) from midtown Manhattan in New York City, has evergreen forests, lakes, and swamps mixed with residential communities. Nearly every day, residents of West Milford and other towns in the Highlands report bears wandering through their backyards.

In the early 1970's, New Jersey's annual bear count varied from 10 to 30 animals. By 1996, the count was up to more than 400. State wildlife biologist Patty McConnell believes two major events triggered the rise. First, in the 1960's, the U.S. Army Corps of Engineers bought up thousands of hectares of farmland along the Delaware River for a dam project, but the project was canceled and the land reverted to forest. And second, neighboring Pennsylvania prohibited bear hunting for several years in the late 1970's. The rise in the number of bears forced younger bears to cross the Delaware and seek new territory in New Jersey's reforested areas. By 1996, bear habitat was pushing against lakeside communities, and bears were attracted to easy-to-get food.

Searching for harmony

Officials are turning to science for ways to control the numbers of undesirable animals in urban habitats. Biologists' major advice is to not leave out anything edible that will attract large animals. People may like to watch deer forage in their backyard, but not the coyotes, bears, or mountain lions that may follow close behind.

On the other hand, some steps are being taken to enhance the urban habitat for desirable species less adaptable to people. Some biologists are collaborating with developers on designs that will preserve woodlands, meadows, and other natural elements of the area. Some communities have left corridors linking large habitats to accommodate seasonal wildlife movements or built tunnels under roads at known crossings to reduce the number of animals killed by vehicles. Most urban dwellers delight in watching animals and birds and applaud such efforts to promote a harmonious relationship between people and wildlife.

For further reading:

Living With Wildlife: How to Enjoy, Cope with, and Protect North America's Wild Creatures Around Your Home and Theirs. Sierra Club Books, 1994.
Swanson, Diane. *Coyotes in the Crosswalk.* Voyager Press, 1996.

For years, people equated Lake Erie with pollution. But vigorous cleanup efforts have restored much of the lake's ecology.

A Comeback for Lake Erie

BY JON R. LUOMA

To the European explorers who first encountered them in the mid-1600's, the Great Lakes no doubt seemed like paradise. The "sweet-water seas," as explorers called the lakes, were bordered by hundreds of miles of unspoiled shoreline. Trout, lake whitefish, blue pike, and sturgeon swam through the clear waters, and wildlife abounded in forests that grew almost to the water's edge. But as the centuries passed and more and more people moved into the region, industry and pollution came to the Great Lakes, transforming large parts of these remarkable inland seas from sweet waters to profoundly dirty waters. The dirtiest was Lake Erie.

Lake Erie, the smallest of the Great Lakes in water volume (and second smallest in surface area), became so polluted by the middle of the 1900's that its name became synonymous with filthy waters, foul odors, and dying fish. By 1970, many observers were even suggesting that the lake was dead.

Yet in the mid-1990's, barely 20 years after Lake Erie's most polluted years, scientists agree that the lake is well on the way to recovery. Thanks to a vigorous cleanup effort by government and industry, the lake is cleaner than it has been in nearly 20 years. Beaches have reopened, and many of the lake's native fish and wildlife are thriving again.

The author:
Jon R. Luoma is a free-lance science writer.

But Lake Erie's story is not all good news. Much pollution persists in the lake, and more hard work and money will be required to continue the cleanup. Government and industry have taken the preliminary steps, and even those were costly. The lake is still contaminated with poisonous chemicals that have built up in the ecosystem, and an invasion by new animal species threatens the long-term survival of the lake's native species. These challenges promise to be much more complex and difficult than the initial cleanup.

A history of ecological abuse

It took 150 years to turn Lake Erie into a cesspool. In the early 1800's, Lake Erie's shores held only a scattering of small ramshackle villages. But a period of explosive growth began in 1825. In that year, the Erie Canal opened, linking the lake with the Hudson River, 584 kilometers (363 miles) to the east and thus with the bustling cities of the Eastern Seaboard. Immediately, the cost of carrying freight to and from the Lake Erie region plummeted. Timber and farm goods began moving east on the canal, and farm equipment, building materials, and people began moving west to the Great Lakes.

By the mid-1800's, railroads had pushed their way into the region. Almost overnight, small harbor villages along the lake became prosperous towns and then major cities. By 1850, Cleveland had blossomed into a town of 17,000 from a tiny village of only 150 people just 30 years earlier.

Even then, human activity in the Lake Erie basin was fouling the lake, and some of the worst pollution came from Cleveland, which was already on its way to becoming a major industrial city. The city's raw sewage and waste from sawmills, factories, and slaughterhouses, were dumped into the Cuyahoga River, which carried them into the lake. That year, in response to a typhoid epidemic, Cleveland moved its drinking water intake from the increasingly contaminated river to a spot 120 meters (400 feet) out into the lake. But the lake was itself growing dirtier by the year. Nonetheless, the city did nothing to stop the pollution.

As Cleveland grew, so did other cities in the region. By the 1900's, the Lake Erie basin—the lands that drain into the lake and its tributaries—had become one of the most populated and industrialized regions in North America. In 1900, some 3.1 million people lived in the Lake Erie basin, an area encompassing northern Ohio, southeastern Michigan, southern Ontario, Canada, and small parts of northwestern Pennsylvania and western New York. Steel mills, refineries, and automobile and chemical plants dotted the lakeshore and the banks of tributary rivers in Buffalo, New York; Cleveland; Lorain, Ohio; and Detroit. Away from the cities, agriculture prospered where forests and swamps had once existed.

The first strong signal of trouble in the lake came when pollution and overfishing began to kill off some fish species. The lake and its tributaries had once been famous for their huge and abundant fish.

Lake Erie's place among the Great Lakes

Lake Erie is the second smallest of the Great Lakes in surface area. Four states (Michigan, New York, Ohio, and Pennsylvania) and one Canadian province (Ontario) border Lake Erie. Almost all of Lake Erie's water comes from Lake Huron through Lake St. Clair and the Detroit River.

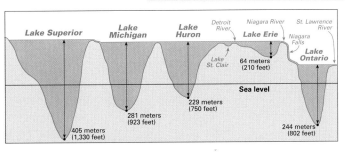

Lake Erie is the shallowest of the Great Lakes, *left, top,* with an average depth of just 19 meters (62 feet) and a maximum depth of 64 meters (210 feet). Because of Lake Erie's shallowness, concentrations of pollutants build up faster there than in the other Great Lakes. More people live around Lake Erie than any other Great Lake, *left, bottom,* a fact that also greatly contributes to pollution in the lake.

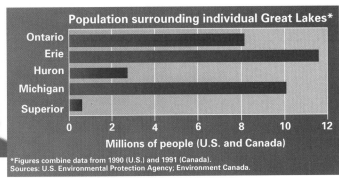

Population surrounding individual Great Lakes*

*Figures combine data from 1990 (U.S.) and 1991 (Canada).
Sources: U.S. Environmental Protection Agency; Environment Canada.

But by the late 1800's, some observers noted that the fish harvest was dropping rapidly. The most rapid decline was in the commercial catch of walleye. Between 1893 and 1900 the yearly catch of walleye collapsed from 5.9 million kilograms (13 million pounds) to only 900,000 kilograms (2 million pounds). The fish stocks recovered, but later in the 1900's walleye harvests crashed again, as did catches of the prized blue pike, which was driven to extinction. Although these disastrous declines were caused mostly by overfishing, pollution also played an increasingly important part.

The degradation of the lake continued for decades. During the worst years, in the 1950's and 1960's, pollutants ranged from acids

How pollution nearly killed Lake Erie

Discharges and wastes from many sources polluted Lake Erie for much of the 1900's. Most of the pollution came from large cities, but farming also contributed.

Tons of runoff from cities and farms, including silt, fertilizers, pesticides, and untreated sewage, entered the lake. Fertilizers and pesticides from farm fields washed away with rains and entered the lake through streams and rivers. Pesticides often accumulated to toxic levels in fish and other wildlife, creating reproduction problems in wildlife and threatening the health of humans who ate contaminated fish. Silt destroyed fish breeding grounds and muddied the water.

Discharges of industrial waste from factories released millions of tons of toxic chemicals into the lake, including mercury, benzene, polychlorinated biphenyls (PCB's), lead, and cyanide.

Agricultural runoff

Urban runoff

Industrial discharges

Sewage and fertilizers contain phosphorus, a plant nutrient that speeded up algae growth and helped kill fish and other aquatic organisms through the process of eutrophication (see diagrams, *right*).

Thick mats of algae resulting from eutrophication covered many parts of Lake Erie in the 1970's and 1980's, including much of the shoreline, *right*.

Air pollution from industrial activities entered Lake Erie. Toxic compounds used in industry, such as PCB's and mercury, were released into the atmosphere and drifted onto the lake or were carried down by rain and snow.

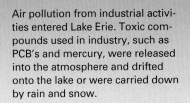

Air pollution

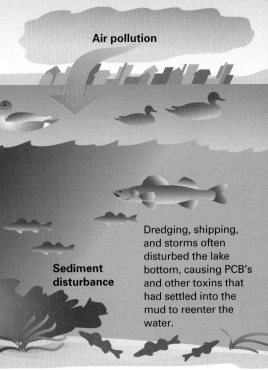

Sediment disturbance

Dredging, shipping, and storms often disturbed the lake bottom, causing PCB's and other toxins that had settled into the mud to reenter the water.

Eutrophication

Eutrophication is a natural process in which the amount of vegetation in a lake gradually increases. After thousands of years, the vegetation clogs the lake, turning it into a swamplike body, and then into dry land. In Lake Erie, however, pollution speeded up eutrophication drastically. Phosphorus from detergents and untreated sewage acted as a nutrient to increase the proliferation of algae and other aquatic plants. Algal blooms formed thick mats on the surface of the lake.

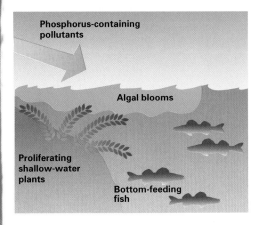

Phosphorus-containing pollutants

Algal blooms

Proliferating shallow-water plants

Bottom-feeding fish

The accelerated eutrophication of the lake had serious ecological consequences. As the algae died, it settled to the bottom. Bacteria decomposed the dead vegetation, using up oxygen dissolved in the bottom water. As a result, fish eggs and bottom-dwelling organisms such as mayfly *nymphs* (insects in the stage of development between an egg and an adult) died from lack of oxygen. Fish that feed on bottom organisms died of starvation.

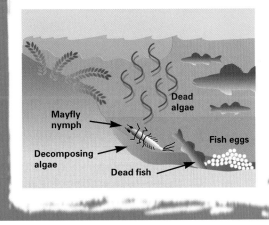

Dead algae

Mayfly nymph

Fish eggs

Decomposing algae

Dead fish

and oils to wood pulp and molten waste from steel mills. In 1968, a U.S. government report estimated that 570 billion liters (150 billion gallons) of industrial wastes from Detroit-area factories poured daily into the Detroit River—the source of most of the water that flows into Lake Erie. In 1969, an incident that captured worldwide attention summed up the ecological assault on Lake Erie: A spill of molten waste metal from a Cleveland steel mill ignited the coating of oil, chemicals, and debris on the Cuyahoga, and the river itself burst into flame.

Phosphorus and eutrophication

Of all the pollutants that poured into Lake Erie, scientists soon discovered that one compound—phosphorus—was particularly troublesome. As investigators learned more about phosphorus, it became a focus in the struggle against the deterioration of Lake Erie.

Phosphorus entered the lake from many sources. Factories were a major source of phosphorus pollution, but so were homes. Due to its power to help water dissolve dirt and stains, phosphorus became a key ingredient in modern detergents after World War II (1939-1945), so large quantities of phosphorus entered rivers and streams in laundry wastewater. Human waste also contains phosphorus, and many outdated and inadequate sewage treatment plants along the lake permitted untreated sewage to enter the lake. In addition, accelerated land use after World War II contributed to phosphorus build-up in the lake by increasing the release of silt into streams and rivers. Silt is muddy material made up of tiny particles of rock and soil. Silt clouds waters and destroys fish breeding grounds, and it also contains small amounts of naturally occurring phosphorus. Intensive construction of suburbs, with their paved streets and parking lots, led to silt build-up in waterways by allowing water to drain away faster during rains, carrying soil with it.

Water runoff from farm fields also added to silt build-up. Farming and livestock practices added to phosphorus pollution in other ways as well. Large amounts of phosphorus-laden animal waste often washed into streams and rivers. And because green plants need phosphorus to grow, farmers increasingly applied it to their crops in fertilizer.

The growing levels of phosphorus created problems for Lake Erie, because it continued to act as a fertilizer—not of crops but of algae. As a result, populations of algae exploded, giving the lake the appearance of a murky pea soup.

The green water signaled the beginning of a deeper problem. The excess vegetation was a sign that the natural process of aging, which occurs in all lakes, had speeded up in Lake Erie. Lakes naturally change over time, becoming richer in nutrients until they are so choked with algae and sediments that they turn into *wetlands* (areas of land where the water level remains near or above the surface of the ground for most of the year). The wetlands eventually become dry lands. But this process, called *eutrophication*, normally takes thousands of years in a large lake such as Erie. Pollution had begun an artificial, extremely rapid eutrophication in Lake Erie.

The proliferation of algae in Lake Erie began to suffocate the lake by depriving it of life-giving oxygen. Like other green plants, algae use sunlight to convert carbon dioxide and water into energy-containing compounds, a process called photosynthesis. During photosynthesis, plants give off oxygen. So as algae continued to grow in Lake Erie, they provided food and oxygen to fish and other organisms—up to a point. Problems began when large amounts of algae died and sank to deeper water and to the bottom. There, bacteria that decomposed them used up oxygen dissolved in the water. The resulting lack of oxygen in the lower depths of the lake killed many fish and fish eggs, as well as bottom-dwelling organisms such as mayfly *nymphs* (insects in the stage of development between eggs and adults) that fish feed on. The lack of oxygen led some observers to claim that the lake was "dead," but it was actually teeming with algae—too much of it.

Algal blooms first became noticeable in the lake's shallower areas near Toledo and elsewhere along the shore in the 1930's. Thick mats of algae washed up on shore and rotted, creating a powerful stench and fouling beaches. Scientists soon discovered negative affects of algal blooms throughout the lake. In 1974, half of the deep-water areas that scientists sampled in late summer, when the algae was at its worst, lacked oxygen.

The problem of organochlorines

As more and more attention focused on the deterioration of Lake Erie, scientists began to suspect that pollutants called organochlorines also posed a major threat to Lake Erie's ecosystem. Organochlorines are compounds containing chlorine and carbon. Chemists synthesize organochlorines in laboratories for use as potent insecticides and as additives in a wide range of products, including paints, oils, plastics, and solvents. Two of the most well-known organochlorines are the insecticide dichlorodiphenyl-trichloro-ethane (DDT) and the group of industrial solvents and insulating fluids called polychlorinated biphenyls (PCB's).

Although they are useful chemicals, organochlorines can harm the health of animals and humans. For instance, DDT disrupts the development of birds' eggs by causing the shells to be extremely thin and fragile, a condition that kills the chicks before birth. High concentrations of PCB's can kill bird embryos. Regulators banned DDT and PCB's in the United States and Canada in the 1970's because of the harm they were causing to wildlife and concerns that the chemicals may cause cancer in humans.

Organochlorines have also been found in many human tissues. Scientists believe that if these compounds build up to high enough levels in the human body, they may cause not only cancer but also a range of other health problems, including disorders of the immune and endocrine systems and damage to embryos.

Major actions that have helped clean up Lake Erie

Since the early 1970's, several actions by the United States and Canadian governments have encouraged communities and industries that border Lake Erie to clean up their operations:

1. **Formation of the International Joint Commission (1909)**
   The governments of the United States and Canada formed the International Joint Commission (IJC) in 1909 to settle questions about the use of boundary waters between Canada and the United States for water power, navigation, sanitation, irrigation, recreation, and scenic beauty. Since 1972, the commission has also coordinated efforts to reduce pollution of the Great Lakes.

2. **Formation of U.S. Environmental Protection Agency (1970)**
   The Environmental Protection Agency (EPA) was formed to protect the nation's environment from pollution. The EPA establishes and enforces environmental protection standards and conducts research on the effects of pollution. It provides grants and technical assistance to cities and states for pollution prevention. Much of the EPA's work involves Lake Erie and the other Great Lakes. In 1995, EPA-proposed legislation took effect that mandates states to substantially limit discharges of harmful chemicals and other pollution into the Great Lakes.

3. **The U.S. Clean Water Act (1972)**
   This act set nationwide water quality guidelines and industrial and commercial limits on the amount of pollution that could be discharged into lakes and rivers. It also established penalties for polluters and committed federal money to upgrading sewage treatment plants in Detroit, Buffalo, and Cleveland.

4. **The Canada Water Act (1972)**
   Similar to the U.S. Clean Water Act, the Canadian legislation set stricter limits on phosphorus content in detergents than did the U.S. law.

5. **The International Great Lakes Water Quality Agreement (1972)**
   This was an agreement between the United States and Canada that set joint goals for Great Lakes cleanup and established a framework for research on environmental problems. The agreement was updated and strengthened in 1978.

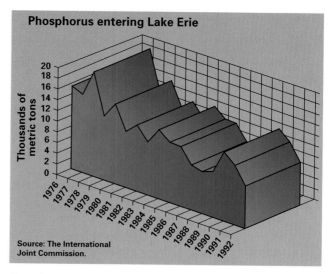

Phosphorus entering Lake Erie

Source: The International Joint Commission.

Phosphorus caused major pollution problems in Lake Erie in the 1950's and 1960's. But beginning in the 1970's, governmental restrictions significantly reduced the amount of phosphorus that entered the lake each year.

Organochlorines and bioconcentration

One of the most disturbing qualities of organochlorines is their tendency to accumulate in progressively higher levels as they ascend the *food web*. Food webs are the chainlike relationships in a habitat by which food energy is transferred from plants to increasingly larger animals. For example, a simple food web in a lake links algae, small animals called zooplankton, small fish that eat the zooplankton, larger fish that eat the smaller fish, and birds that eat the larger fish. The process by which organochlorines or other harmful substances increase in concentration as they move up food webs is called *bioconcentration*.

Bioconcentration occurs with many organochlorines largely because they do not dissolve in water. Inside organisms, organochlorines are absorbed in fatty cells instead of being flushed out with ordinary cellular wastes. Within food webs, tiny, short-lived organisms, such as aquatic insects that only live a few months, may accumulate only small amounts of these chemicals. But longer-lived species, and especially such predators as salmon, gulls, or eagles that eat large numbers of smaller animals, will accumulate far more. Accumulation occurs in fish, for instance, when they eat large amounts of insect larvae or algae contaminated with low levels of organochlorines. The chemicals gradually build up in the fishes' fatty tissues to concentrations far higher than in the algae. If birds then eat large numbers of contaminated fish, the compounds become even more highly concentrated in the birds. Human beings can also accumulate high levels of organochlorines in their tissues if they dine frequently on fish from polluted waters. In this way, molecules of DDT and PCB can remain in cells for years, even decades, and some organochlorines can persist in the environment for as long as 400 years.

Scientists have calculated that a tiny 3 parts per billion of an organochlorine in plankton in Lake Erie can magnify to more than 3,000 times that concentration in small fish such as smelt, up to 60,000 times in walleye, and as much as 1 million times in the fatty eggs of a fish-eating herring gull. (One part per billion is roughly equivalent to a tablespoon of an organochlorine dissolved in a tank of water the size of a football field filled to a depth of 3 meters [10 feet].)

Government actions to clean up Lake Erie

Despite the assault from pollution, Lake Erie's condition improved dramatically during the 1980's and into the 1990's. The lake has not completely returned to its former clarity and abundance of wildlife, but the cleanup has been significant.

Lake Erie is cleaner today because of an unprecedented effort on the part of both the United States and Canada. As long ago as 1909, the two nations agreed to develop an oversight committee, called the International Joint Commission (IJC), to resolve disputes and work for common interests on the Great Lakes and other boundary waters. In the 1970's, the IJC began to help efforts to clean up Lake Erie.

In 1972, the United States and Canada signed the first version of the Great Lakes Water Quality Agreement. With its progress to be monitored by the IJC, the agreement called for the control of industrial pollution and phosphorus and for new or improved sewage treatment plants.

The cleanup of Lake Erie got another boost when the U.S. Congress passed the Clean Water Act of 1972. The act set nationwide standards for water quality, including limits on the discharge of untreated water and harmful chemicals into rivers and other waterways. The legislation mandated penalties for polluters and provided federal money for building and upgrading local sewage-treatment plants. Perhaps most importantly, the Clean Water Act provided money for cleanup efforts. By the late 1980's, the United States alone had spent more than $8 billion on sewage treatment plants on the Great Lakes and their tributaries. At the same time, most Great Lakes states and the province of Ontario imposed strict limits on phosphorus content in detergents.

The Canada Water Act also passed in 1972. The bill was similar to the U.S. Clean Water Act but went further in limiting phosphate use. These major governmental efforts were augmented by agreements among states that border Lake Erie and other measures initiated by private industry.

Lake Erie today

Lake Erie is cleaner today than it has been in decades, and recreational activities, such as ones at Marblehead lighthouse near Marblehead, Ohio, *below*, are common. Serious problems remain, however, including continued pollution and the invasion of foreign species.

The ecology of Lake Erie has changed in the 1900's as a result of pollution and overfishing. Dramatic changes have occurred in the lake's fish populations between 1900 and 1996, *below*.

Lake Erie fish common in 1900:

Blue pike
Lake sturgeon
Lake herring
Lake whitefish
Lake trout
Walleye
Yellow perch
White bass
Freshwater drum
Channel catfish

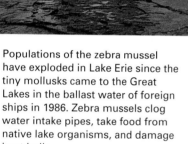

Populations of the zebra mussel have exploded in Lake Erie since the tiny mollusks came to the Great Lakes in the ballast water of foreign ships in 1986. Zebra mussels clog water intake pipes, take food from native lake organisms, and damage boat hulls.

As a result of these programs, the amount of phosphorus from wastewater systems pouring into Lake Erie and the other Great Lakes has decreased by nearly 85 percent compared with 1972 levels. The amount of phosphorus from all sources entering the lake has declined by about 65 percent from 1972—from about 28,000 metric tons (31,000 short tons) per year to about 8,000 metric tons (9,000 short tons), according to the U.S. Environmental Protection Agency (EPA). That total is well below the 11,000 metric tons (12,000 short tons) per year that scientists had established as a restoration target that would prevent algal blooms and allow the lake's ecology to recover.

But the various cleanup actions did more than just reduce phosphorus and algae. In fact, a near miracle seemed to have taken place in Lake Erie by 1996. People now swim safely at beaches once closed by

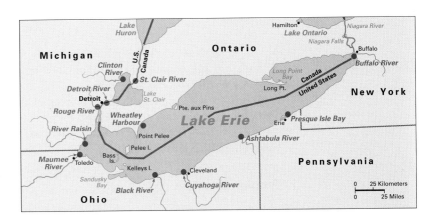

Lake Erie fish in 1996:

Thriving:
Walleye
Lake whitefish
Freshwater drum
Channel catfish

Extinct:
Blue pike

Numbers severely reduced:
Lake sturgeon
Lake herring

Reduced populations:
Yellow perch
White bass

Reintroduced in limited numbers:
Lake trout

Invader species:
Alewife
Carp
Gizzard shad
Smelt
Sea lamprey
White perch

Introduced in limited numbers:
Brown trout
Rainbow trout
Coho salmon
Chinook salmon
Sockeye salmon

The United States and Canada are working together to clean up 12 of the most polluted sites around Lake Erie, *top*. Despite increased cleanup efforts, pollution such as that from an industrial waste pond in Cleveland, *above*, still enters Lake Erie.

health departments because of pollution. The blue pike is gone, but walleye populations have rebounded to record numbers, and the catch of whitefish has grown from a mere 1,800 kilograms (4,000 pounds) in the mid-1980's to nearly 320,000 kilograms (700,000 pounds) in 1995.

The recovery of mayflies, which can breed and complete their life cycle only in clean waters, may be one of the best signals that the lake is getting healthier. Once abundant in Lake Erie, mayflies disappeared completely in the 1960's. Then in 1979, researchers found 20 mayfly nymphs near the mouth of the Detroit River. By 1995, clouds of flying adult mayflies had begun to rise regularly from some parts of the lake.

Additional signs of recovery had appeared by the mid-1990's. The phosphorus content in the lake had fallen below the target level set by the IJC, and summer algal blooms in the lake were less frequent. The number of nesting pairs of bald eagles had increased to 17 along the Ohio shore of Lake Erie, up from just 4 in 1979. And the river that burst into flames, the Cuyahoga, was so much cleaner that posh cafes lined the river's banks in parts of downtown Cleveland.

Continuing cleanup efforts offer further hope for Lake Erie. In

March 1995, the Great Lakes Water Quality Guidance Regulations, an EPA plan to tighten federal control of Great Lakes pollution, became law. The regulations established limits on discharges and concentrations of some 40 toxic chemicals, including PCB's, DDT, and heavy metals such as mercury and lead, into the Great Lakes and their tributary rivers. States bordering the Great Lakes were trying to find ways to meet the new regulations in 1996.

Problems remain

Still, serious ecological problems remain for Lake Erie. Cleanup at a number of contamination sites identified by the IJC for special attention has been slow, and despite dramatic improvements in sewage treatment, there is still a large amount of phosphorus pouring into the lake. About 60 percent of it comes from an array of indirect sources, including silt and fertilizer runoff from lawns and farm fields. Two million metric tons (2.2 million short tons) of silt continue to pour into the lake each year from the Maumee River, at Toledo, alone. Experts hope that more farmers will adopt measures to help prevent runoff, such as not plowing all the way to the banks of streams and rivers. But efforts to reduce such scattered sources of phosphorus pollution have been difficult because they involve changing the habits of millions of people.

And despite the ban on PCB's, they persist in elevated levels in the cells of many birds and fish. After dropping in the 1970's and early 1980's, PCB levels in Lake Erie walleye, for instance, have remained steady since 1984. That fact indicates that PCB's still exist in the lake, where they have concentrated in bottom sediments. Fish that eat aquatic insects and other organisms still become contaminated. Moreover, storms, shipping, and dredging disturb PCB's that have settled into the lake bottom so that they enter the food web again.

The existence of even small concentrations of PCB's in Lake Erie fish concerns scientists and public health officials. Several studies reported in the 1980's suggested that pregnant women who regularly eat lake fish risk exposing their unborn babies to contaminants that may cause learning disabilities or low birth weights. Because of concerns over the persistence of PCB contamination, the four U.S. states and one Canadian province bordering Lake Erie still advise people to limit the amount of certain fish they eat from particular areas of the lake.

Aside from these continuing problems with chemical pollution, Lake Erie is also under assault by "pollutants" of an entirely different kind—harmful species that are not native to the lakes. In 1986, small fingernail-sized invaders called zebra mussels found their way into the Great Lakes from the Caspian Sea, which lies between eastern Europe and Asia. The mussels came over in the ballast water of a foreign ship and entered the lakes when the ship released the water. Today, millions of these tiny, rapidly reproducing creatures infest Lake Erie.

Zebra mussels create several problems. They attach themselves to dock pilings, boat hulls, and water intake pipes of power plants. The invaders even cling to native organisms with shells, such as mollusks and crayfish. Scraping the mussels off encrusted surfaces is both difficult and costly and, as they continue to breed, a never-ending task.

The effects of the zebra mussel invasion on Lake Erie are more complex than clogged pipes, however. The invaders have also changed the ecology of the lake, and scientists worry that the mussels now infesting the lake are crowding out native animal species. The mussels feed on *phytoplankton* (microscopic aquatic plants), including algae, which form the base for much of the lake's food web. By filtering algae from the water, zebra mussels take food away from other filter feeding mollusks, zooplankton, and small fish feeding on algae. Zebra mussels also absorb molecules of PCB's and other toxins that have become attached to phytoplankton. The toxins bioconcentrate when fish such as carp eat the mussels, and birds eat the fish.

One pest, an eellike fish called the sea lamprey, experienced a resurgence in Lake Erie in the 1980's. The sea lamprey found its way into the lake from the Atlantic Ocean in the 1920's. Lampreys attach themselves to larger fish and suck out the fishes' blood and other body fluids. In some lakes, such as Lake Michigan, that were plagued by lampreys, these parasitic invaders nearly wiped out populations of native lake trout. But in the Lake Erie basin, lamprey reproduction remained low because they need clean feeder streams with gravel beds in which to breed. As a "benefit" of pollution, streams in the basin were simply too dirty for the lampreys to prosper. In recent years, however, lampreys have found cleaner waters around Lake Erie. One survey in the late 1980's counted nearly 1 million lampreys in the juvenile, larval stage in Conneaut Creek in Ohio.

The cleanup of Lake Erie has taught scientists and government leaders valuable lessons about the need to prevent pollution. Experts estimate that the cost of cleaning up emissions from factories, wastewater plants, and other sources of pollution would have been 10 to 100 times less than it has cost to restore Lake Erie once those contaminants were allowed to enter the lake. The continued success of Lake Erie's cleanup will require dedication and hard work. But someday, perhaps not too many years in the future, visitors to the lake may look upon the lake's clean, clear waters, and have trouble believing that Lake Erie could ever have been a symbol of everything that human activity can do to harm the environment.

For further reading:
Ashworth, William. *The Late, Great Lakes.* Knopf, 1986.
Burns, Noel M. *Erie: The Lake that Survived.* Rowman & Allanheld, 1985.
Colborn, Theodora E.; Davidson, Alex; Green, Sharon N.; Hodge, Tony; Jackson, Ian; Liroff, Richard A. *Great Lakes, Great Legacy?* World Wildlife Fund/Conservation Foundation, 1990.

Rocket Man

The heroic commander of the real-life
Apollo 13 mission to the moon talks about
the rewards and risks of space exploration.

AN INTERVIEW WITH JIM LOVELL
BY JINGER HOOP

The American astronaut *James Arthur Lovell, Jr., served on four key space flights in the early days of the United States space program. During his first mission, on Gemini 7 in 1965, Lovell and crewmate Frank Borman set an endurance record by spending 14 days orbiting the Earth. Lovell served as commander of the Gemini 12 flight the next year. In 1968, Lovell and two other astronauts became the first people to circle the moon, during the flight of Apollo 8.*

Lovell's fourth and last space flight was the ill-fated Apollo 13, an April 1970 mission to the moon that became a close brush with death. Two days into the flight, an oxygen tank in the craft's supply module exploded, leaving Lovell and his two crewmates, Fred W. Haise, Jr., and John L. Swigert, Jr., with barely enough power to return home. During a four-day journey around the moon and back to Earth, the astronauts endured freezing temperatures and a harrowing series of technical crises. With the world watching on television, the command module made a safe reentry into Earth's atmosphere and splashed down into the Pacific Ocean on April 17.

Twenty-five years later, Lovell reemerged on the public scene with the publication of Lost Moon, *a nonfiction account of the Apollo 13 flight written by Lovell and science writer Jeffrey Kluger. The book was made into an award-winning movie,* Apollo 13, *starring Tom Hanks as Captain Lovell. The film, a critical and popular hit in summer 1995, reestablished Lovell as an American hero.*

The author:
Jinger Hoop is a former
managing editor of
Science Year.

Science Year: In your book, *Lost Moon*, you describe the day you first heard of the plan to put Americans into space. It was 1958, and you were a test pilot in Maryland. You and a few other pilots were summoned to a secret meeting in Washington, D.C., where officials asked for volunteers to sit in a tiny capsule on top of a ballistic missile and be blasted into space.

What was going through your mind as the officials sketched out what must have sounded like a far-fetched and incredibly dangerous project?

Jim Lovell: Actually, to me it sounded like a dream come true. I had been interested in rockets since I was a kid. At first, I wanted to become a rocket engineer—someone like Robert Goddard, who did the early American experiments with liquid fuel rockets, or Wernher von Braun, who developed Germany's V-2 rocket. I wrote a term paper in school on rockets where I said that maybe someday man would go into space using rocket power. I didn't have the money to go to the colleges where they taught rocket engineering, and that's how I ended up at the Naval Academy and became a Navy test pilot. So when I heard about the plan to put men into space, I thought this was my fate. It was just what I had been looking for.

"When I heard about the plan to put men into space, I thought this was my fate. It was just what I had been looking for."

Science Year: But you weren't admitted into the space program at that time.

Lovell: No. I was perfectly healthy, but my physical examination showed an elevated level of a liver pigment called bilirubin, and so they turned me down. It was really disappointing. I'd learned all about space flight before the Alan Shepards and the John Glenns even knew how to spell "rocket." But I got in with the second group of astronauts in 1962.

Science Year: What was it like to be an astronaut in the early days? One of your fellow astronauts, Frank Borman, has said that his stint in the space program was as difficult as eight years of military combat.

Lovell: I kind of disagree with Frank about that, because in combat you see your opponents maximizing all their resources to make your life more risky, and with space flight, everyone is trying to minimize your risks. Everyone was trying to make the systems as accurate and as reliable as possible.

But being an astronaut in those days could be very difficult. Frank says his Gemini 7 mission with me—a two-week flight around the Earth in a very, very small capsule—was a more harrowing and challenging experience than any other flight. We had a lot of problems with malfunctioning fuel cells, and Frank was worried about whether we would hack it for the 14 days. Plus, Frank was an Air Force pilot, so he liked to be over land. Because the Earth is mostly covered with water, 70 percent of the time we were over the ocean. Being a former Navy pilot, I kept assuring Frank that the Navy would be there to pick us up, regardless of where we splashed down. But that was a pretty tough flight.

Science Year: And what about the fateful Apollo 13 mission? What was the worst part of that troubled flight?

Lovell: Just after the oxygen tank exploded. The flight data showed that my heart rate was 130 beats a minute—about twice normal. We thought at first the lunar module had been hit by a meteor. The other two astronauts and I tried to seal the hatch connecting the command module and the lunar module—like a submarine crew trying to clamp off part of the ship that's flooding. We never could get that hatch closed, so if we really had been struck by a meteor, we would have been killed.

Another low point was when we finally realized the severity of what was happening to our command module. We knew we were losing oxygen, which meant that we were losing electricity and losing our propulsion system. But we did not yet have any idea how to get home, and we were way far out into space.

Science Year: It also wasn't clear whether you would really have enough time to do anything about the problem.

Lovell: You are right. One of the most frantic times was when I was manually converting the data from our guidance system in the dying command module to the lunar module before our electric power ran out. The guidance system needed the data to monitor our attitude [position] with respect to the stars. With only about 15 minutes to

An Astronaut's Life

The troubled flight of Apollo 13 was in many ways emblematic of Jim Lovell's own life—filled with obstacles and setbacks, but eventually turning out just fine.

James Arthur Lovell, Jr., was born in 1928 in Cleveland. As a child, he loved the books of the French science-fiction writer Jules Verne, particularly *From the Earth to the Moon* (1865) and a sequel, *Round the Moon* (1870). "Those books describe a flight amazingly similar to my Apollo 8 mission," Lovell says. "Both vessels carried three people, took off from Florida, and landed in the Pacific Ocean in late December. Both crafts were made of aluminum. The only major difference was that Verne's launch required a cannon, while we used a rocket."

Lovell was fascinated with rockets at an early age, and he vividly remembers making a working rocket using gunpowder as fuel. When Lovell was 17, he wrote to the American Rocket Society to find out how to become a rocket engineer. Unfortunately, Lovell and his widowed mother could not afford tuition at the expensive private colleges the society recommended.

An uncle showed Lovell another way into the skies. As one of the Navy's first aviators, Lovell's uncle had flown wood-and-cloth-winged biplanes in an antisubmarine unit during World War I (1914-1918). His uncle's stories of military exploits made Lovell decide to become an aviator, and the boy applied for admission to the U.S. Naval Academy in Annapolis, Maryland.

Lovell was not admitted, however, and so he enrolled in a naval aviation program at the University of Wisconsin in Madison. Two years later, he applied to the Naval Academy again, and this time it accepted him. After graduating in 1952 and receiving his commission as a Navy ensign, Lovell took flight training and became a naval pilot. Within a few years, he took on one of the most important and riskiest jobs in peacetime aviation—testing experimental airplanes at the Navy's Aircraft Test Center in Patuxent River, Maryland.

Lovell was a 30-year-old test pilot and the father of three young children when he learned of the government's plan to create a civilian agency called the National Aeronautics and Space Administration (NASA). He leaped at the chance to become one of the first group of "astronauts," or "star-sailors." But he suffered yet another crushing setback. Harmless but unusual levels of a liver pigment in his blood prevented him from passing the stringent medical tests required for entry into the astronaut corps.

Four years later, Lovell learned that NASA was

Before the fateful Apollo 13 flight, Lovell shows his wife, Marilyn, and four children his intended landing site on the moon.

ready to add a few more astronauts to the ranks, and he applied again. To Lovell's delight, this time NASA selected him despite his slight physical abnormality.

Lovell spent 11 years in the astronaut corps, flying on Gemini 7 and 12 and Apollo 8 and 13. Apollo 13 was scheduled to be the third moon landing. Lovell planned that 1970 mission to be his last trip into space because, as he said in a press conference before the flight, "I can't think of anything to top landing on the moon."

After Apollo 13, Lovell was frustrated at his failure to achieve his dream of walking on the moon and disappointed that the nation wanted to quickly put the unsuccessful mission behind it. Only Lovell's boyhood hero Charles Lindbergh—the first person to make a nonstop solo flight across the Atlantic Ocean—marked the occasion, in a handwritten letter congratulating the astronauts on their achievement.

Lovell left NASA in 1973 to be chief executive officer of a tugboat company, and he later became the executive vice president with the Centel Corporation in Chicago. His two fellow Apollo 13 astronauts also left NASA. Fred W. Haise, Jr., entered the aeronautical industry. John L. Swigert, Jr., was elected to Congress but died before taking office. Through the years, Haise and Lovell made a point of phoning each other on April 13 to mark what the two came to call "Boom Day." In 1995, however, with Lovell's new book *Lost Moon* a success and the movie *Apollo 13* soon to be released in theaters, Lovell, Haise, and their families marked the 25th anniversary of Boom Day with a real party. [J. H.]

make the transfer, I had to use pencil and paper to make the conversion of the angles.

Science Year: Talk about math anxiety.

Lovell: Oh, yes! Luckily, I had NASA controllers to check my calculations. These guys were safe on the ground, so they could sit down and calmly do the conversions. It happened pretty much the way it was shown in the movie.

Science Year: Was the film an accurate portrayal of the entire mission?

Lovell: Yes, I'm very happy with the way the movie turned out. The filmmakers could have set it on Mars if they wanted, but they kept it authentic.

The one thing in the film that disappointed me is that the characters used more profanity than we ever did. After seeing the movie, Fred Haise and I even checked the air-to-ground tapes because he didn't remember saying all those bad words. I understand the moviemakers spiced up the language because they wanted the movie rated PG-13 instead of PG.

Another distortion was making it seem that Fred Haise and I weren't really confident in Jack Swigert's ability at the beginning of the flight. In reality, we had great confidence in him before we ever took off. But the other incidents in the movie rang true. My wife did lose her engagement ring down the shower drain the day before the liftoff. Swigert did forget to pay his income tax.

Science Year: It's hard to believe you three astronauts were so calm during the flight. Is the ability to keep your cool something that you're born with, or did you develop it as a test pilot?

Lovell: I think we developed it as test pilots. The three of us certainly could have panicked. We could have bounced off the walls of the command module for 10 minutes, but afterward we would have been right back where we started.

It was not like an airplane engine quitting or the wing falling off or something else that meant things were going to end in a hurry. As long as the spacecraft's pressure hulls were intact, we had a little time, and we knew the life-support system in the lunar module could give us a little more time. We didn't panic because panic wouldn't have helped us. Logic took over and said, "Okay, here's a problem. Now, what's the solution?"

And of course we had the radio going, so we had help from a lot of people who were comfortably seated in a nice, warm control center and could think things through without worrying about getting killed.

Science Year: It seems to me that the quality people admire in you is your ability to show grace under pressure.

Lovell: I guess so. But you can get too confident, you know, and take foolish risks. And some problems just can't be overcome. If the explosion had cracked our heat shield, there was nothing we or the control center could have done about it. We just had to wade through and find out what would happen on reentry. But then again we felt it was much better to reenter somehow and end the flight—regardless of how things turned out—rather than to be a permanent monument to the space program orbiting the Earth.

Science Year: It's hard to imagine anything worse than being marooned to die in space that way.

Lovell: It's not a very comforting thought.

Science Year: And yet you and your colleagues had decided that such a death was preferable to dying on the ground, as astronauts Gus Grissom, Ed White, and Roger Chaffee did in a 1967 fire on the launch pad, when they couldn't open their spacecraft's escape hatch.

Lovell: You've got to understand the makeup of the first groups of astronauts. We were all test pilots, so we all had a risky life. I was in other crises testing airplanes, where engines would quit, say, and I had to figure out what to do. But that life to me was so much better than a 9-to-5 job. I never cared to be punching a time clock. And so we would say that if you're going to be in this business and for some reason you're not going to make it, it's better to go out in style. Be stranded on the moon. Killed in a rocket spiraling up into space. That's the way we thought. I'm not so sure that today's astronauts feel the same way.

Science Year: How did you react to the Challenger disaster in 1986, when the space shuttle disintegrated in a ball of fire just after liftoff?

Lovell: I felt the way I did when a friend during my test-pilot days crashed and died in an experimental airplane. The rewards of working in that environment and accomplishing things are great. But it's a risky business. Every time you send humans into the vacuum at a high rate of speed, sitting on top of a lot of explosives, it's going to be risky. But that's the name of the game.

Science Year: At the time, some critics said we should not be sending nonprofessionals into space, that it was a mistake to put Christa McAuliffe, a high-school teacher from New Hampshire, on the flight.

Lovell: I agree completely. Sending her up was a public relations stunt that was a big mistake. NASA doesn't do that anymore. Everyone who goes into space now is a professional astronaut. They all understand the risks involved. Christa McAuliffe was also aware of the risks, but the people who were watching the disaster on television at home didn't understand that.

Science Year: Do you see any common thread among the Apollo 13 explosion, the Challenger disaster, and the launch-pad fire that killed Grissom, Chaffee, and White?

Lovell: I see perhaps a lack of foresight. The crew's death in the launch-pad fire was something we should have anticipated. All the astronauts had complained about the escape hatch long before the fire. The hatch was designed to maintain the ship's integrity so there wouldn't be any leaks in space, but to get out of that hatch in a hurry was almost impossible. As far as Apollo 13 goes, it was just a case of everybody missing the fact that we should have replaced one malfunctioning oxygen-tank thermostat with another before the launch. And there was a lack of quality control in the testing of the tank at Cape Canaveral before the flight.

For Challenger, there was too much delay in changing the design of the solid rockets on the shuttle. They knew about the problem and were working on it.

Science Year: What do you think about the changes you've seen in the U.S. space program since you were an astronaut?

Lovell: Well, the purpose of the old Gemini and Apollo missions was essentially pure research designed to develop space flight. The information we got from landing on the moon and from looking at moon rocks, for example, probably won't help you or me in any practical way.

Over the years, NASA matured, and its mission changed from basic research to providing more immediate, practical benefits. NASA today is a support organization. They support the Department of Agriculture by examining the Earth's land masses to monitor the growth of forests or crops. They can study the oceans and monitor weather patterns. And of course NASA supports private industry in many ways, such as by putting up communication satellites.

Another big change in the space program has to do with the public's

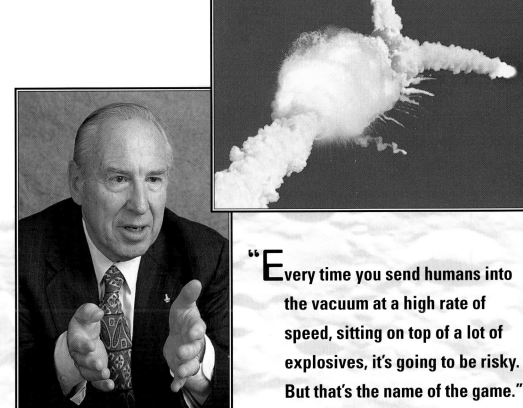

"Every time you send humans into the vacuum at a high rate of speed, sitting on top of a lot of explosives, it's going to be risky. But that's the name of the game."

level of interest in it. In the beginning, the program really captured everyone's imagination. People had been thinking about going to the moon for hundreds of years and we were finally going to do it. Today, people may read about what happens on the flights, but they don't have the same keen interest in them. It's human nature. We've had more than 70 shuttle flights as of this date. No one watches the take-offs on TV anymore, and that's natural. Even way back during the time of Apollo 13, no one was interested in the flight until the explosion.

Science Year: Did your time in space change you as a person? Some astronauts say the experience made them more spiritual.

Lovell: I didn't become more spiritual. The religious beliefs I had

"When I was orbiting the moon and could put my thumb up to the window and completely cover the Earth, I felt a real sense of my own insignificance. Everything I'd ever known could be hidden behind my thumb."

before I got into the program remained with me until the finish. God is down here on Earth with us right now as much as he is out in space, so there shouldn't be any real difference.

The experience did give me a new perspective on our place in the universe. When I was orbiting the moon and could put my thumb up to the window and completely cover the Earth, I felt a real sense of my own insignificance. Everything I'd ever known could be hidden behind my thumb.

Being in space also shows you how relative everything is. In this room, our whole universe is limited to these walls, the ceiling, and the floor. That's all we can see. You get in an airplane, and you start thinking in terms of cities. You think: "I've left Chicago, I'm over St. Louis now, and soon I'll be down to Houston." You get in an Earth-orbiting spacecraft, and your horizon broadens to include whole continents. On the way to the moon, you think in terms of the entire solar system. The moon is up ahead, the sun to your left, the Earth behind you.

Science Year: You see the Earth as just another body moving through space?

Lovell: Yes. I wish everybody could have the experience of looking back at the Earth and realizing it's really no different from a spacecraft. The 5½ billion inhabitants of Earth are all astronauts living on a spaceship that has limited resources. We have to use these resources very wisely if the ship is to keep us alive.

Science Year: Since *Apollo 13* opened, have you been surprised by the public's interest in you and your flight?

Lovell: Totally surprised. It almost makes up for missing my chance to set foot on the moon. The flight of Apollo 13 was technically a failure, but it did prove man's ability to accomplish great things in a crisis. It showed the teamwork, the initiative, and the motivation of the people at NASA. In that respect, I now feel a sense of satisfaction that I really didn't have when I first came back.

The popularity of the movie has also shown me that there are more people interested in the space program than I had imagined. It looks as if the majority of Americans still believe in what we are doing in space, and that the money directed to the program is not ill spent. But they are a silent majority.

Science Year: Have you talked to anyone in Congress, which funds NASA, about that?

Lovell: Yes. Tom Hanks and I were in Washington, D.C., last fall for a reception in the House of Representatives just before Congress voted on funding the space station. A lot of politicians wanted to pose with me for a picture and get an autograph, but when I talked about the future, some said they were voting against the space station. I wish the silent majority of Americans would write to their representatives and say, "I support the space program. NASA is a creative agency that benefits Americans."

Science Year: Why do you think the space station in particular is a worthwhile project? Many scientists claim that it is going to drain funding away from smaller research projects that might produce more significant results.

Lovell: You have to strike a balance between funding basic research projects and funding more practical projects like the space station. The station could be used for manufacturing materials such as alloys, crystals, and serums for medicine. Because of the lack of gravity in space, there aren't any convection currents, and so we can mix things a lot better up there. And if we had a mission to Mars, we could use the space station as a base for assembling a long-range space vehicle.

Today, the plan is to construct the space station jointly with some 14 other countries, including Russia. Now, if we are going to try to help the Russian economy get back on its feet in a more capitalistic way, we might as well get something out of it. And there's a lot of talent in space science in Russia. Why don't we tap it?

The space station enables us to work with other countries on a project that doesn't have the controversy of joint military missions or tariff negotiations, and the process of working together will give us a closer rapport.

Science Year: Yet you entered the space program when its primary

"The 5½ billion inhabitants of Earth are all astronauts living on a spaceship that has limited resources. We have to use these resources very wisely if the ship is to keep us alive."

"We didn't make it to the moon, but Apollo 13 did prove man's ability to accomplish great things in a crisis."

aim was competing with the Soviets. Don't you have any hesitation about joining forces with them now?

Lovell: No qualms. It was a great race between us and the Soviets. Without such heated competition, we might never have gotten the interest ginned up in people about going to space. But now we have a chance at cooperative ventures, and I think that's great.

Science Year: The current NASA chief, Daniel Goldin, emphasizes the importance of doing smaller, simpler, cheaper space missions—for example, sending up unmanned probes rather than manned spacecraft. Do you agree with that philosophy, or do you think that NASA should do something grander—say, establish a moon base or launch a manned mission to Mars?

Lovell: Well, you have to be practical about this. Sometimes you have to get quick results, and the idea of doing things cheaper is always attractive. Goldin has, I think, done a very good job of aiming NASA toward international projects. The United States waffled for years trying to get a solely American space station up. It was too big, too complicated, and too expensive. And NASA didn't immediately realize that everything changed when the Soviet Union dissolved and we no longer

"I believe we will send people to Mars eventually, because human beings are curious animals, and because if America wants to be a leader in the world, we have to stay a leader in technology."

had that great "evil empire" to compete against. I think Goldin has finally got NASA aimed in the right direction. If I were NASA's administrator, however, I would also lay the groundwork for some longer-term programs.

Science Year: Like trying to reach Mars?

Lovell: Yes. We already have the technology to go to Mars. No breakthroughs are required. The last question we had was whether people could safely stay in zero gravity for a space flight of a year's duration. The cosmonauts orbiting for long periods on the Russian space station Mir have essentially proven that it can be done. So all a Mars mission requires is time, effort, and money. Who knows what we might find when we get there? Who knows what practical benefits we might get from the endeavor?

I believe we will send people to Mars eventually, because human beings are curious animals, and because if America wants to be a leader in the world, we have to stay a leader in technology.

Science Year: What advice do you have for young people who might like to be astronauts on that mission to Mars?

Lovell: First, if you want to be successful as an astronaut or as anything else, you have to have keep trying. There will be disappointments in your life. You'll get so far and then there will be a setback. And if you let the setback overcome your drive, your willpower, then you're in trouble.

Look at me—I didn't make it into the Naval Academy the first time I tried. But I got in when I applied two years later. I didn't get in the space program the first time I tried. And I had plenty of setbacks as an astronaut, particularly during Apollo 13. We had crises all the way through the flight, but every time we overcame a crisis, our confidence went up a little bit more that we could probably make it home. Perseverance is really necessary in any field. Now, to be an astronaut today, it's very important to get a good education, but you don't have to become an aviator as I did. You can be a doctor, a physicist, a geologist, an astronomer, just about any kind of scientist. Being an astronaut can even be just a partial career. After your time in space, you can go on to do something else.

Science Year: Do you think you would enjoy being an astronaut today?

Lovell: My bag is packed if someone asks me to go.

Science Year: It would be great public relations for NASA to send you on a shuttle mission.

Lovell: Yes, maybe I ought to push for that. Send the old man up in space another time. And then, of course, there will be a problem with the shuttle, and everyone will be saying, "Holy cow, how are we going to get Lovell down this time?"

For further reading:

Burrows, William E. *Exploring Space: Voyages in the Solar System and Beyond*. Random House, 1990.

The Cambridge Encyclopedia of Space. Ed. by Michael Rycroft. Cambridge, 1990.

Chaikin, Andrew. *A Man on the Moon: The Voyages of the Apollo Astronauts*. Penguin Books, 1994.

Collins, Michael. *Mission to Mars*. Grove Weidenfeld, 1990.

Lewis, Richard S. *Space in the 21st Century*. Columbia University Press, 1990.

Lovell, Jim and Jeffrey Kluger. *Lost Moon: The Perilous Voyage of Apollo 13*. Houghton Mifflin, 1994.

Moore, Patrick. *Mission to the Planets: The Illustrated Story of Man's Exploration of the Solar System*. Norton, 1990.

Spangenburg, Ray, and Moser, Diane. *Space People from A to Z*. Facts on File, 1990.

Wilhelms, Don E. *To a Rocky Moon: A Geologist's History of Lunar Exploration*. University of Arizona Press, 1993.

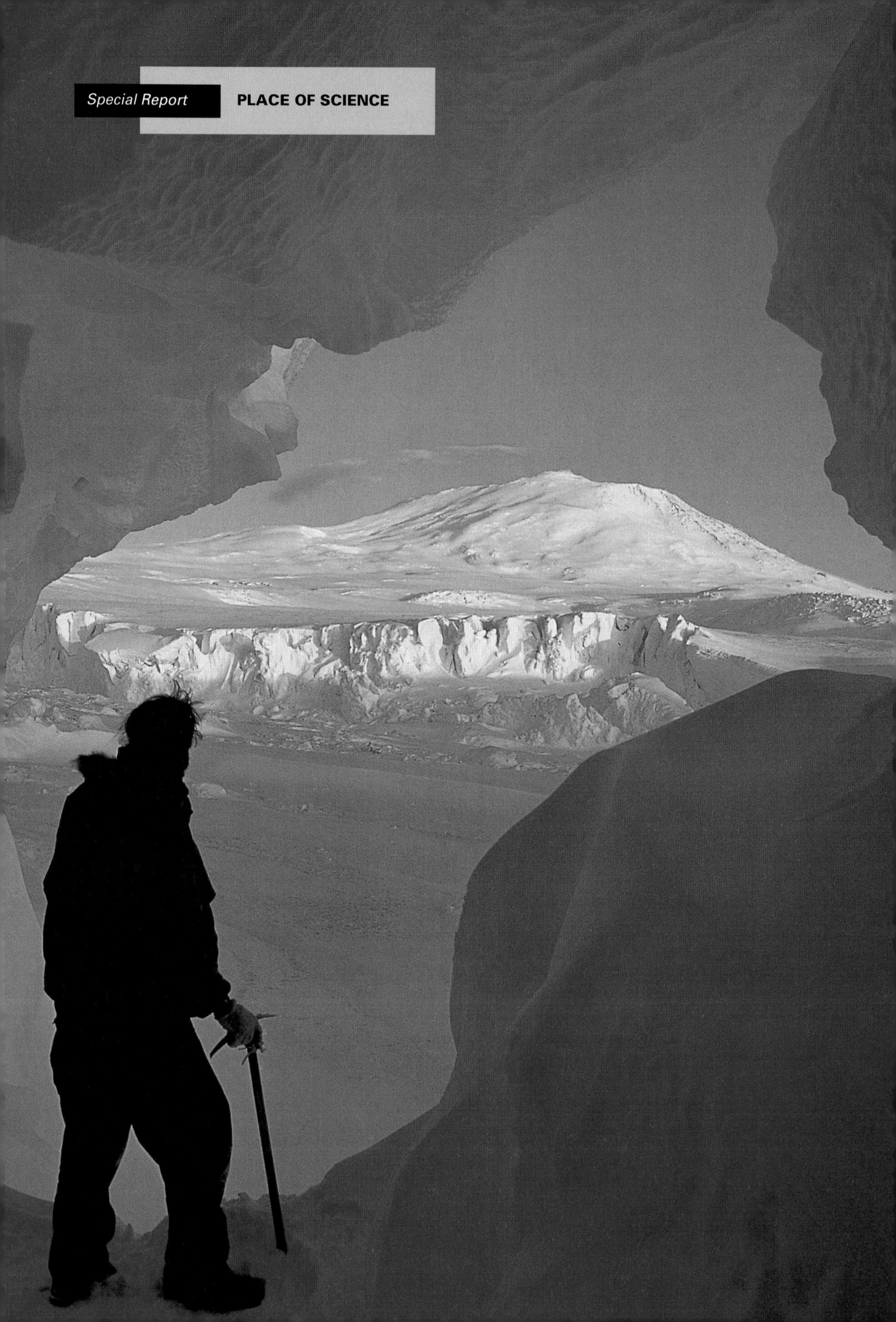

Antarctica's vast expanse of ice and brilliant blue sky offer scientists unparalleled—though frigid—conditions for studying some of our most serious environmental problems and oldest cosmic mysteries.

Science in Antarctica

BY MICHAEL WOODS

B locks of ice bigger than school buses batter the research vessel *Nathaniel B. Palmer* as we steam through the Ross Sea off the coast of Antarctica. The icebreaker, rigged as a floating scientific laboratory, is longer than a football field and towers more than five stories above the water. Yet it lurches with each collision, and the clang of ice against steel sometimes makes conversation in the labs impossible. The deafening noise sounds like lengths of steel chain thrown against a metal barrel.

Harsh conditions are routine for scientists who venture into Antarctica. They work in the world's biggest laboratory, a continent in the Southern Hemisphere larger than the United States and Mexico combined that is reserved by international agreement for science. The investigators come to study some of our most pressing environmental problems and oldest cosmic mysteries. Their research ranges from astronomy to zoology. It involves events as remote in time as the universe's origin 10 billion to 20 billion years ago and as immediate as environmental changes that may alter Earth in the next century. They have found meteorites believed to have landed in Antarctica from Mars, and they have discovered evidence that Antarctica's icecap could melt suddenly, releasing enough water to flood coastal cities.

Antarctica is not an easy place to do research. It is the coldest, windiest, highest, driest continent on Earth. In 1983, scientists recorded the world's lowest temperature, −89.2 °C (−128.6 °F) at Vostok

Station, a Russian research facility in eastern Antarctica. Winds average 70 kilometers (44 miles) per hour, but gusts often reach the coast at 190 kilometers (120 miles) per hour. The continent is surrounded by the ice-clogged Southern Ocean, often called the Antarctic Ocean, where the Atlantic, Pacific, and Indian oceans meet.

A frigid laboratory—even in summer

Most Antarctic research takes place from early spring to early autumn in the Southern Hemisphere—roughly October to March. In 1995-1996, about 650 scientists worked in the U.S. Antarctica program. Barely 200 hardy scientists, technicians, and other intrepid individuals remained for the winter—six months of darkness, terrible storms, and bitter cold that isolates most of Antarctica from the outside world.

Before arriving in Antarctica, scientists and support staff receive special cold-weather clothing on loan. At the South Pole, I often wore heavy, insulated rubber boots with liners and two pairs of socks. I also wore two sets of thermal underwear, flannel trousers and shirt, and an insulated vest. I never ventured out without first pulling down the ear flaps on my cap or putting on gloves. And over everything, I donned a heavy parka with a fur-fringed hood, wind-proof pants, and heavy leather mittens.

Most scientists fly to Antarctica on military cargo planes from New Zealand or by ship or plane from Chile. McMurdo, the main American research station, resembles a small college campus. Scientists and staff sleep in dormitories and work in laboratories. Cold weather and outdoor work create enormous appetites, and the food served in the dining halls is abundant and delicious.

Many scientists stay at McMurdo only a few days before traveling by aircraft, snowmobile, or SnoCat—a large vehicle on treads—to remote outposts, where they live in tents while carrying out various research projects. Other researchers board icebreakers at McMurdo and spend weeks gathering data in the surrounding ocean.

Over several years, I visited scientists working from one end of the frozen continent to the other. One research trip, in January and February 1994, took me on a three-week expedition aboard the *Nathaniel B. Palmer* to study the vast ice sheet of western Antarctica. The ice forms a broad, flat plain with the outermost edge, called the Ross Ice Shelf, floating on the Ross Sea. On another trip, I observed a wide range of research projects near McMurdo Station. McMurdo is on Ross Island off the Ross Ice Shelf. Yet another trip took me to East Antarctica and the desolate deep-freeze of the South Pole. The South Pole is the Earth's southernmost point, where all lines of longitude meet. It is about 3,000 meters (9,850 feet) above sea level. No wildlife or plants can survive in that region, where winter temperatures often plunge below −73 °C (−100 °F).

The South Pole is at such a high elevation because it lies atop a plateau of ice. An icecap that covers 98 percent of the land and is up to 4,800 meters (15,700 feet) thick in some areas gives Antarctica the

Terms and concepts

Ice shelf: A part of the icecap that floats on the ocean.

Ice stream: A river of ice, flowing within a glacier, that moves toward the ocean faster than the surrounding glacier.

Icecap: A thick layer of ice and snow that covers most of Antarctica.

Krill: A shrimplike marine animal on which all the animal life of Antarctica depends.

Polynia: A vast expanse of water in the Southern Ocean that does not freeze like the surrounding water.

West Antarctic Ice Sheet: The ocean-based ice sheet that covers most of western Antarctica.

The author:
Michael Woods is the science editor of *The Toledo* (Ohio) *Blade*.

Icy land in the Southern Hemisphere

Antarctica is the coldest, windiest, highest, driest continent on Earth. It is surrounded by the ice-clogged Southern Ocean, often called the Antarctic Ocean. The South Pole, Earth's southernmost point where all lines of longitude meet, lies at the center of the continent.

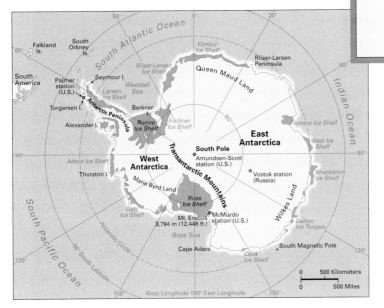

Antarctica covers about 14 million square kilometers (5.4 million square miles). The United States would fit onto the continent with room to spare, *above*. The Transantarctic Mountains cross the entire continent, dividing it into East Antarctica and West Antarctica, *left*. Ice floating on the water forms the Ronne Ice Shelf in the Weddell Sea and the Ross Ice Shelf in the Ross Sea.

highest average elevation of any continent. About 70 percent of the world's fresh water is locked up in the Antarctic icecap.

Antarctica has not always been buried in ice. Research indicates that millions of years ago, Antarctica enjoyed a vastly warmer climate. The continent was part of a land mass called Gondwanaland, which included Africa, Australia, India, and South America. Gondwanaland began to break apart about 140 million years ago, and Antarctica was soon drifting southward. Ice began building up 30 million years ago.

The primary evidence for Antarctica's milder past comes from fossil studies. Scientists have found dinosaur bones, fossilized tree trunks, and the remains of other plants and animals within about 640 kilometers (400 miles) of the South Pole. Researchers have also collected fossil remains of some 800 different species of ancient organisms on Seymour Island, near the Antarctic Peninsula, an S-shaped finger of land in the northwest part of the continent.

Until the 1900's, scientific interest was not a major reason for venturing to Antarctica. Most voyagers of the 1800's visited the frozen continent to hunt seals and whales, seek adventure, and claim territory. In the early 1900's, they came to explore the continent's interior. Real scientific research began during the International Geophysical Year of 1957-1958. In this global cooperative program to study Antarctica, the United States, the Soviet Union, and other countries established permanent Antarctic bases. In 1959, a dozen countries signed a treaty

Sand dunes and volcanoes amid snow and ice

Although about 98 percent of Antarctica lies beneath snow and ice, there are sand dunes in the wind-swept dry valleys of the Transantarctic Mountains, and volcanoes in West Antarctica. The volcanoes are part of the Ring of Fire, a string of volcanoes encircling the Pacific Ocean.

A huge aluminum dome prevents snow from burying buildings of America's Amundsen-Scott South Pole Station, *above*. Hundreds of kilometers away in the Ross Sea, smoke drifts upward from the crater of Mount Erebus, Antarctica's most active volcano, *far right*. Mount Erebus towers nearly 3,800 meters (12,000 feet) above Ross Island. And in Victoria Valley, one of the many dry valleys of the Transantarctic Mountains, *right*, sand ripples under the force of high winds, which sweep away snow before it can accumulate.

that reserved Antarctica for peaceful use, and eventually 40 nations joined the agreement. Several countries—though not the United States—claim parts of Antarctica. But no nation owns the continent.

As scientific interest in Antarctica grew, scientists mapped the continent's land features, studied its weather patterns, gathered data on the surrounding oceans, and cataloged plant and animal life. In the 1990's, however, scientists were studying the continent to learn about the entire Earth—its geologic history, changing climate, and environmental problems. Research in Antarctica is even leading to a better understanding of the nature and evolution of the universe. The South Pole is an ideal place to do some kinds of astronomical research.

The weather seemed almost balmy, only −41.1 °C (−42 °F), on the spring afternoon in November 1991, when I first set foot at the South Pole, a few hundred yards from America's Amundsen-Scott South Pole Station. The research station was named for two great figures of Antarctica's age of exploration. Roald Amundsen, a Norwegian explorer, and Robert Falcon Scott, a British naval officer, battled for the distinction of becoming the first person to reach the South Pole. Amundsen's team won, arriving on Dec. 14, 1911. Scott made it to the pole 35 days later, after Amundsen had headed back to the coast. The Scott expedition ended tragically when he and the other members of his party froze to death trying to return to their base on Ross Island.

The South Pole is not as desolate today as it was in 1911, though it has the same endless expanses of white ice and brilliant blue sky that dazzled Amundsen and Scott. People and supplies arrive in cargo planes equipped with skis in order to land on the ice runway. Near the runway, a huge aluminum dome protects the station's main buildings from being buried by wind-driven snow. A few other small buildings are scattered outside the dome.

In Antarctica's new age of science, astronomers have transformed the South Pole facility into a major observatory. Constructing telescopes at the South Pole was difficult and expensive. But it is a worthwhile effort, because the region's superior viewing conditions exist nowhere else on Earth. The telescopes sit on a mountain of ice, 8,500 feet (2,600 meters) above sea level, which puts them above the densest and murkiest part of the atmosphere. The Antarctic sky is usually cloud free, and the dry Antarctic air does not blur the images of celestial objects the way humid air does.

A window to the universe and into the Earth

Astronomers are able to observe the stars and galaxies of the southern sky continuously in the six-month-long night of the Antarctic winter. And during the other six months of the year, when there is endless daylight, solar astronomers have an uninterrupted view of the sun. Moreover, Antarctica is an especially good place to study the *solar wind*, a stream of high-energy particles released by the sun. Earth's magnetic field deflects most solar wind particles at other locations, but at the South Pole the particles pour in through openings in the magnetic field, called cusps, where lines of the magnetic field converge.

In 1991, the National Science Foundation (NSF), a government agency based in Arlington, Virginia, that funds scientific research, established the first major observatory at the pole. The three main telescopes at the facility, the Center for Astrophysical Research in Antarctica (CARA), are used by scientists from many institutions.

One of the telescopes, the Cosmic Background Radiation Anisotropy telescope (COBRA), detects *anisotropies* (variations) in the normally smooth microwave radiation that permeates space. Microwaves and the other types of radiation in the electromagnetic spectrum (gamma rays, X rays, ultraviolet light, visible light, infrared rays, and radio waves) travel through space at the speed of light—299,792 kilometers (186,282 miles) per second. Microwave radiation is a relic of the big bang, the cataclysmic explosion that scientists think gave birth to the universe 10 billion to 20 billion years ago.

The other two CARA telescopes also gather radiation emitted by celestial objects. The Antarctic Submillimeter Telescope and Remote Observatory (AST/RO) detects electromagnetic waves less than a millimeter long (the thickness of a paper clip). It will also be used for monitoring Earth's atmospheric processes. The South Pole Infrared Explorer detects infrared radiation. The images carry important information about the birth of stars and galaxies.

In contrast, a revolutionary telescope being built 0.8 kilometers (half a mile) under Antarctica's icecap might enable us to learn the universe's fate. This instrument, the Antarctic Muon and Neutrino Array (AMANDA), points into the center of the Earth to detect ghostly subatomic particles called neutrinos that stream out of stars, black holes, and other celestial objects. Neutrinos are difficult to detect because they have no electric charge and little or no *mass* (quantity of matter) and almost never interact with matter. Neutrinos pass unnoticed through everything, even through the Earth.

AMANDA's first phase began operating in 1993. When finished,

Funnel-shaped devices shield a telescope from the distorting influence of sunlight reflected off snow, *above.* The telescope detects variations in microwave radiation that permeates space. It is part of the Center for Astrophysical Research in Antarctica, a U.S. facility that takes advantage of the clear, cold, and dry atmosphere at the South Pole to carry out astronomical research.

AMANDA will consist of a circular array of 10 holes, each 60 centimeters (2 feet) in diameter, bored 1 to 2 kilometers (0.6 to 1.2 miles) into the ice with jets of hot water. Electronic detectors strung inside the holes will watch for neutrinos that enter the Earth at the North Pole and whiz right on through to the South Pole. When a neutrino collides with an atom in the ice, another subatomic particle, called a muon, is produced, emitting a flash of blue light. The clear ice also helps to filter stray particles that might interfere with observations. By January 1996, some detectors were operational and were recording flashes.

Scientists think all of space is swarming with neutrinos. If AMANDA proves that to be true, and if neutrinos have some mass, the conclusion would be that neutrinos make a significant contribution to the total mass of the universe. If enough mass exists, its mutual gravitational attraction would be strong enough to halt, and perhaps reverse, the outward expansion of the universe that began with the big bang. Billions of years from now, everything might collapse inward in a "big crunch." Some scientists speculate that a new universe might then be formed from whatever remains of the collapsed universe in yet another version of the big bang.

Researchers are also boring into the icecap in many locations to extract long cylindrical cores of ice packed with information about Earth's climatic history. Snow falling in Antarctica thousands of years ago absorbed gases and other material during its trip through the atmosphere. The snow was compressed into ice, preserving the material.

In certain areas, the annual layers accumulated undisturbed, one atop the other in chronological order like calendar pages. Scientists drill into these frozen archives to learn how Earth's atmosphere, temperature, and climate have changed over thousands of years. An international science team drilling at Russia's Vostok Station on the East Antarctic ice sheet reached a depth of 3,000 meters (9,800 feet) in 1995. They obtained the world's oldest ice core, with information on Earth's climate dating back 300,000 years.

Some researchers are studying Antarctica's frozen history out of concern for Earth's future, particularly the consequences of global warming due to a phenomenon called the *greenhouse effect*. The greenhouse effect received its name because Earth's atmosphere acts much like the glass or plastic roof and walls of a greenhouse. Sunlight enters a greenhouse and heats the interior. The roof and walls slow the escape of the heat. Similarly, Earth's atmosphere allows most of the sunlight that reaches it to pass through and heat the planet's surface. The Earth sends the heat energy back into the atmosphere as infrared radiation.

Monitoring Earth's atmosphere

Antarctica's clear, dry weather conditions enable scientists to monitor changes in Earth's atmosphere. Researchers at McMurdo Station on Ross Island, America's largest Antarctic facility, send aloft a balloon attached to sensors that measure ozone levels in the stratosphere, *below*. Ozone, a form of oxygen, protects life on Earth from harmful ultraviolet (UV) radiation from the sun. In the mid-1980's, researchers reported the discovery of a hole in the ozone shield above Antarctica.

Much of this radiation does not pass freely into space, because certain gases in the atmosphere absorb it and become warmer. These so-called greenhouse gases include carbon dioxide, ozone (a form of oxygen), and water vapor. The heated gases send infrared radiation back toward the Earth's surface, warming it.

Keeping an eye on the ice

Many scientists fear that higher temperatures worldwide could melt the continent's icecap. If Antarctica's 30 million cubic kilometers (7¼ million cubic miles) of ice melted, sea levels would rise by about 55 meters (180 feet), flooding coastal areas around the world.

Scientists once thought the icecap was extremely stable. But new evidence suggests otherwise. Many studies focus on the West Antarctic Ice Sheet (WAIS), the world's only remaining ocean-based ice sheet. The WAIS rests on bedrock below sea level, though the ice shelves at the periphery float on the ocean.

A scientist adjusts an instrument that measures the amount of UV radiation reaching the Earth from the sun, *below*. Ozone depletion allows more UV radiation to reach Earth's surface. The U.S. Antarctic Research Program maintains UV monitors at all three of its Antarctic research stations.

A researcher collects an air sample at the South Pole, *above*. Antarctic air, far from industrial centers, is the cleanest on Earth. Over the years, measurements of changes in trace amounts of carbon dioxide and other gases in Antarctic air have enabled scientists to document that air pollution has worldwide effects.

Another way scientists monitor the effect of increased UV radiation is by studying Adélie penguin populations on Torgersen Island near the Antarctic Peninsula, *right*. Penguins and all Antarctic life depend upon a shrimplike marine animal called krill, *above,* which in turn feeds on tiny ocean plants called algae. Increased UV radiation has slowed the growth of algae, but the ripple effect on krill and penguins seems minimal.

Hints of instability in the WAIS come from several sources. In one study, scientists drilled holes under the ice and found fossils of a species of algae—tiny aquatic plants—called diatoms that first appeared on Earth 2 million years ago. Their presence indicated to the scientists that this part of the WAIS was open ocean less than 2 million years ago.

Another indication of instability in the ice sheet is the behavior of five immense ice streams that course through the WAIS to the Ross Sea. Unlike glaciers, which are bounded on each side by mountains, the ice streams are bounded by the slower moving ice of the glacier. The ice streams move rapidly, up to 1.8 meters (6 feet) a day, compared with 1.8 meters a year for the glacier through which it flows. Ice streams carry ice from the interior of the continent to the ocean, where chunks break off and float away as icebergs. Some of the ice streams are behaving erratically. One stream, for example, is moving more rapidly than it used to, and another has stopped moving altogether. Unusual movements in the streams could drain ice from central portions of the WAIS, causing the whole sheet to become detached from the sea floor. If more of the sheet became mobile, more ice would enter the ocean and melt, quickly raising global ocean levels.

A number of studies are underway to identify forces influencing the movement of the ice streams, and that research is leading to some interesting findings. For instance, researchers have discovered evidence that active volcanoes exist under the ice. Heat from volcanic eruptions, or geothermal heat escaping from Earth's core through a thin crust, may be melting the ice beneath the streams. And in 1989, California researchers brought up samples of pasty sediments, composed of gravel mixed with water from beneath one ice stream. This finding confirmed a theory that such sediments, not water alone, were the lubricants reducing friction between bedrock and the ice stream above that allowed the ice stream to flow.

Other scientists are examining signs of the WAIS's previous behavior for clues to what it might do in the future. In this research, geologists are using electronic instruments to scan the ocean floor for marks left by the ice sheet thousands of years ago. Evidence indicates that the Ross Ice Shelf once covered huge areas of what now is open ocean and retreated to its current position during several previous meltings. Still other scientists believe the WAIS's fate was determined long ago. They suspect that warmth from the higher global temperatures that have prevailed for at least 10,000 years since the end of the Ice Age has been slowly heating the ice sheet. That warmth, they theorize, is just now reaching the bottom of the ice sheet and is causing the erratic movement of the ice streams. The scientists say that once temperatures rise at the base of the ice sheet, the ice is likely to soften, causing it to flow faster and leading to its catastrophic collapse.

Ozone, ocean currents, and meteorites

Another problem with global significance that is being studied by scientists in Antarctica is damage to Earth's ozone shield. The ozone layer in Earth's upper atmosphere filters up to 99 percent of the harmful ultraviolet (UV) radiation from the sun. Any reduction of this protective blanket allows increased levels of UV light to reach Earth's surface with potentially harmful effects on plant and animal life.

In the mid-1980's, scientists reported that the ozone layer over Antarctica was thinning, apparently because chemicals called chlorofluorocarbons (CFC's) were drifting into the upper atmosphere and breaking it down. At that time, CFC's were widely used as propellants in aerosol spray cans, but today their use is prohibited in the United States and most other countries that had produced CFC's. Nevertheless, the compounds have persisted in the atmosphere.

Atmospheric scientists have found that Antarctica experiences the world's lowest ozone levels every spring, creating an "ozone hole" in the atmosphere. The continent's extreme cold, swirling wind patterns, and complete darkness during the winter set the stage for the hole to form. Then, in spring, the first appearance of sunlight triggers the formation of polar stratospheric clouds in which increased reactions between CFC's and ozone takes place.

Researchers remove an ice core at one of Antarctica's numerous drilling sites, *right*. The ice preserved gases and other material trapped from the atmosphere, forming a frozen climatic history. In 1995, U.S. scientists on Seymour Island found a fossil of a leatherback turtle dating back about 43 million years, *below*. Fossils attest to Antarctica's warm past.

Some experts fear that ozone depletion could damage aquatic *food webs* around the world. A food web is the sum of relationships between animals in a habitat and the foods they eat. Antarctic research already suggests that UV light pouring through the ozone hole reduces the growth of algae in the Southern Ocean. Algae are eaten by *krill,* small shrimplike marine animals, and penguins in turn eat the krill. In fact, all animal life of the continent—fish, birds, seals, whales—depends directly or indirectly on krill. Any major change in the algae population produces a ripple effect up the food web. Fewer algae would mean fewer krill and a decline in all other populations dependent on krill for food.

Antarctica's Adélie penguins are good subjects for monitoring the effects of ozone depletion. These odd creatures with their waddling gait account for about 70 percent of all the birds in Antarctica. Torgersen Island, in Arthur Harbor near America's Palmer Station, is a living laboratory for studying the penguins.

Much of the scientists' work on Torgersen Island involves monitoring the diet of the penguin population, from which they can derive indirect evidence about the state of the algae in surrounding waters. The researchers use a harmless medical procedure that causes the penguins to vomit into buckets. Back in the laboratory, the investigators sift through the partially digested stomach contents for krill eyeballs, which digest slowly. The scientists count the eyeballs to estimate the abundance of krill in the nearby ocean, and they measure the size of the eyeballs to estimate the krill's age and growth rate. Those factors are directly related to the amount of algae available to the krill.

The evidence compiled so far indicates that increased UV levels slow algae growth, but the effect seems to be minimal. The algae adapt and protect themselves by producing pigments that act as a natural sunscreen. The studies suggest that variations in temperature, the amount of sea-ice cover, and other factors have a more important effect on algae growth than do higher UV levels. But further research will be required to back up that conclusion.

Many current studies involve the Southern Ocean. Scientists want to understand how mysterious gaps in the sea ice in the Southern Ocean influence ocean currents and global climate. The gaps, called *polynias,* are vast expanses of ocean that do not freeze in winter like the surrounding water. The open water loses heat to the frigid atmosphere. The frigid water then flows northward in an immense current that influences the temperature and other characteristics of oceans throughout the world.

Contact between the open water and the air also speeds the exchange of gases. This process may be another factor in the Southern Ocean's influence on global climate. The Southern Ocean, because of its immense currents and the great quantity of microscopic plant life it contains, seems to absorb more carbon dioxide than it releases. Carbon dioxide is one of the gases many scientists believe is contributing to the greenhouse effect. Thus, polynias in the Southern Ocean may be a natural mechanism for regulating global warming by removing and storing carbon dioxide.

A researcher grabs a Weddell seal in McMurdo Sound to tag it, *above.* Since the 1960's, tagging has enabled scientists to track the distance the seals travel to feed, their survival rates, and other behavioral factors that have kept the seal population stable in Antarctica's harsh environment. Water sampling in McMurdo, *left,* helps scientists study other life forms that survive in the 0 °C (32 °F) ocean.

Not water, but slow-moving ice attracts scientists to the Transant-arctic Mountains in East Antarctica. Places where the East Antarctic Ice Sheet presses against these mountains have proved to be a rich source of meteorites, bits of extraterrestrial rock that landed on Earth and became buried in the ice thousands or even millions of years ago. The glacier's internal movements transport meteorites to the surface, preserved in their original pristine condition by the natural deep-freeze. Scientists have collected more than 16,000 meteorites in Antarctica, as many as in the rest of the world combined. Some are previously unknown types, including fragments believed to have come from Mars. Some planetary scientists think that the impact of asteroids and comets on Mars sent chunks of Martian rock hurtling into space, where they orbited the sun for millions of years. Finally, they came crashing down in Antarctica and other places on Earth.

Researchers measure a meteorite before collecting it from one of Antarctica's glaciers in the Transantarctic Mountains, *above*. Antarctica has yielded more than 16,000 meteorites, some believed to have come from Mars. They are transported to the surface of the ice in perfect condition by the glaciers' internal movements.

There could be a different type of Martian connection in organisms that cling to life in the ice-free rocky areas of the Trans-antarctic Mountains known as dry valleys. The organisms did not come from Mars, but they survive in Antarctica's Mars-like environment. The microorganisms grow inside the pores of limestone and sandstone rocks, protected from the harsh surface conditions. Knowledge about these organisms may help guide future searches by the National Aeronautics and Space Administration for life on the red planet.

Concerns about Antarctica's future

Clearly, Antarctica's value to science is priceless. The United States and other countries have taken steps to preserve its environment for research. In 1991, the 26 countries that do Antarctic research signed an environmental protection agreement to minimize the effects of human activity. The NSF has completed the clean-up of a big waste dump at McMurdo Station, where trash had accumulated since the station's establishment in 1955. As part of efforts to keep the continent pristine, scientists try to leave no trace of their presence in remote field camps, returning all wastes to McMurdo.

However, other threats to the continent remain. Scientists express concern, for instance, over the effects of commercial krill fishing. Each year Russian, Japanese, and Polish ships harvest krill by the hundreds of thousands of tons. Some experts believe that millions of tons could be harvested annually without harm. But others fear that larger harvests could adversely affect penguins and other Antarctic wildlife.

Tourism is another concern. Antarctica's rugged beauty and remoteness have made it an attractive destination for vacationers. The NSF estimates that tour ships now carry about 8,000 people to Antarctica each year—more than all the world's scientists who go there to work. Tourists must follow strict rules to protect the environment. But scientists worry that increased tourism will result in environmental damage.

They also fear that incidents like the oil spill from the 1989 wreck of the *Bahía Paraíso* may become common. That Argentine vessel, loaded with supplies and tourists, spilled thousands of gallons of fuel oil that killed penguins and other birds.

Government cuts in science budgets may also affect scientific research in Antarctica. Early in 1996, budget problems threatened an NSF proposal to build a $200-million replacement for its aging Amundsen-Scott Station at the South Pole. Russia has been forced to curtail its once extensive Antarctic research program. And the United Kingdom stopped research at its Faraday Station on the Antarctic Peninsula in 1995 and scaled back research elsewhere. Nevertheless, scientists conducted 136 research projects during the 1995-1996 research season as part of the U.S. Antarctic Program operated by the NSF.

With continued international cooperation and care for the Antarctic environment, the frozen continent

Tourists listen to a guide and watch a colony of chinstrap penguins on Deception Island near the Antarctic Peninsula, *below.* Tourists are attracted by Antarctica's remote, rugged beauty, but scientists fear that increased tourism will damage the frigid continent's pristine environment.

will continue to serve as a vast treasure house of information about the Earth's past, present, and future. Research in this living laboratory will also bring us a better understanding of the universe and may guide searches for life on other worlds.

For further reading:

Hackwell, John W. *Desert of Ice: Life & Work in Antarctica.* Macmillan, 1991.

Shapley, Deborah. *The Seventh Continent: Antarctica in a Resource Age.* Resources for the Future, 1986.

Sullivan, Walter. *Quest for a Continent.* McGraw-Hill, 1957.

Woods, Michael. *Science on Ice: Research in Antarctica.* The Millbrook Press, 1995.

A Hubble image of a region of the Milky Way galaxy called the Eagle Nebula reveals details never seen before. Enormous pillars of gas and dust glow from the radiation of nearby young stars. At the top of the left-most pillar, fingerlike projections are tipped with gaseous globules, each about the size of our solar system, that may contain stars in formation.

A New Look at Space

Since its flawed vision was repaired in 1993, the Hubble Space Telescope has produced beautifully detailed images of celestial objects, from the planets in our solar system to galaxies in the farthest depths of space.

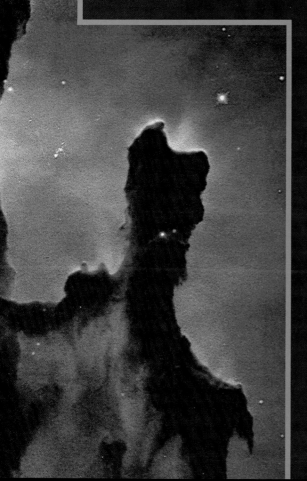

The Hubble Space Telescope (HST), an orbiting observatory circling about 600 kilometers (375 miles) above the Earth, has given us a new eye on the universe. With the Hubble, astronomers have found evidence for supermassive black holes, obtained improved images of the most distant planets in our solar system, and made observations of faraway galaxies that they hope will enable them to determine the size and age of the universe. Engineers with the National Aeronautics and Space Administration (NASA) use radio commands to control the HST. In turn, the telescope transmits data by radio waves to astronomers on the ground. Because the HST orbits above Earth's atmosphere, it can produce much sharper images and observe objects 20 times fainter than is possible with the largest telescopes on the ground. The Hubble was launched by the space shuttle Discovery in 1990, but it was soon found to have flawed optics. The crew of the space shuttle Endeavour repaired the telescope's fuzzy vision in December 1993. Since then, the HST has flawlessly carried out its mission as orbiting observer of our night skies. Here are some of the incredible images it has recorded for us.

The clearest image ever taken of Mars from Earth was made by the HST in February 1995, when the red planet was 105 million kilometers (65 million miles) away. The Hubble photo is surpassed in quality only by the images sent back to Earth by the Mariner and Viking space probes in the 1970's.

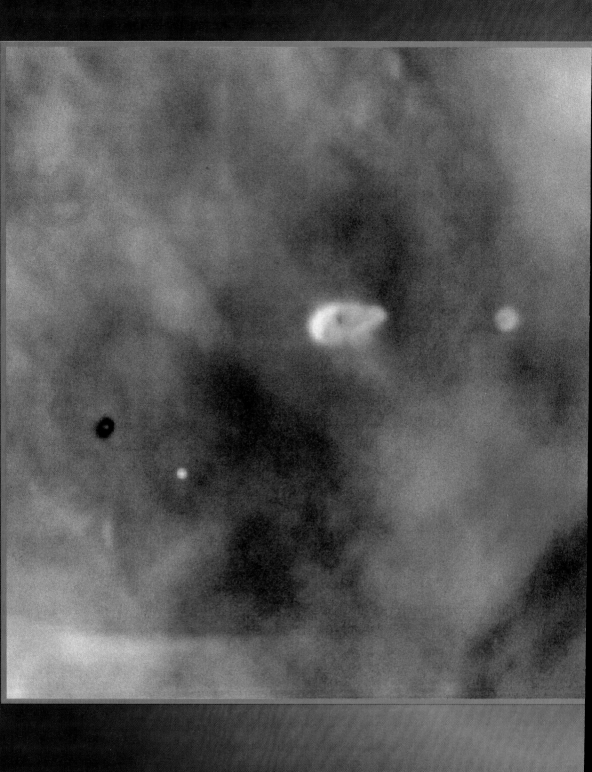

Just after its repair in December 1993, the Hubble photographed a small portion of the Orion Nebula, *left.* With startling clarity, the telescope revealed details of this huge cloud of gas and dust, one of the most prominent features of the Milky Way and the birthplace of new stars. The image shows *proplyds*— disks of material that may form into planets—around four young stars. A *planetary nebula* known as NGC 7027, *below,* shows a star in the process of dying. A planetary nebula is a multilayered shell of gas thrown off by a star as it nears the end of its life, becoming a compact object called a white dwarf.

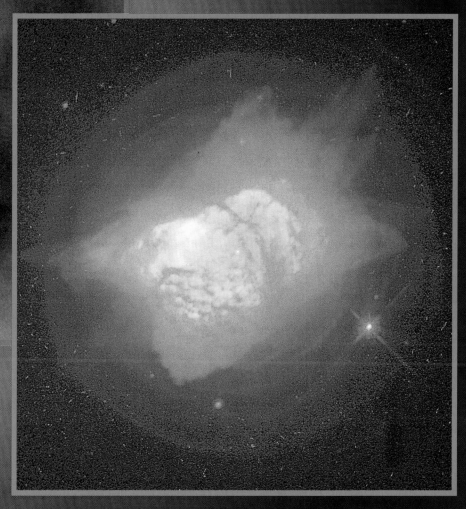

Hubble's look at a planetary nebula known as the Cat's Eye Nebula, *below*, shows that it has an intricate structure. The complex features suggest that there are two stars at the center of the nebula, both exerting various effects on the gases. Twin jets of gas in the Orion Nebula glow as they slam into slower-moving gas clouds, *bottom*, giving astronomers a close look at the dynamics of star birth. The jets were ejected from a whirlpool of gas and dust circling a young star, hidden in the center behind a dark dust cloud. An image of part of a nebula called the Cygnus Loop, *right*—the remnant of a *supernova* (exploding star) that lit up the Milky Way about 15,000 years ago— shows the nebula's expanding gases glowing as they collide with a cool cloud of gas and dust.

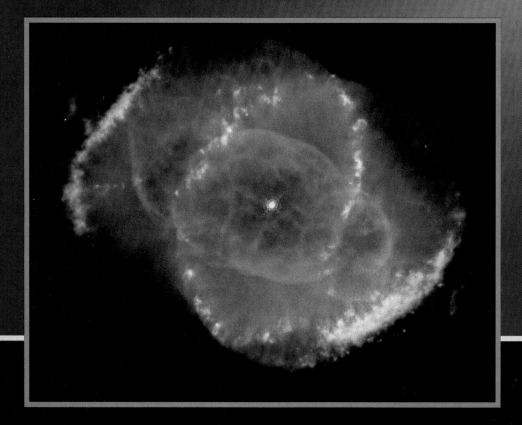

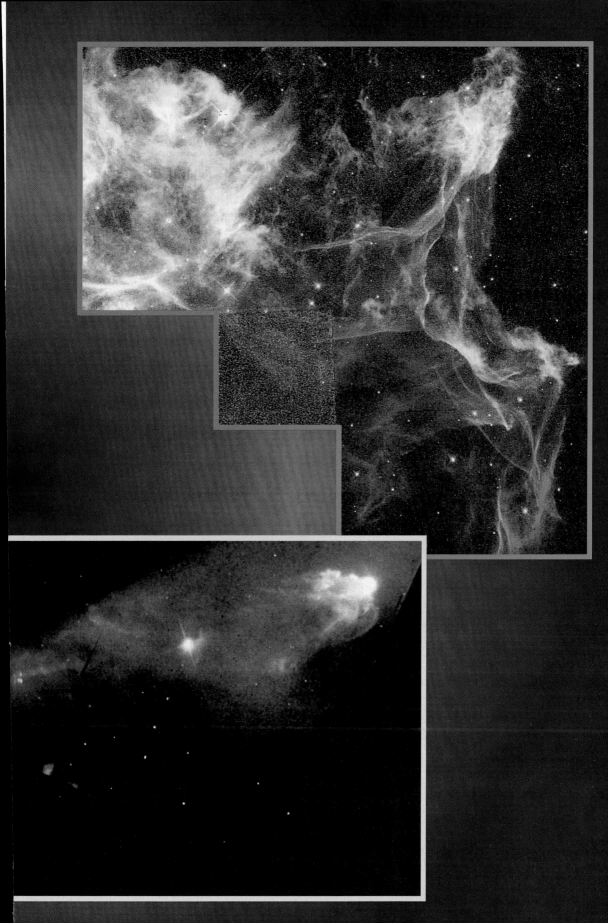

The *core* (central region) of a galaxy known as NGC 1068, about 60 million *light-years* away, shows a huge outpouring of energy. (A light-year is the distance light travels in a year, about 9.5 trillion kilometers [5.9 trillion miles].) Astronomers speculate that the galaxy's energy is being generated by a supermassive black hole, a huge object with such intense gravity that not even light can escape it. The light from the core comes from outside the black hole as matter is ripped apart and drawn toward the hole.

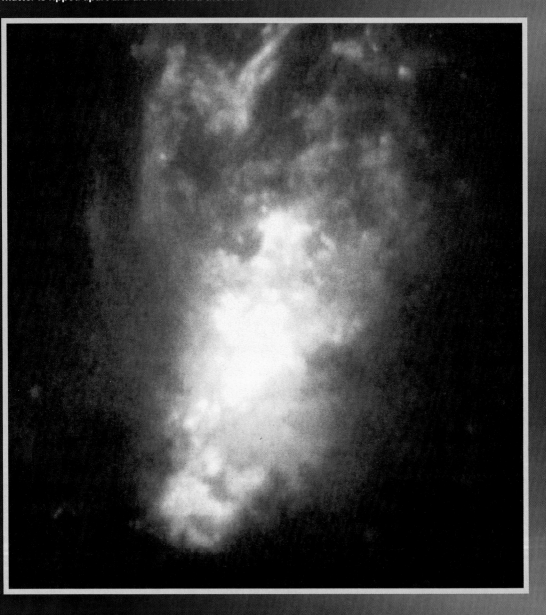

Wisps of matter around Quasar PKS 2349 indicate that the quasar, an extremely bright object several billion light-years away, has merged with a companion galaxy. This Hubble image may require astronomers to rethink their theories about the nature of quasars, which generate more energy than any other objects in the universe. The most widely accepted theory is that a quasar is a galaxy with an extremely bright core powered by a supermassive black hole. But that view did not predict the sort of complex interactions revealed in the image.

An image of a pair of star clusters, *below,* 166,000 light-years away in the Large Magellanic Cloud, a neighboring galaxy of the Milky Way, reveals an unusual detail. Seldom are two groups of stars so close together. Astronomers think supernovae in the larger and older cluster may have compressed gas clouds to form the young stars in the smaller cluster at its right. One of the most spectacular pictures produced by the Hubble, *right,* shows galaxies at the farthest reaches of the universe. Such images from the HST may help astronomers learn the size and age of the universe.

Learning Why Airplanes Crash

By studying airplane crashes to learn their causes, investigators have helped make air travel increasingly safe.

BY EDWARD H. PHILLIPS

On the clear, calm night of December 20, 1995, American Airlines Flight 965 crashed into a mountain as it began its descent to the Cali, Colombia, airport. All but 4 of the 163 people aboard the Boeing 757 were killed.

Within hours of the tragedy, a team of specially trained investigators from the United States National Transportation Safety Board (NTSB) was assembled and began preparations to assist the Colombian government in the intense investigation that was to follow. Besides helping to search the crash site, the safety board—an independent agency of the federal government—also analyzed the plane's flight data and cockpit voice recorders. Within a few weeks, after studying the information provided by the recorders, the investigators were able to piece together a good explanation of why the plane crashed.

The investigation of airplane crashes has changed greatly from the methods Orville Wright used in 1908, when he and a few associates sought to determine why a Wright brothers plane crashed at Fort Myer, Virginia, injuring Orville and killing his only passenger. Today, such investigations require hundreds of skilled people and involve the use of computers, intricate mathematics, and highly specialized procedures designed to identify the causes of crashes. One thing, however, has not changed. Accident investigators, regardless of what methods they use, share Orville Wright's goal—to use what they have learned to prevent similar tragedies from ever occurring again.

In the United States, the NTSB is responsible for investigating major transportation accidents, including all civilian airplane crashes. Its jurisdiction includes both commercial aircraft flown by major and regional airlines and small private planes operated by the general public. The NTSB's primary mission is to determine a probable cause for each accident and to make safety recommendations to the Federal Aviation

Opposite page:
Investigators and rescue workers sift through the wreckage of American Airlines Flight 965, which slammed into a mountain near Cali, Colombia, in December 1995, killing 159 people.

Terms and concepts

Ailerons: The hinged, horizontal parts on the rear edge of a wing that help an airplane turn.

Cockpit voice recorder (CVR): A recorder placed in the cockpit of an airplane to capture noises on the flight deck and conversations between crew members.

Elevators: The hinged, flat segments of the tail that help an airplane climb or descend.

Flight data recorder (FDR): A device, commonly known as a "black box," that uses either electronic memory chips or magnetic tape to record flight information aboard an airplane.

Glass cockpit: A computer-driven electronic display in an airplane that gives the pilot flight information, such as air speed, altitude, and location, on a single screen. It is connected to the FDR, which records all the data.

Go-team: A group of about 10 investigators from the U.S. National Transportation Safety Board that tries to determine the probable cause of an airplane accident.

Microburst: A column of air, often associated with thunderstorms, that blows downward, hits the ground, and then mushrooms out and curls upward. Microbursts are a common cause of wind shear.

Pylon: A structure that attaches the engine to the wing.

Wind shear: A sudden change in wind direction and speed over a short distance that can cause a pilot to lose control of a plane. It is particularly dangerous to aircraft flying at low altitudes and low air speeds.

The author:

Edward H. Phillips is the Transport Editor of *Aviation Week and Space Technology* magazine.

Administration (FAA), a U.S. agency that initiates and enforces air-safety regulations.

The NTSB employs about 300 people, including some 80 investigators and over a dozen laboratory technicians. Because airplanes have become so technologically complex, these people must have extensive training in a variety of technical areas. They must be familiar with a plane's computer-controlled flight control systems, its electronic cockpit displays, and its electric, hydraulic, and environmental systems. They must be experienced in working with aircraft engines, autopilots, and space-based satellites, which many airlines now use to guide planes to their destinations. They must also understand how weather conditions, air traffic control operations, and human factors—such as the way pilots think and react to cockpit situations—may have contributed to a crash.

When a major aircraft accident occurs in the United States or territories under its jurisdiction, the NTSB is notified and dispatches a "go-team" to the crash site. The team consists of an investigator-in-charge, who may be one of five board members appointed by the president of the United States; a group of about 10 technical specialists selected from the staff; and a senior safety board official who is responsible for ensuring that the investigation is conducted according to NTSB rules. Representatives from the FAA, the companies that manufactured the aircraft and its engines, and pilot, flight attendant, and mechanic unions normally also participate in an investigation. In addition, public relations experts accompany the team to assist the news media.

The NTSB is usually also called in to help when an accident occurs outside the United States but involves a plane operated by a U.S. airline or corporation. According to agreements set forth by the International Civil Aviation Organization (ICAO)—an agency of the United Nations that develops standards and procedures for international civil air navigation—the country in which the crash occurred is responsible for conducting the investigation. But nations without investigative teams of their own can, and often do, request help from other ICAO members, including the United States, Canada, the United Kingdom, France, and other Western nations.

At the site: looking for answers

The investigation of a crash site can take anywhere from a few days to several weeks. As they begin their examination of a crash, investigators fan out over the site, looking for clues in the wreckage and terrain that can tell them something about the cause of the accident. If the wreckage is scattered over a large area, it may mean that the airplane came apart at a high altitude, perhaps indicating that it was destroyed by a bomb. This was one of the first clues noted in the investigation of the 1988 crash of Pan American Flight 103 at Lockerbie, Scotland, in which 270 people died. Traces of debris were spread over about 2,200 square kilometers (850 square miles). A terrorist bomb concealed aboard the plane was later found to be the cause of that disaster.

The violent disintegration of an aircraft into small pieces that are confined to a limited area indicates that the plane was intact when it crashed but that it hit the ground at high speed. In the September 1994 crash of USAir Flight 427 near Pittsburgh, Pennsylvania, in which all 132 people aboard were killed, that is exactly what investigators found. All that was left of the Boeing 737, according to rescue workers, were "chunks of metal . . . nothing bigger than a car door." The NTSB later determined that Flight 427 had dropped from the sky at a speed of more than 480 kilometers (300 miles) per hour. On the other hand, if an aircraft remains relatively intact after hitting the ground, investigators know that it struck the ground at a slow speed.

Damage to the terrain at a crash site can also yield important information. The go-team investigating the wreckage of USAir Flight 1016, which crashed at Charlotte, North Carolina, in July 1994, found gouges on the DC-9's turbofan blades left by tree trunks and limbs. These marks were clear evidence that the engines were operating when the plane struck the trees and allowed the investigators to rule out engine failure as the cause of the accident.

Clues in the wreckage

The plane fragments found at the scene of the crash can either hint at causes of the accident or rule them out. First, go-team members document each piece of debris—from the smallest screw to the largest sheet of metal. They photograph it, tag it, log it in, and plot the location at which it was found. Then they transport the debris to a large facility, usually an airplane hangar. There, investigators and technicians organize all of the pieces into the shape of the plane, either by laying them out on a grid or by hanging them inside the shell of a real plane of the same type as the one that crashed. By examining each piece individually and then reassembling the plane, investigators try to learn what caused the plane to crash.

After the 1989 crash of a United Airlines DC-10 near Sioux City, Iowa, NTSB technicians examined a cracked engine compressor disk which a farmer found in his cornfield, far from the accident site. The location of the disk and the pilot's explanation that he had suddenly lost control of the plane led the investigators to conclude that the disintegrating disk had spun out of the engine and cut the hydraulic lines to the wings and tail. With the lines cut, the pilot was unable to manipulate the flight controls. Even so, he and the crew managed to make a crash landing, saving more than half of the 296 passengers aboard.

Cockpit controls, such as flap and landing gear handles, engine thrust levers, rudder pedals, and control wheels, may also be examined by the go-team. However, the information such controls provide is generally less useful than other clues in the wreckage. A severe impact can change the position of the controls or destroy them, making it difficult to determine their actual position before the crash.

Another source of information that is virtually always destroyed in a crash is the *glass cockpit*. A glass cockpit is a computer-driven electronic display resembling a small color television screen. In modern airliners,

Remnants of American Eagle Flight 4184, which crashed in October 1994 near Roselawn, Indiana, *top,* lie scattered in a soybean field. Information retrieved from Flight 4184's flight data recorder (FDR), similar to the one found after the 1994 crash of an Aeroflot Airbus in Siberia, *above,* enabled investigators to quickly determine that the crash was caused by icing on the wings.

both the pilot and the first officer have their own glass cockpit. The screens display all of the flight information that, in older aircraft, was provided by separate instruments—the air speed indicator, altimeter, navigation indicator, and other sources of flight data.

Electronic evidence

Although the glass cockpit itself is destroyed in most crashes, the information it has provided is recorded and stored in the flight data recorder (FDR)—one of the most important pieces of evidence to be retrieved from a crash site. While it is called a "black box" (because early models were encased in black boxes), the recorder is actually in a steel case painted International Orange, with special reflective tape to make it more visible to investigators. The FDR is installed in the plane by the manufacturer, and it may be placed in any of a number of locations within the *fuselage*—the body of the plane. It is usually located behind the cabin section near the tail.

Many FDR's are equipped with locator beacons that emit a sound underwater. Special locating devices can detect the sound. The FDR on Birgenair Flight ALW-301, which crashed into the Atlantic Ocean shortly after take-off from Puerto Plata, Dominican Republic, in February 1996, carried such a beacon. The U.S. Navy, at the request of the NTSB investigators assisting the Dominican government, was able to retrieve the FDR from a depth of 2,195 meters (7,200 feet). Using information from the recorder, the Santo Domingo air traffic control center, and the plane's cockpit voice recorder, investigators determined that the pilots lost control of the Boeing 757 because of problems with the air speed indicators and improper-speed warning alerts. All 189 people aboard the plane were killed.

Flight data recorders are connected electrically to various systems in the airplane. Every few seconds during a flight, specific categories of information, known as parameters, are received from the systems and stored in *digital* format (as a series of 1's and 0's) in electronic memory chips or on magnetic tape. Parameters include air speed, altitude, navigational data, and other valuable information. FDR's can store as much as 25 hours of data before a new recording automatically begins.

Today, the FAA requires that FDR's be able to monitor at least 11 parameters. However, the NTSB believes that even 11 parameters are not enough. The Boeing 737 that crashed near Pittsburgh in 1994 had an FDR that could keep track of 11 parameters of flight information and three additional engine parameters. But, unlike the more modern recorders, it could not monitor the movements of the flight controls— the rudder; the *ailerons* (hinged, movable parts on the rear edge of a wing that help the airplane turn); and the *elevators* (hinged, flat segments of the tail section that help the plane to climb or descend). Investigators insist that the main reason the cause of the accident had not been solved by 1996 was that the aircraft was not equipped with a more up-to-date recorder. Some European airliners are equipped with FDR's that can monitor more than 100 parameters.

One month after the Pittsburgh crash, NTSB investigators unfortu-

Investigators fan out to collect debris at the crash site of United Airlines Flight 585, which plunged to the ground near Colorado Springs, Colorado, in March 1991. Each plane part found at a site is photographed and tagged and its location recorded. The parts are later analyzed to determine which of them—if any—may have contributed to the crash.

From clues to causes

Certain parts of an airplane are more likely than others to cause problems in flight. Investigators at a crash site examine these parts carefully, searching for clues to the cause of the accident.

The flight controls on a plane's tail are operated through hydraulic lines. *Elevators*, the hinged, horizontal flaps on a plane's rear wings, help the airplane rise or descend. The *rudder*, a movable vertical flap on the tail, allows the plane to turn. When a United Airlines DC-10 crash-landed near Sioux City, Iowa, in 1989, the NTSB suspected a problem with the hydraulic lines, based on the pilot's description of the flight. A cracked engine part called a compressor disk that was found far from the accident site was the key to solving the crash. Investigators determined that the disintegrating disk had cut the hydraulic lines, rendering the plane unflyable.

A *pylon* connects a jet turbofan engine to the wing. In the crash of American Airlines Flight 191 during take-off from Chicago's O'Hare Airport in 1979, an engine fell from the plane. NTSB investigators found a microscopic crack in the remnants of an engine pylon. The investigators then determined that a faulty maintenance procedure had caused the crack.

Some defects in a plane may not show up in an examination of the wreckage, but they might be determined from the contents of the *flight data recorder* (FDR). The FDR—commonly known as the "black box"—is located in the fuselage and is connected electrically to various systems in the airplane. It stores information from these systems in its memory. Investigators retrieve the FDR after an accident and extract the data for clues regarding the cause of the crash. After Northwest Airlink Flight 5179 slammed into a mound of iron mining waste near Hibbing, Minnesota, in 1993, data from the FDR revealed that the plane crashed because the pilot had made a too-steep landing approach to the Hibbing airport.

Ailerons, the hinged, movable parts on the rear edge of a wing, help the airplane turn. After the crash of American Eagle Flight 4184 near Roselawn, Indiana, in 1994, NTSB investigators determined that icing on the wings had caused an airflow disruption over the ailerons, leading to the crash.

The spinning blades of a turbofan engine produce the thrust that keeps the airplane aloft. Gouges on the fan blades recovered by investigators after the crash of USAir Flight 1016 at Charlotte, North Carolina, in 1994, showed that the engines were operating when the plane struck a stand of trees. That finding enabled the investigators to rule out engine failure as a cause of the accident.

nately got the opportunity to prove their point. American Eagle Flight 4184, which crashed near Roselawn, Indiana, in October 1994 with a loss of 68 lives, did have an FDR capable of recording the position of flight controls. Data retrieved from the FDR helped the NTSB determine that ice had formed on the wings of the ATR-72 turboprop transport as it awaited clearance to land at Chicago's O'Hare International Airport. The icing created an airflow disruption over the ailerons, causing the aircraft to roll to the right, enter a steep descent, and crash in a soybean field. Because of the additional information provided by the FDR, investigators essentially determined what happened to Flight 4184 in less than a day.

That the investigators were able to obtain this information so quickly was testimony to the sturdiness of the FDR, which survived undamaged. A recorder is designed to withstand incredible impact forces, crushing pressures, and punctures of the steel case. Nonetheless, some crashes are so violent that the recorder is damaged by the impact or by fire. In such rare cases, safety board investigators can still obtain a limited amount of data from special computer chips called nonvolatile memory chips. These chips are computer components that are commonly used in a variety of electronic control units on modern jet transports.

Crises captured on tape

In addition to FDR's, commercial airliners carry cockpit voice recorders (CVR's), which capture noises on the flight deck and conversations between the pilots. A CVR's microphone is located in the cockpit, but the actual recorder is usually placed in a "black box" elsewhere in the body of the plane. In the most modern planes, one black box holds both the FDR and the CVR. Most CVR's can store only 30 minutes of activity at a time. When the tape is full, the next 30 minutes is recorded over the first. Therefore, only the last half-hour before a crash is preserved. However, an increasing number of U.S. and European airlines are equipping new planes with upgraded recorders that can store up to two hours of information. The NTSB would like these units to become standard equipment on all U.S. commercial jet airliners.

The words and sounds captured on a CVR in the last few seconds before a plane crashes are often chilling, but they may provide critical clues about a flight that cannot be obtained from the FDR. The recorded conversation between the pilots of American Airlines Flight 965 and the Cali, Colombia, control tower revealed that the pilots had been totally confused about what the controllers wanted them to do and about where the plane was in relation to nearby mountains. The last words on the tape were those of the plane's automatic ground-proximity warning system: "Terrain, terrain . . . pull up, pull up."

To supplement CVR's, the NTSB is urging development and installation of small color video cameras in the cockpit to provide a visual record of flight deck activity. But equipping a fleet of airliners with video cameras and videotape machines is very expensive, and no airlines had done so as of 1996.

An airplane's FDR, *left*, is enclosed in a steel case and can withstand most crashes, fires, and submersions under water. The FDR is retrieved after a crash and sent to the National Transportation Safety Board's (NTSB) laboratory in Washington, D.C. There, information stored in the recorder by the plane's various electronic systems is retrieved and analyzed. Often, the data are also fed into a computer to produce a video simulation of how the plane probably crashed, *below left*.

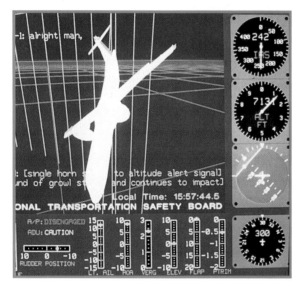

Witnesses to disaster

Besides information from recorders and computer chips, interviews with survivors, eyewitnesses, and other key people such as air traffic controllers can play a vital part in a crash investigation. The accounts of eyewitnesses and survivors must be weighed carefully, however, because people often do not remember traumatic events accurately. After the crash of USAir Flight 427 near Pittsburgh, some eyewitnesses reported seeing "little puffs of smoke" from an engine. But when investigators analyzed data from the FDR and engine parts, they concluded that those witnesses must have been mistaken about what they said they observed.

In addition, most people do not have a technical knowledge of airplanes and how they fly, which may lead them to draw erroneous conclusions about what they see and hear. Aircraft sounds that eyewitnesses report as "booms" and "explosions" often turn out to be normal engine noises. If an eyewitness is someone familiar with aircraft, such as a pilot or an aircraft technician, his or her testimony is usually more credible than that of most others.

When members of a plane's flight crew survive a crash, they become a critical source of information about the accident. The statements of pilots, in particular, are extremely valuable to the NTSB. For example, when investigators spoke with the pilots of USAir Flight 1016, which crashed while landing at Charlotte, they realized that the pilots were unaware of heavy rain at the airport until their plane flew into the edge of the storm. Seeking clear skies, they turned right. Then, one of the pilots reported, "We just dropped." From this description and additional information about weather conditions, investigators determined that the plane had encountered *wind shear* (a sudden change in wind direction and speed over a short distance) from a *microburst* (a column of air that blows downward, hits the ground, and then mushrooms out and curls upward). The plane was lifted when it entered the microburst, then dropped when it hit the microburst's center, causing the pilots to lose control. Wind shears and microbursts are often associated with strong thunderstorms, and they are especially dangerous to aircraft flying at low altitudes and low air speeds. The search for hazardous weather phenomena and ways to avoid them have been an important part of air crash investigations in recent years.

Also of growing importance is the study of human factors in crashes. Such factors include the effects of fatigue, the crew's understanding of how complex electronic flight systems operate, and the ability of the crew to work as a team. Safety board members speak with each pilot's family, friends, and doctors, and anyone else who saw the pilot before the accident flight—such as pharmacists and restaurant workers—to learn what each individual's physical and mental condition was. Investigators need to know what the pilots ate before flying, how long they slept, what medication they took, and what emotional or psychological problems may have affected the pilot's performance.

NTSB investigators determined that human factors were at least partially to blame in the crash of American Eagle Flight 3379 in December

Each part recovered from the crash of Pan American Flight 103 at Lockerbie, Scotland, in December 1988 was taken to an airplane hangar. There, investigators pieced the plane back together to learn what had caused the plane to explode in midair. They determined that an on-board bomb had caused the blast.

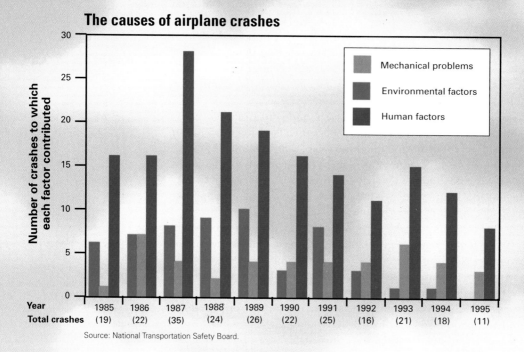

The causes of airplane crashes

Number of crashes to which each factor contributed

Legend:
- Mechanical problems
- Environmental factors
- Human factors

Year	1985	1986	1987	1988	1989	1990	1991	1992	1993	1994	1995
Total crashes	(19)	(22)	(35)	(24)	(26)	(22)	(25)	(16)	(21)	(18)	(11)

Source: National Transportation Safety Board.

In some crashes of major and regional airlines on regularly scheduled flights, *above*, more than one factor is determined to be the probable cause of the accident. Human factors, such as pilot and maintenance-crew errors, are the most common causes of airplane crashes, according to investigators. Aircraft structures, instruments, and equipment are the least common causes of accidents. Mechanical problems did not contribute to any crashes at all in 1995.

1994. The Jetstream Super 31 commuter plane was approaching Raleigh-Durham International Airport in North Carolina when it veered off course and descended into trees about 6 kilometers (4 miles) from the runway. Fifteen of the 20 people on board were killed, including both pilots. The CVR disclosed that the captain thought one engine had failed, when it was actually operating normally. He did not enlist the help of the copilot and standard checklists were not followed. In determining the probable cause of the accident, the NTSB cited the lack of crew coordination and training as a contributing factor in the crash.

Making flying safer

The entire process of investigating a crash—sifting through debris; retrieving information from the FDR, CVR, and other systems; conducting interviews; analyzing clues; performing simulation tests to check hypotheses; and forming conclusions—can take anywhere from a few months to over a year to complete. Once the NTSB has determined a "probable cause" for an accident, it makes recommendations to the FAA for changes in procedures or equipment that could prevent similar accidents in the future. The FAA then considers the recommendations and may issue revised regulations to aircraft manufacturers, the pilots' union, or other groups that are involved in the safety issue that has been raised.

In the aftermath of the Raleigh-Durham crash, the NTSB urged that

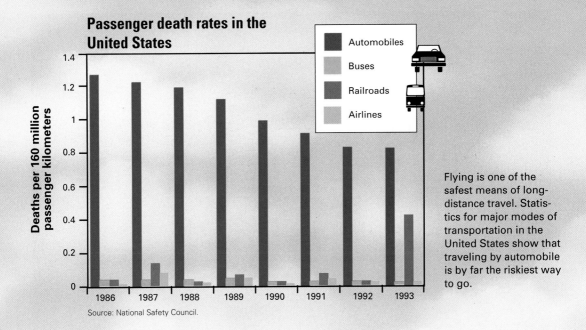

Passenger death rates in the United States

Deaths per 160 million passenger kilometers

Legend:
- Automobiles
- Buses
- Railroads
- Airlines

Source: National Safety Council.

Flying is one of the safest means of long-distance travel. Statistics for major modes of transportation in the United States show that traveling by automobile is by far the riskiest way to go.

every regional airline require its flight crew to attend a training program called crew resource management (CRM). The CRM program teaches pilots to communicate more clearly with each other and encourages lower-ranking crew members to speak up when they see a hazardous situation developing or when standard checklists are not being followed. Pilots for large commercial airlines have been required to participate in CRM for years. Since December 1995, the FAA has required pilots of small regional airlines to receive CRM training as well.

After studying the crash of the American Eagle ATR-72 near Roselawn in October 1994, the NTSB learned that aileron movements could become a serious problem in that type of plane during certain icing conditions. Just days after the crash, NTSB officials made urgent safety recommendations to the FAA. The FAA responded in December 1994, banning commercial airlines from flying ATR-72's in weather conditions that might cause icing.

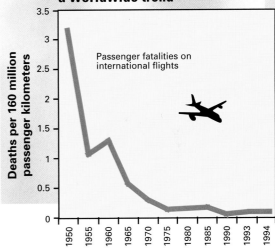

Increasing safety in the air: a worldwide trend

Deaths per 160 million passenger kilometers

Passenger fatalities on international flights

Source: International Civil Aviation Organization.

Internationally, deaths resulting from airplane crashes have dropped dramatically since the 1950's and have remained low throughout the 1990's.

Pilots use a flight simulator to help them learn how to fly safely in situations that investigators have determined can cause accidents. They practice flying through powerful wind currents called microbursts, under icing conditions, and without full engine power. By learning from the accidents of the past, pilots ensure safer flights for the passengers of the future.

Some years earlier, the NTSB uncovered a dangerous maintenance short-cut on McDonnell Douglas DC-10's. In May 1979, American Airlines Flight 191 crashed during take-off from Chicago's O'Hare Airport. FAA control tower personnel saw the plane's left engine tear loose from the wing and watched in horror as the aircraft rolled, plummeted into a field, exploded, and burned. At least 258 passengers, a crew of 13, and two people on the ground were killed. It remains the worst commercial airline accident in U.S. history.

During the investigation, NTSB metallurgists discovered a microscopic crack in the remnants of the engine-mounting *pylon*—the structure that attaches the engine to the wing. Through interviews and maintenance records, investigators learned that mechanics had used an unapproved hoist to remove the engine and pylon from the DC-10's wings for routine maintenance. In addition, the mechanics had removed the two parts as a single unit instead of taking them off the wing separately, as recommended by the manufacturer. These improper procedures caused a crack to form in the pylon. Under the stress of take-offs, landings, and flights, the engine finally broke off. The NTSB then checked the pylons on other DC-10's and found similar damage in eight other pylons. The NTSB's recommendations resulted in the FAA requiring more stringent maintenance procedures for DC-10 operators.

Since it was established in 1967, the NTSB has determined a probable cause for all but five of the airplane crashes under its jurisdiction. Investigators have found that most accidents involving small planes are caused by pilot error, fuel exhaustion, bad weather, or flight-training mishaps. Commercial airline accidents are usually caused by pilot or flight crew errors or adverse weather conditions. Crashes rarely occur because of problems at airports or with a plane's flight-control systems.

Of the five airplane crashes that NTSB investigators have not been able to resolve, two were major accidents with striking similarities. Both the 1994 crash of USAir Flight 427 near Pittsburgh and the crash of the United Airlines plane near Colorado Springs, Colorado, in March 1991 occurred in good weather and for no apparent reason. In each case, the 737 suddenly veered to one side, rolled, and nose-dived, killing all on board. Because the flight data recorders on both of these planes lacked parameters for monitoring the position of flight controls, the NTSB has recommended to the FAA that FDR's capable of monitoring at least 17 or 18 parameters be required on all U.S. commercial flights.

The three other unsolved crashes all occurred over 20 years ago: a Sierra Pacific Airlines Convair crashed at Bishop, California, in 1974, killing 36 people; a Southern Airways DC-9 went down at Huntington, West Virginia, in 1970, killing 75 people, including Marshall University's entire football team; and an Allegheny Airlines Convair crashed at Bradford, Pennsylvania, in 1969, causing the death of 11 people.

What the future holds

As the year 2000 approaches, accident investigators face new challenges. Future airliners will be vastly different from those flying today. To meet the growing demand for rapid, global transportation, designers are envisioning huge airliners known as *Very Large Aircraft (VLA)* that will be twice the size of a Boeing 747. VLA's would carry 600 to 800 passengers. If an immense airliner such as a VLA crashed, an investigation would be very costly and require the expertise of an army of investigators. If a massive and tragic loss of life accompanied the crash of such a huge transport, the NTSB and its foreign counterparts would be under extreme pressure from the airlines, the public, and governments to determine the cause quickly and accurately. In addition, an entire new generation of flight and cockpit data recorders will be needed to adequately monitor the many complex systems that will be installed in the aircraft of the future.

Regardless of how advanced aircraft technology becomes in the years ahead, investigators already know one thing for certain: Each time they track the clues from an airplane crash to a possible cause for the accident, they make air travel a little safer for the millions of people who fly on airplanes each year.

For further reading:

Buck, Robert N. *The Pilot's Burden: Flight Safety and the Roots of Pilot Error.* Iowa State University Press, 1994.

Cohn, Robert L. *They Called It Pilot Error: True Stories Behind General Aviation Accidents.* McGraw-Hill, 1993.

Science Studies

The Computer Comes of Age

In the second half of this century, we have witnessed a computer revolution that has brought massive changes in the way work is done and information is processed. As we move toward the next century, the revolution continues.

Whether aiding in the design of new products and machines, *left,* or simply making it easier for family members to keep in touch, *right,* the computer is becoming an ever more common —and often essential— part of our daily lives.

Introduction

We are in the midst of a technological upheaval known as the computer revolution. A large number of working people today use some type of computer, and nearly all of them can recall when these machines did not exist. A typical secretary may have started her career with a manual typewriter, graduated to an electric one and then to a word processor, and now sits at a sophisticated "workstation" that is networked with many coworkers. Everyday tasks such as grocery shopping involve computers. The gas pump has a computer, we bank through a computer, our household appliances are computerized.

Computer technology changes almost daily as hundreds of thousands of creative minds work to create new computers or new uses for existing models. If we feel dazzled but overwhelmed by all this new technology, it is no wonder. Even experts can be hard-pressed to keep up with the latest developments in every branch of computing. A computer engineer who designs hardware, the physical components of a computer, may not know what's new in software, the programs—instructions—that tell computers what to do. Even fewer people may be aware of the advances occurring at the top computer-science laboratories. There, researchers are developing the computers of the future, machines that are likely to be as far beyond today's computers as a Ferrari is from a Model T.

Nonetheless, the essential nature of computers is likely to remain unchanged. They will continue to be a means for manipulating information in digital form—as a series of 1's and 0's. What will change is the various technologies that are used to carry out computing functions. In addition, computers will continue to become smaller, faster, and more powerful. And they will invade every aspect of our lives.

That may sound like a scary prospect to those who distrust technology, but for people who welcome the future, it is immensely exciting. Nicholas Negroponte, a pioneer in the field of computers, writes in his prophetic book *Being Digital* (1995), "Computing is not about computers anymore. It is about living. The giant central computer, the so-called mainframe, has been almost universally replaced by personal computers. We have seen computers move out of giant air-conditioned rooms into closets, then onto desktops, and now into our laps and pockets. But this is not the end."

What Negroponte and other visionaries see is a world where the microprocessor, the ever-smaller heart of the computer, is in everything we use. Computers will disappear into our surroundings, ready at every turn to serve our needs and enable us to communicate effortlessly with other computer users—on the other side of the room or the other side of the Earth. We will all be digital, and we will all be in touch.

The authors:
Keith Ferrell is an author and the former editor-in-chief of *OMNI* magazine.

Michael Woods is science editor of *The Toledo* (Ohio) *Blade*.

A Look Back

The computer has changed our lives so rapidly and so dramatically that it is hard to remember a time without computers. Yet computers—particularly personal computers, which have had a huge impact on people's daily lives—are a very recent development.

Computers as we know them today are electronic devices that process information digitally. This means that whatever the information's original form—text, sound, image, video—it has been converted into a coded series of digits to be read by the computer.

Computers use the *binary* system, a number system with only two digits: 0 and 1. These digits are called *bits*. Different combinations of bits represent numbers, letters, symbols, and other data. For example, according to one standard comput-

a = 01100001

The language of computers

A computer's ability to store and process information is based on the binary system, a number system using just two digits, 0 and 1. A string of 0's and 1's can represent a numerical value or something entirely different, such as a picture or a letter of the alphabet, *above*. The use of this system in computers and other electronic devices is known as digital technology.

A roomful of computer
The first general-purpose electronic digital computer, called ENIAC, began operating in 1946 at the University of Pennsylvania in Philadelphia. The huge computer was built by two engineers at the university, J. Presper Eckert, Jr., front left, and John W. Mauchly, center.

er code, the binary representation for the letter *a* is 01100001. Such a combination of eight bits is called a *byte*.

Each of a computer's thousands or millions of tiny electronic circuits operates much like an ordinary light switch. When a circuit is off, it corresponds to the binary digit 0. When a circuit is on, it corresponds to the digit 1.

Binary digits, like numbers in the more familiar *decimal system* (the number system using the digits 0 through 9), can be added, subtracted, multiplied, or divided. Thus, using just two digits, a computer can perform all the basic arithmetic operations.

The first computers

The first electronic digital computers, built during the 1940's, filled a large room and used vacuum tubes as their primary component. Vacuum tubes, familiar to anyone who has seen the inside of an early radio or television, controlled the electric currents that were necessary for the operation of the computers. The outer part of a vacuum tube consisted of a glass or metal shell, and inside the shell were wires and small metal plates that controlled the electronic signals. These pioneering computers were slow, taking minutes or hours to perform computations.

In spite of their slow speed, these computers were an important invention, because the calculations they performed would have required days or weeks of human effort—if people could have done them at all.

By the 1950's, an advance in electronics had changed the nature of computers. This was the *transistor*, a simple electronic circuit that had two states: on or off. Using those states to represent the 1's and 0's of digital information, computer engineers were able to make dramatic progress in miniaturizing computers and increasing their speed.

The semiconductor

In the mid-1960's, another revolutionary device was introduced: the *semiconductor*. Semiconductors are materials that conduct electricity better than insulators such as glass, but not as well as conductors such as copper. Silicon is the most widely used semiconductor material. Semiconductor computer components made from ultrapure silicon could hold hundreds, then thousands, of circuits in a tiny space.

Modern-day computer semiconductor devices, known collectively as microchips, are smaller than a person's fingernail, yet they may have millions of transistors embedded in them. Such a construction is called an *integrated circuit*.

From mainframes to PC's

The computers of the late 1960's and 1970's were called mainframes. They were not as large as their vacuum-tube predecessors but were still large and had to be installed in a fixed place. They transformed much of business, governmental, and institutional work. Huge calculations, such as keeping tax records or tabulating census figures, could be done quickly and efficiently and the results stored for later use.

Computers also enabled scientists to conduct research that a few decades earlier would not have been possible, or perhaps even conceivable. In fact, a considerable amount of that research dealt with computers themselves, particularly with ways to further miniaturize transistors and increase the sophistication of semiconductors and integrated circuits.

That research bore fruit in 1975, when the first desktop computer, or microcomputer, debuted. Using a type of integrated circuit chip called a microprocessor, the microcomputer brought a high level of computing power to a box about the size of a portable television set. Microcomputers—soon known as personal computers, or PC's—grew smaller and more powerful at an astonishing rate.

By the early 1990's, the power of a PC rivaled that of mainframes from barely a generation before. Manufacturers were selling tens of millions of PC's worldwide.

Transistor: An electronic circuit that has two states: on or off. When this switch is on, it represents a 1; when it is off, it represents a 0.

Microprocessor: An electronic device consisting of thousands or millions of transistors and related circuitry on a small chip made of the element silicon. Also called a microchip.

Bit: An abbreviation of the term *bi*nary dig*it*; may be either of two digits—0 or 1.

Byte: A group of eight bits that act as a single unit of information, such as a letter or numeral.

Megabyte (mb): One million bytes.

Gigabyte (gb): One billion bytes.

Beyond PC's

The computer revolution shows no signs of slowing. Computers grow more powerful almost daily, offering vast amounts of information storage and ever-faster operating speeds. Computer users also have access to a growing library of information-packed discs called CD-ROM's (*c*ompact *d*isc—*r*ead-*o*nly *m*emory). CD-ROM's can have text, pictures, sound, and even moving pictures stored on them. Programs that combine several of

By the late 1960's, many companies and institutions had installed large computers called mainframes. This type of computer is still used for many large-scale operations.

ENIAC-on-a-Chip

	ENIAC	Chip
Vacuum tubes	18,000	none
Transistors	none	250,000
Clock speed	100,000 hertz	20 million hertz*
Electrical power required to operate	174 kilowatts	0.5 watts*
		*estimated

Digital revolution: The first 50 years
In 1996, computer engineers at the University of Pennsylvania created ENIAC-on-a-Chip. The computer chip, *above,* similar to ones used in modern personal computers, was the size of a fingernail but could perform the same functions that the 27-metric-ton (30-ton) ENIAC did. The ENIAC used vacuum tubes to perform the computations that miniature transistors do now. Each of the computers used the same measurements of speed and power. Clock speed is the rate at which bits travel through a computer as pulses of electric current and is measured in *hertz* (cycles per second).

The components of computers became smaller and smaller until the first desktop computers were created in the 1970's. Soon known as personal computers, or PC's, they operated by use of an integrated circuit chip called a microprocessor. By the early 1990's, the power of a PC rivaled that of mainframes from barely a generation before.

these forms of information are called multimedia programs.

The next invention that expanded the usefulness of computers was the *modem,* a device that connects a computer to telephone lines and from there to other computers around the world. More and more computers in businesses, institutions, and private homes are being linked in this way, forming a global network of interconnected computer networks called the Internet.

Future historians may view the development of the computer as the most important event of the 1900's. Some observers, in fact, say that the computer revolution is the most important technological advance in human history. But it is a revolution still in progress.

Computer power is growing at a staggering rate, even as the cost of that power drops to new lows. Tens of millions of homes now have personal computers, and new computer trends promise to shape our lives and our world in the years to come.

Advances in Hardware

Before long, according to electronics experts, it will be possible for us to carry wallet-sized computers. These machines will do for us what the desktop personal computers (PC's) of today can do, and more. A wallet PC will perform complex calculations, send and receive electronic mail (e-mail), display schedules and memos, and even hold many books' worth of information. It may also contain electronic money: credits, transferred to the PC from the owner's bank account, that could be used to make purchases or pay bills.

Computer industry leaders foresee such technology resulting from the increasing miniaturization of the electronic components, or *hardware*, that make up a computer. Over the years, size reductions in electronic components have enabled computers to work faster and do more.

Many PC users remember with amusement when 20 megabytes (MB) of memory, or information storage, seemed so big that they could not imagine ever using all of it. One megabyte is a million bytes of data. A byte is a group of eight *bits* (*bi*nary digi*ts*), the 0's and 1's that are used to represent information, such as a letter or number, in a form that can be easily manipulated by a computer. Computers operating with this system—which includes virtually every general-purpose computer—are known as digital computers.

Today, an ordinary word-processing program, such as the one used to type the letters on this page, requires 30 to 40 MB of memory. Storing complex graphics, images, and other information requires even more megabytes. Experts predict that PC users in the future will be amused at the 1.2 *gigabytes* of data-storage capacity found in most new machines today. A gigabyte is 1 billion bytes.

The heart of the computer

In order to understand how these advances in miniaturization and data-handling capacity have been achieved, we must look at the "brain" of a computer. This is the *microprocessor*, an electronic device consisting of thousands or millions of transistors and related circuitry on a chip smaller than a fingernail. This chip is usually made of the element silicon.

Tiny transistors control the flow of electric current, rapidly manipulating the electric charges that represent the 0's and 1's of digitally encoded information. As the transistors move the charges about, the electronic circuits carry out all the data-processing operations.

When smaller transistors can be packed closer together, the electronic signals have less distance to travel, thereby shortening the time it takes for each bit to be processed. Miniaturization advances in chip-making technology have led to faster and faster microprocessors.

To gain a sense of this, we can look at the 8088 processor introduced by Intel Corporation of Santa Clara, California, in 1979. The 8088 was used in the first PC's and contained 29,000 transistors. It had a *clock speed* (the rate at which bits travel through the computer as pulses of electric current) of 4.77 *megahertz* (MHz). A megahertz is 1 million cycles per second. Intel's latest Pentium

The Navigator wearable computer, developed at Carnegie-Mellon University in Pittsburgh, Pennsylvania, is controlled manually or by voice commands and can hold large volumes of information that an aircraft inspector needs to check a plane for defects. A head-mounted unit displays the information on a small screen positioned in front of the inspector's eye.

chip, the P6, or Pentium Pro, was packed with more than 5.5 million transistors and whizzed along at 150 to 200 MHz.

Microprocessor speed has been doubling every 18 months and will continue to do so for at least another 10 years, according to experts at Intel, the world's leading computer chip manufacturer. These new chips will run programs faster and will give computers a number of new features. The expanded capabilities of computers will include the ability to respond to voice commands, display more realistic graphics and animation, and automate routine tasks. Computers will also be able to more efficiently use the *Internet,* the worldwide network of computer networks operating through the telephone system.

Improvements in computer architecture

Other improvements in hardware that will increase the speed and power of computers will come from changes in computer architecture—that is, the way components of microprocessors are organized and interconnected. The typical PC of the mid-1990's, for instance, is a *complex instruction set computer* (CISC), meaning its microprocessor can carry out many programmed instructions. By handling so much work, though, the chip is slowed down.

A new architecture, the *reduced instruction set computer* (RISC), overcomes this limitation. RISC architecture limits the number of instructions that a chip can execute to a bare minimum, mainly the most frequently used instructions. This optimizes a chip for the fastest possible performance, and RISC chips run 50 to 75 percent faster than CISC chips. The RISC hardware systems can do this because they depend upon *software* to perform the functions that CISC microprocessors did themselves. Computer software consists of programs, or instructions, that are entered into a computer to enable it to perform certain tasks.

RISC chips were once used mainly in high-performance scientific computers. Then in 1994, Apple Computer, Incorporated, of Cupertino, California, introduced its Power Macintosh computer with the PowerPC chip, which was based on RISC technology. Experts predicted that other home computers with the RISC architecture would become more common in 1996 and 1997.

Future microprocessors will also take greater advantage of a technology called *pipelining* to improve speed and performance. Pipelining is the execution of commands in continual, consecutive stages. As an analogy, consider how people do large batches of laundry that must be separated into several loads. When wet clothes from the first load go into the dryer, a second load of dirty clothes goes into the washer. The launderer keeps the three-stage pipeline full—constantly washing,

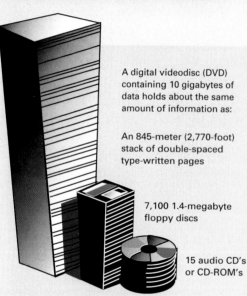

A digital videodisc (DVD) containing 10 gigabytes of data holds about the same amount of information as:

An 845-meter (2,770-foot) stack of double-spaced type-written pages

7,100 1.4-megabyte floppy discs

15 audio CD's or CD-ROM's

The power of data compression
In 1996, manufacturers planned to offer the first digital videodisc (DVD) products. These discs play motion pictures and use the same technology as audio CD's, which store recorded music, and CD-ROM's, which store audio and visual data to be viewed on a computer screen. The DVD's hold far more data than other CD's, though, because new technology has allowed the data to be greatly compressed. One type of DVD requires a special player, *above,* that is hooked up to a television.

drying, and folding—until the whole batch is done. A nonpipelined approach to laundry would involve completing one series at a time: washing a load, drying it, and folding it before starting the second load. With this method, doing one's laundry would take much longer.

Pipelined chips speed the processing of commands from their programs. The greater the number of stages, the faster the performance. The first Pentium chips had a pipeline with five stages, but the P6 has a superpipelined architecture consisting of 14 stages. Upcoming chips may use even more stages.

New chips will also be able to execute more commands in each stage of the pipeline, thanks to a "superscalable" architecture that can be scaled, or adjusted, to suit different applications. Superscalar chips contain extra data-manipulation circuitry and special control equipment that keeps the various parts of that circuitry functioning in unison. A conventional microprocessor solves a complex math equation, for example, one step at a time. It may first perform a multiplication problem, then an addition problem, then a subtraction problem, and finally a division problem. A superscalar processor might perform all of those operations at the same time. Intel's Pentium Pro chip uses a superscalar architecture that processes two program instructions simultaneously.

Computers that can perform *parallel processing* use many individual microprocessors to work on different parts of a problem at the same time— in parallel—and then combine the results. This approach was pioneered in the 1980's in supercomputers with expensive, custom-made microprocessors. But only a few government agencies, universities, and corporations could afford these machines. Future supercomputers will be more affordable because they will use mass-produced microprocessors, like the Pentium's, that work together. The U.S. Department of Energy, for instance, was planning in 1996 to link 9,000 Pentium P6 processors in a machine that would work 10 times faster than existing supercomputers.

More memory and greater speed

Tomorrow's microprocessors will have increased *random access memory* (RAM), memory in which data being used at the moment by the operator of the computer are quickly available to the processor. RAM is temporary memory that is lost when the computer is turned off, as opposed to the permanent data stored on a rigid internal disc called the hard drive.

RAM chip capacity has quadrupled every three years. But speed in accessing RAM has not kept up with the speed of processors. Computer designers have compensated for this by placing a small memory compartment, called a cache (pronounced *kash*), right on the microprocessor. The cache holds the most frequently used parts of a program, allowing the microprocessor to work without calling on the slower external RAM chips or the hard drive. Some microprocessors of the mid-1990's already devoted as many transistors to the cache as they did to the rest of the processor.

Hardware: The physical parts of a computer system.

Disc: A small plastic or metal platter on which information is stored in digital form.

About 90 percent of computers sold in 1995 were *multimedia* machines, able to combine traditional text and graphics with video clips, animation, and sound. Multimedia computers have a *CD-ROM* (*Compact Disc-Read Only Memory*) drive that runs plastic discs similar to the shiny plastic audio CD's used for music. Read-only means that new information cannot be put onto the disc. As of 1996, CD-ROM's held an amazing 650 megabytes—more than many hard drives.

The first in a new generation of specialized microprocessors designed for multimedia computers was being readied for the market in 1996. Intel was working on a multimedia version of the Pentium, and MicroUnity Systems Engineering, Incorporated, of Sunnyvale, California, was developing a microchip called Mediaprocessor. These new chips were being customized for video and audio in some of the same ways that traditional chips were modified to handle text.

Accessing multimedia data was frustratingly slow with the first generation of CD-ROM drives, called double-speed, or 2X drives. Most computers now come with a 4X, or "quad-speed" drive, and 6X drives may be common by 1997, followed by 8X drives. The new drives mean faster searches and retrievals of information, and better performance of new games and other software that uses full-motion video. Future CD-ROM innovations are expected to include super-high-density discs with a capacity of many gigabytes of data and a recordable CD, called a CD-R. A CD-R would allow a computer user to record large amounts of data—as much as a hard drive might hold—and that information would then be portable.

In 1996, manufacturers planned to offer the first digital videodisc (DVD) products. These discs play motion pictures and use the same technology as audio CD's. The DVD's hold far more data than other CD's, though, because new technology has allowed the data to be greatly compressed. There will be two types of DVD's: one that requires special hardware that is hooked up to a television, and one that can be played on a computer with a special CD-ROM drive.

Computer users will also benefit from advances in the design of *modems* (*mo*dulator-*dem*odulators), which are making it faster and easier to use the Internet. A computer's modem communicates with other computers through telephone lines. When someone sends out a message, the modulator in the person's modem translates the computer's digital signals into *analog* (continuous, or nondigital) electronic signals that can travel over phone lines. In the modem attached to a computer receiving that transmission, the demodulator translates the analog signal back into digital language. Modem speed determines how long it takes for information to transfer. Slow modems frustrate many people who download information—especially images—from the Internet and on-line services into their computers.

But modems are becoming faster. Their speeds for sending or receiving information have increased from a few hundred bits per second (bps) in the early 1980's to thousands of bits per second. The industry standard in the early to mid-1990's was 14,400 bps, but by 1996 the majority of modems being sold operated at 28,800 bps.

Even faster modems are available, including units that operate at 128,000 bps, but outdated telephone lines and switching equipment prevent their widespread use. The usefulness of superfast modems depends on the installation of new telephone technology, such as high-capacity *optical fibers*. Optical fibers are thin glass filaments that carry information as pulses of light. They can convey far more data in a second than can be transmitted over conventional copper lines.

The Internet's potential as an information source is fostering what may be the most fundamental redesign of personal computers in history. Several companies announced plans in 1996 for development of a bare-bones PC that would sell for about $500 and be used mainly for retrieving information from the Internet. The Oracle Computer Corporation in San Francisco said in February that it had designed an Internet computer called the Network Computer, or NC. In March, Microsoft said it was working with two other computer manufacturers to develop a similar machine called the Simply Interactive Personal Computer (SIPC). The SIPC could be connected to either a television or a computer monitor and be able to transfer data at very high speeds.

Off of the desktop . . .

One of the more exciting advances in hardware for everyday use has been the portable, battery-run laptop computers that became more com-mon in the mid-1990's. But their battery packs often die in the middle of a lecture, a meeting, or a long airplane flight. Most laptops operate less than three hours between battery charges.

New kinds of batteries may solve that problem. One of the most promising is a zinc-air battery, the PowerPro, introduced in some laptops in late 1995. It produces electricity by passing oxygen from the air over a zinc surface and works up to 12 hours before needing to be recharged. A lighter, more powerful version of the battery was expected by the end of 1996.

. . . and off the lap

Tomorrow's computers may become an even more intimate part of everyday life. Researchers at Carnegie-Mellon University in Pittsburgh, Pennsylvania, for instance, have developed a wearable computer that they call the Navigator. The computer weighs 0.9 kilogram (2 pounds) and fits around a person's waist. A monitor the size of a postage stamp displays information. The monitor is mounted on a headband and can be positioned in front of the user's eyes.

An experimental version of the Navigator has a map of the Carnegie-Mellon campus in its memory and is programmed to understand the spoken names of 200 people and places. If the user says, "Find the library," the monitor displays a map with a red guide line and a photograph of the library. If the user names a library employee and room number, the Navigator displays the person's picture and a map of the library interior.

The first commercial use of the Navigator has been as an aid to aircraft inspectors, displaying information in maintenance manuals. With the Navigator, inspectors are able to consult a manual without having to look away from their work. Some airplane manuals contain up to 70,000 pages of information, which can all be contained in the small wearable computer.

Wearable PC's are part of the natural evolution of computer hardware. Some people already carry small pocket computers known as personal digital assistants to keep track of appointments, phone numbers, and other information. The wallet-sized PC is the logical next step in this trend.

As computers continue to shrink in size, it becomes possible to include computer power in many products and devices. The microprocessors in today's automobiles and kitchen appliances are more powerful than the huge, corporate-owned computers of 40 years ago. Building computing power into these items is called *embedded computing*, and it is becoming increasingly common. It is clear that unique computer hardware will become ever more prevalent in people's lives in the years to come.

Advances in Software

More computers are being produced that respond to such cues as speech and handwriting. The smARTwriter handheld computer, *above,* which went on the market in late 1995, was reportedly able to read users' writing with up to 97 percent accuracy.

Imagine a computer equipped with a staff of electronic helpers to assist you with your daily tasks. These so-called intelligent agents, who might be represented by friendly faces on your computer's *monitor* (screen), would store information on your habits and preferences and then act independently for you. They would trash unwanted pieces of electronic mail (e-mail), schedule you for meetings, purchase tickets for trips and concerts, even order merchandise for you. Software developers predict that intelligent agents will make tomorrow's powerful computers easier to use.

New programs

Intelligent agents, also called software assistants, are a new generation of computer programs that are now being developed. Programs, referred to collectively as software, are the coded instructions that tell microprocessors and other computer components—the hardware—what to do.

There are two kinds of software. Operating-system (OS) software are the master programs that tell computers how to interpret commands, process information, and store data. Application software are programs that tell computers how to perform particular tasks. Much of the new application software that will be developed in coming years will be improved versions of programs for everyday tasks such as word processing or producing financial spreadsheets. That type of software accounts for about 60 percent of all programs al-

ready being sold. But more exciting software, such as that used for intelligent agents is expected to become common.

Many computer users follow routines that software assistants could learn and automate. For an example, consider the daily schedule of a writer who works at home. She starts her day by turning the computer on. She then connects to the *Internet,* the global network of computer networks, to check for new e-mail. She may read some mail and leave the rest for later. Next, because it is Tuesday—Tuesdays and Thursdays are her days for writing—she starts up a word-processing program to work on a magazine article. When she finishes writing, she gives the computer a command to store the article in its memory. Finally, done for the day, she shuts down the computer.

How would intelligent agents help our writer? They would turn on her computer for her in the morning, then automatically connect her to the Internet and display important mail, saving or trashing the rest. On Tuesdays and Thursdays, the agents would display her magazine article files. When she finished writing, her agents would display unread e-mail. Lastly, they would shut down the computer— perhaps after sending e-mail requests for meetings to other people's computers and printing out the next day's appointments.

People could use software assistants to search the Internet for information that would take hours to find by looking at hundreds of different sources. The assistants would serve as personal librarians, tirelessly scanning hundreds of sources for needed materials and storing them in the user's computer files.

Individual agents might work together as a team on especially complex tasks. For instance, a purchasing assistant that has been asked to search for a particular item of mer-

Software: The programs that tell a computer what to do.

Program: A set of instructions to be carried out by a computer, written in a computer language.

Operating system (OS): The master program that controls a computer's basic functions.

Application software: programs that instruct a computer on how to perform particular tasks.

Multimedia: The combination of text, graphics, video, animation, and sound in a computer format.

RAM (*random access memory*): Digital information that can be searched or replaced.

ROM (*read only memory*): Information that a computer cannot change.

Electronic helpers

A new type of software called an intelligent agent will be designed to carry out a computer user's routine tasks. By building up a database of information about the user, an agent will be able to anticipate the person's needs and carry out actions that he or she wants performed.

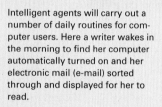

Intelligent agents will carry out a number of daily routines for computer users. Here a writer wakes in the morning to find her computer automatically turned on and her electronic mail (e-mail) sorted through and displayed for her to read.

While the writer relaxes, her software agent searches for specific information the writer needs for an article she is working on. The agent will browse the Internet, the worldwide network of computer networks, where many libraries, universities, and other institutions supply information.

The writer's editor receives a notification of a meeting on his computer. The writer's intelligent agent has contacted his software agent and those of other people in the company involved in a current project to set up a meeting time when all are available.

chandise might spot a bargain after comparing prices in scores of on-line catalogs and alert the financial assistant, which manages credit accounts and bank accounts. Working together, they would order the item and charge it to your credit card.

Software agents are part of an effort to endow computers with traits associated with human intelligence, an area known as *artificial intelligence*. Such traits include the ability to understand spoken languages and to infer or guess the meanings of imprecise terms. Making computers behave more like human beings relies on a type of programming that computer scientists call "fuzzy logic." Conventional programs make decisions in a clear-cut, yes-or-no fashion. Fuzzy logic deals with the imprecise circumstances that so often surround situations in the real world.

For example, a fuzzy logic program developed for use in elevator systems synchronizes the movements of elevator cars to the best advantage of the users. Let's say a passenger on the 7th floor of a 14-floor hotel summons an elevator. The system has two choices: Send car 1, which is on the 10th floor, heading downward with several passengers; or send car 2, which is on the 12th floor with no passengers. The simple answer is to send the nearest one, but in this case it would be better to send the one with no passengers. The fuzzy logic system can add several bits of information together,

such as how full the cars are as well as how close each one is to a particular floor, and respond in a highly efficient manner.

New operating systems

New operating systems will also be an important part of many upcoming software advances. About 90 percent of the world's PC's use operating systems developed by the Microsoft Corporation of Redmond, Washington. These systems, which include MS-DOS (*disc o*perating *s*ystem) and Microsoft Windows, are for IBM and IBM-compatible personal computers (PC's). IBM-compatible PC's are ones that use the same software and hardware as IBM PC's. Macintosh (Mac) computers, manufactured by Apple Computer, Incorporated, of Cupertino, California, use a different operating system and different application software.

The first OS was DOS, which worked by typing in commands. Then Apple created a Graphical User Interface (GUI), with easy-to-use commands that involved moving an electronic pointer on the screen and clicking on *icons* (pictorial symbols). Microsoft followed the Mac lead and created Windows with those same easy-to-use functions.

In 1995, with worldwide fanfare, Microsoft launched its Windows 95 OS, which had many new features and was very similar to the Macin-

The writer starts her vacation plans by giving her agent the details of where and when she wants to go. The agent will carry out the task of contacting other agents to find airplane flight times and the lowest fares. When the writer makes her selection, the agent will book the reservation and pay for the ticket.

The writer avoids browsing the shopping malls by using the many electronic catalogs available. She gives her agent information about what items she is seeking, and the agent browses for her. After the agent presents some choices, she can make a selection and the agent will purchase it.

At the end of the day, the writer returns to her desk. She reads any new e-mail, finishes making travel plans and shopping selections, and sets up her work for the next day. Her computer screen displays a message reminding her that tomorrow is her niece's birthday and asks, "Shall I send flowers?"

tosh OS. However, even as computer users were learning this new system, Microsoft was working on its successors. One with minor improvements, scheduled for release in 1996, allowed PC's easier access to the Internet, better *multimedia* performance, and other new features. Multimedia products combine traditional text and graphics with video clips, animation, and sound.

A major update of Windows, code-named "Memphis," was to be ready by 1997 or 1998. Memphis would further integrate Windows with the Internet in order to make Internet data as accessible as the information on a computer's hard drive. Apple Computer's 1996 version of the Macintosh OS had improved multimedia capabilities as well as other features. Its successor, an OS called "Gershwin," was in the works in 1996. Gershwin would be the first major update of the internal architecture of the Mac OS since 1984.

Windows 95 was the first *32-bit* operating system widely used in home PC's. Bits are the 1's and 0's used in computer language. Different combinations of bits represent numbers, letters, symbols, graphics, or other information, and a combination of eight bits is called a *byte*. The first personal computers ran 8-bit programs, and most programs today are 16-bit.

A 32-bit computer performs like a multilane superhighway, carrying twice as much "traffic"— data—per second as a 16-bit machine. Programs adapted to the 32-bit format are more powerful and versatile than earlier machines. Even more advanced 64-bit programs were on the horizon in 1996. Many software manufacturers were rewriting older programs for the 32-bit format, and many of their revised programs were showing up in stores in 1996 as the 32-bit format became standard. These new programs included more animation, video, games, and many other new features.

Internet software and other advances

Many experts believe that the Internet and the World Wide Web (WWW) will further revolutionize the way software is written, distributed, and used. The WWW is a segment of the Internet that allows computers anywhere in the world to share files and other data such as graphics, video, and audio information.

Experts predicted that the World Wide Web would break down the barrier between Macs and IBM-compatible PC's. On the WWW, information is processed in a computer language called *hypertext markup language (HTML)*, which is accessible to any computer with any operating system. Reading HTML requires a "browser," software specific to the user's OS that understands HTML. A program called Netscape Navigator is the most popu-

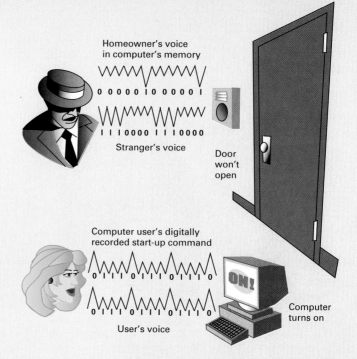

Homeowner's voice in computer's memory

0 0000 I0 0000 I

I I I0000 I I I0000

Stranger's voice

Door won't open

Computer user's digitally recorded start-up command

0 I I I 0 I I I 0 I I I 0

0 I I I 0 I I I 0 I I I 0

User's voice

ON!

Computer turns on

lar browser used on the WWW. Through HTML, web users can exchange documents regardless of which OS they have on their computer or which OS the information came from.

More software in the future may use the hardware-independent format of HTML. A move in that direction was the Java programming language developed in July 1995 by Sun Microsystems Incorporated of Mountain View, California. Java greatly increased the range of possibilities for Internet users by allowing them to get animation, moving pictures, and other advanced features on their own screens without having to purchase all of the necessary software. Java enables computer users to obtain required chunks of software, called "applets," over the phone lines. The applets are on the Internet and can be summoned to one's computer whenever they are needed. Java attracted attention in 1995 when Microsoft announced a plan to make it work well with Windows and to develop programs that could easily be distributed on the Internet.

Many computer experts expected the Internet distribution of software to end the necessity of buying new programs or program updates on discs. Instead, computer users would download programs and updates directly from the Internet onto their hard drive, even multimedia materials. This would enable consumers to obtain continuous improvements for their software rather than having to wait a year or more for a single massive update. Software companies might charge users an annual fee to use a program and its updates.

New WWW-compatible programs might also blur the traditional distinction between software and data. New programming languages such as Java are *object-oriented* systems—ones that merge software and data into a single "object." An object named Smith's Catalog, for example, might contain data encompassing all the items in the company's mail-order catalog plus software for ordering over the Internet. Future software of this kind might be disposable. A computer user would use an object-oriented program only once, and then it would be erased from their computer. But all such programs would still be available on the Internet to be used as needed.

Home computer programs that respond to voice commands were also expected to become common. These voice-recognition programs would eliminate the need to give the computer commands with a keyboard or mouse. By saying "file," for instance, the user could make the file menu in a word-processing program appear on the screen with all of its options. The user would then pick the desired option with a voice command such as "save," "close," or "delete."

Voice-recognition software programs would provide a simple way to interact with intelligent agents. While working on a document, a computer user might simply ask, "Do I have any new e-mail?" The program's electronic mail agent would check and respond with a "yes" or "no." Advanced versions of this technology might allow the user to make further spoken requests, such as "Read it to me," "Trash it," or "Send copies to Bill and Sue."

Software assistants, voice-recognition software, and Internet-oriented programs will fundamentally change the way we use computers. Computers will be more complex than ever, but software advances will make it increasingly simple to use these amazing machines.

Computer Networks

While personal computers (PC's) dramatically increase the amount of work that individuals can accomplish independently, much of our work—whether for school or business—depends upon interaction with others. Lawyers need references from past cases. Bankers require large amounts of financial information. Students seek information from many different sources. Nearly every computer user, no matter how powerful his or her machine, occasionally needs to draw on resources not available at the desktop. For this reason, many computers are part of a *network*, two or more connected computers that can communicate with each other.

With computers connected together, each computer user gains the resources of larger computers, the opportunity to share and compare work with others, or to use peripheral devices, such as printers, that might be in short supply. For example, a bank customer can use a neighborhood automated teller machine to withdraw or deposit money. That computer is networked to a computer at the main bank that will keep track of the customer's transactions. Electronic mail (e-mail) travels across networks, allowing users to communicate with one another.

Network: Two or more connected computers that can communicate with each other.

Internet: The worldwide network of computer networks.

Modem: A device attached to a computer that allows it to communicate with other computers through telephone lines.

Types of networks

There are two basic types of networks: *local-area networks* (LAN's) and *wide-area networks* (WAN's). LAN's are generally confined to a single office, classroom, or building. WAN's connect several—or many—smaller networks together. A typical LAN consists of a number of PC's, called workstations, linked by wires and cables to a larger central computer called a *server*. The server holds data files that can be accessed by anyone on the network. In some cases, a server also holds the software that is used by the workstations.

Whatever the physical nature of a network may be, the uses of networks are changing rapidly. Although networks have primarily been a means of exchanging information and sharing resources, they are increasingly being used for a much wider range of tasks, including some made possible only through networking. An example of this is *collaborative software*. This type of software lets many people, using different computers, work together on the same project—making notes, offering suggestions, correcting errors, and adding insights. Everyone's contributions are immediately visible to all the members of the network.

Collaborative software is altering the way many companies operate. Bringing many points of view to bear on problems simultaneously can enable employees to work more efficiently and effectively, with the added benefit of building teamwork and cooperation.

WAN's are created by enabling computers to send and receive information over telephone lines. The device that makes this possible is the *modem* (*mo*dulator/*demo*dulator). A modem is a small electronic device that converts *digital* information (information encoded as a series of 1's and 0's) from a computer into *analog* (continuous) signals that can travel over telephone lines. The modem also translates incoming analog telephone signals back into digital information for a computer to process.

The Internet

Ultimately, except for networks kept apart for security reasons, all networks may eventually join the single global network known as the Internet. Originally created by the United States Department of Defense as a means of keeping communications in place in the event of nuclear war, the Internet has evolved into the largest computer network on Earth, with as many as 50 million computers linked together by the mid-1990's. The computers hooked into the Internet range from PC's to huge mainframes at universities, government offices, and corporations. All are linked together through the telephone system.

The Internet enables individuals to obtain huge amounts of information from all over the world. Any computer connected to the Internet can access any information source on the network.

Experts estimate that the information available on the Internet is doubling every few months, and the number of people who have access to that in-

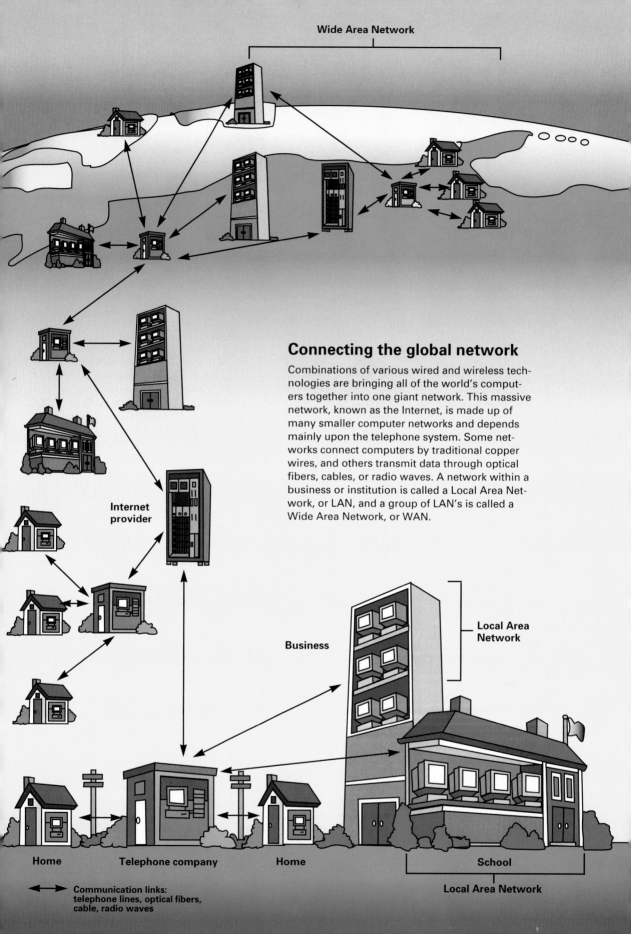

Wide Area Network

Connecting the global network

Combinations of various wired and wireless technologies are bringing all of the world's computers together into one giant network. This massive network, known as the Internet, is made up of many smaller computer networks and depends mainly upon the telephone system. Some networks connect computers by traditional copper wires, and others transmit data through optical fibers, cables, or radio waves. A network within a business or institution is called a Local Area Network, or LAN, and a group of LAN's is called a Wide Area Network, or WAN.

Internet provider

Local Area Network

Business

Home   Telephone company   Home   School

Local Area Network

Communication links: telephone lines, optical fibers, cable, radio waves

Using solar-powered equipment, a health-care worker in Sudan communicates with faraway colleagues through a computer network based on high-frequency radio technology. A group called Volunteers in Technical Assistance established the network in 1989 for the United Nations.

formation is increasing at an equally rapid rate. We are witnessing the creation of a global database that may one day contain all of the world's information—even artwork, music, and motion pictures.

However, modem-based networks, upon which most of the Internet relies, have been limited because such networks are too inflexible. Part of that inflexibility comes from the fact that telephone lines are fixed in place. A larger limitation, though, is the information-carrying capacity of traditional copper telephone lines. Essentially, these lines were designed to carry voices, not huge volumes of complex information. A typical phone line can carry about 28,000 bits of data per second. At that rate, transmitting large data files takes many minutes.

Increasing speed and volume

One solution to this problem has been ISDN (Integrated Services Digital Network) lines, which use copper wire but have special modems and other equipment that allow data to be transmitted at a rate of 128,000 bits per second. *Dedicated* (reserved for a particular purpose) ISDN lines must be specifically installed for customers wishing this particular service.

Other types of lines that increase transmission capacity include those known as T1 and T3. T1 lines use copper wire and special switches and other equipment to transmit digital information at about 1 million bits (1 megabit) per second. The larger T3 line is made with optical fiber and can carry 45 megabits of information per second. T1 and T3 lines are generally used to carry information in bulk rather than to individual users.

Cable television lines offer an alternative for bringing digital information to individual customers. These lines can carry hundreds of megabits of information per second. Many computer users are now accessing the Internet through their cable provider rather than through the telephone system.

However, cable connections to the Internet have a limitation. Because cable systems are delivering dozens—in some cases, hundreds—of television channels at once, the lines can become quite crowded.

The ultimate in high-speed data transmission is offered by *optical-fiber* technology. Optical fiber is a type of filament made from a special type of ultraclear glass composed of silicon or quartz, and less than 0.1 mm (1/250 inch) thick. In most digital optical communications, the optical fibers carry information as pulses of laser light. A laser is a device that emits a narrow beam of light of a single *wavelength* (color).

Optical fiber can transmit a tremendous volume of data per second, making even the transmission of sound, graphics, video, or animation virtually instantaneous. The information travels at the speed of light, though light moves somewhat slower in glass than it does in space. (The speed of light in a vacuum, where there are no atoms to impede it, is 299,792 kilometers [186,282 miles] per second.)

Optical fiber is expensive, however, and it requires amplifiers built into the system at regular intervals in order to maintain the strength of the transmission. For these reasons, fiberoptic networks are used mainly in single locations, such as a building or factory.

Gradually, though, traditional telephone and cable-television lines are being replaced with optical fibers, making fiberoptic networks more practical over longer distances. Optical transmissions are the wave of the future.

Going wireless

Optical technologies are also being used to create wireless networks. Wireless networks, which were developed in the early 1990's, offered a solution to some of the limits of wire-based networks, mainly in freeing computers from fixed *topologies* (interconnections of devices and communication channels).

Most wireless networks employ radio frequencies such as the ones cellular telephones use. In a typical wireless network, special *cards* (circuitry) are added to workstations. The cards include transmitters and receivers that do the work formerly done by wire or cable connectors.

Using a wireless-network computer, a user might enter a request into the computer for information from a central server. The request is transmitted by radio signal, received by the server, processed, and the requested information returned by a signal received by the user's computer. The entire process takes an instant.

Because these networks do not require the costly installation of wires and cables, they are less expensive to install and operate than networks that do. Additionally, computers can be added or removed from the network simply by installing or removing the wireless-network card. Thus, workers can join or leave a wireless network in a matter of minutes, rather than having to wait for technical specialists to establish or sever their network connection.

Perhaps more importantly, wireless networking capacity has made network membership more mobile. For example, a doctor in a particular network, by carrying a laptop computer equipped with a wireless network card, can link to the network from many different locations, including a patient's room in a hospital.

The same flexibility is available to other professionals. Teachers can move from classroom to classroom, even school to school, taking their computer along. Manufacturing personnel can do their work at various stations on a production line or at remote locations. Traveling salespeople with cellular network cards can connect to their offices from any location that affords them a cellular signal.

Using light for wireless transmissions

The drawback of wireless networks that depend on regular radio waves is the relatively small amount of information radio signals can carry and the slow speeds at which that information is transmitted. Using light to transmit data can be the answer to that problem.

Many wireless optical networks use *infrared waves* to transmit and receive information. Infrared waves lie just beyond the red end of the visible light spectrum and cannot be seen by the human eye. Some additional features are required on the network card to make it work, including a device to translate the electronic information into pulses of light and, in some cases, a lens to focus the infrared beam for efficient transmission.

Lasers, too, are effective tools for wireless optical networks. Again, a transmitter/receiver, along with translator and lens, are required for laser-networked installations.

Wireless laser and infrared digital signals are only good for short distances, because they depend upon the light beams passing uninterrupted from sender to receiver. Moreover, it is doubtful that wireless optical transmissions—or any wireless technology—will ever be able to match the data-carrying capacity of cable or optical fibers. Still, these technologies offer all the advantages of freedom from wires and cables.

As use of the Internet and on-line services grows, many kinds of traditional information lines are being combined with various wireless technologies. New approaches to data transmission are constantly being invented and perfected, making the global network more and more extensive.

On the Far Frontier

The computer revolution has grown mainly through continuous improvements to electronic *integrated circuits*. An integrated circuit consists of thousands or millions of transistors and other tiny parts on a small chip of silicon. These chips—*microchips*—make up the heart of a computer. But the most exciting areas of research, and the ones most likely to lead to the computers of the future, are moving beyond the integrated circuit.

There are several reasons for this. Chief among them is that there is a speed limit to electronic computing. Electronics is based on the movement of *electrons* (negatively charged subatomic particles), which are pushed through tiny wires and connections. But the wires exert a certain *resistance*, or physical opposition, to the movement of the electrons. Resistance slows the speed of computer operations and generates heat that must be disposed of. Researchers are seeking ways of computing that involve little or no resistance.

Researchers are also trying to find ways for computers to tackle larger and larger problems. Many complex mathematical problems that scientists would like to solve would take years for current computers to calculate.

In the quest to build these superadvanced computers, nearly every major field of science is involved, including physics, chemistry, and biology. Each of these disciplines offers potential new directions for computing.

Computing with light

One promising avenue of research is *optical computing*, the use of light rather than electrons to perform computations inside the computer. Optical computing employs miniature *lasers* (devices that emit narrow beams of light) to process information. The advantage of using light for computing is its tremendous speed—299,792 kilometers (186,282 miles) per second.

Because computing is a *digital* process—one in which all information is expressed as a series of 1's and 0's, it is easy to see how a computer could be based on light. A laser could be turned on to represent a 1 and turned off for a 0. A series of tiny lasers and mirrors would be arranged to direct and receive the digital signals. Some scientists estimate that optical computers could operate millions of times faster than current personal computers.

Smaller, faster, more powerful

Another approach to computing that has attracted a great deal of attention involves using the nature of atoms as a basis for manipulating data. This emerging technology, called *quantum computing*, rests upon the fact that atoms and their subatomic components—electrons, neutrons, and protons—exist in various levels of energy, called quantum states. An electron, for example, changes quantum states when it absorbs or gives off a packet of energy called a photon. The electron jumps from one energy level to another. If scientists could systematically raise and lower the energy level of an electron, one quantum state could represent a digital 1 and the other a 0.

The challenge in building a quantum computer is in the difficulty of altering the quantum level of a single, specific electron. In addition, quantum states can change as a result of outside influences, such as atoms combining with other atoms. One possible solution to this problem would be to alter

In February 1996, world chess champion Garry Kasparov competed against a chess-playing computer known as Deep Blue, designed by engineers at the International Business Machines Corporation (IBM). Deep Blue won one round in the face-off, causing many people to wonder if the computer could think. Computer experts said no. Nonetheless, some experts predict that thinking computers will be developed in the future.

The house of tomorrow

Designers and engineers working for General Electric Company have created a futuristic house, *right,* in Pittsfield, Massachusetts. Throughout the house are embedded computers that work together to make the entire house computerized. Every major system and many smaller functions can be operated through computers.

The kitchen, *above, right,* contains a control panel, *inset,* with which features throughout the house can be operated. Residents can adjust the heat, air conditioning, and lighting for various rooms and even set the water temperature for a bath. A security system photographs a guest at the door and prints his picture for the resident to view. The house uses futuristic materials and technologies while following a traditionally elegant design, *right.*

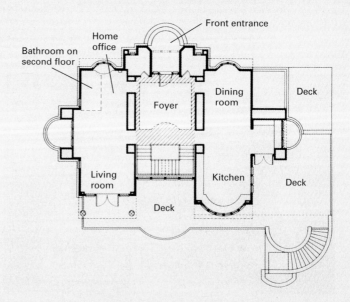

Bathroom on second floor

Home office

Front entrance

Foyer

Dining room

Deck

Living room

Kitchen

Deck

Deck

the energy states of billions of subatomic particles at once for each step of a computational process. The computer would operate by calculating the average result of each operation. This would adjust for any errors that could occur as a result of random factors affecting individual atoms. Quantum computing is no more than a scientist's dream so far, but its potential is truly amazing. A quantum computer could be smaller than a grain of salt, yet contain trillions of individual atoms, each of which would hold a bit of information.

Another field of research that could lead to salt-grain-sized computers is *nanotechnology*, an experimental science that seeks to build machines on a molecular scale. By manipulating atoms, some visionaries say, it would be theoretically possible to build machines, including computers, so small they could be seen only with a microscope.

One scientist has speculated that a nanocomputer might work best if it was mechanical rather than digital. Mechanical—or *analog*—computers use moving parts to perform calculations rather than the electronic switches of digital computers. More than a century ago, attempts were made to build mechanical computers. By turning gears in such computers, other gears moved in sequence, resulting in the solution to mathematical problems. Such computers were huge and unwieldy and ultimately proved impractical.

Suppose, however, that scientists could create incredibly tiny gears and that those gears could be turned at phenomenal rates of speed and accuracy. It would be possible—again, theoretically—to build an analog computer the size of a grain of salt that would be more powerful than all of the world's digital computers combined.

Another futuristic avenue of research is the possibility of using *DNA* (*deoxyribonucleic acid*, the molecule genes are made of) to create what scientists are calling an organic or molecular computer. DNA is composed of four compounds called nucleotides that join together in specific ways. Various paired arrangements of those nucleotides encode all the information needed to create the billions of features of all living things. This ability of DNA to store enormous amounts of information and to use that information to form complex structures strikes some scientists as very computer-like. Because DNA can be custom-made in the laboratory by stringing nucleotides together, some researchers speculate that it might be possible to put whatever information we want into DNA.

Scientists could combine the four nucleotides in many ways to represent information, just as the 0's and 1's of the binary system are combined to represent numbers and letters. Because those compounds naturally bind with each other in particular ways, scientists could create long strands of DNA that would recognize and bind with certain other strands. In this way, they could use certain pieces of DNA to "find" and bind to specific pieces of information encoded in other DNA strands. Complex mathematical problems could be solved in this way.

There would be many advantages to molecular computing. For one, millions of trillions of DNA molecules would be involved in solving a problem, all working in unison. This is called *massively parallel computing*, and it is one of the goals of all branches of computer research. A DNA computer might be capable of carrying out a thousand trillion operations a second, making it as much as a thousand times faster than the most powerful present-day electronic supercomputers.

Glimpses of the future

The frontier that most captures the human imagination may be artificial intelligence. In February 1996, world chess champion Garry Kasparov faced a chess-playing computer known as Deep Blue, designed by researchers at the International Business Machines Corporation (IBM). Deep Blue won one round in the competition, causing people to ask: Can this machine think? Most experts said the computer could not be said to think because it merely performed massive numbers of individual calculations at a high rate of speed. Deep Blue decided what move to make by running every possible move and outcome through its memory and picking the best one.

In order to really be a thinking machine, computer experts say, a computer would have to have what we call common sense, an ability to take in and respond to new information and unique circumstances. So far, the most advanced computers are only able to act upon the thousands of pieces of information that have been fed into them. But some experts say that it is just a matter of time before actual thinking computers are developed.

Some long-predicted computer technologies, like the so-called house of the future are already here. The General Electric Company has built such a house in Pittsfield, Massachusetts, to demonstrate the use of advanced materials and computerized control systems. A central computer controls all of the systems in the house, from heating and air conditioning to lighting and security. Throughout the house, embedded microchips respond to the environment and to the homeowner's commands. These all work together with the central computer.

The computer revolution is far from over. Even the most accurate predictions of the past have fallen short of the reality we now experience. So perhaps even the most visionary of present-day predictions about the future of computing will seem to have been short-sighted in tomorrow's reality.

Science Year contributors report on the year's major developments in their respective fields. The articles in this section are arranged alphabetically.

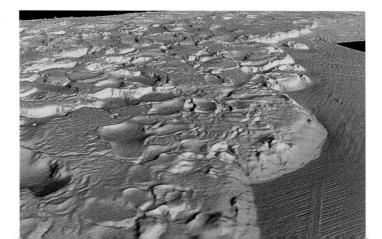

Page 273

Page 207

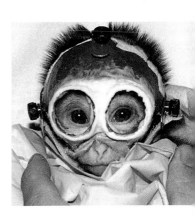

Page 245

Public health officials in the United Kingdom announced in March 1996 that people who eat beef from cattle with a brain disease known as bovine spongiform encephalopathy (BSE) may risk developing Creutzfeldt-Jakob disease (CJD). CJD, thought to be closely related to BSE, is a rare, fatal brain disease that usually strikes people in middle and late life. British officials said that there was weak evidence linking the consumption of infected beef with 10 cases of CJD in patients much younger.

BSE is caused by a type of protein called a prion, but scientists do not know how prions act to produce the disease. The brain of an infected cow becomes full of holes, and the cow stumbles in circles, making it appear crazy. Thus, BSE is commonly called mad cow disease. Cooking beef from BSE-infected cows to 130 °C (266 °F) does not destroy prions, as it does other microbes.

British scientists believe that BSE spread among domestic cattle through feed supplements made of sheep by-products. Many of those sheep had been stricken with a disease called scrapie, which is closely related to BSE.

The European Union (EU), an organization of 15 nations including the United Kingdom, banned British beef exports and demanded that Britain kill its herds. British beef sales and prices fell sharply, bringing the beef industry to near-collapse. Britain promised to kill 42,000 cattle most at risk for BSE in return for a lifting of the export ban. On April 30, the EU budgeted $1.1 billion to help cover the cost of Britain's eradication program, but retained the ban.

The United States banned British beef in 1989 to protect domestic herds from BSE. In May 1996, the U.S. Food and Drug Administration proposed a regulation that sheep by-products not be used in cattle feed. The United States has had no documented cases of BSE.

Soybeans for science. Researchers at the U.S. Department of Agriculture (USDA) and Iowa State University of Science and Technology in Ames announced in September 1995 that they had discovered a variety of soybean plants that do not produce pollen, particles containing a plant's male reproduc-

Dyed medflies die
Agricultural Research Service (ARS) scientists in Hawaii apply a mixture of red dye and bait to a wick, *left*, before offering it to Medflies, insects that feed on hundreds of different crops. The scientists tested various combinations of dye, bait, and an appetite stimulant to induce a Medfly to eat enough dye to turn its abdomen red, *below*. Sunlight reacts with the dye, killing Medflies that have eaten the bait, according to a January 1996 ARS report.

A camera at the end of an arm of a robotic mushroom picker scans a bright round spot of reflected light in the center of a mushroom cap. The camera sends an image to a computerized system that can tell the size of mushrooms by the size of the bright spot on each one's cap. Another arm descends to pick the mushrooms and place them in a tray. Engineers in the United Kingdom, who announced the prototype in November 1995, said the robot's top harvesting speed is one mushroom every six seconds, about the same as for a human picker. But they expect a commercial version of the machine to pick a mushroom every three seconds.

tive cells. But the male-sterile plants are capable of being pollinated in the field by bees, resulting in a bounty of hybrid seeds. Breeders need numerous seeds in order to develop plants with new, valuable traits, such as increased yield.

The flowers on a normal soybean plant are fertilized with pollen from the same plant, a characteristic called self-pollination. Plant breeders have had to cross-pollinate by hand and cultivate plants for several years to ensure that a desirable trait has been passed on.

The new soybean plants bear white flowers without pollen instead of the normal purple flowers with pollen. Genetic tests of the white-flowering plants revealed that they had inherited two genes for male sterility, which caused them to be male-sterile. The genes were located close to a gene that codes for flower color on the same *chromosome*. (Chromosomes are tiny, threadlike structures in the cell nucleus that carry the genes.) This proximity meant that soybean plants lacking pollen produced only white flowers, making them easy to identify. Also, the stem of a sprout from

a male-sterile seed is green. The stem from a fertile seed is purple.

In the field, researchers pulled up the purple-stemmed seedlings, leaving rows of sterile green-stemmed plants to grow next to rows of normal plants. Bee pollination resulted in hybrid seeds that the researchers offered to plant breeders.

New rice resists disease. For the first time, scientists in 1995 isolated a rice gene that conveys resistance to blight, a disease that causes plants to wither and die. They then successfully transferred the gene to other rice plants, making them blight-resistant. Rice is the staple food for more than half the world's population, and blight has reduced rice yields by 50 percent in parts of Asia.

The scientists, led by plant pathologist Pamela Ronald of the University of California at Davis, reported in December 1995 that they had identified a gene called Xa21 as the blight-resistance gene among eight genes that seemed likely candidates because of their location on a particular rice chromosome. The location was similar to that of known disease-resistance genes on a corresponding soybean chromosome.

The researchers transferred the eight genes and a "marker" gene into rice cells in a Petri dish. The marker gene enabled the scientists to track how the rice cells incorporated the other eight genes. The scientists grew 1,500 rice plants from the genetically altered cells. They tested for disease resistance by trimming the leaves with scissors dipped in a solution containing the bacterial blight organism. Ten days later, of the 1,500 test plants, all but 50 had gray streaks on their leaves—a symptom of bacterial blight. The investigators found that those 50 healthy plants were the only ones that contained the Xa21 gene.

Mare vaccine protects foals. *Foal* (baby horse) diarrhea is a contagious disease, caused by a virus, that can be fatal if not properly treated. Until now, treatment was lengthy, and surviving foals grew slower than normal. But in January 1996, after 10 years of research, the USDA approved a vaccine for mares that prevents diarrhea in their foals.

The vaccine was developed by researchers at the Gluck Equine Research Center at the University of Kentucky in Lexington. Since foals are most susceptible to foal diarrhea in the first two months of life, and a foal receives *antibodies* (disease-fighting molecules) from its mother's milk only during the first 12 to 18 hours after birth, the scientists administered the vaccine to pregnant mares near delivery. Tests showed that the vaccine passed to foals in mares' milk, and immunity lasted about 60 days. Foals from vaccinated mares had 50 percent fewer cases of diarrhea than foals from unvaccinated mares.

Hybrid poplars. Harvest was scheduled for 1996 of a new hybrid poplar species that matures in nine years— decades ahead of other hardwoods. The trees were planted on thousands of hectares in the Pacific Northwest in 1987. On average, they grew 3 meters (10 feet) in height and 3.3 centimeters (1.3 inches) in diameter each year. Geneticists at Washington State University in Pullman developed the hybrid as an economical wood for paper making and other timber products.   [Steve Cain]

In WORLD BOOK, see AGRICULTURE.

Anthropology

Fossil bones discovered in Kenya belong to a 4-million-year-old *hominid* species, according to an August 1995 report. (Hominids include human beings and their close prehuman ancestors.) A team of anthropologists led by Meave G. Leakey of the National Museums of Kenya found 21 fossil bones from the species at Kanapoi and Allia Bay, near Lake Turkana in northern Kenya.

The bones were assigned to the early prehuman genus *Australopithecus,* well known from other fossil sites in eastern and southern Africa. But the remains were unique enough to justify designating a new species. Leakey's team named the species *Australopithecus anamensis,* from *anam,* the word for lake in the language of the Turkana people.

Walking on two legs. The fossils of *A. anamensis* include a shinbone shaped for *bipedalism* (walking on two legs). *A. anamensis* is the oldest prehuman species for which bipedalism has been fully demonstrated. However, the species also possessed numerous apelike features, including a chin that sloped sharply backward and large *canine teeth*

(pointed teeth next to the incisors). Another important feature is lower first premolars—the teeth just beyond the lower canines—of a characteristic shape. In *A. anamensis,* as in apes, these two teeth—one on either side of the lower jaw—have an oval outline and only one distinct *cusp* (point).

In later hominids, the chin region is less sloping, the canine teeth are smaller, and the first lower premolar has a round outline and two conspicuous cusps. Some of the apelike features of *A. anamensis* also occur in *A. afarensis,* an early hominid species that lived in east Africa between 3.9 million and 3.0 million years ago. This led Leakey's team to suggest that *A. anamensis* evolved into *A. afarensis,* the ancestor of all later hominids, including human being.

But there is a problem with this theory. *A. anamensis* coexisted 4 million years ago with another early prehuman species, *Ardipithecus ramidus,* discovered in 1992 at Aramis, Ethiopia, by Tim D. White of the University of California at Berkeley. White proposed that *A. ramidus* may be the ancestor of *A. afarensis.*

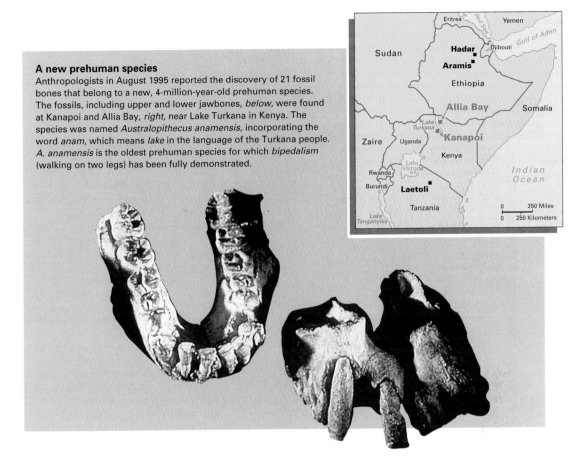

A new prehuman species

Anthropologists in August 1995 reported the discovery of 21 fossil bones that belong to a new, 4-million-year-old prehuman species. The fossils, including upper and lower jawbones, *below,* were found at Kanapoi and Allia Bay, *right,* near Lake Turkana in Kenya. The species was named *Australopithecus anamensis,* incorporating the word *anam,* which means *lake* in the language of the Turkana people. *A. anamensis* is the oldest prehuman species for which *bipedalism* (walking on two legs) has been fully demonstrated.

A. *ramidus* differs from A. *afarensis* and A. *anamensis* in some important respects, such as the thickness of the enamel covering the molar teeth. Thicker enamel, which allowed early hominids to feed on harder or grittier foods, may have evolved when seeds and other hard or abrasive items became more important in prehuman diets. Both A. *anamensis* and A. *afarensis,* like later hominids, had very thick enamel. But A. *ramidus* had thinner enamel more like that of the chimpanzee and the gorilla.

Based on this and other characteristics, Leakey and her colleagues suggested that A. *ramidus* was not a direct human ancestor but belonged instead to a separate, extinct hominid line. They noted that A. *ramidus* was found with the fossils of forest animals, indicating that it was a tree-dwelling creature—more ape than human. A. *anamensis* and A. *afarensis,* in contrast, were found with the fossils of animals that inhabited a *savanna* environment (grassland with scattered trees), the same kind of environment favored by our early ancestors.

The conflicting interpretations can be explained in at least two ways. First, A. *ramidus* may have been a strange humanlike ape rather than a prehuman species. By studying A. *ramidus* leg bones discovered in 1994, researchers expected to determine whether A. *ramidus* was bipedal and thus could have been part of the human line. If the answer is yes, then a second possibility must be considered—that at its beginning, the human family tree may have included at least two branches. Only one branch could have led to modern human beings, however. Future fossil discoveries should help anthropologists decide which species was our ancestor.

The oldest-known upright ape. A fossil skeleton discovered in Spain is the oldest-known skeleton to show the *orthograde* (upright) body structure of modern apes, according to a January 1996 report. Salvador Moyà-Solà and Meike Köhler of the Miquel Crusafont Institute of Paleontology in Sabadell, Spain, found the 9.5-million-year-old skeleton at Can Llobateres, Spain. The partial skeleton includes major bones of the arms, hand, vertebral column,

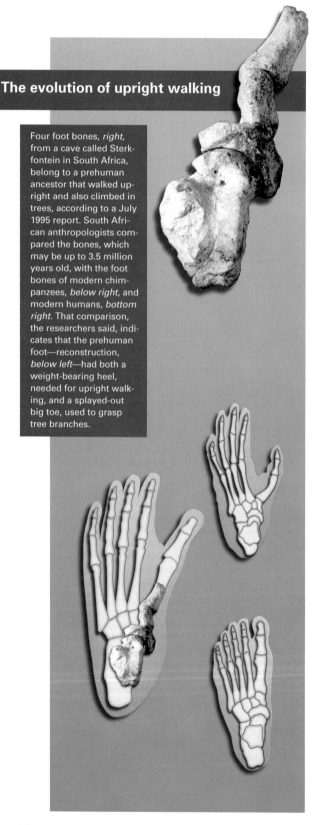

The evolution of upright walking

Four foot bones, *right*, from a cave called Sterk-fontein in South Africa, belong to a prehuman ancestor that walked up-right and also climbed in trees, according to a July 1995 report. South African anthropologists com-pared the bones, which may be up to 3.5 million years old, with the foot bones of modern chim-panzees, *below right*, and modern humans, *bottom right*. That comparison, the researchers said, indi-cates that the prehuman foot—reconstruction, *below left*—had both a weight-bearing heel, needed for upright walk-ing, and a splayed-out big toe, used to grasp tree branches.

and legs, along with a partial skull. The skull shows that the skeleton is from a species called *Dryopithecus laietanus*, one of several species of apes that lived in Europe from about 14 million to 8 million years ago.

Many jaws and teeth of *Dryopithecus* have been found in the past, but anthro-pologists had discovered only a few iso-lated bones from below the neck. The new fossil is the most complete skeleton of an ape or early hominid that has been discovered from the time between *Proconsul africanus*, an ape that lived in Kenya about 18 million years ago, and *A. afarensis*.

Present-day apes and human beings are built for orthograde posture, in which the vertebral column is held per-pendicular to the ground. This contrasts with the *pronograde* posture of monkeys and most other mammals, in which the vertebral column is held parallel to the ground. Most paleontologists believe that orthograde posture evolved when apes began using their arms for climb-ing hand over hand in trees and hang-ing or swinging below branches. Mod-ern apes are clearly built for these sorts of movements. Monkeys, in comparison, are adapted for jumping from branch to branch and walking or running on all fours on top of branches.

The evolution of apelike orthograde posture was probably essential for the later evolution of bipedalism. Anthro-pologists are thus interested in learning when orthograde posture first evolved.

There are several skeletal characteris-tics that indicate orthograde posture. These include a shortening of the *lum-bar* (waist) section of the vertebral col-umn, a change in the shape of the chest from narrow and deep (as in a dog or monkey) to broad and shallow (as in a chimpanzee or human being), a length-ening of the arms, and a reshaping of the arm and hand bones.

The 18-million-year-old skeleton of *Proconsul africanus* possesses no ortho-grade features and shows that early apes were pronograde. The Can Llobateres skeleton's orthograde features indicate that the body form necessary for bi-pedalism had evolved by 9.5 million years ago.

Dryopithecus laietanus probably became extinct about 8 million years ago. Al-though the species lived only in Europe, it may have had orthograde cousins in Africa. One of those African species may have given rise to two separate evolutionary lines—one leading to human beings and the other to modern apes—between 7 million and 5 million years ago.

A hominid fossil in central Africa. The first discovery of a very early hominid fossil in central Africa was announced in November 1995, by an international team of archaeologists led by Michel Brunet of the University of Poitiers, France. The researchers discovered the front portion of a lower jaw near Koro Toro, Chad. Animal fossils found with the jaw indicated that it is between 3.5 million and 3.0 million years old. Before this fossil was found, the only known prehuman fossils that old came from east Africa (Ethiopia, Kenya, and Tanzania), 2,500 kilometers (1,500 miles) to the east.

Like other very early hominid jaws, this one retains some apelike features, including the relatively large size of the canine teeth. In this and other traits, the jaw resembles ones from Ethiopia and Tanzania that have been placed in the species *A. afarensis*. But Brunet's team announced in May 1996 that the creature was different enough from other known hominids to rank as a new species, which they named *A. bahrelghazalia*, after the Arab name of a nearby riverbed. Further study was expected to determine whether *A. bahrelghazalia* is ancestral to human beings or whether *A. afarensis* should retain that role.

The fact that the jaw was found with the fossils of savanna-dwelling animals suggests that hominids evolved many of their human traits as they adapted to life on the open plains of Africa, outside the forests that apes prefer. The new fossil finding also extends the known geographic range of the earliest hominids, suggesting that even the earliest prehuman species were widely dispersed in the region of Africa around the equator. Until now, most anthropologists had assumed that human beings originated in east Africa and reached other parts of Africa much later.   [Richard G. Klein]

See also ARCHAEOLOGY. In WORLD BOOK, see ANTHROPOLOGY; PREHISTORIC PEOPLE.

Archaeology

The frozen mummy of an Inca girl was discovered in the Andes Mountains of South America in September 1995. The Inca ruled Peru before the Spanish conquest in the 1500's. American archaeologist and mountaineer Johan Reinhard, affiliated with the Field Museum of Natural History in Chicago, found the body on Mount Ampato in southern Peru, at an elevation of 6,300 meters (20,700 feet). The 12- to 14-year-old girl, dubbed Juanita, died about 500 years ago.

An Inca sacrifice. Two bodies of Inca boys were later found at the Mount Ampato site, but unlike Juanita they were not well preserved. The three young people had been sacrificed, perhaps while in a drug-enhanced stupor, to appease gods that the Inca believed were the source of rain and the cause of earthquakes and avalanches.

The discovery was made possible by the eruptions of a nearby volcano. Falling ashes had been melting the icecap on Mount Ampato. Reinhard and a Peruvian colleague, Miguel Zarate, noticed feathers sticking out of ice and snow on the mountain slope. They knew that the summit of Mount Ampato had been sacred to the Inca and immediately suspected they had found an Inca sacrifice. Searching the area, they found the girl's body, which was wrapped in cloth. It had already been exposed to the elements and the face had been damaged.

Near the area where the body was discovered, Reinhard and Zarate found about a dozen figurines made of shell, bronze, silver, and gold, clothed with textiles and feathers. The figurines ranged in height from 6.5 to 16.5 centimeters (2.5 to 6.5 inches). These objects were also offerings to the Inca gods.

A campsite nearby was apparently left by the Inca on their way to the summit to make sacrifices. At the campsite, the archaeologists found pottery, sandals, and the remains of mat-covered tents that had been used to insulate the Inca campers from the cold.

Reinhard and Zarate wrapped the body in foam sleeping pads to keep it from thawing any further and took

Andean ice maiden
The frozen mummy of a young Inca woman, sacrificed to Inca gods 500 years ago, was found in September 1995 atop Mount Ampato in Peru. American archaeologist Johan Reinhard and a colleague found the body along with several small figurines, *right*. The figurines were also offerings to appease gods that the Inca believed were the source of rain, earthquakes, and avalanches.

it back down the mountain. By burro and bus, they transported the body to the Peruvian city of Arequipa. Juanita and the two other bodies, found the following month, were placed in a freezer at the Catholic University of Santa Maria to ensure their preservation.

The National Geographic Society of Washington, D.C., funded research on these unique remains. Studies of the well-preserved tissues and body fluids revealed that the girl's diet had been good. She was apparently in excellent health at the time of her death.

A shipwreck from the 1500's. In July 1995, a team of underwater archaeologists led by Barto Arnold of the Texas Historical Commission announced the discovery of a remarkably well-preserved shipwreck off the Texas coast. The sunken vessel, the *Belle,* was one of four ships used by the French explorer Sieur de La Salle.

In 1684, La Salle and a party of about 300 settlers departed from France aboard four ships to establish a colony at the mouth of the Mississippi River. But navigational errors took them past the Mississippi into shallow uncharted bays on the central part of the Texas coast. La Salle established a settlement, which he called Fort Saint Louis. He and several of his men struck out on foot to try to reach French garrisons in Illinois. La Salle was murdered along the way.

Meanwhile, the *Belle* had been blown aground by a storm, and the settlement had been wiped out by the Karankawa Indians. The *Belle* gradually settled to a depth of about 4 meters (12 feet) to rest at the bottom of what is now Matagorda Bay. Over time, the wreck was covered by *silt* (fine particles carried by moving water) and sand.

Arnold and his team searched the bottom of Matagorda Bay using a *magnetometer,* an electronic device that can detect iron or metal remnants of shipwrecks. Divers discovered artifacts from the *Belle* on the first dive of their exploration. Searching further, they found portions of the ship itself. By brushing away the silt over part of the wreck, Arnold and his colleagues found musket balls, pottery, small bronze bells, a brass buckle, and cannon handles in the form of arched leaping dolphins. Arnold called the *Belle* "the earliest and most

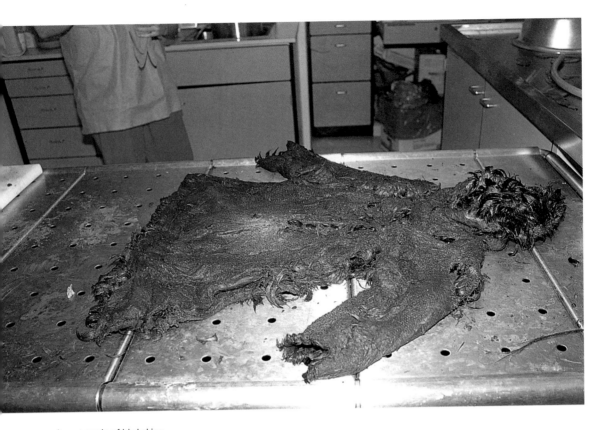

A coat made of bird skins and feathers was worn by a young girl buried in about A.D. 1200 near present-day Barrow, Alaska. The burial site was discovered in August 1995. The girl was a member of the Thule (*THOO* lee) culture, people who traveled along the coast to hunt whales. An autopsy performed on the body suggested that the girl died of starvation.

significant French vessel found in this hemisphere."

Arnold and his team decided that only the cannon would be raised, because lengthy and tedious excavation would be required to raise the whole ship. The 320-kilogram (700-pound) cannon, bearing the name of a French admiral, was lifted from the sands by a barge-mounted crane and transported to the Corpus Christi Museum of Science and History for preservation and restoration.

It is estimated that 15 to 20 percent of the *Belle* has survived. The archaeologists covered the ship's remains with sand to protect it from erosion and treasure hunters. The research team planned to return to the site in summer 1996 to set up a steel *cofferdam* (temporary dam) around the ship and pump out tons of seawater to expose the ship's remains. After that, they expected to spend about six months making painstaking excavations to document how the ship was built and what goods it carried and to shed light on other mysteries of La Salle's ill-fated expedition.

Early peoples in Siberia. A vast archaeological site known as Diring, located on the Lena River in Siberia, has provided new evidence that human beings occupied that region over 250,000 years ago—10 times earlier than scientists had thought. A husband-and-wife Russian archaeological team, Yuri Mochanov and Svetlana Fedoseeva, announced these findings in January 1996.

Archaeological digs at Diring have turned up thousands of stone tools chipped from large flint pebbles. Other finds include stone anvils on which the pebbles were shaped into tools. Mochanov and Fedoseeva believe that an early form of modern human beings lived briefly at Diring. According to a collaborating scientist, geoarchaeologist Michael Waters of Texas A&M University, these people endured a severe climate "requiring fire, clothing, shelter, and a sophisticated subsistence strategy to deal with the Siberian environment." The evidence from Diring is not isolated. The Russian archaeologists have found at least a dozen sites in the Lena River Basin with similar stone tools.

The excavations at Diring have been conducted on a massive scale, with more than 60,000 cubic meters (80,000 cubic yards) of earth removed. But it was difficult for the scientists to find materials that could be dated using scientific techniques. Then Waters and a colleague, Vatche Tchakerian, discovered soils ideal for a procedure called thermoluminescence (TL) dating.

The TL method involves reheating objects, such as pottery or soil samples, that have been heated long ago and measuring the amount of light energy they emit. The longer the interval since the object was first heated, the more light energy it gives off. Scientists at Ohio State University conducted the TL dating, which indicated that the soil was about 250,000 years old.

Though the Russian archaeologists believe the site may be much older, the TL dates show that early humans were living in Siberia at the same latitude as modern-day Anchorage, Alaska, during the bitter cold of the Ice Age. This new information provides insight into the spread of human populations out of Africa and into Europe. More significantly, the findings at Diring demonstrate the adaptability of humans to severe environments much earlier than scientists had thought possible.

The lost city of Urkesh. The discovery of Urkesh, the ancient capital of the 4,000-year-old Hurrian civilization, was announced in November 1995 by a team of California archaeologists. The people who inhabited the city, known as the Horites, are described in ancient Egyptian and Biblical texts as having lived in a region of what is now Syria. Urkesh was reputedly a place of great wealth, but information about its location had been lost, and some archaeologists doubted that it had even existed.

The keys to finding the city were two bronze lions, uncovered by farmers digging graves near a site called Tell Mozan, 650 kilometers (400 miles) northeast of Damascus, Syria. The lions had been smuggled out of Syria and acquired by the Louvre Museum in Paris and the Metropolitan Museum of Art in New York City. Translations of inscriptions on the bases of the statues re-

Artifacts and human remains dating to about 2500 B.C. were found in a group tomb on the banks of the Euphrates River in northern Syria, according to a September 1995 report by archaeologists at the University of Pennsylvania in Philadelphia. The objects, which included daggers, beads, and pottery, *below,* provide insights into the lives of people in the Bronze Age.

The foundation of an ancient temple, *above,* at the site of the Roman city of Caesarea on the coast of Israel was cleared of rubble in July 1995. Volunteers used buckets to remove the last remaining debris from the ruins, *above right.* The temple, constructed to honor the Romans, was built 2,000 years ago by Herod the Great, a ruthless king mentioned in Biblical stories.

vealed the name of a temple and the king who built it. The inscriptions also identified the site where the lions were found as Urkesh.

The translations attracted the attention of Giorgio Buccellatti, professor of archaeology at the University of California at Los Angeles. Buccellatti and his team, including his wife, Marilyn Kelly-Buccellatti of California State University, Los Angeles, began excavations at Tell Mozan in 1987. Finally, after eight years of digging, the archaeologists exposed the ruins of a large temple and what they believed to be a royal storeroom. Buccellatti reported in November 1995 that the contents of this storeroom provided direct evidence identifying the site as Urkesh.

On the floor of the storeroom, the archaeologists found dozens of clay seals with impressions bearing hundreds of examples of writing, as well as depictions of humans and animals. One seal depicts a banquet, another shows a king on his throne with a lion crouching near his feet, and still others appear to be royal portraits. Seals of this sort

have been found at sites throughout the Near East, and scholars have used them to attempt to unravel the history of writing and record keeping.

From the Tell Mozan seals, archaeologists have learned that the storeroom probably contained the property of a queen named Uqnitum. Her name is of the Akkadian language of the ancient nation of Sumer in southwest Asia. This finding indicated that Uqnitum was part of a royal marriage intended to foster an alliance between Urkesh and Sumer. The rest of the inscriptions are in the Hurrian text, further supporting Buccellatti's claim that the site is Urkesh.

The investigators said they had probably uncovered no more than 1 percent of the site. They estimated that Urkesh was populated by 10,000 to 20,000 people. Scientific dating techniques indicated that the city was occupied as early as 2200 to 2300 B.C. and that it flourished for several centuries.

The downfall of Urkesh, the archaeologists said, may have resulted from falling *water tables* (ground water levels) and increased *aridity* (dryness). These conditions probably destroyed the agriculture of the area. Although the city disappeared, the Sumerians and other ancient Middle Eastern cultures developed numerous myths about the glories of Hurrian civilization. Kumarbi, the principal god of the Hurrians, continued to be revered throughout the region and was long identified with the city of Urkesh.

Mastodon butchering site. Evidence that the early inhabitants of North America butchered and ate mastodons was reported in August 1995 by archaeologist John Broster and paleontologist Emanuel Breitburg, both with the Tennessee Division of Archaeology. The mastodon, now extinct, was a relative of the modern elephant. It stood about 3 meters (10 feet) tall at the shoulders and weighed about 2.7 metric tons (3 short tons).

The first humans who entered the Western Hemisphere during the late Ice Age, perhaps 12,000 years ago, hunted a number of animals that have long been extinct. Archaeologists in North America have found a number of sites at which these early hunters, known as Paleo-Indians, killed and butchered mammoths, also now-extinct relatives of the modern elephant. But very few sites have been found with clear evidence of human association with mastodons.

Broster and Breitburg carried out their research on mastodon bones that were uncovered in a ravine in Williamson County, Tennessee. The bones, which lay about 2 meters (6 feet) below the surface of the ground, were from the second mastodon to be found at this location, known as the Coats-Hines Mastodon Site. However, the first find was only a partial skeleton, with no artifacts around it.

The new find was better preserved and carefully excavated. Along with the bones, the investigators found a number of flint tools, including a *prismatic blade*, a parallel-sided flake of flint used as a knife. Such blades were among the tools that Paleo-Indians brought to the Western Hemisphere.

Also found with the mastodon bones were many small flint flakes that were apparently produced when the hunters

Pharos sculpture
A sculpture of a woman's torso, *right,* inset, was lifted from the underwater ruins of the ancient Lighthouse (or Pharos) of Alexandria, Egypt, in October 1995. The lighthouse, shown in a speculative illustration, was one of the Seven Wonders of the Ancient World. Built in the 200's B.C., it stood for 1,500 years on the island of Pharos in the harbor of Alexandria until it was finally toppled by an earthquake. The sculpture probably represented a goddess or a queen. It was one of about 30 sculptures recovered from the site, including sphinxes, granite columns, and a headless statue of the Egyptian pharaoh Ramses II.

resharpened their stone tools. This finding led the archaeologists to suggest that up to eight different knives and scrapers were used in butchering the mastodon. Because there were no stone spear points associated with the bones, it is unclear whether the Paleo-Indians killed the mastodon themselves or came upon its carcass after it had been killed by animal predators.

The most striking evidence that human beings and mastodons coexisted was discovered when the scientists examined some of the mastodon bones under a microscope. They found numerous cut marks with distinctive V-shaped cross sections, indicating that a stone flake or knife had been used in removing meat from the bone. These were not accidental marks—they appeared in clear patterns on the bone, particularly in areas where muscles had to be severed as part of the butchering process. Nor were the scratches the result of animals chewing the bones. Animal teeth leave behind marks that are very different from the cut marks of human tools.

The Coats-Hines site is the third site in the Eastern United States that has revealed the definite role of humans in killing or butchering mastodons. There are sites in Florida and Ohio that have produced similar evidence.

Broster and Breitburg theorized that in Tennessee and parts of the Eastern United States, the mastodon was much more common than the mammoth. This theory reflects the different diet of the two elephant species. The Tennessee region had few grasslands that mammoths would have preferred, while the mastodons would have found a rich diversity of plants and shrubs in the developing forests of the region.

The archaeologists noted that there are over 60 locations in Tennessee where mastodon remains have been found, compared with just 3 sites with mammoth remains. Because only three sites have provided clues about the association of mastodons and human beings, it remains uncertain just how important these beasts were in the early Paleo-Indian diet.   [Thomas R. Hester]

See also ANTHROPOLOGY. In WORLD BOOK, see ARCHAEOLOGY.

Astronomy

One of the most exciting astronomical discoveries of recent years occurred in October 1995, when researchers reported finding a planet orbiting another star. Their news was quickly followed with several other reports of new planets. While none of the new planets closely resembles Earth, their existence adds fuel to the expectation that solar systems, including ones with Earth-like planets, are common in the universe. (See CLOSE-UP.)

Galileo arrives at Jupiter. A probe released by the Galileo spacecraft reached Jupiter in December 1995, becoming the first artificial device to enter the atmosphere of one of the giant outer planets of our solar system. The probe survived for less than an hour before being destroyed by the high temperature and pressure of the planet's atmosphere. But the information it collected is causing astronomers to reevaluate much of what they thought they knew about Jupiter.

Scientists had studied Jupiter's atmosphere for years with ground-based telescopes and remote-sensing instruments aboard the National Aeronautics and Space Administration's (NASA) Pioneer and Voyager spacecraft. They concluded that Jupiter is more like the sun than is any other planet, but none of their previous instruments had been able to directly sample the planet's atmosphere. That was one of the reasons that NASA scientists designed the probe, which was carried into space aboard the Galileo spacecraft, launched by the space shuttle Atlantis in October 1989.

Galileo released the probe in July 1995. The probe slammed into Jupiter's atmosphere on December 7 and began its one-hour drop by parachute. Galileo arrived at Jupiter a few hours later and went into orbit.

As the probe fell, instruments packed into its capsule took measurements that the probe relayed to Galileo. The spacecraft, in turn, radioed the data to Earth. Researchers reported their preliminary results during a January 1996 press conference.

The probe's first unexpected discovery was the detection of only a thin layer of ammonia clouds during the early part of the probe's descent and no hint of the water clouds that astronomers had expected to find. The concentration of water vapor in Jupiter's atmosphere was lower than expected. That expectation had been based on the abundance of oxygen, a constituent element of water, in the sun. Measurements made by Voyager and Pioneer spacecraft in the 1970's and experiments conducted after Comet Shoemaker-Levy hit Jupiter in July 1994 had led them to expect the planet's atmosphere to have 20 to 100 times as much water vapor as was found.

The probe also measured the amount of complex organic molecules made up of various combinations of carbon, oxygen, and nitrogen, which could indicate the presence of life. However, only methane and possibly ammonia, which contains nitrogen, were found in higher-than-expected concentrations.

The probe also found that Jupiter's winds behave quite differently than scientists had predicted. Unlike winds on Earth, which form when the sun heats our atmosphere, Jupiter's winds seem to be caused by heat rising from the planet's depths. Instead of decreasing as the probe fell, the winds actually increased in strength the deeper the probe penetrated.

Finally, the probe tested for signs of lightning. It found that Jupiter has 3 to 10 times less lightning than the Earth.

One reason for all of the surprising findings could be that the probe descended into an unusual patch of Jupiter's atmosphere that was dry and cloudless. These dry regions can be seen from Earth, but they make up only about 1 percent of Jupiter's atmosphere. This dry spot seems to have opened up just 3 months before the probe reached Jupiter, by which time it was too late to retarget the probe.

Despite the probe's fall into a less-than-ideal part of Jupiter's atmosphere, the data it collected gives us an extremely valuable direct look at the most primitive atmosphere in our solar system. Scientists hope that this information—as well as that which Galileo will gather over a two-year period—will help them answer a myriad of questions about how our solar system was formed.

Two new comets in the heavens

Comet-Hale Bopp, *left*, discovered in July 1995 by amateur astronomers in America, was captured in a Hubble Space Telescope image released in October 1995. Hale-Bopp was expected to reach its closest point to Earth in spring 1997, and astronomers predicted that it would put on a spectacular display. Comet Hyakutake, *below*, was found by an amateur Japanese astronomer in January 1996. This image was taken in March 1996, when Hyakutake was easily visible to the naked eye.

The Galileo spacecraft, shown in an artist's conception, reached Jupiter in December 1995 and went into orbit around the giant planet. A probe (not shown) that Galileo had released in July 1995 preceded the spacecraft to Jupiter and plunged toward the planet to obtain data on the atmosphere. Galileo is depicted passing over one of Jupiter's moons, Io, on which a volcano is erupting.

A tale of two comets. Two newly discovered comets thrilled amateur and professional astronomers alike in 1996 and contributed to scientists' growing core of knowledge about these "dirty snowballs" of our solar system. American amateur stargazers Alan Hale and Thomas Bopp independently spotted Comet Hale-Bopp in July 1995, and Japanese amateur astronomer Yuji Hyakutake discovered Comet Hyakutake in January 1996.

Comets are small objects, usually less than 10 kilometers (6 miles) in diameter, composed mainly of rock and water ice. Astronomers think that they were created from the same cloud of gas and dust that gave birth to the sun and planets about 4.6 billion years ago.

Astronomers also believe that comets come from two regions beyond the outer edge of our solar system. One of these is the so-called Kuiper Belt, named after the Dutch-American astronomer Gerard Kuiper, who first predicted its existence. The Kuiper Belt begins just beyond the orbit of Pluto. Comets that circle the sun in periods of

200 years or less generally come from the Kuiper Belt.

The other source of comets is even more distant from the sun. Named the Oort Cloud after Dutch astronomer Jan Oort, it is a spherical region extending for trillions of kilometers that contains debris flung outward by the giant planets after they formed. Comets that orbit the sun in periods of thousands or millions of years usually come from the Oort Cloud.

Comet Hyakutake, an exceptionally bright comet that became easily visible to the naked eye in March 1996, probably came from the Oort Cloud. Hyakutake glowed because the sun's heat vaporized its water ice and the *solar wind* (a flow of charged particles from the sun) drove its dust into a huge circular halo and tail, causing the comet to reflect even more of the sun's light. Scientists speculate that Hyakutake's orbit will bring it back to our inner solar system 10,000 to 20,000 years from now.

A surprise finding about Hyakutake was made by ROSAT, a German X-ray satellite. On March 25, as the comet passed very close—only 15 million kilometers (9 million miles)—to Earth, astronomers at the Max Planck Institute for Extraterrestrial Physics in Germany noted that it was emitting powerful X rays, the first ever detected from a comet. Scientists do not yet know what caused the radiation, but they are considering theories that may help us to better understand comets.

Comet Hale-Bopp, which became visible with binoculars in the spring of 1996, also probably originated in the Oort Cloud. Astronomers estimate that Hale-Bopp's orbit takes it around the sun once every 3,000 to 4,000 years. Although Hale-Bopp will not reach its closest point to Earth—about 192 million kilometers (120 million miles)—until the spring of 1997, it has already caused much excitement because of its great size. Astronomers estimate that it may be 160 kilometers (100 miles) in diameter—10 times the size of Halley's comet. They will be tracking Hale-Bopp throughout 1996 and early 1997, seeking answers to many questions about this icy visitor from space.

Learning more about the sun. The Japanese Yohkoh spacecraft has been taking pioneering images of the sun from Earth orbit ever since its launch in August 1991. In December 1995, the solar research group at Lockheed Martin Palo Alto Research Laboratories in California reported that Yohkoh had detected holes in the sun's *corona* (outer atmosphere).

The portion of the sun that we can see, its *photosphere* (surface), plays only one part in transferring energy from deep in the sun's interior outward to space. Beyond the photosphere lies the corona, a gaseous region heated to millions of degrees by physical processes that scientists still do not understand well. In visible light, we can see the corona from Earth only during a solar eclipse. At other times it is obscured by the brilliant disk of the sun. But Yohkoh can produce very sharp images of the corona by capturing the X rays that it emits.

The holes that Yohkoh observed in the corona produce plumelike structures—some hotter than the corona

A Hubble Telescope image of the first confirmed *brown dwarf* (a celestial object larger in mass than a planet but smaller than a star) was released in November 1995 by a team of astronomers at the California Institute of Technology. The large, fiery object at the left in the photo is a star called Gliese 229. At right is the small, dim brown dwarf, dubbed GL 229B. The long white streak is a lens flare. Although astronomers have long believed that brown dwarfs exist, GL 229B is the first one that has actually been seen and verified by calculating its radiant energy and measuring its surface gases.

itself—extending far out into space. Astronomers had viewed coronal holes, which appear to be regions from which the solar wind emanates, with other X-ray cameras in the past. However, Yohkoh has been able to track the holes over time and in sharp detail. Learning how these holes form, and what their relationship is to other coronal features like flares or eruptions, may lead to a better understanding of how Earth's upper atmosphere is affected by charged particles coming from the sun.

Dark matter in the outer galaxy. Scientists know that a large quantity of invisible matter—as much as 90 percent of all the matter in our Milky Way galaxy—resides in the *halo*, the outer portion of the galactic disk. They do not know exactly what this matter is, though everything from exotic subatomic particles to black holes has been proposed. In late 1995 and early 1996, astronomers in the United States and France reported that they had finally found some clues to the nature of the invisible mass.

One of the techniques scientists use to detect dim objects in the halo is called *gravitational lensing*. When light passes near an object in space, the gravitational pull of the object bends and distorts the light. Astronomers confirmed in the 1970's that very massive objects such as galaxies can create noticeable gravitational lensing effects. It was only recently, however, that they realized that even relatively small objects like stars and planets can also cause gravitational lensing.

In January 1996, astronomer David Bennett of the Lawrence Livermore National Laboratory in California reported the findings of his group's lensing studies. The group had made repeated images of the Large Magellanic Cloud, a galaxy just outside the Milky Way, and recorded seven instances of "brightening." This is a lensing effect in which light from stars in that galaxy was intensified by the gravity of unseen objects in the Milky Way's halo as the objects passed between Earth and the stars. The intensity and duration of the brightening episodes enabled Bennett's group to determine that all of them were caused by objects less than half the mass of the sun. These bodies are probably white dwarfs, compact remnants of stars like

the sun which have consumed all of their nuclear fuel. Bennett and his group estimate that as much as 50 percent of the unseen dark matter in our galactic halo may consist of white dwarfs.

In a similar study, a group at the Saclay Research Center in France looked for lensing events that might be caused by very low-mass objects, such as planets or objects known as brown dwarfs. No such events were found, leading this group to announce in December 1995 that the dark matter in the galactic halo is almost certainly not made of bodies in this mass range. Astronomers now face the task of determining exactly what the remainder of the dark matter may be.

Brown dwarfs at last. Astronomers have long predicted the existence of brown dwarfs—elusive celestial objects smaller in mass than stars but larger than planets. But in searches for these bodies, most of the likely candidates turned out to be dim, but real, stars. In November 1995, however, two groups announced that they had finally found a real brown dwarf.

Brown dwarfs have been so difficult to find because of their small size and dim glow. When a contracting cloud of gas and dust forms an object with more than about 80 times the mass of Jupiter, its core becomes hot enough to trigger nuclear reactions, and the object becomes a star. It then has enough energy to glow brightly for billions of years. But if the body contains less than 80 Jupiter masses, it cannot get hot enough to ignite nuclear reactions. Although the object will glow for a while, its glow will become ever weaker as it cools. It is not a star but a brown dwarf.

A team led by Tadashi Nakajima of the California Institute of Technology detected a small object orbiting a star known as Gliese 229 (GL 229). Nakajima and his colleagues first spotted the object (dubbed GL 229B) with a telescope at the Mount Palomar Observatory in California that uses special techniques to block out the light from the brighter star and at the same time corrects the blurring caused by Earth's atmosphere. Then the team observed the object with the Hubble Space Telescope, to see GL 229B more clearly. Finally, they used a telescope that collects infrared data, which revealed the presence of methane in the surface gases of the object. Methane had been detected in Jupiter but not in any star.

The group also precisely calculated the radiant energy of GL 229B by comparing it with the energy of the parent star—and the energy reading fell well within the range expected of a brown dwarf. Astronomers are now convinced that GL 229B is a genuine brown dwarf.

At the same time that Nakajima and his colleagues were reporting their results, astronomers Gibor S. Basri and James R. Graham of the University of California at Berkeley and Geoffrey W. Marcy of San Franscisco State University were completing their study of a dim object in the Pleiades star cluster. Basri, Graham, and Marcy used a new technique involving the element lithium to establish that the object is a brown dwarf.

Lithium is rare in the universe and nonexistent in stars, because the element is destroyed at temperatures lower than those required to ignite the hydrogen-burning reactions that fuel ordinary

stars. Thus, if lithium is found in a brown dwarf candidate, we can be sure the object has never been hot enough for nuclear reactions to occur.

When Basri, Marcy, and Graham studied the light from the dim Pleiades object, known as PPL 15, they found signs of lithium. Moreover, when the team measured PPL 15's mass, they found it to be just under the limit that separates brown dwarfs from stars. Nonetheless, some astronomers are not convinced that PPL 15 is a brown dwarf, though many are convinced that it is.

Now that at least one brown dwarf has been found, astronomers want to know how common they are. Earlier estimates suggested that there might be enough brown dwarfs to account for the large quantity of dark matter known to exist in our galaxy. The failure to find many of them suggests that this may not be so—the conclusion reached by the Saclay group in France. As astronomers try to gauge the number of brown dwarfs, they expect to learn more about how our stars and planets were formed as well.

A dark disk of material at the center of a galaxy named NGC 4261, astronomers believe, is whirling around a black hole more than a billion times as massive as the sun. NGC 4261 may have captured a smaller galaxy to "feed" the black hole. As matter in the disk spirals into the hole, it emits tremendous amounts of radiation. The image, released in December 1995 by astronomers at Johns Hopkins University in Baltimore and the Leiden Observatory in the Netherlands, was made with the Hubble Space Telescope.

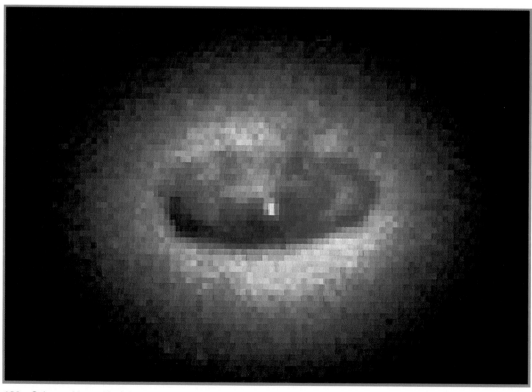

The *nucleus* (center) of galaxy M82 is captured in the midst of a violent burst of star formation in an image released in February 1996 by astronomers working with the University of Hawaii's 2.2-meter (7.2-foot) telescope. M82 is one of our nearest neighbors at a distance of just 10 million *light-years* from Earth. (A light-year is the distance light travels in a year, about 9.5 trillion kilometers [5.9 trillion miles].) The heat and radiation from the newly forming stars cause clouds of gas and dust to pour from the galaxy's nucleus.

A look at star formation. Scientists have long theorized about how stars form, but until recently no one had actually seen star formation in progress. Now, images made by two teams of astronomers using the Hubble Space Telescope and released in November 1995 have provided a vivid look at star birth.

Astronomers believe that stars form when clouds of gas and dust contract because of the force of gravity. As this matter becomes compressed, it gets steadily hotter until it is hot enough to ignite nuclear reactions. Researchers have calculated that the quantity of matter likely to be drawn together in this way is many times the mass of an ordinary star. They have also learned that one way that small, isolated stars manage to keep from becoming too massive is by ejecting infalling matter in high-speed jets of gas. The jets, or bipolar outflows, arise when gas spiraling in toward a forming star is caught in the star's magnetic field and shot outward from the star's north and south poles.

Astrophysicist John Bally of the University of Colorado in Boulder and his colleagues observed and photographed bipolar outflows from a number of young stars. Bally's Hubble images show that the outflows extend much farther into space than astronomers had previously thought. The group found gas jets extending as far as tens of *light-years* from their parent stars. (A light-year is the distance light travels in a year, about 9.5 trillion kilometers [5.9 trillion miles].) At those distances, the jets sometimes break through to the outside of the gas and dust cloud in which the stars are forming.

Jeff Hester of Arizona State University in Tempe and his colleagues used the Hubble to study a region known as the Eagle Nebula. Their images show in spectacular detail the effects of newly formed stars on their surroundings. In the images, the intense radiation from young, hot stars has eroded the outer layers of large gas clouds. At the edge of one dense cloud are a number of pillars of gas that extend into lower-density regions where the gas has been evaporated by the radiation.

Both Bally's and Hester's images may

A Panorama of Planets Circling Other Suns

The discoveries of four planets orbiting four distant stars that resemble our sun have put to rest the idea that our solar system is unique in the universe. In fact, astronomers say, systems of stars and their planetary companions may be quite common. So far, however, Earth is unique in being the only known planet supporting life. Astronomers think that none of the *extrasolar* planets—planets outside our solar system—found so far is likely to be inhabited.

In October 1995, astronomers Michel Mayor and Didier Queloz of the Geneva Observatory in Switzerland reported finding a planetary companion to 51 Pegasi, a star in the constellation Pegasus, about 40 *light-years* from Earth. (A light-year is the distance light travels in one year, about 9.5 trillion kilometers [5.9 trillion miles].) The startling discovery was soon confirmed by astronomers Geoffrey Marcy and Paul Butler of San Francisco State University and the University of California at Berkeley.

Marcy and Butler soon created a sensation of their own. On Jan. 17, 1996, they reported finding two more extrasolar planets, about 35 light-years from Earth—one orbiting 70 Virginis, a star in the constellation Virgo, and the other circling 47 Ursae Majoris, a star in the constellation Ursa Major, also known as the Big Dipper. Then, on April 12, Butler announced that he and Marcy had identified still another planet, this one orbiting a star called Rho[1] Cancri in the constellation Cancer, about 40 light-years away.

All four stars, which are visible from Earth without the use of a telescope, are similar in mass, temperature, color, brightness, and age to our sun. All four planets are massive—ranging from at least half as massive as Jupiter, the largest planet in our solar system, to eight or nine times as massive. Jupiter is about 320 times as massive as Earth.

The new planets stand in sharp contrast to what may be the first two extrasolar planets ever discovered. In 1992, astronomers Alexander Wolszczan of Cornell University in Ithaca, New York, and Dale A. Frail of the National Radio Observatory in Socorro, New Mexico, reported finding two, perhaps three, planets orbiting a pulsar, a rapidly spinning remnant of a *supernova* (exploding star). But some astronomers speculated that those planets may actually be objects formed from the debris of the supernova that created the pulsar. They may not be regular planets like Earth and the other members of the solar system, which

were created from the same cloud of gas and dust as the sun.

The Swiss and California astronomers have not seen any of the newly discovered extrasolar planets through their telescopes. In all cases, the planets, massive as they are, are obscured by the bright light of their parent stars. Instead, the astronomers deduced the existence of the planets from tiny but systematic changes in the wavelength of visible light from their stars. These changes were caused by the planets' slight gravitational pull on the stars.

To detect these shifts, the astronomers used a visible-light spectrometer, an instrument that breaks down visible light into its component colors. As a planet moves along the part of its orbit that takes it in the direction away from Earth, the force of its gravity tugs the star in that direction a slight bit. This gravitational pull causes the star's light to be shifted toward the longer-wavelength, or red, end of the light spectrum. When the planet moves back toward the Earth on the opposite side of its orbit, the light of the star is shifted toward the shorter-wavelength, or blue, end of the spectrum.

Because astronomers have no procedure for naming planets beyond our solar systems, the four extrasolar planets were named according to the system for naming a *binary* (two-star) system. For example, 51 Peg b, the planetary companion to 51 Pegasi, is so called because it belongs to the 51st star in the constellation Pegasus in a catalog published in 1725. The "b" in its name indicates that it is dimmer than 51 Pegasi.

The most surprising characteristic of 51 Peg b may be its closeness to its parent star—only about 8 million kilometers (5 million miles) away. It is so close, in fact, that it must be orbiting within 51 Pegasi's corona, the outermost layer of its atmosphere. At that distance, 51 Peg b zips around its parent star in just 4.2 days. In contrast, Mercury, the innermost planet in our solar system, is 58 million kilometers (36 million miles) from the sun and takes 88 days to complete one revolution. Because the estimated mass of 51 Peg b is about half that of Jupiter, astronomers believe the planet is surely a huge gas ball. Its surface temperature is an estimated 1,000 °C (1,832 °F).

Rho[1] Cnc b, the planetary companion of Rho[1] Cancri, is about three-quarters as massive as Jupiter and almost certainly a gas ball as well. Only 16 million kilometers (10 million miles) from its parent star, it completes an almost perfectly circular orbit once every two weeks. Its surface temperature is an estimated 500 °C (932 °F).

The close-in orbits of 51 Peg b and Rho[1] Cnc b have challenged widely accepted theories that gaseous planets always form far from their stars.

In our solar system, the gaseous planets—Jupiter, Saturn, Uranus, and Neptune—lie far beyond Earth and the other rocky planets of the inner solar system. Jupiter, for example, orbits at a distance of about 780 million kilometers (480 million miles) from the sun.

A possible resolution of this discrepancy was proposed in April 1996 by Douglas Lin of the University of California at Santa Cruz. He theorized that giant gaseous planets normally form far from their star in the flattened cloud of gas and dust from which a solar system is created. But the gravitational interactions between a giant gas-ball planet and farther-out remnants of the flattened cloud may cause the planet to spiral inward toward the star. At some point, the planet reaches a stable, close-in orbit around the star.

In contrast to 51 Peg b and Rho[1] Cnc b, the other two newly discovered planets—70 Vir b and 47 UMa b—orbit at safer distances from their parent stars. 70 Vir b, the planetary companion of 70 Virginis, is truly a giant planet with a mass at least 6.6 times, and perhaps as much as 9 times, that of Jupiter. Its highly elliptical orbit takes it an average of 64 million kilometers (40 million miles) from its parent star, and the planet completes one revolution every 116.6 days.

Marcy and Butler estimate the surface temperature of 70 Vir b at 90 °C (190 °F), about that of scalding water. Thus, liquid water, perhaps suspended as tiny droplets, may cloud the planet's atmosphere. Water is widely regarded as a necessary ingredient for the origin and evolution of life, though astronomers have no way of determining if there is life on 70 Vir b. They speculate that this planet could have a solid moon with warm oceans, conditions perhaps more conducive to the evolution of life.

47 UMa b, which orbits 47 Ursae Majoris, is at least 2.3 times as massive as Jupiter and follows a roughly circular orbit at a distance of 315 million kilometers (195 million miles) from 47 Ursae Majoris. It circles its parent star, which is slightly hotter and brighter than our sun, every 1,100 days. Its surface temperature is an estimated –90 °C (–112 °F). If it were located in our solar system, 47 UMa b would lie in the asteroid belt, between the orbits of Mars and Jupiter. At that distance, 47 UMa b would be too cold to have liquid water, except perhaps deep below the surface.

All four of the new planets were discovered with relatively small telescopes. Now the search for extrasolar planets is moving to the world's largest telescope, the Keck Telescope on the Mauna Kea volcano in Hawaii. Astronomers are hopeful that other very large telescopes coming on line in the near future, including the Hobby-Eberly Telescope at the University of Texas's McDonald Observatory at Mount Locke in Texas, will lead to the

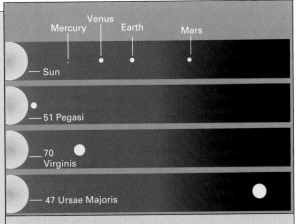

New planets around other suns
The discoveries of three planets orbiting stars like our sun were reported by astronomers from October 1995 to January 1996. The first of these to be found, a planetary companion of a star named 51 Pegasi, is about half as massive as Jupiter, the largest planet in our solar system, and it seems to be, like Jupiter, a gaseous body. The planet is so close to 51 Pegasi that it must be orbiting within that star's outer atmosphere. A planet orbiting a star known as 70 Virginis is probably a solid planet like Earth, and it is the most massive planet known—up to nine times as massive as Jupiter. A planet circling a star called 47 Ursae Majoris, which is about 3½ times as massive as Jupiter, is also likely a rocky planet. The search continued for other new planets in 1996, and in April a fourth one was discovered orbiting a star called Rho[1] Cancri. This planet (not depicted) is probably a gaseous body and is about three-fourths as massive as Jupiter.

Source: Geoffrey W. Marcy / San Francisco State University

discovery of even more of the planets that are now believed to be circling other stars like the sun. Astronomers think that those telescopes should also be able to detect somewhat smaller planets, comparable to Saturn. Even our largest telescopes, however, would not be powerful enough to make out planets as small as Earth.

In January 1996, the National Aeronautics and Space Administration (NASA) announced that it would make the search for planetary systems, particularly ones that might have habitable Earth-type planets, one of its highest priorities over the next 25 years. NASA said it would use both ground-based and space-based telescopes, such as the Hubble Space Telescope and a proposed network of small infrared telescopes that would be deployed deep in space, to search for such planets and make images of them.

Meanwhile, the Swiss and California teams are continuing to analyze the information they have already gathered on more than 100 stars. After the discovery of his third planet, Butler predicted that we might soon expect to find a new planet every month.   [Stephen P. Maran] help to explain why some condensations of gas and dust become large stars, while others, having ejected their building material as jets or lost it through erosion, remain small stars or objects such as brown dwarfs. (In the Special Reports section, see A NEW LOOK AT SPACE.)

Watching baby galaxies grow. How the universe organized itself into a vast structure of galaxies is one of the burning questions of modern astronomy. To see galaxies in the act of forming has therefore been an important goal. In January and February 1996, three groups of astronomers reported that they had begun finding the long-sought primeval galaxies.

The key to observing the past is the time that light requires to travel the enormous distances of space. The farther away in space we look, the longer ago the light we are seeing was emitted. Some astronomical objects have been observed at distances greater than 10 billion light-years, which means that we are seeing them as they were more than 10 billion years ago. But galaxies more remote than that have been difficult to locate, largely because they are so dim.

In January 1996, Robert Williams, director of the Space Telescope Science Institute in Baltimore, along with a team of collaborators, released a composite of images from the farthest reaches of the universe taken with the Hubble Space Telescope. Williams and his colleagues had pointed the telescope at a single region of sky for 10 days, taking hundreds of repeated exposures.

The composite Hubble image that was made, called the Hubble Deep Field Image, was incredible. Where the largest ground-based telescopes revealed nothing but blank sky, the Hubble image contained some 1,500 objects showing a variety of colors and shapes. Many, if not most, of these are thought to be very young galaxies. Their irregular shapes suggest that these objects were in the process of formation when their light began the long journey to Earth. Astronomers planned next to try and verify that the objects are indeed very distant galaxies, seen as they were when the universe was young.

A group of astronomers headed by Charles Steidel of the California Institute of Technology announced in February 1996 the discovery of remote galaxies whose *red shifts* (shifts in their light toward the red end of the spectrum, showing that the objects are moving away from Earth) indicate that they lie some 13 billion light-years away. The light received from these galaxies was therefore emitted 13 billion years ago, when the universe was perhaps only about 15 percent of its present age.

Steidel's team found the galaxies using a novel technique based on the theory that remote galaxies should be deficient in emissions at short (ultraviolet) wavelengths of light because these wavelengths are absorbed by hydrogen gas in the space between the galaxies. Therefore, Steidel and his group looked for faint objects with no ultraviolet emissions. The astronomers then used the Keck Telescope in Hawaii to determine the red shifts of those objects. They discovered 23 galaxies with the enormous red shifts expected of primeval galaxies.

A third group of astronomers found a baby galaxy quite by chance. This group, headed by astronomers Howard Yee of the University of Toronto in Canada and Erica Ellingson of the University of Colorado, discovered an odd, unusually bright object, whose spectrum revealed a red shift corresponding to a distance of 12.5 billion light-years. Yee and his colleagues deduced that the object is a galaxy in the process of forming, consisting largely of gas that has yet to be incorporated into stars.

All of the images of primeval galaxies reveal very immature systems, not yet displaying the regular shapes of modern galaxies. Astronomers hope that these images will help them to understand how and when galaxies formed.

The age of the universe. One of the great debates that continues to interest astronomers concerns the age of the universe. In 1994, astronomers using the Hubble Space Telescope calculated that the universe is about 10 billion years old. In 1996, another group calculated the age as at least 15 billion years. Now astronomers are working at reconciling the contrasting measurements. (In the Special Reports section, see HOW OLD IS THE UNIVERSE?)

[Jonathan I. Lunine
and Theodore P. Snow]
In WORLD BOOK, see ASTRONOMY.

On Nov. 30, 1995, an international group of atmospheric scientists agreed for the first time that human activity has contributed to global warming in the 1900's. In its report, the International Panel on Climate Change (IPCC)—a United Nations (UN)-sponsored group comprising more than 2,500 climate experts from 75 nations—said that global temperature increases in the 1900's, especially those of the late 1980's and mid-1990's are "unlikely to be entirely due to natural causes, and that a pattern of climatic response to human activities is identifiable in the climatological record."

Global warming is a gradual rise in Earth's average surface temperature, apparently resulting from an increase in *greenhouse* (heat-trapping) gases in the atmosphere. Many heat-trapping gases, such as carbon dioxide and methane, occur naturally. But human beings also emit massive amounts of these gases, mostly as a result of burning *fossil fuels* (coal, gasoline, and natural gas). Scientists fear that global warming could produce widespread droughts and more intense storms, shift the prime farming belt farther north, and melt some polar ice, leading to a rise in sea levels that could flood coastal cities or low-lying islands. Some scientists also fear that a warmer Earth would cause certain disease-carrying insects to flourish.

The IPCC report attributed at least part of the 0.5- to 0.6-Celsius-degree (0.9- to 1.1-Fahrenheit-degree) rise in average annual global temperature in the 1900's to the burning of fossil fuels and the destruction of forests, activities that release carbon dioxide into the atmosphere. If the release of carbon dioxide and other greenhouse gases continues at the same high rate, the IPCC warned, global temperatures could increase by 1 to 3.5 Celsius degrees (1.8 to 6.3 Fahrenheit degrees) by the late 2000's. The higher end of that temperature range would be roughly equivalent to the warming that ended the last Ice Age more than 10,000 years ago.

The IPCC report marked the first time that scientists had reached such a broad consensus on the role that human activity plays in global warming. Scientists do not dispute that Earth's average surface temperature has risen in the 1900's, but some scientists have been reluctant to attribute the rise to human activity. These scientists claim that natural climate variability could have caused the temperature increases observed during the 1900's.

The IPCC based its conclusion largely on improvements in the complex computer climate *models* (simulations) scientists use to predict possible changes in Earth's weather patterns. Such models predict how global weather may change as a result of various factors, such as the amount of carbon dioxide entering the atmosphere, sea-surface temperatures, and the amount of sunlight reaching Earth's surface.

Until 1994, these computer models did not work very well. When using data from the 1900's, for instance, including increasing emissions of greenhouse gases, the models usually indicated that the Earth should be much warmer than it is. Critics thus dismissed predictions of dramatic global warming based on computer models, since the models apparently could not even predict what had already happened.

Scientists now believe that these early models left out the effect of sulfate aerosols on climate. Sulfate aerosols are tiny droplets of sulfur dioxide produced along with carbon dioxide when fossil fuels burn. The aerosols provide a cooling effect by creating a haze that blocks sunlight, and their absence in the early models caused the models to overemphasize the warming effects of carbon dioxide. Those models generally predicted that Earth's temperature should have warmed by about 1.4 Celsius degrees (2.5 Fahrenheit degrees) by the 1990's—more than twice the warming that has occurred.

Beginning in early 1995, atmospheric scientists at the British Meteorological Office's Hadley Centre for Climate Prediction and Research in Norwich, England, began using computer simulations that included the cooling effects of the aerosols. Their simulations produced warming of 0.5 Celsius degree—a number within the actual range.

In July 1995, a team of atmospheric scientists led by Benjamin D. Santer at the Lawrence Livermore National Laboratory in Livermore, California, further refined the improved global climate models, isolating the effects of sulfate aerosols and carbon dioxide. They found that sulfate aerosols produced cooling as great as 7 Celsius degrees (12.6 Fahrenheit degrees) in the Norwegian Sea but that the cooling varied widely around the globe. When the scientists added the effects of warming from carbon dioxide to the model, it accurately reproduced complex patterns of weather changes around the globe since the mid-1940's. Many scientists believed the model provided the first clear sign of human involvement in global warming.

Warmest year on record. American and British scientists said in January 1996 that 1995 was the warmest year since researchers began recording global temperature averages in the mid-1800's. The average temperature for 1995 surpassed the average for 1990, the previous record year. Atmospheric scientists at the British Meteorological Office and the University of East Anglia and the U.S. National Aeronautics and Space Administration's (NASA) Goddard Institute for Space Studies in New York City made the anouncement.

The British and U.S. teams came up with different averages. According to the British team, Earth's average surface temperature in 1995 was 14.84 °C (58.72 °F). The Goddard measurement was 15.39 °C (59.7 °F). The measurements differed because the two teams used a different combination of surface temperatures to calculate the final average. Both teams' recordings also showed that the period from 1991 to 1995 was the warmest five-year span on record.

Active tropical storm season. The hurricane season of 1995 (June 1 to November 30) in the Atlantic Ocean nearly broke the record for the most tropical storms and hurricanes in a year. There were 19 named tropical storms, 11 of which reached hurricane intensity. Not since 1933, with 21 named storms, 10 of which became hurricanes, had there been so many tropical storms in the Atlantic.

Scientists do not clearly understand why some years produce far more hurricanes than others. But they suspected that two main factors contributed to the high level of storm activity in 1995.

One factor may have been the disappearance in mid-1995 of the longest-lasting El Niño on record. El Niño is a complex change in ocean circulation and winds in the tropical Pacific Ocean that disrupts temperature and rainfall patterns around the world. El Niños usually occur every four to five years and last about a year and a half. The El Niño that ended in 1995 had lasted more than four years, however, and atmospheric scientists believe winds blowing east toward Africa as a result of El Niño may have prevented some potentially hurricane-producing storms from entering the eastern Atlantic Ocean.

Scientists said that unusually wet weather in the West African Sahel—the hot, arid region just south of the Sahara—may have also aided hurricane formation. Storms from this region travel west into the Atlantic Ocean, where warm ocean water imparts increased energy to the storms and causes them to gain strength.

Ozone hole continues. The annual thinning that develops in the protective layer of ozone in the upper atmosphere above Antarctica set a record for duration in 1995. This thinning, the so-called "ozone hole," usually forms every year above Antarctica in mid- to late September and lasts into November.

But the ozone hole in 1995 began forming in August and lasted until late December, according to the UN World Meteorological Organization. By mid-October, the ozone hole had grown to 19.9 million square kilometers (7.7 million square miles), an area about twice the size of Europe.

Ozone is a molecule made up of three oxygen atoms. A layer of ozone in the upper atmosphere protects Earth's surface from most of the sun's damaging ultraviolet radiation. Scientists are concerned that increased levels of ultraviolet radiation passing through a thinner ozone layer will damage plant life, greatly increase the incidence of skin cancer in people, and possibly damage the eyesight of people and animals.

Researchers think the ozone hole has been caused by chemicals called chlorofluorocarbons (CFC's) that have drifted into the upper atmosphere. CFC's are chlorine-containing gases that have been widely used since the 1930's as industrial solvents, coolants in air conditioners and refrigerators, and as propellants for aerosol sprays. In the 1980's, scientists identified chlorine as the key chemical in the destruction of ozone.

Climate model, sea-level study shed light on global warming

Data on global temperatures and sea-surface levels, reported by atmospheric scientists in the United States in July and October 1995, indicated that Earth's atmosphere is heating up—most likely because of human activities—and that this worldwide warming is starting to raise ocean levels.

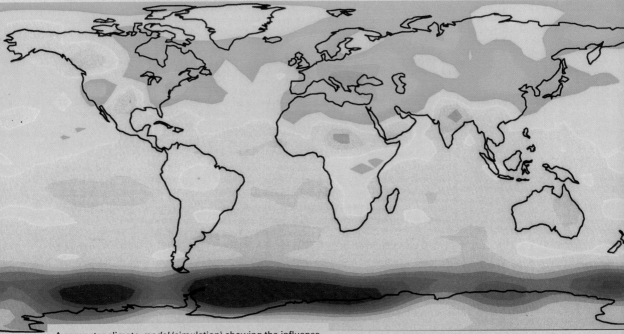

A computer climate *model* (simulation) showing the influence of human activity on the atmosphere since the mid-1940's, *above,* is the first such model that corresponds to actual temperature changes recorded over that period. The model was announced in July 1995 by researchers at Lawrence Livermore National Laboratory in California. Orange and red regions mark areas of higher-than-normal temperatures; blue areas were cooler than normal. The model shows the effects of two air pollutants on climate: carbon dioxide, which traps heat in the atmosphere, and *sulfate aerosols* (microscopic particles from industrial emissions), which form a sun-reflecting haze. The scientists' conclusion was that increasing average global temperatures are most likely due to the *greenhouse effect,* a build-up of heat in the atmosphere due to carbon dioxide and other gases released by human activity.

A satellite-generated map released in October 1995 by the National Oceanic and Atmospheric Administration (NOAA), *below,* shows rising ocean levels around the world from 1993 through early 1995. Orange and red areas mark areas of greatest increase. NOAA scientists said sea levels rose nearly 5 millimeters (0.2 inch) per year in that time, more than twice the annual rate for the 1900's. Many scientists believe global warming may be causing the rapid rise by increasing the melting of glaciers and polar ice.

In the lower *stratosphere* (upper atmosphere), where ozone concentrations are greatest, solar radiation breaks CFC molecules apart, releasing chlorine. The freed chlorine atoms act as *catalysts* (substances that speed up chemical reactions without themselves being affected) to help destroy ozone molecules in the stratosphere.

This process occurs throughout the lower stratosphere. But it is particularly intense over Antarctica from late September through November—spring in the Southern Hemisphere. Darkness, extreme cold, and swirling winds during the winter months create the atmospheric conditions for the hole to form. Then, with the return of sunlight in the spring, clouds full of ice crystals form in the stratosphere, providing surfaces for CFC's and ozone to interact.

CFC ban takes effect. A UN-sponsored international treaty banning the production of CFC's in the world's industrial nations went into effect on Jan. 1, 1996. Scientists first hypothesized a connection between CFC's and ozone destruction in the mid-1970's, and they confirmed the link in the early 1980's. In 1987, responding to the scientists' findings, scientists and world political leaders drafted an agreement called the Montreal Protocol to gradually phase out CFC production, beginning in 1989. World leaders revised the agreement several times after 1987, leading to the January 1996 total production ban. Developing countries have longer to comply with the ban.

Falling chlorine levels. Evidence reported in March 1996 suggested that the CFC ban is working. According to atmospheric scientist Steven Montzka of the U.S. National Oceanic and Atmospheric Administration, chlorine levels in the atmosphere peaked in 1994 and have declined about 1 percent per year since. Montzka measured levels of chlorine in the stratosphere at seven sites around the globe. Scientists cautioned, however, that even with the CFC ban, ozone levels in the upper atmosphere will not return to normal until around the year 2100. [John T. Snow]

See also OCEANOGRAPHY. In WORLD BOOK, see METEOROLOGY; OZONE.

Awards and Prizes

Insights into the chemical processes leading to the destruction of Earth's protective layer of atmospheric ozone, the subatomic particles that make up matter, and the genes that control the development of embryos were the achievements awarded the 1995 Nobel Prizes for chemistry, physics, and physiology or medicine. Student high-achievers won recognition for projects delving into the topics of "surreal" numbers, programmed cell death, and many other subjects.

The Nobel Prize for chemistry was shared by F. Sherwood Rowland of the University of California at Irvine, Mario Molina of the Massachusetts Institute of Technology in Cambridge, and Paul Crutzen of the Max Planck Institute for Chemistry in Mainz, Germany. The Nobel committee honored the three scientists for their research on the chemical destruction of ozone molecules. (Ozone consists of three oxygen atoms. Ordinary oxygen gas molecules have only two atoms.) The prize-winning research showed that pollution can deplete the ozone layer in Earth's atmosphere. The layer protects life by screening out much of the sun's harmful radiation.

In 1970, Crutzen showed that a group of chemicals called nitrogen oxides could destroy ozone. In 1974, Rowland and Molina discovered that other chemicals, chlorofluorocarbons (CFC's), could also break down ozone molecules. At the time, CFC's were commonly used in refrigerants and spray-can propellants, and the research findings led to an international ban on the chemicals. The Nobel committee cited the three chemists for work that "contributed to our salvation from a global environmental problem that could have catastrophic consequences."

The Nobel Prize for physics went to Martin L. Perl of the Stanford Linear Accelerator Center in Palo Alto, California, and Frederick Reines of the University of California at Irvine. The scientists won for discovering two different types of subatomic particles called leptons. Leptons and a family of particles called quarks are the smallest known constituents of matter in the universe.

In the 1950's, Reines and Clyde L.

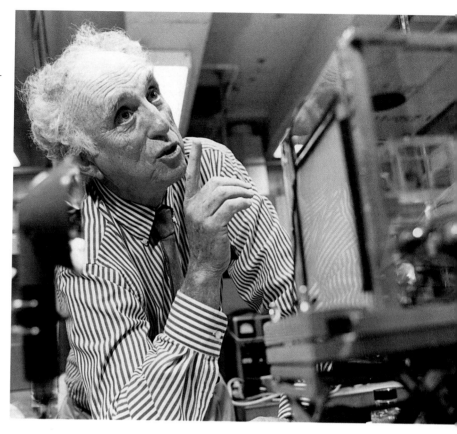

Martin L. Perl of the Stanford Linear Accelerator Center in Palo Alto, California, shared the 1995 Nobel Prize in physics for his 1977 discovery of the tau lepton, a subatomic particle that is one of the smallest constituents of matter in the universe.

Cowan, Jr., who has since died, detected a type of lepton called the neutrino. The existence of neutrinos had been predicted in the 1930's, but because these particles have little or no mass and no electric charge, they were extremely hard to detect.

Perl discovered a type of lepton called the tau in 1977. Tau leptons are heavy, unstable particles that quickly break down into lighter particles.

The prize for physiology or medicine was shared by Edward B. Lewis of the California Institute of Technology in Pasadena; Eric F. Wieschaus of Princeton University in Princeton, New Jersey; and Christiane Nüesslein-Volhard of the Max Planck Institute for Developmental Biology in Tübingen, Germany. The scientists studied the genetic makeup of fruit flies in order to understand how genes control an animal's embryonic development. Because fruit flies have large, easily observed *chromosomes* (the structures that carry the genes), they proved ideal for such studies. The research deepened scientists' understanding of the development of not only ani-

mal embryos but human embryos, too.

Lewis began his research in the late 1930's by breeding flies and exposing them to radiation to cause genetic *mutations* (changes). In this way, Lewis identified the master-control genes that guide the development of each segment of the fly's body, such as the head and abdomen. Lewis discovered that a mutation in a single master-control gene could create extra body segments.

In the 1960's, Wieschaus and Nüesslein-Volhard built upon Lewis's work by searching for genes that determine earlier stages of development. The scientists discovered that 139 of the fruit fly's 20,000 genes control the transformation of a fertilized egg into a fully segmented body.

Student awards. Winners in the 55th annual Westinghouse Science Talent Search were announced on March 11, 1996, and winners of the 47th annual International Science and Engineering Fair were named on May 9. Both competitions are conducted by Science Service, a nonprofit organization based in Washington, D.C. Other student science

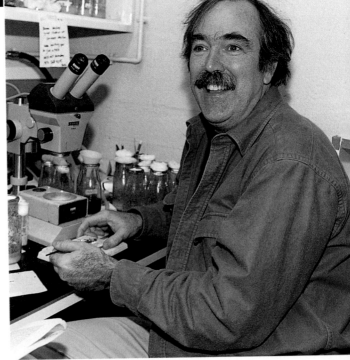

Nobel winners in physiology or medicine
Research into the genes that cause a fruit fly
to develop from a fertilized egg into a segmented organism earned the 1995 Nobel Prize for
Edward B. Lewis of the California Institute of
Technology in Pasadena, *above;* Christiane
Nüesslein-Volhard of the Max Planck Institute
for Developmental Biology in Tübingen, Germany, *above right;* and Eric F. Wieschaus of
Princeton University in Princeton, New Jersey,
right. The scientists' research helped explain
how specific genes control embryo development
in human beings as well as flies.

competitions included international olympiads in chemistry, mathematics, and physics, all held in July 1995.

Science and Engineering Fair. Approximately 1,200 students in grades 9 to 12 competed in the 47th annual International Science and Engineering Fair in Tucson, Arizona.

Seven students were the recipients of Grand Awards, which included all-expenses-paid trips to attend international science fairs or awards ceremonies. Grand Award recipients were Naomi Sue Bates of Franklin (West Virginia) High School; John Paul Tassinari of Braintree (Massachusetts) High School; Mark Mason Esformes and Jason Adam Gerstenberger of Manatee High School in Bradenton, Florida; and David James Matsumoto, Marvin Taichi Kawabata, and Christopher Chi Yuen To of the Saint Louis School in Honolulu, Hawaii.

First Award winners in 16 categories were:

Behavioral and Social Sciences. Jason Christopher Oraker of William J. Palmer High School in Colorado Springs, Colorado, and Nathan Daniel Doty of Pensacola (Florida) High School.

Biochemistry. William Dennis Kunz of the Academy of Science and Technology in Conroe, Texas; Ting Luo of Stuyvesant High School in New York City; and Bart Martel Bartlett of Metro High School in Saint Louis, Missouri.

Botany. Jeremy Hatton Mills of Clear Lake High School in Houston, Jennifer Louise Jelkin of Hildreth (Nebraska) Public High School, and Marta A. Kamburowski of Sylvania (Ohio) Northview High School.

Chemistry. Andrew Anthony Nelson of Saint Petersburg (Florida) Senior High School and Sidney Hsiao-Ning Chang of Half Hollow Hills High School in Dix Hills, New York.

Computer Science. Christopher Michael Stark of the Center for the Arts and Sciences in Saginaw, Michigan.

Earth and Space Sciences. Naomi Sue Bates of Franklin (West Virginia) High School.

Engineering. Sabrina R. Perri of Marianopolis College in Montreal, Canada; Daniel Paul Weitz of Morristown (New Jersey) High School; John Paul Tassinari of Braintree (Massachusetts) High School; and Paul Saitta of Leigh High School in San Jose, California.

Environmental Sciences. Cathy Joy Kindem of Mankato (Minnesota) West High School; Katherin Marie Slimak of West Springfield High School in Springfield, Virginia; Justin Lee Herreman of Stevens High School in Rapid City, South Dakota; and Kirk Bennett Doran of Walt Whitman High School in Bethesda, Maryland.

Gerontology. Grace I-Chen Liu of Edison High School in Fresno, California.

Global Change. Sophie Elizabeth Weirich of Yale Secondary School in Abbotsford, British Columbia.

Mathematics. James Andrew Fowler of Mankato (Minnesota) West High School; Jason Charles Stone of Westmoore High School in Oklahoma City, Oklahoma; and Lauren Kiyomi Williams of Palos Verdes Peninsula High School in Rolling Hills Estates, California.

Medicine and Health. Adam Paul Mikkelson of Lake Crystal (Minnesota) Wellcome Memorial High School, Diane Loreli Downie of Winona (Minnesota) Senior High School, Ceen-Yenn Cynthia Lin of Lexington (Massachusetts) High School, and Adam Amiel Friedman of Saint Andrew's Episcopal School in Ridgeland, Mississippi.

Microbiology. Blayne Kauli Welk of Rossland (British Columbia) Secondary School; Thomas Arthur Allen of Marjory Stoneman Douglas High School in Parkland, Florida; and Ruchi Mishra of Detroit Country Day School in Beverly Hills, Michigan.

Physics. Charina Terranova Cameron of Wolfville (Nova Scotia) Junior High School and Carmella Maria House of Evansville (Indiana) Day School.

Team Project. Mark Mason Esformes and Jason Adam Gerstenberger of Manatee High School in Bradenton, Florida; Belazs Benedek, Tamas Nagy, and Sandor Mezei of Neumann Janos in Budapest, Hungary; Renee Jeanne Filion and Stefane Robert Filion of Ecole Secondaire Algonquin in North Bay, Ontario; Selvan Masilamany and Rajarsmi Banerjee of Saint Paul's School in London; and David James Matsumoto, Marvin Taichi Kawabata, and Christopher Chi Yuen To of the Saint Louis School in Honolulu, Hawaii.

Zoology. Carol Anne Fassbinder of Valley Community High School in Elgin, Iowa; Andrew Allen Farke of Armour (South Dakota) High School; Eugenia

Westinghouse Talent Search winners
The first-, second-, and third-place winners in the 1996 Westinghouse competition were Jacob Lurie of Maryland, Ting Luo of New York, and Matthew David Graham of Florida.

Jacob Lurie

Ting Luo

Matthew David Graham

Anne Amelung of Boca Raton (Florida) Community High School.

Westinghouse Talent Search. Forty finalists were chosen from among 1,863 U.S. high school seniors to compete for $205,000 in scholarships in the prestigious Westinghouse Science Talent Search. The finalists were interviewed in Washington, D.C., by a panel of judges.

First place and a $40,000 scholarship were awarded to Jacob Lurie, a student at Montgomery Blair High School in Silver Spring, Maryland. Lurie examined the possibility of computing "surreal numbers," which include numbers that are infinitely small or infinitely large.

Second place and a $30,000 scholarship went to Ting Luo of Woodside, New York, a student at New York City's Stuyvesant High School. She investigated the process by which cells die after being exposed to toxic drugs.

Third place and a $20,000 scholarship were awarded to Matthew David Graham of Stanton College Preparatory High School in Jacksonville, Florida. Graham developed a sensor to detect the buildup of ice on airplane wings.

Fourth place and a $15,000 scholarship were won by Bruce Mizrahi Haggerty of New York City.

Fifth place and a $15,000 scholarship went to Aaron Michael Einbond of New York City.

Sixth place and a $15,000 scholarship were awarded to Daniel Paul Weitz of Morristown, New Jersey.

Seventh place and a $10,000 scholarship went to Brian Palmer Hafler of West Newton, Massachusetts.

Eighth place and a $10,000 scholarship were won by Simon Joseph DeDeo of New York City.

Ninth place and a $10,000 scholarship were awarded to Sidney Hsiao-Ning Chang of Dix Hills, New York.

Tenth place and a $10,000 scholarship went to Vezen Wu of Jacksonville, Florida.

Two alternates, Naomi Sue Bates of Franklin, West Virginia, and William David Garrahan of Gloucester, Rhode Island, as well as the 28 other finalists, each received $1,000 cash awards.

Chemistry Olympiad. The U.S. team finished 15th out of more than 40 countries participating in the 27th International Chemistry Olympiad in Beijing, China. Teams from China, Iran, and Romania finished first, second, and third.

Silver medals were awarded to Jason Wong of Thomas Jefferson High School for Science and Technology in Alexandria, Virginia, and Prashant Mishra of Detroit Country Day School in Beverly, Michigan. Elliot Waingold of Central York (Pennsylvania) High School and G. Michael Sawka, Jr., of Henry M. Gunn High School in Palo Alto, California, won bronze medals.

Math Olympiad. Each member of the U.S. team won a medal in the 36th International Mathematical Olympiad, held in Toronto, Canada. The U.S. team placed 11th out of the record 74 countries enrolled in the competition. The teams from China, Romania, and Russia placed first, second, and third. In all, 412 students participated in the event.

Aleksandr Khazanov of Stuyvesant High School in New York City; Jacob Lurie of Montgomery Blair High School in Silver Spring, Maryland; and Josh Nichols-Barrer of Newton South High School in Newton Center, Massachusetts, won silver medals. Jay H. Chyung of West High School in Iowa City, Iowa;

Christopher C. Chang of Henry M. Gunn High School in Palo Alto, California; and Andrei C. Gnepp of Hawken School in Gates Mills, Ohio, won bronze medals.

Physics Olympiad. The U.S. team took second place at the XXVI International Physics Olympiad in Canberra, Australia, achieving its highest team finish ever. China placed first, and Iran finished third. The two-day competition involved 250 students from more than 50 nations.

Rhiju Das of the Oklahoma School for Science and Mathematics in Oklahoma City tied for the second-highest overall score and won a gold medal. Other gold-medal winners were Paul Lujan of Lowell High School in San Francisco, California, and Joon Pahk and Benjamin Rahn, both of Thomas Jefferson High School for Science and Technology in Alexandria, Virginia. A silver medal was awarded to Daniel Phillips of Concord-Carlisle High School in Concord, Massachusetts.

[Kristina Vaicikonis and Jinger Hoop]
In WORLD BOOK, see NOBEL PRIZES.

Biology

A method for speeding up the flowering of plants was reported by American and Swedish biologists in October 1995. The researchers modified a single gene that, when inserted into a plant, forced the plant to develop complete flowers much earlier than normal plants. The gene acted like a switch that "turned on" other genes needed to produce flowers. The research was conducted by molecular biologists Detlef Weigel of the Salk Institute for Biological Sciences in La Jolla, California, and Ove Nilsson of the Swedish University of Agricultural Sciences. The scientists also reported that they had transferred the gene switch of one plant to a plant of a different species, causing that plant to produce flowers early.

Normally, plants make leaves and flower parts from a tiny mass of embryonic cells known as the shoot meristem, which is buried deep in the middle of a bud. Leaves and flower parts develop from microscopic outgrowths called primordia on the flanks of the meristem. When a plant is growing, the primordia always develop into leaves. But

when a plant gets ready to make flowers, the primordia develop into all the parts of a flower—sepals, petals, stamens, and pistils.

For many years, plant biologists have sought to learn how primordia "know" when to become leaves and when to develop into flower parts. They have usually worked with *Arabidopsis thaliana*, a plant whose small size and small number of genes make it useful for genetic experiments. Researchers have identified several *Arabidopsis* genes that are activated early in the transition from the leafy phase to the floral phase of development. *Mutations* (changes) in these genes have given rise to *Arabidopsis* plants with abnormal flowers. Geneticists have examined these mutant plants to identify the genes that control flowering, and they named one such gene LEAFY because the plant tended to produce only leaves instead of flowers.

For their experiments, Weigel and Nilsson inserted a modified version of the LEAFY gene into *Arabidopsis*. They altered the LEAFY gene by inserting a piece of a plant virus gene called a promoter. A promoter determines when, where, and how strongly the gene is activated. The researchers used a promoter known to be a strong activator of gene activity in all plant cells.

The *Arabidopsis* plants with the modified gene flowered earlier than normal *Arabidopsis* plants. The researchers said this result demonstrated that activation of the LEAFY gene caused the primordia to begin to develop into flower parts. Once it was activated, they explained, the LEAFY gene switched on the other genes needed to make complete flowers. Weigel and Nilsson went on to insert the modified LEAFY gene into immature aspen trees, and the trees began to flower after only five months. Normally, aspen trees grow 8 to 20 years before they flower.

Weigel and Nilsson concluded that the same molecular mechanisms that control flowering in the tiny *Arabidopsis* plant also control flowering in aspen trees and probably all other flowering plants. These experiments bring researchers one step closer to being able to genetically engineer plants to make them flower sooner. This trait would be an advantage for a number of reasons. For example, crop plants engineered to flower early could be grown in areas with a short growing season. The flowers then would be available for fertilization by insects, thus producing a valuable crop in areas previously unsuited for the plant.

The mechanics of hopping. Large kangaroos use their hind limbs like giant springs as they hop. They can do this because the structure of the kangaroo hind limb is especially suited to store elastic energy, according to anatomists M. B. Bennett and G. C. Taylor of the University of Queensland, Australia, who reported that finding in November 1995. Furthermore, the researchers said, kangaroos do not use energy at an increased rate as they hop faster. All other mammals use more energy the faster they run. Large kangaroos can hop as fast as 50 kilometers (30 miles) per hour for short distances.

The Australian researchers measured the ability of the muscles and tendons of the hind limbs of kangaroos to store and release energy while the animals were jumping. The scientists found that a 50-kilogram (110-pound) kanga-

roo stores more than six times the energy of other mammals the same size. The researchers also watched high-speed films of kangaroos hopping and discovered that the kangaroo's crouched posture on the ground and the structure of the hind limbs makes jumping energy-efficient.

As a kangaroo's size increases, the amount of elastic energy stored in the hind limbs also increases, but so does the risk of breaking tendons. Bennett and Taylor said the optimal size for energy efficiency in kangaroos is 50 to 60 kilograms (110 to 132 pounds). Within this weight range, kangaroos store the most energy in their hind limbs without risk of tendon injury.

Bennett and Taylor also speculated that extinct giant kangaroos, which weighed about 150 kilograms (330 pounds), probably had slower hopping speeds, which may have contributed to their extinction. These creatures may not have been able to escape faster-moving predators.

Cloning sheep. Scottish scientists reported in March 1996 that they had successfully cloned sheep. A clone is an organism that is genetically identical to a parent organism. Natural cloning includes growing plants by cuttings, graftings, or separating clusters of bulbs or tubers. It is an important technique in growing plants with desirable traits, such as commercial varieties of apple trees, potatoes, and tulips.

Reproductive physiologist K.H.S. Campbell and his co-workers at the Roslin Institute in Edinburgh, Scotland, used a technique called nuclear transfer to clone sheep. Nuclear transfer has long been used to clone mice in the laboratory. Until now, however, the technique has been unsuccessful with farm animals.

Campbell and his colleagues removed the normal nucleus from sheep *oocytes* (egg cells that are ready to develop into embryos). The nucleus is the part of a cell that contains the genes, which carry an organism's hereditary information. The researchers then inserted a nucleus from another line of sheep into the oocytes and implanted the altered oocytes in female sheep. The lambs that developed from the modified oocytes were clones because their nuclei were identical.

Tibet's rugged isolation—a biological asset

A team of British, French, and Spanish scientists came across dozens of previously unknown horses in an isolated valley of northeastern Tibet in October 1995. In December 1995, another international team reported the discovery of 200 Tibet red deer, a species not seen in the wild for 50 years and thought to be extinct.

A Riwoche horse, *above,* stands in the isolated Tibetan valley for which it was named. With its short stature—only about 1.2 meters (4 feet) at the shoulder—and bristly mane and tail, the Riwoche resembles horses drawn up to 30,000 years ago on the walls of European caves. French anthropologist Michel Peissel, who led the expedition that discovered the animal, took blood samples back to England for analysis to determine the Riwoche's place in the evolution of the horse.

A Tibet red deer, *left,* ascends a hill in its home range in the southeastern Himalayas along the border with India. The deer, which is related to the North American Elk, is actually gray-brown in color, and males have a distinctive white patch on the rump. The antlers bend inward at an angle that distinguishes the species from other types of red deer.

Exactly why nuclear transfer previously had been unsuccessful in farm animals is uncertain. One theory is that a transplanted nucleus needs time to become "reprogrammed" into an embryonic state.

Campbell and his colleagues used two tricks in their experiment. First, they developed a special line of cultured cells derived from sheep embryos. These cells grew and reproduced in culture and were *totipotent*. Totipotent means the embryonic cells retained the potential to differentiate into all the different cell types that make up an adult sheep. The researchers also pretreated this cell line so that the nuclei achieved a "resting stage" before transfer. This stage readied the nucleii for reprogramming once they were transferred into an oocyte.

If cloning farm animals were to become routine, biologists would have a means of producing unlimited numbers of animals with desired genetic traits. Sexual reproduction shuffles genes, and favorable combinations of genetic traits are often lost.

The origins of lichens. Lichens, a biological partnership between fungi and algae, formed independently at least five times during the course of evolution. That conclusion was reported in June 1995 by botanists Andrea Gargas and Paula DePriest of the Smithsonian Institution in Washington, D.C.; Martin Grube of the University of Graz, Austria; and Anders Tehler of Stockholm University in Sweden. Their work shows how DNA (deoxyribonucleic acid, the molecule that encodes an organism's genetic information) can be used to reveal the evolutionary history of living organisms.

Lichens, commonly found growing on rocks and tree trunks throughout the world, are a life form that unites an alga and a fungus into a close and long-lasting relationship that benefits both partners, a relationship called a symbiosis. The fungal cells provide protection, mineral nutrients, and living space for the algal cells. In return, the algal cells share food they make with the fungal cells. Algal cells use energy from sunlight to make food from carbon dioxide and water.

A cluster of primitive oak flowers estimated to be 90 million to 94 million years old remains forever open, perfectly preserved in amber. They are the oldest intact flowers ever found in amber. Entomologist David Grimaldi of the American Museum of Natural History in New York City announced in February 1996 that he had found the specimen at a site in New Jersey. Amber is fossilized tree resin, usually from ancient pine trees, that often contains insects and bits of plants that were covered by resin and preserved.

Fungi take the active role in forming this partnership, but how they evolved this lifestyle is shrouded in mystery. Equally mysterious is the evolutionary relationship between these fungi and other fungi that do not form lichens.

In an attempt to solve the second mystery, Gargas and her colleagues compared DNA *sequences*—the order of molecular units called bases—for a specific gene obtained from 75 different fungus species, including 10 species that form lichens. Similarity in DNA sequence is commonly used to judge how closely one species is related to another. Thus, by comparing the DNA sequences of the 75 fungus species, the researchers were able to identify those that were genetically very similar to one another and those that were very dissimilar.

From this information, the scientists constructed an evolutionary tree showing the relatedness of the 75 fungus species. If the lichens of today originated from one common ancestor, the DNA sequences from the lichen-forming species would all be found on the same branch of the evolutionary tree. On the other hand, if lichen-forming species originated independently on several occasions during evolution, they would be found on different branches.

Gargas's research team found that the lichen-forming fungi were located on five different branches of the evolutionary tree. Thus, they concluded that lichens constitute not a single evolutionary group but rather a collection of independently evolved symbioses that may have formed for some common, but unknown, ecological reasons.

A propelling protein. American cell biologists reported in July 1995 that they had identified a key bacterial protein responsible for organizing the microscopic machinery that powers cell motion. The researchers, Marcia Goldberg of the Albert Einstein College of Medicine in New York City and Julie Theriot of the Whitehead Institute for Biomedical Research in Cambridge, Massachusetts, said their discovery may help reveal how cancer cells spread in the human body.

Ordinary bacteria use several mechanisms to move about in their environment. Some infectious bacteria spread throughout the body of their host by penetrating the host cells and commandeering the host cell's own chemical machinery for motion. The bacteria do this by recruiting a protein called actin from the host cell and using the protein to build a rigid tail that is used for propulsion. As their tails grow, the bacteria are "rocketed" through the host cell, gaining sufficient force to break through the cell membrane into adjacent cells and spread the infection.

Actin is made by *eukaryotes*, cells in which the chromosomes—the tiny threadlike structures that carry the genes—are packaged in a nucleus. Actin and another protein called myosin work together and are responsible for muscle contraction in animals. The two proteins also provide the major mechanism for movement in nonmuscle cells in the human body. And it is the actin-myosin complex in cancerous cells that enables the cells to move around in the human body, causing cancer to spread from the original site to other locations. Cell biologists have yet to discover, however, how actin and myosin organize themselves into an interacting complex.

Goldberg and Theriot discovered that a single bacterial protein is sufficient to organize actin molecules into a stiff tail that can give a bacterium the power of movement. The protein is called IcsA. Normally this protein is found on the surface of shigella, an infectious bacterium that causes diarrhea.

The researchers took the IcsA gene from shigella and inserted it in *Escherichia coli,* a common bacterium that lacks both IcsA and an actin tail. The researchers placed *E. coli* bacteria with IcsA into a cell extract containing actin. The bacteria quickly grew actin tails and began to move about at a rate of nearly 1 millimeter (0.04 inches) per hour. That may not seem fast, but it meant that the *E. coli* were travelling a distance equivalent to about 200 times their length in an hour. This result indicated that the IcsA protein could organize the actin proteins into a tail and cause the shigellalike form of locomotion.

Goldberg and Theriot also believe that these findings give clues as to how actin is organized in normal human cells and how it may become modified when cells turn cancerous. Cancer cells multiply uncontrollably and invade surrounding tissue.   [Daniel J. Cosgrove]

In WORLD BOOK, see BIOLOGY.

Here are 16 important new science books suitable for the general reader. They have been selected from books published in 1995 and 1996.

Archaeology. *Ancestral Passions: The Leakey Family and the Quest for Humankind's Beginnings* by Virginia Morell recounts the lives of Louis, Mary, and Richard Leakey and describes their accomplishments. The Leakeys have been at the forefront of the search for the earliest remains of human ancestors. Their discoveries, especially at Olduvai Gorge in Kenya, have shaped our understanding of how the human species evolved. (Simon & Schuster, 1995. 639 pp. illus. $30)

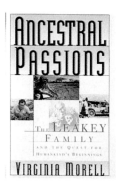

Astronomy. *Hubble Vision: Astronomy with the Hubble Space Telescope* by Carolyn Collins Petersen, a science writer, and John C. Brandt, an astronomer, highlights the Hubble telescope's scientific odyssey. Even before its flawed optics were repaired in 1993, the Hubble was revealing the universe in striking detail never before seen from Earth. Abundant color illustrations show comets crashing into Jupiter, the remains of exploded stars, and galaxies near the edge of the universe. (Cambridge University Press, 1995. 252 pp. illus. $39.95)

Biology. *Bombardier Beetles and Fever Trees: A Close-Up Look at Chemical Warfare and Signals in Animals and Plants* by William C. Agosta, a biochemist, provides an entertaining and informative introduction to some unusual forms of communication. When we think of communication, we think of sound, of words, of people talking. But many plants and animals communicate with chemicals. Insects attract mates using pheromones, chemicals that signal their interest in one another. Lima beans release a chemical alarm, to which their neighboring plants respond, when attacked by mites. Bombardier beetles eject a spurt of hot liquid to repel intruders. Agosta explains the workings of these and other remarkable chemical signals. (Addison-Wesley, 1995. 240 pp. illus. $25)

The Way Life Works by Mahlon Hoagland and Bert Dodson provides an entertaining survey of modern biology, from DNA to enzymes and from embryology to evolution. Hoagland, a noted molecular biologist, provides a wealth of authoritative detail about how living creatures function on the molecular, structural, and ecological levels. Dodson, an artist, contributes clever sketches and cartoons that make difficult concepts understandable to the average reader. (Times Books, 1995. 222 pp. illus. $35)

Chemistry. *The Same and Not the Same* by Roald Hoffmann, a Nobel Prize-winning chemist and poet of some note, presents his outlook on science in a series of short essays. Some essays deal with the technical and creative problems chemists face in the course of their work, such as distinguishing one molecule from another or designing and synthesizing new molecules from old ones. Others explore ethical issues, such as how to deal with the applications of science and what role scientists should play in education and government. (Columbia University Press, 1995. 294 pp. illus. $29.95)

Cosmology. *Einstein's Greatest Blunder? The Cosmological Constant and Other Fudge Factors in the Physics of the Universe* by Donald Goldsmith outlines the mysteries of modern cosmology and describes the solutions astronomers are proposing. One of the mysteries concerns the age of the universe. Some measurements indicate that our universe is only about 10 billion years old, while others lead to the conclusion that the oldest stars are some 15 billion years old. How can the universe be younger than the stars it contains? Another topic is the possibility that gravitation repels, rather than attracts, bodies at very large distances. This possibility was considered by Einstein, who later rejected it as a "blunder." Perhaps he was right after all. (Harvard University Press, 1995. 216 pp. illus. $22.95)

General Science. *The Demon-Haunted World: Science as a Candle in the Dark* by Carl Sagan explores a variety of ideas based on superstition and pseudo-science—from alien abductions to channeled entities and spirits—and points out how the scientific method can help us distinguish fact from fantasy in the world around us. (Random House, 1996. 416 pp. $25)

Mathematics. *A Tour of the Calculus* by David Berlinski is not a textbook of mathematics, but rather an exploration of the power of calculus and the history of its inventors and of the people who have used it. Anyone who does not think that calculus has relevance to our daily lives will be surprised to find how much of our understanding of the world is tied to the great ideas of calculus. (Pantheon Books, 1996. 331 pp. $27.50)

Medicine. *The Case of the Frozen Addicts* by J. William Langston and Jon Palfreman is the intriguing account of how Langston, a physician, treated a number of drug addicts displaying the symptoms of Parkinson's disease. Langston traced their symptoms to the use of tainted drugs and found a way of curing at least some of the damage. (Pantheon Books, 1995. 309 pp. $25)

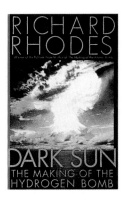

Natural History. *The Rarest of the Rare: Vanishing Animals, Timeless Worlds* by Diane Ackerman recounts Ackerman's travels to areas inhabited by vanishing species. In one memorable scene, she visits a remote Pacific island, home to one of the last nesting colonies of albatross, which once were as common as the pigeon or the sparrow. Part travelogue, part natural history, the narrative evokes a sense of loss at the disappearance of so many remarkable creatures. (Random House, 1995. 184 pp. $23)

Dinosaur in a Haystack: Reflections in Natural History by Stephen Jay Gould is a collection of essays about everything from fungi to baseball. The individual essays contribute to a harmonious whole, illustrating the role of evolution in the shaping of all plants and creatures. (Harmony Books, 1996. 496 pp. illus. $25)

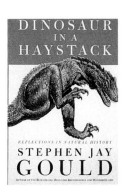

Physics. *The Physics of Star Trek* by Lawrence M. Krauss, a professor of physics at Case Western Reserve University, explores the question of how much is science and how much is fiction in one of television's most popular shows. Krauss discusses possible designs for warp drives, transporters, and phaser guns, with an eye to showing how such things might work in the high-tech world of the future. Along the way he gives some entertaining lessons in quantum mechanics, relativity theory, and many other branches of physics. (Basic Books, 1995. 208 pp. illus. $18)

Lise Meitner: A Life in Physics by Ruth Lewin Sime is an absorbing biography about a little-known scientist. In the 1920's and 1930's, Meitner was recognized as one of the great physicists of Europe, codiscoverer of the element

protactinium, and a leader in the new science of radioactivity. In 1939, however, she was forced to leave Nazi Germany, just as she and her co-worker, Otto Hahn, had discovered the fission of the uranium nucleus. Hahn won a Nobel Prize for this work, but in the turmoil of World War II (1939-1945) and its aftermath, Meitner's greatness was slighted. This absorbing biography may finally afford Meitner the recognition she deserves. (University of California Press, 1996. 512 pp. illus. $30)

The Simple Science of Flight: From Insects to Jumbo Jets by Henk Tennekes, a professor of earth sciences and an avid amateur pilot, describes how shape and weight, wind and weather, affect the flight of any flying creature or flying machine. There are also instructions for making simple paper airplanes. Although you won't learn how to make a Boeing 747 from this book, you will come to understand much better how such a plane manages to keep its many tons of metal aloft with grace and ease. (MIT Press, 1996. 152 pp. illus. $25)

Technology. *Dark Sun: The Making of the Hydrogen Bomb* by Richard Rhodes follows up his history of the atomic bomb with an equally readable account about the hydrogen bomb. Pulitzer Prize-winner Rhodes describes both the science and the politics of mankind's most powerful weapon. While the atomic bomb was developed for use as a weapon at the height of the Second World War, the hydrogen bomb, thousands of times more destructive, was born at the height of the Cold War, in which the United States and the Soviet Union threatened each other with total annihilation. (Simon & Schuster, 1995. 736 pp. $32.50)

Longitude: The True Story of a Lone Genius Who Solved the Greatest Scientific Problem of His Time by Dava Sobel recounts how John Harrison, a British craftsman, devised a practical method for determining longitude at sea. Until the late 1700's, navigators had no way of measuring their position east or west upon the globe, and sailors crossing the great oceans could do little but guess at how far they had traveled. Harrison's story, and the story of navigation in his time, makes interesting and illuminating reading. (Walker and Company, 1995. 224 pp. $18)   [Laurence A. Marschall]

The first three-dimensional simulation of aspirin in action was reported in August 1995 by researchers at the University of Chicago. Aspirin works by blocking the action of two *enzymes* (substances that speed up biochemical reactions) called PGHS-1 and PGHS-2. In the image, an aspirin molecule (yellow) splits apart as it encounters PGHS-1 (blue). One aspirin segment then bonds with the enzyme, inhibiting its function. But this action can lead to stomach upset and other of aspirin's side effects. Scientists hoped to design a new form of aspirin that blocks PGHS-2—the source of pain—while leaving PGHS-1 alone.

A new and simple method for preparing unusual types of *polymers* (long chainlike molecules) called dendrimers was reported in August 1995 by chemist Jean M. J. Fréchet of Cornell University in Ithaca, New York. Unlike ordinary polymers, which usually consist of long linear chains with occasional branches from the side, dendrimers do not have a central backbone. Some of them are star-shaped molecules, with chains of atoms branching out in all directions from a single carbon or nitrogen atom. Others have highly branched structures but lack a central core.

Dendrimers have many important potential applications because chemists can control their size and shape very precisely. In particular, they can add selected groups of atoms to the outer branches of dendrimers to give the molecules properties that might make them useful in a variety of products. For example, dendrimers might be used to extract toxic chemicals from industrial wastewater or to produce more durable paints and coatings.

Since their discovery in 1980, however-

er, dendrimers have not lived up to that promise because their preparation has required a long series of slow and tedious chemical reactions. Fréchet's new synthesis allows chemists to make many types of dendrimers in a single step.

Fréchet started with a carbon-based molecule containing a *vinyl group* (two carbon atoms connected by a double bond) and a chlorine atom. He dissolved the molecule in a solvent containing stannic chloride, which acts as a *catalyst* (an agent that speeds up reactions without itself undergoing change). The catalyst attracted the chlorine atom away from the molecule, leaving behind a positively charged molecule called a cation (pronounced *CAT ion*).

The cation and the catalyst reacted with the vinyl group of another starting molecule to form a larger molecule that contained two positively charged carbon atoms. This doubly positive molecule reacted with the catalyst and the vinyl group in yet another starting molecule, forming a still larger molecule with more positive charges. These reactions repeated themselves in the solution un-

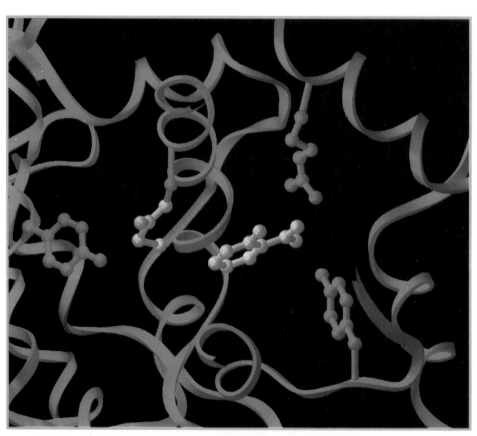

Strips of grass that were treated with a type of *gibberellin*—a group of chemicals plants produce to regulate growth—have stopped growing, compared with untreated grass strips. Australian and Canadian biologists reported in June 1995 that while studying these chemicals, they found one had degraded and was highly effective at stunting plant growth. The investigators patented a more powerful, synthetic version of the growth-inhibiting chemical in the hope that gibberellin can be used as a biodegradable chemical lawnmower or as an agent to control weeds.

til a highly branched polymer formed.

Because starting molecules containing the vinyl group are easy to make and cheap, the new synthesis could open the door to low-cost dendrimers, along with all the useful products that could be made from them.

Element 112. Scientists at the Society for Heavy Ion Research (GSI) laboratory in Darmstadt, Germany, announced in February 1996 that they had created element 112—the newest and heaviest element yet reported. Only 14 months earlier, GSI researchers had disclosed that they had created element 111.

The investigators made the new element by *fusing* (joining) the nuclei of lead and zinc atoms. They did this by bombarding a small chunk of lead with a stream of zinc *ions* (electrically charged atoms) that were accelerated to tremendous speeds by a magnetic device called a heavy-ion accelerator. The new element did not last long enough to be detected directly. It *decayed* (broke down) into progressively lighter atoms in about 280-millionths of a second. But when it decayed, the element gave off

alpha particles (the nuclei of helium atoms) in a pattern that only element 112 could have produced. Element 112 has 165 neutrons and 112 protons in its nucleus. As of June 1996, the element had yet to be named.

Element 112's lifetime was so short that the GSI researchers could not determine the element's physical and chemical properties. But they were intrigued by the relatively long lifetime of one of the lighter atoms that was produced during the decay process. It was a form of element 110 containing 161 neutrons in its nucleus, and it took 19.7 seconds to decay—far longer than most atoms of its type. This finding confirmed theoretical predictions that elements with about 162 neutrons in their nucleus should be fairly stable.

A nanotube gun. Physicists have made a miniature electron "gun" out of a bundle of carbon *nanotubes* (microscopic hollow cylinders made of carbon atoms), according to a November 1995 report by a team of researchers in Switzerland and Brazil. It was the first working device to use nanotubes.

Chemists imitate nature's skeletons

Marine microorganisms form skeletons in myriad patterns that chemists have long sought to reproduce. In November 1995, Canadian chemists reported using *organic* (carbon-containing) and inorganic compounds to synthesize materials that resemble tiny, porous skeletons (photos, *below*). The synthetic structures could have a wide range of uses, including as filtration materials and artificial bone.

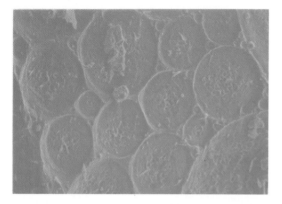

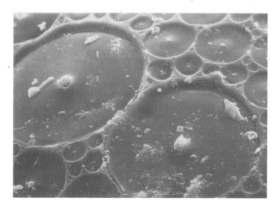

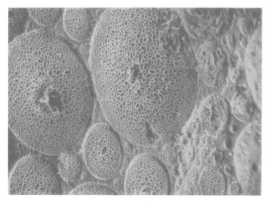

Led by physicist Walt A. de Heer of the École Polytechnique Fédérale de Lausanne in Switzerland, the scientists made the device out of thousands of nanotubes having diameters of about 15 nanometers (600-billionths of an inch). They made the nanotubes from the deposit of an electrically heated device called a carbon arc. They then dispersed the tubes in *ethanol* (grain alcohol) and passed the ethanol solution through a ceramic filter, which produced a film of the tubes on the surface of the filter. Next, they pressed a sheet of electrically conductive plastic against the filter surface, which transferred the tubes upright onto the plastic. When the investigators attached the plastic containing the upright nanotubes to the negative end of a 200-volt battery, they found that the nanotubes began to function like tiny electron guns, firing streams of electrons at a target plate attached to the positive battery terminal.

Electron guns are the heart of the heavy and bulky cathode ray tubes (CRT's) found in television sets and computer monitors. Current CRT's employ electrically heated metal filaments to generate streams of electrons that strike a screen coated with *phosphors* (light-emitting chemicals). A device incorporating nanotube guns as the source of electrons would be much lighter and more compact than any CRT now on the market. It would also provide a much brighter image and wider viewing angle than the liquid crystal displays used in current laptop computers.

Before nanotubes can replace CRT's, however, a way must be found to selectively direct tube bundles so they can form meaningful images on a screen. The Swiss and Brazilian researchers said they thought that eventually this should be fairly easy to do.

Microchips record reactions. The time involved for chemists to make new molecules that can be used as drugs could be shortened by tiny electronic memory chips that track the chemical process taking place in test beakers. Chemists at IRORI Quantum Microchemistry and the Scripps Research Institute, both located in La Jolla, California, reported in October 1995 that they had used the microchips to improve a high-speed chemical synthesis method called combinatorial chemistry.

Combinatorial chemistry allows laboratory workers to rapidly produce very large numbers of different molecules from a few simple compounds placed on plastic beads. The beads are immersed in beakers, each containing a different *reagent* (a compound that causes chemical reactions). Chemical "tags" mark the compounds on the beads so that scientists can identify the newly created molecules. But tagging is a slow and tedious process.

The microchips made the process much easier. The researchers placed the chemically sensitized chips inside the plastic beads. The chips detected the reactions of the reagents with the test compounds on the beads by electronically encoding the identities of all the reagents they encountered. The chips converted the information to radio signals and transmitted the signals to a receiver, which decoded the information and stored it in a computer. The chemists used the data to find out what molecules had formed.

New catalysts. New types of catalysts may eliminate the use of the poisonous and polluting solvents now used to prepare many common drugs and agricultural pesticides. That finding was reported in August 1995 by researchers at Los Alamos National Laboratory in New Mexico.

Chemicals used in drugs and pesticides often exist as two *isomers* (molecules with the same formula but different structures) that are mirror images of each other. Usually, only one isomer is biologically active, and the other form may be not only inactive but even harmful. To get the active isomer, chemical manufacturers usually must promote its formation with a substance called a chiral (pronounced *KY rhul*) catalyst. Such catalysts, however, are usually soluble only in benzene, chloroform, methylene chloride, and other solvents that are hazardous to people and wildlife.

But by tinkering with the molecular structures of some chiral catalysts, the Los Alamos team created compounds that dissolve readily in a harmless solvent called supercritical carbon dioxide. The compounds produce almost exclusively the biologically active isomers.

Supercritical carbon dioxide is an intermediate between a liquid and a gas.

It exists only at a pressure of 73 atmospheres (73 times the air pressure at sea level) and at a temperature of 31 °C (88 °F). Once dissolved in this solvent, the new chiral catalysts produce up to 99 percent of the desired isomers of various forms of amino acids, the building blocks of proteins.

Atoms of antimatter. Scientists at the European Laboratory for Particle Physics (CERN) in Geneva, Switzerland, disclosed in January 1996 that they had produced the first atoms of antimatter in a laboratory. The atoms were a form of hydrogen called antihydrogen. Researchers have made subatomic particles of antimatter for many years in laboratories around the world, but never before had complete antiatoms been made.

Atoms of antimatter have the same structure as ordinary atoms but opposite charges. For example, an atom of hydrogen has a nucleus made of a positively charged proton and a negatively charged electron. Antihydrogen, by contrast, is made up of a negatively charged antiproton nucleus and a positively charged electron, called a positron. When matter and antimatter collide, they annihilate each other in a burst of energy. The newly created antihydrogen atoms at CERN, for example, lasted for only about 40 nanoseconds (40-billionths of a second) before being annihilated by ordinary matter.

The CERN team made the antihydrogen atoms by firing a beam of antiprotons through xenon gas. A small number of antiprotons, as they passed through the electromagnetic field surrounding a xenon atom, interacted with the field and produced an electron and a positron. In a few instances, the positron went into orbit around the antiproton, giving birth to an atom of antihydrogen.

Only 11 atoms of antihydrogen were produced. The researchers detected the antihydrogen atoms from *gamma rays* (a form of high-energy radiation) the atoms released upon colliding with ordinary matter. Later in 1996, the CERN group was attempting to trap antihydrogen atoms in a way that would prevent the antimatter atoms from coming in contact with ordinary matter. (See PHYSICS [Close-Up].)   [Gordon Graff]

In WORLD BOOK, see CHEMISTRY.

The intersection between the personal computer (PC) and the global telecommunications system continued to be the most exciting spot in the computer world during 1995 and 1996. Dominating that world was the explosive growth of the Internet (the Net), a global connection of tens of millions of computers and computer networks belonging to universities, government, businesses, institutions, and individuals.

Traffic on the Internet grew at a rapid pace in 1996 with estimates of the number of individuals tapping into the Internet reaching as high as 30 million. In the United States, commercial enterprises had claimed nearly 250,000 Internet *sites* by April 1996, according to Network Solutions, Incorporated, a U.S. government-funded company that manages registration services for the Net. (Sites are storage locations for resources, each of which has its own electronic address.) Tens of thousands of other sites have been established by individuals or institutions. And virtually all personal computers sold after mid-1995 contained a *modem* (a device that allows computer information to be transmitted over telephone lines) and telecommunications software designed to make Internet access easier.

Nevertheless, only about 35 percent of U.S. households owned a PC in 1995, according to an August survey by sociologists at the University of Maryland in College Park. More than 90 percent of U.S. households had at least one television set and telephone. The sociologists also found that about 7.5 percent of PC owners were using the Internet.

Information on the Internet spans the breadth of human knowledge and interests, with text, pictures, animation, computer software, and even recorded sound and video on virtually every subject. With a personal computer, a modem, and special software, anyone can now access the international resources of the Internet.

And those resources proliferated at an amazing rate in 1995 and 1996. New services and sites included Internet-based soap operas and games, electronic magazines called *digizines* (digital magazines), and software called *knowbots* that searched for materials of particular interest. The Net also offered discussion groups for people with similar interests,

interactive novels, electronic art galleries and theaters, advertising, and public-opinion polls.

Until the early 1990's, most of the information on the Internet consisted of text-based files. The development of the World Wide Web (the Web), a network within the Internet, made possible the inclusion of pictures, sounds, and video on the Net. These features made the Internet far more accessible and popular.

Netscape takes off. In order to see the images at a Web site, software called a *browser* is required. A browser enables a computer to display the text and images—and, increasingly, to play the videos and sounds—at a site. The most popular browser in 1995 and 1996 was Netscape Navigator, produced by Netscape Communications Corporation of Mountain View, California. By 1996, an estimated 80 percent of consumers using the Internet did so via Netscape.

In August 1995, Netscape Communications, which began as a private company, offered 5.75 million shares of stock for sale to the public. The price was $28 at the start of trading but quickly jumped to $74.75 in one of the largest and most dramatic single-day price increases in the history of the U.S. stock market. At the end of the first day of trading, the stock sold for $58.25.

Netscape was expected to help businesses sell products over the Internet, while protecting the privacy of those transactions. New features introduced by Netscape in the year after its stock offering enabled the browser to handle animation, video, and sound more efficiently, increasing its popularity. But in 1996, Netscape's dominance was challenged by the Microsoft Corporation of Redmond, Washington, which offered a browser called Microsoft Explorer.

Censoring the Net. Among the more controversial sites on the Internet were those offering "adult" or pornographic material. On Feb. 8, 1996, President Bill Clinton signed the Communications Decency Act (CDA), which allows the U.S. government to restrict on-line speech and conduct. The law, a part of the Telecommunications Reform Bill, prohibits the transmission of indecent material over public computer networks to which minors have access. Violators would be subject to penalties ranging up to $250,000 in fines and five years in jail.

Within a week, a federal judge had temporarily blocked enforcement of the act. Lawsuits challenging the act were filed almost immediately by a group of 20 civil liberties and free-speech groups, including the American Civil Liberties Union, and by a broad coalition of computer companies, software manufacturers, information providers, and Internet service providers. The suits contended that the CDA was an unconstitutional infringement of freedom of speech and of the press and that it was imprecise and unenforceable. Many people feared that the act would be used to censor much legitimate information. On June 12, the U.S. Court of Appeals in Philadelphia struck the act down.

Network computer. In one of the largest gambles ever undertaken by a software company, the Oracle Corporation of Redwood City, California, announced in May 1996 the development of software for an inexpensive computer designed almost exclusively for accessing the Internet. The computer was expected to sell for less than $500.

Called a *network computer* or an *infor-*

mation appliance, the device would connect to a television set and would not require disc drives, memory, or other computer equipment that drive up the cost of PC's. Software for a network computer would be downloaded from the Internet itself or from private computer networks rather than stored inside the computer. Also in May, Oracle announced that at least 15 electronics manufacturers, including Mitsubishi Corporation of Japan, had agreed to produce network computers using Oracle's software.

Many industry experts considered network computers a risky proposition because PC's continued to increase in power and decline in price. In mid-1996, the average price of a fully equipped PC fell below $2,000, with continued price cuts expected. Nonetheless, some analysts viewed network computers as a superior alternative to PC's. They said network computers would not only be cheaper and easier to operate than PC's but would also offer the potential for expanding computer services and products to a vast market.

Personalized cartoon faces representing up to four family members allow customers of the RCA Digital Satellite System (DDS) to create an individual menu of channels. The icons allow viewers quick access to their favorites among the 175 channels offered by DDS. The menus, locked in by a four-digit code, also enable parents to restrict their children's viewing to channels whose programming the parents approve of.

Access provider competition. As the popularity of the Internet has grown, telecommunications, software, and computer hardware companies have hurried to take part in its expansion. Among the most competitive of all the Internet businesses are those offering telephone access to the Net. Computer users, whether accessing the Net via Netscape Navigator or another browser, must first dial special telephone numbers, called Internet providers (IP's). These numbers provide the hookup to the Internet for the price of a local telephone call in most communities. IP service charges average $35 a month for about 20 hours of Internet access.

In August 1995, the AT&T Corp. introduced AT&T Worldnet Services to provide Internet access to its 80 million customers around the world. The company's customers were offered unlimited Internet access via Worldnet for $19.95 a month. The service included *electronic mail* (messages sent virtually instantly from one computer to another), protected business transactions, and video and voice conferencing.

Other telephone companies also looked to the Internet as a new marketplace. In April 1996, regional Bell operating companies Nynex Corporation and Bell Atlantic Telephone Company announced plans to merge. The consolidated company would service 36 million customers in an area extending from Maine to Virginia. According to the companies, the spur for the merger was the increased amount of Internet and computer-oriented traffic that the consolidated company would be able to accommodate.

Microsoft weighs in. Software giant Microsoft also entered the Internet access business in 1995 through its Windows 95 operating software and by redefining its Microsoft Network (MSN) as an Internet service. Windows 95, introduced in August, was a major upgrade of the operating system used in most of the world's PC's. An operating system consists of software that controls and coordinates a computer's most basic functions. It handles the communication between the computer's hardware—the physical components, such as the disc drives—and the application programs that tell the computer how to perform particular tasks. Among Win-

dows 95's advanced features was a direct portal to the Internet. With a single click of the mouse on an *icon* (symbol) on the computer screen, users were automatically connected to the Internet via the MSN.

The MSN had been introduced in late 1994 as an on-line service for which customers paid a monthly fee plus hourly charges. Many on-line services in 1995 and 1996 offered access to the Internet as part of their menu. They also offered software, pictures and videos, and special electronic events that could not be reached from the Internet. By April 1996, the MSN had attracted about 1 million customers, far fewer than the 6 million subscribers to America Online, the biggest on-line service.

In April, Microsoft announced that it was shifting MSN News, which supplied informational services to the MSN, to the World Wide Web. As a Web service, MSN News was available without a subscription charge. In May, the company began offering unlimited access to the non-news contents of the MSN to consumers with Microsoft's Explorer browser via the Web for $6.95 a month. The company planned to expand the service to users of other browsers and computers by late 1996. Despite uncertainties with the MSN, Microsoft posted record earnings in 1995.

Apple problems. In contrast, Apple Computer, Incorporated, of Cupertino, California, suffered so disastrous a year in fiscal year 1995-1996 that for a time many industry observers thought the company would be sold. One of the best-known makers of personal computers, including the popular Macintosh, Apple had achieved success by differentiating its computers from standard PC's. Macintoshes were among the first computers to feature icons for ease of use. Apple also pioneered in desktop publishing and desktop video.

By the mid-1990's, however, software such as Microsoft Windows had made visual tools commonplace on standard PC's. While Microsoft products ran on more than 90 percent of the world's computers, Macintosh's share of the U.S. computer market dwindled to less than 8 percent. With fewer applications being written for Macintoshes, the computers appeared increasingly isolated from mainstream business and personal

Computerized ID

Unique individual characteristics enable new computerized identification systems to provide more foolproof security for financial transactions and classified files or for areas where access must be controlled. The systems bypass badges that may be counterfeited or codes that may be broken.

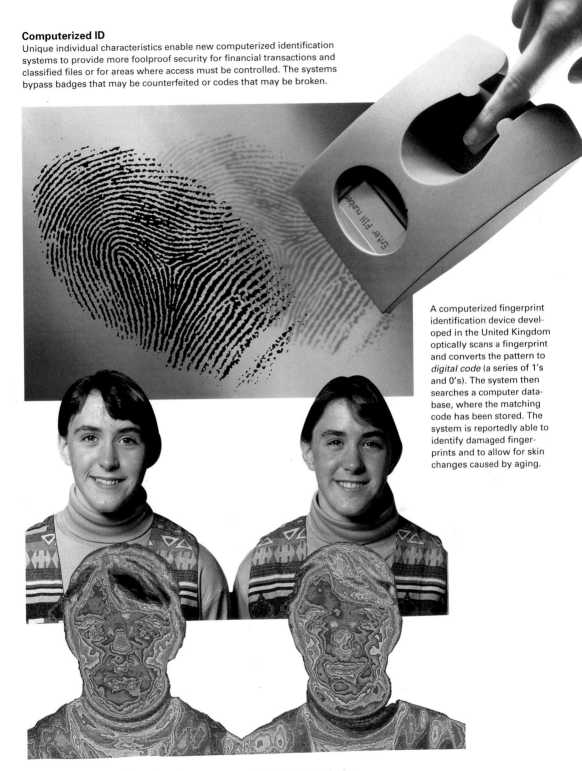

A computerized fingerprint identification device developed in the United Kingdom optically scans a fingerprint and converts the pattern to *digital code* (a series of 1's and 0's). The system then searches a computer database, where the matching code has been stored. The system is reportedly able to identify damaged fingerprints and to allow for skin changes caused by aging.

Heat patterns radiated from the unique arrangement of blood vessels in the face are the basis of an identification system developed by Technology Recognition Systems of Alexandria, Virginia. Images called facial thermograms are produced by an infrared camera and then compared digitally to thermograms stored in a computer. The company says the system is able to distinguish even between identical twins, *above*, and is not fooled by plastic surgery.

computing. They were also more expensive than standard PC's.

In fall 1995, Apple sought to regain its polish by cutting prices on its computers in time for the Christmas buying season. The strategy both succeeded and failed. Between October 1 and December 1, Apple sold more than 1 million computers, but the computers went for such low prices that the company lost money on them. In April 1996, Apple reported losses of $740 million for the second quarter of the 1995-1996 fiscal year. The company also announced plans to lay off another 1,500 employees in addition to 1,300 workers already cut. Earlier in 1996, the company reorganized, and replaced its chief executive officer.

In an effort to boost its low market share, Apple in May agreed to license its Macintosh operating system to International Business Machines (IBM) of Armonk, New York, the world's largest computer company. Under the agreement, IBM would contract with smaller computer makers to produce Macintosh *clones* (copies). In 1994, Apple, which had long refused to license its operating system, began permitting a few manufacturers to make clones. The company hoped the licensing arrangement with IBM and its reorganization efforts would at least ensure its survival and perhaps enable it to make a comeback.

Multiresource computer. In October 1995, Be, Incorporated, of Menlo Park, California, introduced the BeBox computer, which uses available technology in innovative ways to let users synchronize sound, video, and communications to create audiovisual multimedia presentations for both computers and the Internet. Priced at less than $2,000, the BeBox uses a new operating system that draws on multiple resources such as hard disks and the Internet. Be is headed by Jean-Louis Gassee, former president of Apple's product division.

Computers and the movies. *Toy Story*, the first completely computer-animated movie, became one of the great motion-picture successes of 1995. The movie was produced by Pixar Animation Studios of Richmond, California, whose president, Steven Jobs, was a cofounder of Apple.

Collaborating on the Net. In October 1995, IBM announced plans to use software acquired in its June purchase of the Lotus Development Corporation of Boston as the cornerstone of an effort to market so-called collaborative software that works over the Internet. The IBM-acquired software, Lotus Notes, is an innovative program that allows multiple users to work together over corporate computer networks. Collaborative software is expected to become increasingly important as computer networks grow. Also in October, IBM introduced InterNotes, a program that allows documents created with Lotus Notes to be published on the World Wide Web.

Many observers considered IBM's acquisition of Lotus to be a smart step in helping the giant corporation recover from business difficulties it faced in the early 1990's. Lotus, with its enormously popular Lotus 1-2-3 financial and business spreadsheets program, had been one of the early giants of the PC software industry. Lotus's business during the 1990's, however, had been badly eroded by Microsoft's dominance of the software industry.

A new CD. One of the biggest developments in consumer electronics in 1995 was the introduction in October of the digital videodisc (DVD), a new approach to consumer entertainment, including prerecorded movies. The DVD, also known as the digital versatile disc, represented an agreement among the world's leading consumer electronics and entertainment companies on a new standard for CD-based prerecorded entertainment and information.

DVD's can hold about 15 times as much data as traditional audio CD's. The increased storage capacity was the result of three advances in technology. The first of those was the use of smaller pits and lans on the disc surface. *Pits* (indentations) and *lans* (smooth spots) represent the *bits*—the 1's and 0's—of digital information. The second advance was the development of small lasers that emit the very-short-wavelength beams required to read that information. And the third advance was progress in *data compression*—squeezing greater amounts of information onto a disc.

A single DVD can hold about two hours of motion-picture footage, with enough room for the soundtrack to include multiple languages as well as closed-captioned text for the hearing-impaired. Dual-layer DVD's offer an even larger storage capacity. Two-layer DVD's use two discs, stacked one on top of the other, and hold up to four hours' worth of motion-picture footage and multilanguage soundtrack.

The first DVD players were expected to reach the market in late summer 1996 with an average price of $700. DVD-ROM's (*d*igital *v*ideo *d*isk *r*ead-*o*nly *m*emory) were also expected to debut in 1996. If consumers responded enthusiastically, the price of DVD players was expected to drop quickly. Industry analysts predicted that DVD's eventually would replace videocassettes as the standard medium for distributing prerecorded movies.

The video game industry picked up a major new competitor with the September 1995 introduction of the Sony PlayStation, a $299 game machine that quickly became the most popular such unit on the market. Using 32-bit technology similar to that of some computers, the PlayStation featured advanced graphics and sound that helped it sell more than 1 million units during its first six months on the market.

Competition in the video game industry heated up further in May 1996 when Nintendo of America, Incorporated, of Redmond, Washington, introduced a new video game machine, the Nintendo 64. The device's name describes its ability to handle data in 64-bit increments. Higher data capacity makes possible more realistic animation, faster speed, richer colors, and more dramatic music and sound.

The Nintendo 64 was designed to use cartridges as its software medium, though the company expected to introduce CD-ROM and ultimately DVD discs for the machine. Additionally, the Nintendo 64's more muscular data-handling power may make it possible for the device to offer other features, such as keyboards and printers, that are traditionally found only on PC's. Some industry analysts speculated that the new game machine would ultimately incorporate a modem and offer access to the Internet.   [Keith Ferrell]

In the Science Studies section, see THE COMPUTER COMES OF AGE. In WORLD BOOK, see COMPUTER.

Conservation

Conservationists became concerned in late 1995 over a quickly fatal disease of rabbits called rabbit calicivirus disease (RCD) that biologists had been testing on a remote island off mainland Australia. Testing on the island was aimed at confirming that RCD could control Australia's exploding rabbit population, estimated to be 300 million in 1996, without harming other wildlife. Despite extensive precautions on the island, dead rabbits infected with RCD were found on the mainland in October. Conservationists worried that RCD, by killing off rabbits—an important food source for many predators—could harm many Australian wildlife communities.

RCD first appeared mysteriously in China in 1984, killing millions of rabbits. It spread elsewhere in Asia and to Europe. Infected rabbits experience extensive internal blood clotting, lapse into a coma, and die within 36 hours.

Rabbits have created massive environmental upheaval in Australia since they were introduced in 1859. They have severely overgrazed the land, which has brought on widespread soil erosion.

Fences and poisons could not control their population growth. In 1950, biologists introduced a disease known as myxomatosis as a means of controlling rabbits. Myxomatosis kills rabbits without infecting kangaroos and other native animals. Up to 80 percent of the rabbit population died, though some developed a resistance to the organism that causes the disease, and populations began to surge once again.

Biologists searched for another means to control the rabbits, and RCD seemed a strong candidate. Thus, biologists brought RCD to Australia in 1991 under tight security. A research facility was established on Wardang Island, 4 kilometers (2.5 miles) off the coast of South Australia. Elaborate measures were taken to quarantine RCD while the disease was tested on captive rabbits. No more than 10 rabbits were infected at any one time, and the test area was enclosed with rabbit-proof fences. Electric fences also surrounded the pens. Scientists exposed to the disease underwent disinfection procedures and changed their clothing when entering or leaving the pens. The

A rare giant anteater lumbers through the grass of Kaa-Iya del Gran Chaco National Park, one of two areas in Bolivia that the Bolivian government established as national parks in September 1995. Gran Chaco, covering 3.5 million hectares (8.6 million acres) in southeastern Bolivia along the border with Paraguay, is the world's largest protected dry forest, a type of forest area that contains open grassland, swamps, and scrubby trees. Conservationists said Bolivia's actions indicate a new concern for protecting the nation's plant and animal life.

site was heavily sprayed with insecticides to assure that mosquitoes and other insects could not transmit RCD to other areas. All tests indicated that RCD infected only rabbits and was effective at controlling their numbers. Despite all these precautions, RCD for reasons unknown escaped before it could be released under the control of scientists.

Conservationists worried that the wholesale elimination of millions of rabbits would most likely collapse food chains in wildlife communities throughout Australia. In such a scenario, predator populations would plummet as the number of hares dwindled, but perhaps not before the predators switched to eating livestock and pets. Conservationists knew that in Spain, where RCD had ravaged rabbits, national park rangers discovered starving lynxes. Similar consequences could be in store for the wedgetailed eagle, Australia's largest bird of prey and a major predator of rabbits.

With the prospect of fewer rabbits competing with livestock for grass, ranchers may be tempted to increase the size of their herds. If they were to do so, soil erosion and other environmental damage could probably continue at the same pace as it did with an ever-growing rabbit population. Moreover, millions of rotting rabbit carcasses would produce a temporary plague of blowflies.

On the plus side, some species of native plants, long suppressed by the rabbits, could again flourish in the Australian outback. Seedlings of some trees would, researchers hoped, survive to maturity and produce seeds that could restore the nearly depleted supply of ungerminated seeds now in the ground. The land might respond "as if a long drought had just ended," said Ian Noble, an expert in land degradation at the Australian National University. However, if RCD produces only a short-term reduction in the rabbit population, the few remaining seeds will have germinated for nothing if the surviving rabbits later eat the seedlings.

Conservation prize winners. Mountain gorillas, one of the world's best-known endangered species, have long

Young sandhill cranes follow biologist Kent Klegg in his ultralight plane as he heads south from Idaho in October 1995 to a winter migratory site in New Mexico. The sandhills were substituting for endangered whooping cranes in an experiment to establish a safer wintering site than along the heavily trafficked Gulf of Mexico, where whooping cranes currently spend the winter. The sandhills were conditioned as hatchlings to follow the plane as they normally would follow their parents. Klegg planned to lead whooping cranes to New Mexico in 1997.

been victims of poaching, but the ravages of a civil war in the central African nation of Rwanda posed even greater threats to their survival. The war lasted from 1990 to 1994, with tragic impact on the human population. Throughout most of the turmoil, however, the staff at Rwanda's Parc National de Vulcans, home of about half of the world's remaining population of some 650 mountain gorillas, stayed at their posts. Soldiers of the warring factions repeatedly damaged the park's buildings and pillaged valuable records, but the guards continued their patrols in the forest instead of fleeing to the safety of nearby Zaire. As a result, not one gorilla was lost during the war, though one was later killed by a land mine.

For their courageous dedication, the park's guards and administrators received the prestigious 1995 J. Paul Getty Wildlife Conservation Award of $50,000 in May 1996 during ceremonies at the park. The award, administered by the World Wildlife Fund, recognizes outstanding achievement for the conservation of wildlife and their habitats. In

announcing the award recipients in January 1996, fund president Kathryn S. Fuller praised the staff's "heroic efforts" in protecting the park. The prize money will be used to help rebuild the facilities at the park, according to Henri Nsanjama, the fund's vice president for Africa.

Supreme Court defines habitat. Conservationists hailed the 6-to-3 vote of the United States Supreme Court on June 29, 1995, that affirmed the federal government's authority to regulate habitat used by endangered species. The decision, however, may add fuel to the bitter debate in the U.S. Congress concerning renewal of the Endangered Species Act of 1973. The act's renewal has been stalled largely because of a thorny issue concerning the regulation of land serving as habitat for the more than 800 species officially designated as threatened or endangered by extinction. About 90 of the species depend to some extent on habitat located on private land.

The case before the Supreme Court, *Babbitt v. the Sweet Home Chapter of Communities for a Greater Oregon*, pitted log-

Romeo, a diademed sifaka, nibbles at a blossom at the Duke Primate Center of Duke University in Durham, North Carolina. Diademed sifakas, the largest of the 32 species of lemur, are endangered in their native Madagascar, where Duke biologists captured Romeo and two other sifakas in1993. Back at the center, Romeo was the only one that survived. The Duke scientists had planned to return to Madagascar in spring 1996 to find a mate for Romeo and another breeding pair. But the expedition was delayed. The researchers said the minimum mating age for sifakas was 5 years, and Romeo was still only 3 years old in 1996.

ging interests against the government's plan to protect forest habitat on public and private lands in the Pacific Northwest, home to the endangered northern spotted owl. At issue was interpretation of what constitutes "harm" to the habitat. The Department of Interior, led by Secretary Bruce Babbitt, said that in the Endangered Species Act's language, harm included habitat modifications that subsequently injured or killed endangered animals, and lumbering fulfilled this definition. But the timber industry claimed that harm had a more restrictive meaning, limited to trapping or killing the owls.

The high court's ruling made it clear that logging harmed the owls as much as killing them outright. Speaking for the majority, Justice John Paul Stevens said, "Given Congress's clear expression of the Endangered Species Act's broad purpose to protect endangered and threatened wildlife, the secretary's definition of harm is reasonable."

New blood for Florida panthers. Fewer than 50 Florida panthers roam in and around the Everglades in southern Florida, their last remaining habitat. The latest threat to their survival is inbreeding, which has caused increasing inherited physical problems, such as weakened immune systems and sterility. To combat the threat, conservation biologists in 1995 released eight female mountain lions from Texas into the Everglades, hoping a new gene pool would strengthen the Florida panther population.

In Texas and other Southwestern and Western states, mountain lions are thriving. Conservationists reasoned that in the past some Western mountain lions and Florida panthers occasionally strayed into each other's range and mated, thereby exchanging genes in the days before highways and other human development prevented these chance encounters. Assuming such cross-breeding occurred, concerns for maintaining Florida panthers as a genetically "pure" subspecies became less important than previously believed.

Biologists released the last of the eight mountain lions from Texas into the Everglades in July 1995. Before being freed, the animals were quarantined for medical testing to rule out any health problems. Then, each was fitted with a radio collar to enable the biologists to track the animal's movements. To improve the chances of mating, the Texas mountain lions were released in areas where there were male but not female Florida panthers.

Biologist Darrel Land of the Florida Game Commission said that once they have raised their cubs, the Texas mountain lions may be recaptured and returned to their original habitat in Texas. If successful, mountain lion introduction may also be repeated about every 10 years, which would mimic the frequency of mating among lion subspecies that probably occurred in nature before the Florida panther became an endangered species.

Grand Canyon experiment. On March 6, 1996, the U.S. Bureau of Reclamation opened the gates of the Glen Canyon Dam on the Colorado River upstream from Grand Canyon National Park in northeast Arizona. The river flowed unimpeded by the dam for one week in an effort to restore habitats downstream in the park. The water flowed at a rate of 1,275 cubic meters (45,000 cubic feet) per second—fast enough to fill Chicago's 110-story Sears Tower in just 17 minutes.

Before the Glen Canyon Dam was completed in 1964, the Colorado was a dynamic river that fluctuated with the seasons, rainfall, and the runoff from side canyons. These conditions created sandbars and backwater areas where many species lived. After the dam became operational, it generated electricity for the area. But in so doing, it greatly reduced the normal downstream flow of sediment-enriched water through the huge canyon. As a result, beaches eroded along the lower Colorado River, and many wildlife habitats deteriorated.

The renewed flow was expected to restore backwater areas, which is the habitat of the humpback chub, an endangered species of fish. The increased flow was also expected to create new beaches as well. Interior Secretary Babbitt said that the Glen Canyon Dam release represents the first attempt under a new federal policy to manipulate water flow into the Grand Canyon for environmental and conservation purposes rather than to suit the needs of power companies.   [Eric G. Bolen]

In WORLD BOOK, see CONSERVATION.

Notable scientists and engineers who died between June 1, 1995, and June 1, 1996, are listed below. Those listed were Americans unless otherwise indicated.

Asch, Solomon (1907-Feb. 20, 1996), Polish-born social psychologist whose research on the effects of social pressure on individual thought shaped the field of social psychology. During World War II (1939-1945), Asch studied the effects of propaganda, concluding that propaganda is most effective when people are fearful and ignorant. He believed that humans would, however, behave morally if properly informed. Asch produced a classic study on human conformity in 1951 that influenced the work of others.

Chandrasekhar, Subrahmanyan (1910-Aug. 21, 1995), astrophysicist, born in colonial India, who shared the 1983 Nobel Prize in physics for research on the evolution and death of stars. Chandrasekhar was best known for his work on white dwarf stars—the compact final state in the evolution of certain stars. Chandrasekhar discovered that white dwarfs with a mass 1.4 times greater than the mass of our sun collapse from their own gravity. Eventually, they become neutron stars—stars with the density of an atomic nucleus—or collapse even further to become black holes. The maximum mass a white dwarf star can have before it begins to collapse is known as the Chandrasekhar limit.

Hanford, William E. (1908-Jan. 27, 1996), industrial chemist whose work led to the development of polyurethanes, a type of tough, chemical-resistant plastic. In 1936, working for E.I. du Pont de Nemours & Company, Hanford and his colleagues developed the first method for linking organic molecules into long chains to produce polyurethanes. Hanford developed more than 120 patented items during his career. He directed projects that made Teflon into a commercially viable product and that led to the creation of the first liquid detergent.

Hawkes, Jacquetta (1910-March 18, 1996), English archaeologist and author of books about archaeology, geology, and the history of mankind. Her archaeological expeditions took her to Palestine, Ireland, and France, as well as around England. In her many books, Hawkes searched for humanity within science. She was also a poet and novelist

and, in collaboration with her husband, a playwright. She held several government posts. Her 1951 book, *A Land*, was based on her work as an archaeological adviser in Britain. Hawkes's books included *A Woman as Great as the World* (1953), a collection of fables and a science fiction novelette; *Providence Island: An Archeological Tale* (1959); *King of the Two Lands: The Pharaoh Akhenaten* (1966); and *Dawn of the Gods* (1968), a study of Greece in the Bronze Age.

Hill, Julian W. (1904-Jan. 28, 1996), research chemist who discovered nylon. In 1930, Hill was working for the Du Pont Company studying long chainlike molecules called polymers when he noticed that a material that he and his colleagues had formulated had a remarkable stretching quality. The new material became known as nylon and has been used in many products, including stockings, parachutes, rope, and tents.

Keller, Fred S. (1899-Feb. 2, 1996), behavioral psychologist and early associate of behaviorist B. F. Skinner. Keller was the author of the Personalized System of Instruction, or Keller Plan, introduced in 1964, which divides college courses into units that students master at their own pace with the help of tutors. Keller also created the so-called code-voice method of teaching Morse code in the armed forces, a method that speeded training by about a third and came to be widely used. Keller also wrote several textbooks on psychology and education.

Langsdorf, Alexander (1912-May 24, 1996), physicist who produced the plutonium used to make the first atomic bomb, exploded in 1945 as a test in the New Mexico desert, and the third bomb, dropped on Nagasaki, Japan, near the end of World War II. (The Hiroshima bomb was made with uranium.) The plutonium—some of the first usable samples of that radioactive element—was produced with a *cyclotron* (atom smasher) that Langsdorf and a colleague had built. After the first sustained nuclear chain reaction at the University of Chicago in 1942, Langsdorf was one of the chief designers of the first nuclear reactor. Opposed to using the atomic bomb in World War II, Langsdorf was among 70 scientists to petition President Harry Truman not to employ the weapon.

Subrahmanyan Chandrasekhar

Jacquetta Hawkes

Julian W. Hill

Fred S. Keller

Jonas Salk

Julian Samora

McIntire, Ray (1918-Feb. 2, 1996), chemical engineer for the Dow Chemical Company who invented the material trademarked by Dow as Styrofoam. Styrofoam, a form of *polystyrene*—a colorless, transparent plastic—is used in many products from cups to building materials to flotation devices. In the early 1940's, McIntire was trying to develop a rubberlike polymer to be used as a flexible insulator. He combined styrene with isobutylene, a volatile liquid, and discovered that the styrene had formed a polymer. But the isobutylene had evaporated, leaving a polystyrene foam 30 times lighter and more flexible than existing polystyrene materials.

Packard, David (1912-March 26, 1996), electrical engineer and cofounder of the Hewlett-Packard Company of Palo Alto, California, the second-largest computer company in the United States after the International Business Machines Corporation (IBM). Packard and his partner, William Hewlett, began their company in a garage in 1938 with $538. Their first products were electronic testing and measuring devices. The company invented the first hand-held calculator and many other products. The company also became a model of innovative and successful management techniques. Packard, one the nation's wealthiest men, left most of his money to the David and Lucille Packard Foundation, making it one of the nation's largest charitable trusts.

Salk, Jonas (1914-June 23, 1995), research scientist who developed the first effective vaccine against poliomyelitis in the early 1950's. Epidemics of polio had been common, and victims of the disease were often left paralyzed. In 1953, Salk announced the development of a trial polio vaccine, which he tested on himself, his wife, and their three sons. It was further tested on 440,000 schoolchildren in 1954. In April 1955, the vaccine was pronounced safe and effective, and it was soon being widely used. From 1963, Salk was the director of the Salk Institute for Biological Studies in La Jolla, California. In addition to his work on poliomyelitis, Salk added significantly to the understanding of influenza.

Samora, Julian (1920-Feb. 2, 1996), well-known Mexican American sociologist and a leader in Mexican American studies. After growing up in southern Colorado, where he was often exposed to ethnic taunts, Samora decided to combat prejudice and work for Mexican Americans. In 1953, he became the first-known Mexican American to earn a doctorate in sociology and anthropology. Samora produced many research papers on the status of Mexican Americans and attracted many students to the subject while a professor of sociology at the University of Notre Dame in Indiana.

Smoluchowski, Roman (1911-Jan. 12, 1996), physicist, born in the Austro-Hungarian Empire, who studied the structures of both atoms and planets. As a professor of solid-state physics trying to understand how materials interact on a microscopic scale, Smoluchowski realized he could look to the field of astrophysics for his answers. He saw, for instance, that studying the structure of a large planet can lead to a better understanding of how atoms and molecules interact under conditions of high temperature and pressure. Smoluchowski escaped Warsaw, Poland, at the outbreak of World War II with the assistance of the Jewish underground and then took a position offered to him by Princeton University in New Jersey. Smoluchowski served on advisory boards for the U.S. Department of Defense and the Oak Ridge National Laboratory.

Solomon, Gustave (1931-Jan. 31, 1996), mathematician whose work influenced the computer revolution. In 1960, Solomon and Irving S. Reed invented what became known as the Reed-Solomon codes. The codes are used to get rid of errors that occur in the transmission or storage of digital information—that is, information encoded as a series of 0's and 1's. The Reed-Solomon codes have been used in spacecraft, compact discs, digital audiotapes, and high-definition television systems.

Walton, Ernest Thomas Sinton (1903-June 25, 1995), Irish nuclear physicist who shared the 1951 Nobel Prize in physics with Sir John Cockcroft for their work on *transmuting* (changing) atomic nuclei by bombarding them with subatomic particles. They jointly discovered the phenomenon of transmutation in 1932, and they constructed the first *particle accelerators* (atom smashers). Their work confirmed physicist Albert Einstein's theory that mass and energy are equivalent. [Mary Carvlin]

Three drugs offering a new approach to the treatment of AIDS (acquired immunodeficiency syndrome) were approved by the United States Food and Drug Administration (FDA) in late 1995 and early 1996. The drugs are the first members of a class of anti-AIDS drugs called protease inhibitors that researchers hope will significantly prolong the lives of AIDS patients.

The first of the drugs, saquinavir—sold under the trade name Invirase—was approved in December 1995. Ritonavir, marketed under the name Norvir, and indinavir, sold under the name Crixivan, won approval in March 1996.

Previously, the only drugs approved for combating AIDS were nucleoside analogues, such as zidovudine (also known as AZT). Both nucleoside analogues and protease inhibitors hinder the ability of the AIDS virus to reproduce within cells, but they do so at different stages in the virus's reproductive process.

In clinical studies, protease inhibitors reduced symptoms and raised survival rates for patients with advanced cases of AIDS. The FDA also approved the use of the drugs to delay the development of symptoms and prolong the lives of patients with less advanced cases of the disease, though further research is needed to confirm these benefits.

The new drugs also appear to reduce the amount of HIV—the virus that causes AIDS—detectable in the blood. And they boost levels of crucial disease-fighting cells of the immune system that are reduced by HIV infection. In clinical studies, protease inhibitors reportedly produced only mild side effects in relatively few patients.

Questions remain about the drugs' long-term effectiveness, which, like that of nucleoside analogues, may decrease over time. Patients who benefited most from the new drugs took both a protease inhibitor and a nucleoside analogue. Medical researchers expressed hope that the combination of drugs would provide a double-barreled approach to delaying and reducing the damage to the immune system caused by the AIDS virus.

Treatment for Lou Gehrig's disease. The first effective drug for the treatment of amyotrophic lateral sclerosis (ALS) received approval from the FDA in December 1995. ALS, whose cause is poorly understood, is a rare and fatal disease that gradually destroys the nerves that control the muscles. It affects about 25,000 Americans. ALS patients generally survive three to five years after being diagnosed with the disease. ALS is also known as Lou Gehrig's disease, after the famous baseball player who died of it in 1941.

Clinical studies of the new drug, called riluzole—marketed as Rilutek—indicated that it slows the rate of deterioration of muscle strength and extends the survival of some ALS patients with a form of the disease that begins with the nerve cells in the brain. Another form of the disease that begins with nerve cells in the spinal cord was less responsive to the new drug.

Researchers are as uncertain about how riluzole slows deterioration and extends life as they are about the biochemical cause of ALS. Some evidence suggests that the drug interferes with the action of an amino acid that stimulates nerves controlling muscles. That amino acid, investigators think, may be present in excessive amounts in ALS patients.

Osteoporosis treatment. The first of a new class of drugs that appear to build bone tissue in patients with osteoporosis, a condition in which there is a progressive loss of bone mass, won FDA approval in October 1995. Osteoporosis affects an estimated 25 million Americans, most of them women.

This disabling and sometimes life-threatening disorder results from an imbalance in the body's bone replacement cycle. In healthy young adults, the amount of bone broken down by the body generally equals the amount rebuilt. But in patients with osteoporosis, bone breakdown outpaces bone replacement. Bones weaken and become more prone to fracture.

The new drug, alendronate sodium—marketed under the name Fosamax—belongs to a class of drugs that slow the biochemical processes that cause bone to break down and so help the body's bone-building cells restore bone tissue lost to osteoporosis. The drugs may provide an alternative to the hormone estrogen, widely used to treat patients with osteoporosis. Although effective in preventing and slowing the progress of the disease, estrogen increases the risk of

Thalidomide Makes a Comeback

Thalidomide, a drug that gained worldwide notoriety in the early 1960's when it was linked to severe birth defects in thousands of children, was in the news again in 1995 and 1996—with a surprising new spin. Many researchers were exploring whether thalidomide could benefit patients with some diseases that had no effective treatment.

When thalidomide was introduced as a sedative in 1957 by a West German pharmaceutical firm, sales of the drug soared in dozens of countries, spurred by its apparent virtues: It was inexpensive and nonaddictive, and even large overdoses of the drug were not lethal. But thalidomide was never approved for sale in the United States, largely because of safety concerns raised by an official at the U.S. Food and Drug Administration.

Not long after thalidomide became available, Europe experienced a rise in the number of children born with a rare birth defect that resulted in missing or stunted limbs. A 1961 study pinpointed thalidomide as the cause of these defects, and the drug was quickly withdrawn from the world market. Health experts estimated that 10,000 women took thalidomide during the critical second month of pregnancy when arms and legs begin to form in the fetus.

Despite four years of clinical research on thalidomide in West Germany, it became evident that the drug had not been sufficiently tested before being placed on the market, because these studies had not revealed that the drug interfered with the growth and development of a fetus. Later research found that thalidomide interferes with the body's synthesis of folate, a vitamin necessary for rapidly growing fetal tissue, and that it also may block the development of new blood vessels crucial to the development of a fetus's arms and legs. These effects, investigators concluded, were responsible for the abnormal limbs of babies exposed to the drug in the womb.

Just a few years after thalidomide's tragic effects on developing fetuses became known, however, a surprising new use for the drug emerged. In 1965, an Israeli doctor who had given the drug to patients with leprosy to ease pain and sleeplessness found that their conditions improved dramatically. Today, thalidomide is the treatment of choice for many patients with leprosy.

Since the mid-1980's, thalidomide has also shown promise as a treatment for a host of other difficult-to-treat diseases. These include tuberculosis; certain *autoimmune disorders* (diseases in which the immune system attacks the body's own tissues), such as rheumatoid arthritis; ulcerative colitis, a condition (possibly also caused by an autoimmune reaction) involving inflammation of the colon and rectum; and Behçets syndrome, a rare disorder that causes recurrent mouth ulcers and other symptoms. Researchers have also discovered that the drug helps prevent a sometimes fatal side effect of bone marrow transplantation, when transplanted marrow cells attack tissues in the recipient's body it perceives as "foreign."

Ongoing research also indicates that thalidomide may be a useful treatment for late-stage symptoms of AIDS: painful sores of the mouth and esophagus and *wasting* (severe weight loss). Moreover, laboratory studies have shown that the drug prevents some of the cells infected with HIV—the virus that causes AIDS—from producing new copies of the virus. But whether the drug will actually slow the spread of HIV in infected individuals is unknown.

While the precise mechanism for thalidomide's beneficial effects is unknown, researchers at Rockefeller University in New York City discovered in 1989 that the drug decreases the body's production of a protein called tumor necrosis factor-alpha (TNFa). This protein, named for its anticancer effects, plays a key role in regulating the body's immune response.

TNFa is involved in initiating inflammation, which is one of the ways the body fights infection. But when this protein is present at low levels for excessively long periods—as it is in patients with AIDS, cancer, and other chronic diseases—it is associated with the wasting that accompanies those diseases. Because thalidomide effectively decreases TNFa levels, scientists believe it might prove useful in treating these debilitating illnesses. Other diseases or processes that involve inflammation, such as diabetes and infections, also represent potential targets for thalidomide.

Another effect of thalidomide—the drug's ability to inhibit the growth of blood vessels—may be helpful in treating other conditions. Researchers in 1995 and 1996 were exploring whether the drug might help prevent two eye diseases, diabetic retinopathy and macular degeneration, by inhibiting the uncontrolled growth of tiny blood vessels in the back of the eye that can result in vision loss. Other ongoing animal studies were examining whether the drug could help "starve" tumors that require blood vessels for their growth.

Will thalidomide rise like a phoenix from the ashes of its dark history to help patients with such conditions? Or will it be replaced by new drugs that offer similar benefits without thalidomide's risks and reputation? Only time—and further research—will tell. [Robert J. Linhardt]

Countering bone loss

A new drug called alendronate sodium slows the process of *osteoporosis*—loss of bone mass—and helps patients build new bone. The drug works by inhibiting the action of bone-destroying cells called osteoclasts.

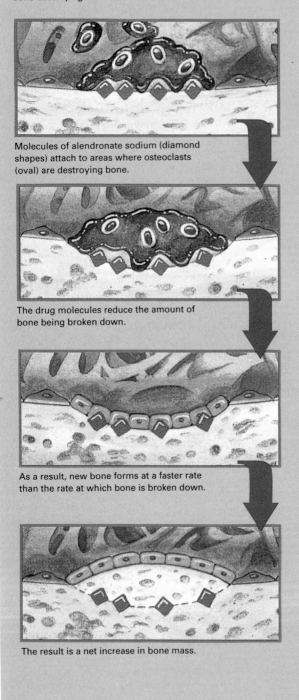

Molecules of alendronate sodium (diamond shapes) attach to areas where osteoclasts (oval) are destroying bone.

The drug molecules reduce the amount of bone being broken down.

As a result, new bone forms at a faster rate than the rate at which bone is broken down.

The result is a net increase in bone mass.

cancer of the uterus and may also increase the risk of breast cancer.

In clinical studies, alendronate sodium appeared to restore the balance between bone formation and destruction by slowing the rate at which bone was broken down. As a result, more bone was rebuilt than was destroyed. Researchers reported that the drug reduced the risk of new spinal fractures. Side effects were generally mild.

Drugs for diabetes. Two new drugs for reducing high blood sugar levels in people with Type II diabetes became available in late 1995. Type II diabetes, also known as non-insulin-dependent diabetes mellitus or adult-onset diabetes, is characterized by the body's inability to properly use the hormone insulin. Insulin regulates the amount of *glucose* (blood sugar) entering body cells.

In people with Type II diabetes, some glucose enters the cells, but most builds up in the blood. High blood sugar levels may cause a variety of complications, including blurred vision and kidney and nerve damage.

About 16 million people in the United States have Type II diabetes, which typically occurs in overweight people over 40. The primary treatment for patients with this illness consists of a well-planned diet, weight control, and exercise. If blood sugar levels remain high, however, medication may be required.

One class of drug used to treat Type II diabetes stimulates insulin production by the pancreas, thus making more insulin available to move glucose from the bloodstream into the cells. In December 1995, the FDA approved a new member of this class, glimepiride, marketed under the name Amaryl. The new drug is more powerful than other drugs of its type and works over a longer period.

A second new drug approved for the treatment of Type II diabetes in September 1995 takes a different approach to reducing blood sugar levels. That drug, acarbose, marketed under the name Precose, helps to lower blood sugar levels by blocking the absorption of glucose from the intestinal tract. Acarbose inhibits enzymes responsible for breaking glucose down into smaller fragments, which are then absorbed into the blood. (See also MEDICAL RESEARCH.)

[Thomas N. Riley]

In WORLD BOOK, see DRUG.

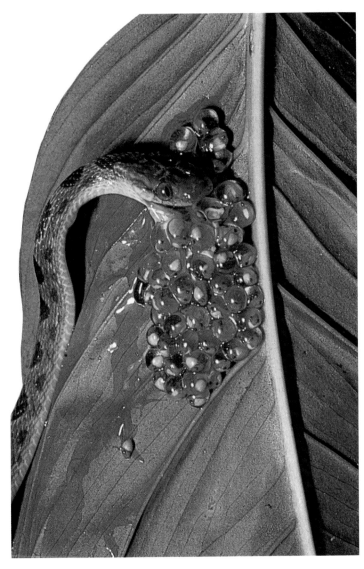

A cat-eyed snake bites into a favorite food—a jellylike clutch of red-eyed tree frog eggs deposited on a leaf overhanging a pond. Biting causes the tough jelly mass to vibrate. This alerts the embryonic tadpoles to danger, causing some to hatch early and slide down toward the water to escape the hungry predator. This unusual survival mechanism was reported in August 1995 by Karen Warkentin, a graduate zoology student at the University of Texas at Austin. Warkentin said the frog eggs have to be at least five days old to respond to a snake attack by hatching early. In experiments, eggs not under attack stayed on a leaf for up to 10 days before hatching.

Canadian ecologists reported a landmark study in August 1995—they announced that they had discovered the cause of mysterious population fluctuations known as the snowshoe hare cycle. Ecologists have long been interested in solving this puzzle, in which snowshoe hare populations increase from low numbers, reach very high numbers, and then decrease again over a 10-year period. Theories to explain the phenomenon have ranged from disease to sunspot cycles, which also occur over periods of about 10 years. The only other such population cycle known in nature involves voles (field mice), which takes only four years to complete.

Landmark study. Ecologist Charles J. Krebs and his colleagues at the University of British Columbia in Vancouver and other Canadian universities began a large-scale study of snowshoe hares in 1987. Their "laboratory" was the *boreal* (northern) forests of the Yukon Territory in northern Canada, just one area in the Northern Hemisphere where the cycle takes place. During a cycle, environmental factors change as the density of snowshoe hares change. Krebs chose to manipulate two of these factors in his experiment—the availability of food and the number of predators.

To accomplish this, the ecologists mapped out five sections of forest, each one measuring 1 square kilometer (0.4 square mile) in area and spaced at least 1 kilometer (0.6 mile) apart. Each square was subdivided into smaller squares about 30 meters (100 feet) on a side. Three of the large squares were designated as control areas in which no manipulations would be made.

In the remaining two large squares, the investigators fertilized the plant life and provided additional food for the hares to test the effect of abundant food on the hare population. They surrounded one of those squares with an electric fence to keep out mammal predators and strung fishing line over part of it to exclude owls and hawks. This section was to test the effects of increased food and exclusion of predators, though the netting failed to keep out all the birds. The scientists captured, tagged, and released hares in the control and experimental areas every March and October for eight years.

Krebs found that the exclusion of

Honey bee ball of death
A ball of about 400 Japanese honey bees encases a giant Japanese hornet, *top,* that had invaded their hive to carry off honey bees to feed to hornet larvae. The closely packed honey bees cause the hornet's body temperature to rise to 47 °C (116.6 °F), high enough to kill the hornet but not the bees, *bottom.* The temperature of a ball of bees remains at the lethal high for about 20 minutes on average, according to Japanese scientists from Tamagawa University in Tokyo who reported these findings in 1995. They said the giant hornet can kill European honey bees, which have not evolved this defensive behavior, at the rate of 40 a minute by seizing and biting them with its mandibles.

predators doubled the hare density compared with the control populations. Increased food supply tripled the hare population compared with the controls. But the greatest increase in hares occurred in the section with both increased food supply and no predators. There, hare densities were an average of 11 times greater than in the control areas. The ecologists said the experiment demonstrated that neither lack of food nor predation alone could account for the snowshoe hare cycle. A combination of those factors must be the cause, they concluded.

But the results of the experiment were not all so clear-cut. For example, in some sections with increased food supply and no predators, hare populations declined slightly rather than increasing. Krebs attributed this to either the fact that some hawks and owls were able to get through the fishing-line barrier or, less likely, that some unknown factor was at work. The investigators also could not explain why hare populations remained low for three or four years after bottoming out. At the end of a decline, there should be ample food for the hares and low numbers of predators.

Frogs in forest fragments. General ecological theory suggests that species diversity—the relative numbers of species in a given area—is dependent on the size of a habitat. The larger the habitat, the greater the species diversity, and conversely, the smaller the habitat, the fewer the species. However, an international research team studying frog species in patches of Amazon forest reported in July and August 1995 that frog species diversity increased in patches of forest left after ranchers and farmers cleared the surrounding land for agricultural use.

The study data covered the last 10 out of 15 years of a study called the Biological Dynamics of Forest Fragments Project, begun in 1979 by ecologist Thomas Lovejoy, now at the Smithsonian Institution in Washington, D.C. Lovejoy wanted to discover how large a reserve needed to be to save frog species, known to be in decline nearly worldwide.

Lovejoy had established patches from 1 to 100 hectares (2.5 to 250 acres) in size in the rain forest near Manaus, Brazil. The international team of ecologists took up the study in the mid-

heaviest hours of usage, from about 2 p.m. to 10 p.m.

Solar cell efficiency record. Energy engineers in Colorado reported in March 1996 that they had obtained a record efficiency for thin-film *photovoltaic* (PV) cells. PV cells, also called solar cells, are panels that convert sunlight into electricity. Thin-film PV cells are so named because they are about 30 times thinner than the most common type of PV cells, called crystalline silicon cells.

A solar cell's efficiency measures the percentage of sunlight striking the cell that is turned into electricity. Thin-film PV cells are about 2 percent less efficient than crystalline silicon cells. But energy engineers predict that thin-film cells hold the most promise for wide-scale use because they are cheaper, more flexible, and easier to make than crystalline silicon.

The new efficiency record was announced by researchers at the National Renewable Energy Laboratory in Golden, Colorado. They reported that they had developed a thin-film photovoltaic cell with an efficiency of 17.7 percent. The previous efficiency record was 17.1 percent.

The ability of PV cells to produce electricity directly from sunlight results from the *photovoltaic effect.* The photovoltaic effect is a phenomenon in which the energy in sunlight causes electrons to flow through layers of a conductive material to produce a useful electric current.

PV cells are made with two thin layers of extremely purified silicon, the material used to make computer chips. Different chemicals are added to each layer as it forms so that an electric field exists where the two layers meet. When a ray of sunlight strikes the PV cell, the sunlight dislodges electrons from the silicon atoms. The electric field forces the freed electrons from the bottom layer into the top one, creating a useful electric current.

PV cells are usually constructed in panels that are arranged in groups called arrays. The cells are used mostly in remote areas, where extending electric power lines would be too difficult or too costly. PV cells are used to operate such devices as remote weather stations, irrigation pumps, and ocean navigation aids.

Huge methane hydrate deposits. Scientists in November 1995 confirmed the existence of a huge deposit of methane hydrates beneath the ocean floor off the coast of South Carolina. Methane hydrates are tightly packed ice crystals containing methane gas molecules. The newly discovered deposit, one of the largest ever found, lies in sediment beneath the sea floor about 320 kilometers (200 miles) east of Charleston, South Carolina, in an 8,000-square-kilometer (3,000-square-mile) area called the Blake Ridge.

Methane hydrates are created from methane gas excreted by bacteria when they digest *phytoplankton* (tiny aquatic plants) and the flesh of other decayed organisms. The gas dissolves and forms crystals in the cold waters and extreme pressure at the bottom of the ocean. Scientists estimate that the energy in methane hydrate deposits under the ocean floor in many parts of the world may be double that contained in all the Earth's other known deposits of *fossil fuels* (coal, oil, and natural gas).

Geologists had estimated that the Blake Ridge deposit contains as much as 37 trillion cubic meters (1,300 trillion cubic feet) of methane gas, about 60 times the estimated 1996 U.S. consumption of natural gas. But those estimates were derived indirectly by bouncing sound waves off the ocean floor. Different kinds of sediments produce different patterns of reflected sounds, and scientists wanted a more accurate picture of the extent of the deposit.

To confirm the amount of methane in the deposits, marine geologist Charles Paull of the University of North Carolina in Chapel Hill led a group of scientists aboard the research ship *JOIDES Resolution* to take sediment samples of the gas deposits. The scientists found that 1 to 8 percent of the sediment layer contained methane hydrates, an amount roughly equal to previous estimates.

Despite the potential of methane hydrates as an energy source, significant obstacles to their commercial use exist. Reduced surface pressure releases the methane from the ice crystals, and scientist have not figured out a way to capture it efficiently.   [Pasquale M. Sforza]

In WORLD BOOK, see ENERGY SUPPLY; SOLAR ENERGY.

The successful mass production of the world's smallest micromotors that can do work was announced by engineers at the Sandia National Laboratories in Albuquerque, New Mexico, in March 1996. The devices, which consist of a motor about one millimeter square—the thickness of a paper clip—linked to electronic control circuitry, have many potential uses, including in activation systems for automobile air bags and miniature pumps that continuously deliver medication to the body.

The micromotors drive external gears 100 times thinner than a sheet of paper and smaller in diameter than a human hair. The gears turn at the rate of 200,000 revolutions per minute.

Both the micromotors and their electronic controls are built using the same fabrication techniques used to produce silicon computer chips. The motors' microscopic electrical contacts, gears, linkages, and other components are chemically carved or etched onto wafers of silicon. The unneeded silicon is then removed, leaving only the motor. Mass production is thus simple and inexpensive. Thousands of fully assembled and completely operational micromotors can be produced in a single batch.

New concrete technology. A new construction technology called Cubic-Crete, based on the use of a special cement additive, was planned for use in the construction of 1 million low-cost homes in South Africa. The agreement was announced by American and South African officials in August 1995.

The Cubic-Crete System was developed by researchers at Grassroots Technology Group, a company in White Plains, New York, devoted to producing energy-efficient, low-cost housing and creating jobs for semiskilled workers in the process. Cubic-Crete consists of a liquid latex *polymer* (a long, chainlike molecule) mixed with ordinary cement.

The polymer additive binds cement together strongly, producing a concrete with superior properties. According to Michael Byfield, managing director of Grassroots Technology, the polymer-modified material resists cracking because the additive prevents the it from expanding and contracting with temperature changes. Byfield said that buildings constructed with Cubic-Crete are waterproof, fireproof, hurricane and earthquake resistant, and safe from termites, mold, and mildew. He claimed they can also save owners 30 to 60 percent in heating and cooling costs and are four times as strong as a typical wood-frame home.

The cement-polymer mixture was first used mainly to repair in-ground swimming pools. But builders and engineers at Grassroots Technology later incorporated it into a construction system using foam-coated plastic panels reinforced with steel bars. Workers either spray the material onto the panels or apply it with a trowel. The coated panels form walls and other structures usually built from wood framing in a standard house. Three workers can build a typical Cubic-Crete home in about two weeks.

Stronger wood. Civil engineers from the University of Maine at Orono began monitoring the world's first ocean pier built of "fiber wood" in September 1995. Fiber wood, a new, extremely strong and light construction material, may make it possible to use low-grade timber for many construction projects.

To create fiber wood, researchers coat wooden beams with a thin layer of fiber-reinforced plastic (FRP), a plastic strengthened by minute strands of glass, carbon, ceramic, or other fibers. FRP has long been used in airplane and automobile components, tennis racquet frames, and other products.

According to Habib Dagher, an associate professor of civil engineering at the University of Maine and the developer of fiber wood, FRP greatly increases the strength of wooden beams. A 30-centimeter (12-inch) hemlock beam becomes 50 percent stronger when coated with about 13 millimeters (½ inch) of FRP. The beams are made by gluing together 2-by-4's, construction boards about 5 centimeters (2 inches) thick and 10 centimeters (4 inches) wide. While an ordinary hemlock beam can support about 3,600 kilograms (8,000 pounds), the fiber-wood beam can support 5,300 kilograms (11,750 pounds).

The 38-meter (124-foot) pier, located at Bar Harbor, Maine, will be used to test the feasibility of making wider use of fiber wood. Habib believes that fiber-wood beams will last longer and cost less than ones made of corrosion-prone steel because they require no painting and little maintenance. The demonstration

Bright lights

Space Hall at the National Air and Space Museum in Washington, D.C., *right,* is brightly illuminated by a new lighting system developed by Fusion Lighting of Rockville, Maryland. Just three "light pipes" spanning the ceiling, each lit by a single sulfur bulb at one end, provide three times as much light in the hall as 94 mercury-vapor fixtures once did, museum officials said in 1995. They said the new system was also producing a 25-percent energy savings.

The golfball-sized sulfur bulb, *left,* dwarfed by the conventional high-intensity bulb next to it, is one of the most energy-efficient light sources ever developed, according to Fusion Lighting. The quartz bulb contains a pinch of sulfur mixed with argon gas. When the bulb is bombarded with microwaves from a device called a magnetron, the sulfur becomes "excited" and emits a brilliant white light.

pier may help open new markets for wood in heavy construction projects such as bridges and commercial and industrial buildings.

Largest synthetic diamond. Engineers at the University of Florida in Gainesville announced in February 1996 that they had created the world's largest synthetic diamond. The diamond weighed 1,600 carats, or 320 grams (11.5 ounces), and had the shape of a thin disk—a diamond film— 30 centimeters (1 foot) in diameter and 1.5 millimeters (0.06 inch) thick.

James Adair and his associates made the diamond—which, like all diamonds, consists of crystallized carbon—by depositing carbon vapor on a *substrate* (surface) coated with crystals that served as "seeds" for the diamond's growth. This approach produc-ed the unusually large diamond film.

Diamond film is used to make protective coatings for cutting tools and other surfaces. Diamond is also an excellent conductor of heat, so diamond films may one day be used to remove heat from computer chips. But their cost will have to come down before they can find wide use in such an application.

Advances in optics. A major advance in producing lenses, prisms, and other optical devices was announced by mechanical engineers at the University of Rochester in September 1995. These devices are used in airplane guidance systems, laser printers, fax machines, supermarket check-out scanners, cameras, and many other applications.

John Lambropoulos, a professor of mechanical engineering and materials science, and his associates developed the first technique to predict how different kinds of glass will respond to grinding. Grinding, which gives a piece of glass the shape necessary to precisely focus light rays, is a key step in making precision optical components. It prepares glass for polishing, which removes tiny cracks and other imperfections that make the surface hazy and prone to breakage.

Craftsmen have always relied on experience and trial-and-error when grinding the more than 250 kinds of glass used in optical devices. When working with an unfamiliar kind of glass, they often spoil many pieces of it before finding the right grinding procedures. Lam-

bropoulos and his team found a way to eliminate the guesswork by noting that just two properties—hardness and resistance to fracturing—determine how a specific type of glass will hold up during grinding. The researchers plan to develop a master list of specifications on both characteristics for each type of glass. Technicians will then be able to enter the specifications for a particular kind of glass into a computerized grinding machine and immediately produce high-quality ground surfaces.

Auto stability control system. A new automotive safety system that prevents vehicles from skidding out of control on sharp or slippery curves was introduced on a Mercedes-Benz sedan in November 1995. Similar systems are being developed for other domestic and foreign cars and will be adapted for use in buses and trucks as well.

Experts said that the new antiskidding technology, developed by Robert Bosch GmbH and Mercedes-Benz AG, both of Stuttgart, Germany, can help drivers recover from skids and prevent deaths and injuries resulting from single-car spinouts. Such spinouts account for about 4 percent of all traffic deaths that occur each year.

Stability control systems use electronic sensors that calculate—1,000 times each second—whether a car is going in the direction in which the driver is steering. If the car is going in a different direction, the system concludes that a skid or spinout is underway and corrects the car's path by adjusting engine speed and applying an individual wheel brake. While antilock brake systems prevent skids when the driver applies the brakes, stability control systems operate independently of the driver, and more quickly. They can react in about 40 thousandths of a second, 7 times faster than the average human.

Improved milking machines. The development of a new, energy-saving device for use in milking cows was announced in February 1996 by engineers at Cornell University in Ithaca, New York. According to David Ludington, professor of agricultural and biological engineering, the device controls vacuum levels on milking machines. The vacuum is used to draw milk from a cow's udders.

Electric pumps on milking machines

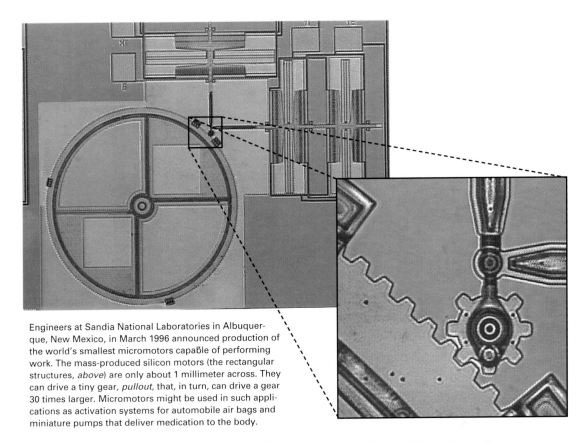

Engineers at Sandia National Laboratories in Albuquerque, New Mexico, in March 1996 announced production of the world's smallest micromotors capable of performing work. The mass-produced silicon motors (the rectangular structures, *above*) are only about 1 millimeter across. They can drive a tiny gear, *pullout*, that, in turn, can drive a gear 30 times larger. Micromotors might be used in such applications as activation systems for automobile air bags and miniature pumps that deliver medication to the body.

operate throughout the day on some dairy farms and are a major expense in the production of milk. They often run at maximum capacity to compensate for vacuum leaks, which occur when the udder attachments on milking machines fall off a cow's udder. The new device monitors the milking system's vacuum and adjusts pumps to run only as fast as necessary. If the vacuum strength decreases during milking, the device sends a signal that increases the speed of the pumps. Research on dairy farms in New York and Hawaii showed that the device could save farmers as much as half of the cost of milking.

Careers in engineering. Many jobs will be available in coming years for those interested in engineering as a career, according to a report published in January 1996 by the American Association of Engineering Societies (AAES). The report, based on data from the U.S. Bureau of Labor Statistics, predicted that more than 865,000 new jobs for engineers and engineering managers will open by the year 2005. Most of the jobs will be in computer and data processing consulting companies, research and de-velopment laboratories, and management and accounting firms.

Computer engineering and engineering and scientific management were the two specialties projected to grow most rapidly. By 2005, computer engineering will replace mechanical engineering as the second largest specialty, the report predicted. Electrical and electronic engineering will remain the largest specialty. If the projections are accurate, more than 40 percent of all engineers will work in computer and electrical engineering by 2005. Relatively little growth will occur in manufacturing, once the most important engineering sector.

In a report in October 1995, AAES estimated that more than 1 million bachelor's degrees in engineering and related fields like computer science are awarded around the world each year. The estimate were the first ones ever made for the entire world. Russia produced the most engineers, followed by China, Japan, the United States, Ukraine, Germany, India, the Philippines, South Korea, Mexico, the United Kingdom, France, and Brazil.   [Michael Woods]

In WORLD BOOK, see ENGINEERING.

Frequent exposure to elevated levels of some common pesticides may weaken people's immune systems, making them more susceptible to infectious diseases. That conclusion was reported in March 1996 by two investigators, Robert Repetto and Sanjay Baliga, of the World Resources Institute (WRI), an environmental research organization based in Washington, D.C.

Repetto and Baliga based their finding on a comprehensive study of scientific reports from the former Soviet Union, eastern European and Baltic countries, and Canada. Most of the studies examined the effect of pesticides on the immune systems of animals. But two studies—one in Chisinau, Moldova, and the other from the Hudson Bay region in northern Canada, looked at the effects of pesticides on the human immune system.

Some of the pesticides studied included chlorine-containing substances called organochlorines and compounds called organophosphates, which contain phosphorus. One common organophosphate, malathion, is used by farmers to protect their crops against many insects. DDT, a well-known organochlorine, is also used to combat a variety of insects. But DDT has been banned in the United States and Canada since the 1970's because scientists found that it caused certain birds to lay eggs with thin shells, resulting in the death of chicks. There was also concern over DDT's role as a possible cancer-causing agent in human beings. Many other countries still permit the use off DDT, however.

The Chisinau study found that concentrations of T cells, types of disease-fighting white blood cells, fell in people in proportion to their exposure to pesticides. In an ongoing study cited in the WRI report, Inuit (Eskimo) children who were breast-fed milk containing high levels of organochlorines faced a highly elevated risk of infection. Some Inuit children's immune systems had weakened so much, according to Repetto, that they were unable to make *antibodies* (disease-fighting molecules of the immune system) in response to vaccinations.

CO's effect on the heart. Federally permissible levels of carbon monoxide may worsen the condition of many people who suffer from congestive heart failure. That was the conclusion of a study reported in October 1995 by epidemiologist Robert D. Morris of the Medical College of Wisconsin in Milwaukee. About 3 million Americans suffer from congestive heart failure, a condition in which the heart weakens and is unable to pump blood efficiently. Congestive heart failure leads to the build-up of fluids in the lungs and can be fatal if not treated.

Morris compared hospital admissions for heart failure in seven major U.S. cities (Chicago, Detroit, Houston, Los Angeles, Milwaukee, New York, and Philadelphia) over a four-year period with daily records of air pollution levels in the same cities. He found that admissions for heart failure among people with heart disease increased when carbon monoxide levels rose. The increase in admissions occurred regardless of the levels of other air pollutants, such as sulfur dioxide or ozone, according to Morris. The study showed that between 2 and 11 percent of admissions for heart failure could be traced to elevated carbon monoxide levels.

Combustion of *fossil fuels* (coal, oil, gasoline, or natural gas) in trucks, buses, automobiles, and power plants releases carbon monoxide. The gas is odorless and colorless, and it binds to hemoglobin, an oxygen-carrying protein found in red blood cells. By binding to hemoglobin, carbon monoxide lowers the oxygen-carrying capacity of the blood. This, in turn, causes the heart to beat faster. In patients suffering from heart disease, carbon monoxide places additional stress on the heart.

The current standard for carbon monoxide levels in the United States is 8 parts per million. (One part per million equals .0001 percent of a volume of air). Regulators base current standards for carbon monoxide exposure in the United States on the pollutant's ability to stimulate *angina* (chest pain) in susceptible people. Since physical exertion causes angina, reduced oxygen in the blood brought on by higher carbon monoxide levels makes it easier for angina to occur.

Admissions for heart failure rose 20 to 40 percent for each 10-parts-per-million rise in carbon monoxide levels, according to Morris. The increase in admissions began even when carbon monox-

An oil tanker lies stranded in January 1996 near the Trustom Pond National Wildlife Refuge near Green Hill, Rhode Island. The tanker leaked 3.1 million liters (820,000 gallons) of home heating oil onto the shores surrounding the refuge and into the Atlantic Ocean, killing thousands of lobsters and dozens of ducks and other birds.

ide levels were well below federal safe limits, indicating that there seemed to be no threshold below which carbon monoxide's negative influence vanished, he said. If further research confirms Morris's results, some researchers believe, it may be necessary to lower federal air pollution standards for carbon monoxide.

Plant bacteria clean up oil spills. Plants—or, rather, the bacteria around them—may have the ability to clean oil spills, according to a July 1995 report by Kuwaiti scientists. Terrestrial oil spills such as those resulting from the sabotage of oil wells during the 1991 Gulf War in Kuwait cause considerable damage to plants and wildlife. But botanist Samir Radwan and his colleagues at the University of Kuwait in Safat found that bacteria found in soil around the roots of certain plants can break down oil in moderately polluted soils.

Radwan's team found that desert wildflowers belonging to the same family as sunflowers (*Compositae*) flourished around the edges of oil lakes where the sand contained less than 10 percent oil by weight. No plants grew in more severely polluted sand. According to the researchers, toxic compounds in the oil should have killed the plants, but the scientists found the plants' roots healthy and free of oil.

The researchers found that bacteria in the sand around the wildflowers' roots broke down and *metabolized* (used as energy) toxic *hydrocarbon* molecules (molecules containing hydrogen and carbon) in the oil. The researchers said that the roots of the wildflowers release sugars, *amino acids* (molecular building blocks of proteins), oxygen, and vitamins that promote bacterial growth. But oil also appeared to stimulate the growth of the petroleum-eating bacteria, Radwan said.

Lead danger for adults. A study reported in April 1996 suggests that long-term exposure to levels of lead considered safe for adults may lead to *hypertension* (high blood pressure). Researchers led by environmental toxicologist Howard Hu at the Harvard School of Public Health in Boston reported the study.

Hypertension is an elevated pressure of blood against blood vessel walls that results from a narrowing of blood vessels. Hypertension raises the risk of many serious disorders, including heart disease, *stroke* (an interruption of normal blood flow to the brain resulting from a burst or blocked blood vessel), blindness, and kidney damage.

Scientists have known for many years that high concentrations of lead can delay mental development and stunt physical growth in children. For this reason, the U.S. government forbids lead in gasoline, paint, and food and issues guidelines for acceptable levels of lead in children's blood. The government's permissible level of lead in children's blood is 10 micrograms (10 millionths of a gram) per *deciliter* (tenth of a liter).

Few studies exist on lead's long-term effects on adults, but scientists generally believe that adults are less susceptible than children to lead. The permissible lead level in adults' blood is 40 micrograms per deciliter.

To test the connection between long-term exposure to lead and hypertension, Hu used advanced X-ray equipment to measure the concentration of lead in the bones of 590 middle-aged to elderly men. He also measured their blood pressure for four years. Bone tests more accurately reflect long-term exposure to lead than blood tests because lead stays in bone longer, according to the researchers.

Hu found that the men with the highest lead levels in their bones were 1.5 times more likely to have high blood pressure than those with the lowest lead levels. High lead levels were also more closely related to high blood pressure than other traditional risk factors, including cigarette smoking, drinking, and high salt intake.

When Hu measured the blood levels of the men, he found that they were far below the generally recognized danger level. The men's blood lead levels ranged from less than 1 microgram per deciliter to 26 micrograms per deciliter. These levels represent the average American's exposure to lead since about 1950, Hu said.

[Daniel D. Chiras]
In WORLD BOOK, see ENVIRONMENTAL POLLUTION.

Fossil Studies

One of the mysteries of life on Earth is the relatively late appearance of *metazoans* (multicelled organisms). These animals are thought to have appeared as much as a billion years later than single-celled organisms. Why did this evolutionary step take so long, and why was the subsequent proliferation of animal species, known as the Cambrian Explosion, so rapid? In July 1995, biogeochemist Graham Logan of the Australian Geological Survey Organization presented a new explanation for the enigma of the Cambrian Explosion.

Logan argued that about 580 million to 540 million years ago—toward the end of Precambrian time and just before the beginning of the Cambrian Period—multicellular organisms developed a digestive system. They captured food from the water, processed the food, and then eliminated unusable remains. According to Logan, the evolution of feces was the trigger for the Cambrian Explosion.

In late Precambrian time, the sea was populated mostly by simple organisms such as bacteria, algae, and single-celled plankton. Algae and blue-green bacteria that lived near the surface of the sea underwent *photosynthesis*, a process in which the energy of sunlight is used to produce food from carbon dioxide (CO_2) and water. Other types of bacteria *metabolized* (converted into energy) the remains of these organisms. In the process, the bacteria used up much of the oxygen produced as a by-product of photosynthesis. Also, little food made its way to the sea floor.

When multicelled organisms with digestive systems appeared, they ate the photosynthesizing organisms and "packaged" the leftover organic matter into fecal pellets that were dense enough to sink rapidly to the sea floor, thus depriving the bacteria of their food source. The resulting decrease in the bacteria population left more nutrients available in the seawater. It also freed up large amounts of oxygen, which escaped to the atmosphere and accumulated to levels that allowed new animals to evolve.

A completely different explanation of the Cambrian Explosion was proposed in June 1995 by paleontologist Geerat

Nesting dinosaur

The fossilized skeleton of a small predatory dinosaur called *Oviraptor,* crouched on a nest of eggs, *below,* was discovered by American fossil hunters in Mongolia's Gobi Desert, according to a December 1995 report. The 80-million-year-old fossil provides the first strong evidence of parental care among dinosaurs.

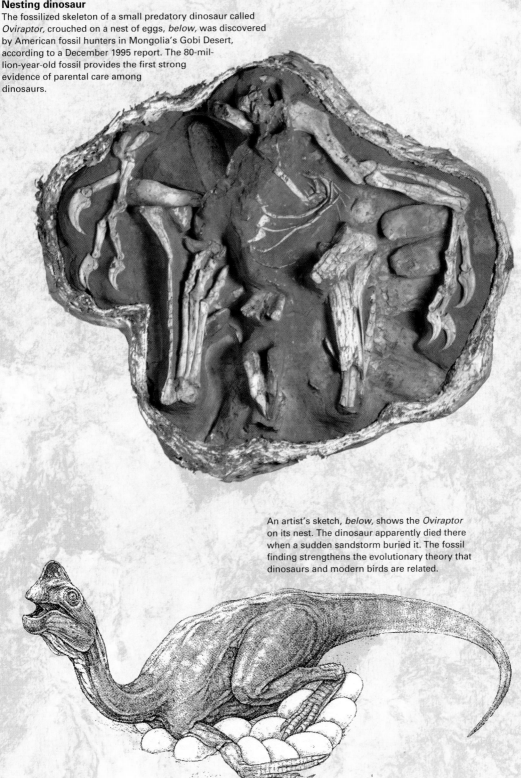

An artist's sketch, *below,* shows the *Oviraptor* on its nest. The dinosaur apparently died there when a sudden sandstorm buried it. The fossil finding strengthens the evolutionary theory that dinosaurs and modern birds are related.

New Titans from the Dinosaur Age

About 90 million to 100 million years ago, during the Cretaceous Period, giants ruled the plains of southern Argentina and northern Africa. In 1995 and 1996, paleontologists announced the discovery of fossils from two fearsome *carnivores* (meateaters) that would have outweighed the somewhat later *Tyrannosaurus rex*, previously the largest-known land-dwelling predator. Also found were fossils from a *herbivore* (plant-eater) that may have towered over *Ultrasaurus*—the previous recordholder among herbivores—and fossils from what may have been the fastest-known large predator. That carnivore, found in the Sahara in Morocco, was built for speed with unusually long and slender limbs. Named *Deltadromeus agilis* (agile delta runner), it was 8 meters (26 feet) long and had a running stride of about 3 meters (10 feet).

The first of the new fossil finds were made in Argentina. In September 1995, scientists led by paleontologist Rodolfo Coria of the Carmen Funes Museum in Plaza Huincul, Argentina, reported finding about 70 percent of the fossilized skeleton of a huge predator, named *Giganotosaurus carolinii*, that walked upright on powerful hind legs. Its massive head, which was about 1.5

meters (5 feet) long, was equipped with saberlike teeth up to 20 centimeters (8 inches) long, with *serrations* (sharp notches) on their cutting edges.

From the *femurs* (thigh bones), which are useful for estimating height and weight, Coria calculated that *Giganotosaurus* was about 13 meters (43 feet) long and weighed up to 8 metric tons (9 short tons). The femurs are about 5 centimeters (2 inches) longer than those of the largest known *T. rex* fossil. If these estimates are correct, *Giganotosaurus* would have weighed almost 2.7 metric tons (3 short tons) more than *T. rex*, which lived about 70 million years ago in North America.

Coria also reported finding the pubic bone and lower jaw of a huge herbivore whose fossilized bones he has been excavating for several years. Slightly older than *Giganotosaurus*, it is named *Argentinosaurus huinculensis*. Among the fossils recovered were seven *vertebrae* (spinal bones), each weighing up to 1.8 metric tons (2 short tons). Although Coria has not found a femur, he unearthed a *tibia* (shin bone) and, from it, estimated that *Argentinosaurus* may have weighed about 100 metric tons (110 short tons), measured 30 meters (100 feet) long, and stood 7 meters (23 feet) at the shoulder. Such an animal would have outweighed what had been the largest-known dinosaurs, *Seismosaurus* and *Ultrasaurus*, which lived about 180 million years ago in North America.

The discovery of a skull and teeth from a dinosaur called *Carcharodontosaurus saharicus* (sharktoothed reptile of the Sahara), an equally large

At a May 1996 press conference in Washington, D.C., University of Chicago paleontologist Paul Sereno is framed by a model of the dinosaur skull he discovered in Morocco. The skull came from a huge meat-eater called *Carcharodontosaurus,* which lived about 90 million years ago. The awesome predator, bigger and heavier than the legendary *Tyrannosaurus rex,* was one of several huge dinosaurs whose fossilized bones were found in 1995 and 1996.

African cousin to *Giganotosaurus*, was reported in May 1996 by paleontologist Paul Sereno of the University of Chicago, the discoverer of *Deltadromeus*. Previously known only from a few bones unearthed in 1927, *Carcharodontosaurus* was also found in Morocco. The skull is 1.6 meters (5.3 feet) long with teeth 13 centimeters (5 inches) in length.

Sereno estimated that *Carcharodontosaurus* was about 14 meters (45 feet) long and weighed about as much as *Giganotosaurus*. But both he and Coria believe *T. rex* was taller, had more powerful jaws, and could run faster than *Carcharodontosaurus* or *Giganotosaurus*. It also had a brain that was about twice the size of those dinosaurs' brains.

Despite having some general similarities to the younger *T. rex*, *Giganotosaurus* and *Carcharodontosaurus* were apparently more closely related to each other than to that famous predator. The huge carnivores may have been overgrown descendants of the significantly smaller *Allosaurus*, a North American predator that lived about 150 million years ago, during the Jurassic Period.

The suggestion that these dinosaurs were close cousins runs counter to widely accepted theories about the breakup of Pangaea, an ancient supercontinent that millions of years ago included all of Earth's major land masses. Most geologists think that by 150 million years ago, South America and Africa had already separated from North America and were well on their way to splitting from each other. But if *Giganotosaurus*, which lived 100 million years ago, and *Carcharodontosaurus*, which lived 90 million years ago, were as closely related as scientists think, Africa and South America must have remained connected longer than believed.

The huge carnivores are also fueling the debate over whether dinosaurs were warm-blooded or cold-blooded. (Warm-blooded animals maintain a constant body temperature regardless of their surroundings.) In recent years, the theory that dinosaurs were warm-blooded has increasingly gained scientific support. However, some recent studies, including a November 1995 report that dinosaurs lacked a nasal bone common to all living warm-blooded animals, have argued against true warm-bloodedness in dinosaurs.

The enormous predators may have been able to maintain a nearly constant body temperature simply because of their size. Indeed, their bulk argues against warm-bloodedness. Paleontologist James Farlow of Indiana University-Purdue University in Fort Wayne, Indiana, calculated that to maintain the high bodily energy production of a warm-blooded animal, these dinosaurs would have had to eat almost constantly. That requirement would have limited their populations to unrealistically small numbers. [Carlton E. Brett]

Vermeij of the University of California at Davis. Vermeij linked major evolutionary changes in both the Cambrian Period and the late Jurassic and early Cretaceous periods (170 million to 100 million years ago) to an increase in underwater volcanic eruptions. The volcanic gases, especially CO_2, bubbled up to the atmosphere and had a warming effect on the climate. CO_2 is a so-called greenhouse gas—its presence in the atmosphere helps trap heat from the sun, just as the glass of a greenhouse does.

Ash emitted by surface volcanoes counteracts this phenomenon by blocking sunlight. But in the case of underwater volcanoes, ash would stay in the seawater and so would not produce its cooling effect. Vermeij argued that greenhouse heating of the earth greatly increased rates of biochemical reactions, which led to major evolutionary developments.

Oldest multicellular fossils. Evidence that multicellular organisms may have evolved much earlier than previously believed was reported in October 1995 by paleontologists Zhu Shixing and Chen Huineng of the Chinese Academy of Geological Sciences in Tianjin, China. Scientists had thought that multicellular organisms first appeared about 900 million years ago. But the Chinese researchers claimed to have found fossils of multicellular algae that lived 1.7 billion years ago.

The researchers reported that fossils of small leaflike plants, found in *shale* (rock formed from hardened clay or mud) east of Beijing, represent brown algae, a group that includes modern kelp and other seaweeds. If so, the new fossils are about 800 million years older than the next-oldest fossil seaweeds.

Were dinosaurs cold-blooded? Anatomical evidence suggesting that dinosaurs were *ectothermic* (cold-blooded) was reported in November 1995 by John Ruben, a physiologist at Oregon State University. The key to Ruben's theory is a thin sheet of cartilage or bone called the *basal turbinate*, found in the noses of all living mammals and birds, which are warm-blooded animals.

The turbinate bone is considered critical in controlling the loss of heat and water from animals' bodies and therefore in maintaining constant body temperatures. The turbinate is found not

The world's longest set of dinosaur tracks was discovered in summer 1995 by American researchers. Found in central Asia, the 150-million-year-old footprints of *Megalosaurus* (a general term for large, little-known meat-eating dinosaurs) are about 45 centimeters (18 inches) long on the average. The main set of prints is about 310 meters (1,020 feet) long. The tracks are the same age as similar ones found in North America, supporting the theory that 150 million years ago Asia and North America were connected, enabling dinosaurs to roam freely across the huge region.

only in present-day warm-blooded animals but also in fossil birds up to 70 million years old and all mammal and mammallike reptile fossils as old as 250 million years. But dinosaurs lacked these bones. On this basis, Ruben argued that dinosaurs were ectotherms, and that they probably maintained nearly constant body temperature because of the large bulk of their bodies.

Nesting dinosaurs. Paleontologist Mark Norell of the American Museum of Natural History in New York City in December 1995 reported a new fossil finding at a site long famous for dinosaur eggs—the Flaming Cliffs of the Gobi Desert in Mongolia. Norell discovered an 80-million-year-old skeleton of an adult dinosaur called *Oviraptor* crouched on a nest of eggs. A sudden sandstorm had apparently buried the nesting dinosaur alive.

Oviraptor was a small, ostrichlike predatory dinosaur that was once thought to have raided the nests of other dinosaurs to obtain eggs—*Oviraptor* means "egg stealer." But embryos preserved in the eggs proved that they belonged to *Ovi-*

raptor. The *Oviraptor* fossil found by Norell provided evidence of parental care among dinosaurs and strengthened the evolutionary theory that modern birds and dinosaurs are related. Many paleontologists believe that the egg *brooding* (incubating) habits of birds were inherited from dinosaurs.

New chordate discovered. In October 1995, a team of paleontologists, led by Jun-yuan Chen of the Nanjing Institute of Geology and Paleontology, reported the discovery of a remarkable 525-million-year-old animal fossil. The fossil, found in a Cambrian Period fossil bed in the Yunnan province of China, is about 2 to 4 centimeters (0.8 to 1.6 inches) long. It clearly shows the mark of a *notochord,* a rod of cartilage that supported a nerve cord.

The fossil, which was named *Yunnanozoon,* is thus clearly a *chordate,* a member of the group of organisms that possess a notochord at early life stages. This group includes the *vertebrates* (animals with backbones). *Yunnanozoon* is about 10 million years older than *Pikaia,* a fossil from the Burgess Shale in Cana-

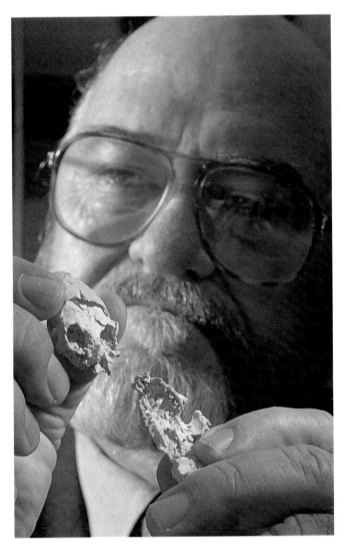

Paleontologist Elwyn Simons of Duke University in Durham, North Carolina, holds fossilized skull fragments of a squirrel-sized monkey called *Catopithecus*, which may be the oldest ancestor of apes and human beings. Simons reported in June 1995 that he had discovered the 36-million-year-old fossils near Cairo, Egypt. *Catopithecus* had features such as joined forehead bones and bony eye sockets, which indicate that it belongs on the evolutionary line leading to human beings.

da that had been considered the oldest chordate.

The oldest vertebrates. For many years, paleontologists have puzzled over *conodonts*, tiny toothlike fossils of now-extinct creatures that existed from late Cambrian to Triassic times (about 510 million to 220 million years ago). In 1995, these enigmatic creatures were confidently identified as chordates, and researchers concluded that they were probably vertebrates as well.

For many years, researchers had only the toothlike fossils to go on, but in 1982 a Scottish paleontologist found the fossil of a whole conodont animal in a museum drawer. The creature was eel-like and about 3 centimeters (1.2 inches) long, with a cluster of teeth at the front end. It also had the notochord and muscle bundles typical of chordate animals.

In April 1995, researchers at the University of Leicester in England reported the discovery in South Africa of a conodont fossil with preserved muscle tissue. This find revealed that conodonts had large rings of cartilage in their heads that almost certainly supported a pair of large eyes.

In light of the new discoveries, paleontologist Mark Purnell and his colleagues at the University of Leicester began making models of the conodont and then flattening them to simulate fossilized impressions. Purnell's team located places where the conodont teeth would come together if used in biting. They then examined fossil groupings of teeth and found that the teeth showed chipping and wear at just those contact points. They concluded that conodonts were eellike predators—vertebrates—that used their conelike teeth to grasp and bite.

Ancient frog and turtle fossils. Paleontologists in 1995 reported the discovery of a new fossil frog and several fossil turtles. The newly discovered frog, called *Prosalirus bitis*, was reported in September 1995 by vertebrate paleontologists Neil Shubin of the University of Pennsylvania in Philadelphia and Farish Jenkins of Harvard University in Cambridge, Massachusetts. The 190-million-year-old fossil was found in shale in Arizona, predating what had been the oldest-known fossil frogs by about 15 million years.

But the newly discovered frog was surprisingly advanced, with long, powerful hind legs and a flexible shock-absorbing pelvis. Like modern frogs, *Prosalirus* had no tail and was able to make long leaps.

Fossil turtles discovered in Argentina in 1995 provided the basis for researchers to reevaluate the origin of modern turtles. The 210-million-year-old fossils were the same age as turtle fossils found in Greenland, Germany, and Thailand, but they were found in Argentina, suggesting that turtles had spread widely early in their history. The discovery of the fossil turtles was first reported in May 1995 by paleontologist Guillermo Rougier of the American Museum of Natural History in New York City.

Fossils come to life? Amber, a hardened resin from conifer trees, has been shown to have remarkable preservational properties. But can bacteria from amber come back to life after being dormant for tens of millions of years?

Raúl Cano, a biogeochemist at California Polytechnic State University, contends that the answer to that question is yes. Since May 1995, Cano has painstak-

ingly cultivated bacteria, yeasts, and fungi extracted from the stomach contents of insects found in Dominican Republic amber. By mid-1996, Cano claimed to have revived over 2,000 of those species. But many microbiologists argued that Cano's "revived" species are just modern microorganisms that contaminated his experiments.

In April 1996, researchers also announced the first discovery of mammal bones preserved in amber. The partial backbone and ribs from a mammal that weighed about 142 grams (5 ounces) and was 10 to 12.5 centimeters (4 to 5 inches) long were found in the Dominican Republic. The mammal, estimated to have lived from 18 million to 29 million years ago, probably ate insects and may have been related to the opossum.

The fossil mammal may help scientists understand when mammals arrived in the West Indies. The fossil indicated that mammals had lived there much longer than scientists had previously thought.   [Carlton E. Brett]

In WORLD BOOK, see DINOSAUR; PALEONTOLOGY.

Genetics

Researchers reported finding two defective genes in 1995 that may be responsible for virtually all cases of a common form of Alzheimer's disease. In June, Canadian researchers reported finding a defective gene that causes many cases of familial, or early-onset, Alzheimer's disease. In August, United States researchers reported finding another gene connected with the same form of the disease.

Alzheimer's disease is marked by the degeneration and death of *neurons* (nerve cells) in the brain. It causes a progressive deterioration of memory, reasoning powers, and judgment. There is no known cure for Alzheimer's disease, which afflicts an estimated 4 million people in the United States.

More than three-fourths of Alzheimer's cases strike people over age 65. The remaining cases strike younger people, most of them in their 40's or 50's. This early-onset or familial form of the disease has long been recognized as a genetic disorder that runs in families. The discoveries bring to four the number of genes scientists have linked to the

disease, including three linked to the early-onset form. The two newly discovered genes are thought to cause all but 2 to 3 percent of familial Alzheimer's cases.

In August 1995, two teams of geneticists announced the discovery of a gene called STM2 that accounts for about 20 percent of early-onset Alzheimer's cases. People who suffer from this form of Alzheimer's are sometimes called Volga Germans, because they are descended from a colony of ethnic Germans who lived in the Volga Valley of Russia in the 1700's and 1800's. Gerard Schellenberg of the Veteran's Affairs Medical Center and the University of Washington in Seattle led one team, and Rudolph Tanzi of Massachusetts General Hospital in Boston led the other team.

Schellenberg and Tanzi found the STM2 gene after investigating a clue uncovered by Canadian researchers looking for a separate gene, named S182, linked to a more common form of early-onset Alzheimer's. The researchers studied people with early-onset Alzheimer's as well as people who were unaffected.

In March 1996, Scottish researchers at the Roslin Institute in Edinburgh announced that they had *cloned* (produced without sexual reproduction) two sheep from a single sheep embryo. The scientists placed individual cells from the embryo into sheep egg cells from which the genetic material had been removed. They then implanted the egg cells into female sheep, where the cells developed normally. The researchers said the technique could be used to produce unlimited numbers of genetically identical sheep or other animals. The experiment marked the first time that scientists had cloned a large mammal.

Eventually, the investigators found a gene that was defective only in people with Alzheimer's.

Although the two genes have similar structures, they occur on different chromosomes, the structures that carry the genes. Human cells normally have 23 pairs of chromosomes, and the Canadian researchers found their gene on chromosome number 14. Schellenberg and Tanzi found STM2 on chromosome 1.

Researchers at the University of Toronto had announced the discovery of S182 in June 1995. Geneticist Peter St. George-Hyslop led the international research team that made the finding. According to the Canadian researchers, defects in S182 are responsible for about 80 percent of cases of early-onset Alzheimer's. The team identified the gene by studying seven families with a high incidence of early-onset Alzheimer's. The researchers identified five different *mutations* (changes) in the S182 gene that occurred only in family members with Alzheimer's.

Besides finding the S182 gene, the St. George-Hyslop team noticed that segments of its DNA—deoxyribonucleic acid, the molecule genes are made of—strongly resembled a DNA segment from an unstudied human gene they found in a computerized database of human DNA. Although the Toronto team did not know the location of the gene resembling S182, they suspected that it might play a role in the less common form of familial Alzheimer's seen in the Volga Germans.

Schellenberg and Tanzi located the gene on chromosome 1. They found that all of the afflicted members of the Volga German descendants in their study shared a defective form of the suspect gene. None of the unaffected family members had the defective gene.

The researchers said that one of the most noteworthy aspects of these two findings is that the new genes seem to have similar functions. Both genes seem to have a role in the build-up of beta amyloid, a gluelike protein found in abnormal levels in the nerve endings of Alzheimer's patients' brains. The excess protein destroys neurons. Scientists hope that finding these genes will lead to a better understanding of how Alzheimer's develops and to the development of drugs to block the production of beta amyloid in the brain.

AT gene. Israeli researchers in June 1995 announced the discovery of a gene responsible for a rare but devastating disease known as ataxia telangiectasia (AT). The researchers were led by geneticist Yosef Shiloh at Tel Aviv University. AT can cause many problems, including a balance disorder called ataxia, a high risk of certain cancers, and an extreme sensitivity to X rays. About 500 people in the United States have AT.

People normally carry two copies of the AT gene, and the disease develops when both copies are defective. The team from Tel Aviv University discovered the AT gene by isolating genetic mutations that occur only in people with AT. Researchers thus called the gene ATM for *AT M*utated.

The investigators were particularly interested in the role that the ATM gene may play in the development of some cancers. They found that the gene is very similar to some genes known to be important in controlling the growth of cells. Defects in such cells had previously been implicated in the development of some forms of cancer, which is uncontrolled cell growth.

About 38 percent of people with AT develop *leukemia* or *lymphoma* (cancers involving the production of abnormal white blood cells or lymphatic cells). Statistics also show that women with one copy of the defective AT gene are five times more likely to develop breast cancer than women with two normal copies of the gene.

New gene map. The most complete map to date of human chromosomes was announced in December 1995 by scientists at the Massachusetts Institute of Technology (MIT) in Cambridge. Geneticist Eric Lander of the Whitehead Institute for Biomedical Research at MIT led the international effort to produce the map.

The map provided more than 15,000 special landmarks called *sequence tagged sites* in human DNA. These sites are made up of particular sequences of nucleotides, the chemical building blocks of DNA. The landmarks are distributed throughout the 23 pairs of human chromosomes. The map did not show the location of specific genes, but it should give scientists a rough idea of where a given gene might be located and thus help track down the precise locations of the body's estimated 100,000 genes.

The new map was the latest of a series of genetic maps that researchers have compiled. Putting the new map together with the other maps will yield a more detailed picture of human chromosomes than was previously available. A complete map of human genes may be completed by the year 2005. Such a map should help in understanding many diseases in which genes are involved.

Other mapping milestones. Genetic researchers in the United States announced in July 1995 that, for the first time, they had worked out the genetic blueprint of an entire free-living organism, a bacterium called *Haemophilus influenza.* Geneticist Craig Venter at the Institute for Genomic Research in Gaithersburg, Maryland, led the mapping team.

In April 1996, an international team of researchers announced that they had completed mapping the genetic structure of the most complex organism to date—the yeast *Saccharomyces cerevisiae,* commonly called brewer's yeast. Yeast is a single-celled organism used to make bread, beer, and wine.

The project marked the first time that scientists had mapped all of the genes in an organism containing a nucleus. Such organisms, called eucaryotes, include all multicelled plants and animals. The yeast gene mapping took seven years to complete and involved research centers throughout Canada, Europe, Japan, the United Kingdon, and the United States.

The researchers discovered that brewer's yeast contains many genes resembling those found in other organisms, including humans. They planned to study the map for clues about human disease and evolution.

Designer Medfly genes. Scientists in Greece announced in December 1995 that they had discovered how to introduce new genes into the Mediterranean fruit fly. This insect, commonly called the Medfly, is one of the world's most destructive agricultural pests. A research group at the Institute for Molecular Biology and Biotechnology in Crete made the discovery. The achievement ended a long series of frustrating attempts to genetically alter an insect other than *Drosophila melanogaster,* the fruit fly commonly used in laboratory experiments.

Scientists expressed hope that the discovery will enable them to introduce genes into the Medfly that would control the pest, such as by inhibiting its reproduction. Until 1995, chemical pesticides had been the only way of combating the Medfly. Researchers also hoped that the same approach may work in other insects that plague human beings.

The Greek scientists introduced a gene that controls eye color in the Medfly. The researchers began with flies whose chromosomes contained an abnormal gene that made their eyes white instead of the normal multihued color. When the investigators introduced the normal version of the gene into Medfly embryos, the insects were born with normal-colored eyes.

Previous experiments had failed at delivering new genes into Medfly cells because scientists had not found an efficient method to incorporate the genes into the flies' chromosomes. The Greek researchers succeeded with a segment of DNA called a jumping gene from another fly species that was able to transport the new gene into the chromosomes of Medfly embryos.

Although the use of the eye-color gene served only as a "marker" to demonstrate that the gene-insertion technique had worked, the scientists were optimistic that it would be possible to introduce other, more useful genes in the same way. They said it might be possible, for instance, to introduce genes that would make male Medflies sterile.

Premature-aging gene found. In April 1996, researchers in the United States reported finding a gene that causes Werner's syndrome, a rare disease that results in premature aging. People with this disorder develop gray hair in their 20's and soon develop cancers, *cataracts* (clouding of the lens of the eye), heart disease, and other disorders of old age. People with Werner's syndrome usually die before age 50. Only about 500 people in the United States have Werner's syndrome, but scientists hope that the newly discovered gene will yield clues about what controls aging. Geneticists Gerard Schellenberg of the University of Washington in Seattle and John Mulligan of the Darwin Molecular Corporation in Bothell, Washington, led the research team that found the defective gene.

The researchers traced the gene, named WRN, to chromosome 8. They said that WRN is inherited recessively, meaning that a person must receive a defective copy of the gene from each parent before he or she gets the disease.

According to Schellenberg, the normal gene controls the production of an *enzyme* (a protein that speeds up biochemical reactions) called helicase. Helicase plays a vital role in uncoiling DNA molecules so that other enzymes can repair genetic damage and orchestrate DNA *replication* (reproduction). If helicase production is defective, DNA damage may not be repaired, and cells will not function properly.

The investigators studied genetic material from preserved tissue samples from families in which Werner's syndrome was prevalent to find the defective gene. They compared these samples with ones from unaffected people to confirm their finding.

Pancreatic cancer gene. In January 1996, a research team led by molecular biologist Scott Kern of Johns Hopkins University School of Medicine in Baltimore announced that they had found the gene responsible for more than 50 percent of pancreatic cancers. Although it is fairly rare, pancreatic cancer is devastating. Once diagnosed, half of the patients die within six weeks, and less than 1 percent survive for five years or more. About 25,000 people in the United States die from the disease each year.

The researchers found the gene by studying the chromosomes in tumor cells taken from people with pancreatic cancer. The scientists found that one small piece of chromosome 18 was consistently missing in cells from more than 90 percent of the tumors. But this small piece of the chromosome contained several genes, and only detailed comparisons of tumor cells from different patients revealed exactly which gene was responsible for pancreatic cancer.

The researchers called the gene DPC4 for *d*eleted in *p*ancreatic *c*ancer. The number 4 designates the fourth site on the chromosome that the scientists investigated. [David S. Haymer]

In WORLD BOOK, see CELL; GENETICS.

A 40-million-year-old boulder found in the Swiss Alps has challenged geological theory about the movement of rock between Earth's outer crust and the *mantle*. (The mantle is a layer of hot semimolten rock between the crust and inner core, extending from about 40 to 2,900 kilometers [25 to 1,800 miles] below the surface.) Mantle rock is rarely brought to the surface by geologic forces because it is denser than the crustal rock above it.

However, scientists led by geologist Larissa Dobrzhinetskaya of the University of California at Riverside reported in March 1996 that the Swiss rock came from a depth of at least 400 kilometers (250 miles). This distance is at least 100 kilometers (60 miles) greater than the original depth of any other rock ever found at the surface.

The boulder, which is about 800 meters (2,600 feet) long and 500 meters (1,600 feet) wide, was found on a Swiss mountain called Alpe Arami. It consists mainly of olivine, believed to be the most common mineral in the mantle.

The Alpe Arami olivine is most unusual, however. Sprinkled throughout are thousands of microscopic rods of ilmenite, an iron-titanium oxide. Normally, olivine's simple crystal structure is too small to incorporate titanium, which has a large crystal structure, even when subjected to great pressure and heat.

But, the scientists noted, laboratory studies have shown that at pressures encountered below 400 kilometers, olivine is transformed into another mineral, wadsleyite. Wadsleyite's crystal structure is large enough to incorporate significant amounts of titanium. This suggests that the Alpe Arami rock came from a depth of at least 400 kilometers. The scientists theorize that as the rock rose through the mantle and as temperatures and pressures fell, the wadsleyite was converted to olivine and the rods precipitated out of the olivine.

How did such a dense piece of rock rise through lighter rock to the surface? Dobrzhinetskaya and her colleagues theorize that when Europe and Asia collided about 50 million years ago, forming the Alps, some continental crust became sandwiched between slabs of mantle

A sonar image of the floor of the Mediterranean Sea southwest of the island of Crete shows (in blue) one of three underwater lakes filled with extremely salty water. The lakes, whose discovery was reported by geologists in August 1995, lie on the sea floor more than 3,300 meters (10,800 feet) below the surface, and they may explain why Mediterranean water is saltier than typical ocean water. The lakes formed when seawater dissolved deposits of salt-rich rocks on the sea floor. The U-shaped lake in the sonar image, named Urania, has an average depth of 80 meters (260 feet).

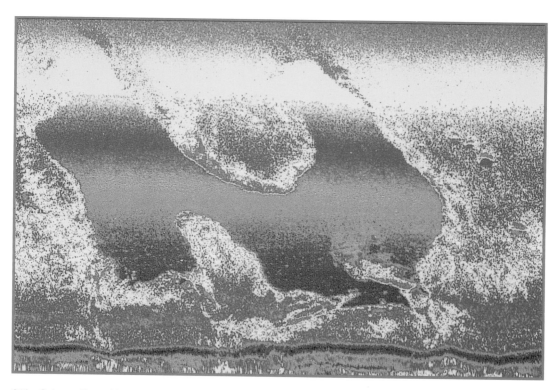

Shifting colors chart the shrinking of Mount Etna on the island of Sicily during the last half of an eruption from May 1992 to October 1993, according to a report published in June 1995. French researchers combined time-lapse radar pictures made by an orbiting satellite to create an image that reveals movement to within a fraction of an inch. Such images may improve scientists' ability to predict eruptions by monitoring the expansion of volcanoes as they fill with magma.

rock that underlay the continents. As the "sandwich" was pushed deeper into the mantle by the collision, the heat in the interior warmed and weakened the descending mantle rock. Eventually, the lighter crustal rock was able to slide out of the sandwich and bob back to the surface, bringing a sizable section of mantle rock—the Alpe Arami boulder—with it.

Sliding rocks. Ice may explain how rocks weighing up to 320 kilograms (700 pounds) have made strange tracks on the surface of the Racetrack, a lake bed in California's Death Valley National Park, according to a September 1995 report. The puzzle of the sliding stones, whose motion has never been witnessed, has long intrigued geologists.

The Racetrack is marked by dozens of tracks up to 100 meters (330 feet) in length. At the end of each track sits a boulder. Geologists have long assumed that the angular boulders were somehow blown across the extraordinarily level surface of the Racetrack when it was wet and slippery. The lake bed is usually dry but may be covered by up to

5 centimeters (2 inches) of water after winter rains.

However, experiments conducted in 1953 with a wind machine suggested that a wind blowing at least 180 kilometers (110 miles) per hour—rare in the area—would be needed to move blocks the size of those on the Racetrack. In 1955, a California geologist, George M. Stanley, suggested that wind might be able to push the rocks if they were embedded in the ice that sometimes forms on the surface of the water after a winter rain.

Between 1987 and 1994, geologists led by John B. Reid, Jr., of Hampshire College in Amherst, Massachusetts, visited the Racetrack seven times and produced detailed maps of the tracks. The geologists found that one major episode of rock movement occurred in the late 1980's and another in late 1992 or early 1993. They also noted that the tracks were often curved and marked by ridges and grooves, indicating that the stones did not rotate as they moved. In addition, they found that all the tracks from each episode of movement were parallel and displayed the same pattern of turns.

The geologists wet the lake bed and measured the force needed to move rocks of varying sizes. They confirmed that wind alone could not move the boulders. They concluded, however, that if the rocks became embedded in a thick sheet of ice floating on the surface of the water, wind could blow the ice and the rocks together as one piece across the lake bed.

Chesapeake crater. The seventh largest impact crater ever found on Earth lies buried beneath the southern half of Chesapeake Bay, according to a March 1996 report by an international team of scientists. The report also concluded that the crater, formed when a meteorite crashed into the Earth millions of years ago, is the long-sought source of distinctive bits of rock found across North America.

To find the crater and determine its structure, the scientists relied chiefly on seismic reflection profiling. In this technique, scientists beam sound waves into the Earth and then record echoes reflected off buried rock *strata* (layers).

The pattern of the echoes is then used to create an image of the buried rock.

The seismic profiles revealed that the crater is 90 kilometers (55 miles) in diameter and is buried from 300 to 500 meters (1,000 to 1,650 feet) below the floor of the bay. Comparisons of the crater's rock strata with strata exposed on land indicated that the crater was formed about 35.5 million years ago, at the end of the Eocene Epoch.

The scientists also retrieved rock samples from holes drilled into the crater. The samples indicated that the rock contains mineral grains that had been *shocked*, that is, subjected suddenly to very great pressure such as that occurring during a meteorite impact.

The authors of the report proposed that the Chesapeake crater is the long-sought source of the North American *tektites*. Tektites are small glassy rocks composed of previously melted bits of crustal rock. They form during a meteorite impact as the surface rock is crushed, melted, and thrown into space. The pieces of rock harden as they fall back to Earth over a broad area. The

One vast sheet of semimolten rock from Earth's mantle may feed volcanoes from the Canary Islands in the Atlantic Ocean to Mount Etna on the Mediterranean island of Sicily. Geochemist Kaj Hoernle of GEOMAR, a marine geology institute in Kiel, Germany, reported in 1995 that chemical analysis of volcanic rock and computerized scans of Earth's interior suggest that a sheet of hot rock extending 2,400 by 4,000 kilometers (1,500 by 2,500 miles) underlies the eastern Atlantic, northern Africa, and southern Europe.

North American tektites have been found in Late Eocene rock in parts of the United States and Canada. Tiny fragments of the tektites have been found as far away as Indonesia. Comparison of the chemical composition of the Chesapeake rock and North American tektites indicates the tektites were blasted out of the Chesapeake crater.

Permian extinctions. Contrary to common belief, Earth's forests should be counted among the casualties of the Permian Extinction, the greatest mass extinction in Earth's history. That conclusion was reported in March 1996 by an international team of scientists headed by paleobotanist Henk Visscher of Utrecht University in the Netherlands.

During the Permian extinction 245 million years ago, as many as 80 percent of all species of ocean-dwelling animals, as well as many species of land animals, were wiped out. Scientists had assumed, however, that most land plants had survived the die-off.

Visscher and his colleagues based their conclusion on the discovery of numerous specimens of normally rare fossilized saprophytic fungi in plant fossils. Saprophytic fungi live on decaying wood and other dead plant matter. The fungi fossils were found in sedimentary rocks from Italy and Israel dating from the Late Permian Period and the Early Triassic Period that followed. Abundant fossilized saprophytic fungi also has been found in Late Permian rock from every continent except South America. The presence of so much fungi, the scientists concluded, indicates that huge numbers of dead trees must have littered the Earth at that time.

The scientists linked the extinctions to massive volcanic eruptions in what is now Siberia that occurred at about that time. The outpouring of lava from those eruptions was so enormous that, if spread evenly, it would have covered the Earth's surface to a depth of 6 meters (20 feet). The eruptions would have boosted levels of atmospheric carbon, warming the climate. Sulfur and chlorine emitted by the eruptions would have produced acid rain that poisoned the air and water.   [William W. Hay]

In WORLD BOOK, see GEOLOGY.

Medical Research

Medical researchers made progress against several major diseases in 1995 and 1996.

Chemicals that fight AIDS. The isolation of three chemicals called chemokines, which are naturally produced by the immune system and may interfere with the activity of the human immunodeficiency virus (HIV), the virus that causes AIDS, was reported in December 1995 by Robert Gallo, a leading AIDS researcher. Gallo, who in 1996 became director of the Institute for Human Virology at the University of Maryland in Baltimore, isolated the chemicals while he was with the National Institutes of Health in Bethesda, Maryland.

The three chemical inhibitors, which are released by white blood cells, may be capable of blocking the *replication* (reproduction) of HIV. The substances had been sought by investigators since 1986, when evidence of their existence surfaced. Scientists dispute whether the chemokines could be used, at high dosage levels, to extend the lives of HIV-infected people who have not developed full-blown AIDS.

According to Gallo, the CD8 lymphocyte, a type of disease-battling white blood cell, secretes the three chemicals as a response to foreign substances in the body. Gallo claimed that the compounds, working together, interfered with HIV multiplication in a test tube.

Additional research may determine whether chemokines can play a role in drugs designed to enhance the immune system's ability to fight HIV. Some experts believe that it may be possible to synthesize the compounds for therapeutic use.

HIV proteins. In May 1996, Anthony S. Fauci, director of the National Institute of Allergy and Infectious Diseases in Bethesda, announced that institute scientists had discovered the "co-factor" protein necessary for HIV to gain entry into a human immune-system cell. Scientists have long known that for infection to take place—that is, for cell walls to be penetrated—the virus must find both a receptor molecule, called CD4, and a surface protein. The elusive protein uncovered by institute scientists was named fusin because it promotes fusion between the coating of the virus and the outer membrane of the immune system cell. The protein also facilitates the injection of the virus's genetic material into a cell. Fauci hailed the discovery as "a tremendous advance" in unlocking the basic biology of HIV. Understanding how the virus works may aid in the development and testing of new drugs and vaccines.

Breast cancer genes. In 10 percent of women with breast cancer, there is a family history of the disease. Research into the genetics of breast cancer accelerated after the 1994 isolation of the gene known as BRCA1. In families at high risk for breast cancer, women with *mutated* (changed) BRCA1 genes have an 80 to 90 percent likelihood of developing breast cancer. A study published in November 1995 suggested that a defective BRCA1 gene is also present in nonfamilial cases.

Researchers at the University of Texas Health Science Center at San Antonio confirmed that BRCA1 is linked to the inherited form of the disease by producing or encoding an abnormal protein. But in nonfamilial, or "sporadic," cases, mutations produce a normal-appearing protein that is unable to make its way into the nucleus of cells to do its work of regulating cell division. As a result, the protein permits, rather than suppresses, abnormal cell growth, which can result in breast cancer.

Studies carried out by investigators at Boston's Massachusetts General Hospital and Seattle's Fred Hutchinson Cancer Research Center, published in January 1996, evaluated the DNA of young breast cancer patients. The scientists discovered that the BRCA1 gene was flawed in a large number of the patients, including women with no family history of the disease. In women under age 30, the genetic defect was found in 38 percent of all cases of breast cancer among Jewish women and 8 percent of cases among non-Jewish women.

In December 1995, investigators at the Institute of Cancer Research in Sutton, United Kingdom, and at the Duke University School of Medicine in Durham, North Carolina, reported finding a second breast cancer susceptibility gene, which was named BRCA2. The gene is believed to be responsible for most familial breast cancers not related

to BRCA1, including many that occur at an early age.

Researchers believe that ongoing genetic research into breast cancer may result in the development of tests that could screen women for the genetic mutations associated with breast cancer. One pharmaceutical company announced that it expected to have a combined BRCA1 and BRCA2 genetic predisposition test available by 1997. In response, critics noted that while a genetic susceptibility to breast cancer might eventually be detectable, strategies for keeping a woman cancer-free remained uncertain.

Obesity gene. A gene that appears to play a role in obesity drew continued interest in 1995. The mutated gene, called *ob* (for obese), can cause weight problems if it is defective or absent. The gene was first identified in 1994 in mice. A similar gene was found in humans.

In July 1995, three groups of researchers—from Rockefeller University, in New York City; Hoffman-LaRoche International, in Nutley, New Jersey; and Amgen, Inc., in Thousand Oaks, California—announced that they had isolated a protein they thought was produced by the mouse *ob* gene. They found that the protein contributes to obesity.

The investigators named the protein leptin, from *leptos*, the Greek word for thin. After meals, they theorized, the human protein, if it is functioning normally, sends to the brain a fullness signal that suppresses appetite. According to this theory, the brain of obese individuals does not receive this important signal, either because the leptin protein is not functioning normally or because it is not present.

The three teams of researchers manufactured leptin and injected it daily into obese mice. Not only did the appetite of the mice wane, but the speed of their calorie-burning metabolism increased— they became more physically active, and their body weight decreased by 30 percent. Mice of normal size lost weight as well, but to a lesser extent.

Researchers have speculated that injections of leptin in overweight individuals could produce similar results. Pharmaceutical companies in 1996 had begun investigating the production of a leptin-based drug.

But scientists at Thomas Jefferson

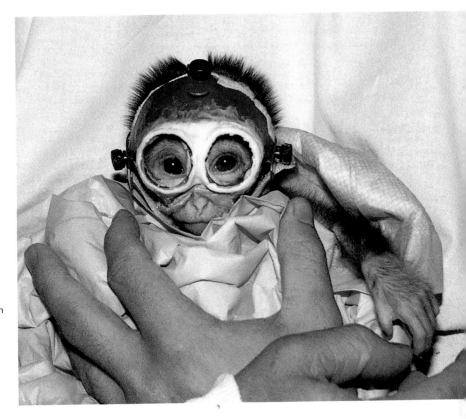

A three-week-old rhesus monkey at the University of Houston wears special glasses as part of an experiment on eye-growth control. Reporting on the experiment in 1995, University of Houston vision scientist Earl Smith said that eyes grow in such a way that the retina—the light-sensitive area at the back of the eye—is put in the right position for the most effective sight. He concluded that it may be possible to correct certain eye problems in infants and toddlers by fitting them with glasses that force the eye to develop in a particular way.

University in Philadelphia, in a study reported in February 1996, raised questions about the use of leptin in treating obese people. The group examined blood levels of the protein in 275 volunteers, approximately half of whom were obese. They found leptin at levels up to four times that in normal-weight people in approximately 95 percent of the individuals in the overweight group. The discovery led some weight-control researchers to speculate that the problem for many obese people may not be a lack of leptin but rather an insensitivity to the effects of the protein.

Cholesterol-lowering benefits. A long-term study at the University of Glasgow in Scotland, published in November 1995, concluded that reduced blood cholesterol levels saved lives among men who have never had heart disease. Earlier studies revealed that lowering cholesterol readings minimized the risk of heart attacks among people who already had heart disease by retarding or even reversing build-up of fatty deposits in the arteries. The new research demonstrated that reducing

cholesterol levels over time correlated with lowered risks of heart disease in healthy men.

The research involved approximately 6,600 men, aged 45 to 65 years, who appeared to be in good health but who had cholesterol levels between 250 and 300 milligrams per deciliter of blood and who were unable to control their cholesterol with diet. Approximately half of the men were placed on pravastatin, a cholesterol-reducing medication. The other half of the study group were given a *placebo* (inactive substance).

After five years, cholesterol levels among the men who had taken the medication had plummeted, on average, by 28 percent. The same group experienced an average of 31 percent fewer heart attacks, 28 percent fewer deaths from coronary artery disease, and a 22 percent lower overall mortality rate than the group given the placebo.

Hypertension treatment. Two studies published in August and September 1995 concluded that a commonly prescribed, short-acting form of a calcium-channel blocker called nifedipine can

Transplants from Animal Donors

At a time when the demand for transplantable human organs far exceeds the supply, a growing number of scientists are investigating the possibility of transplanting animal organs or tissues into human beings. Although much more research is needed before cross-species transplants can be anything but experimental, investigators were making considerable progress in 1995 and 1996.

Perhaps more than anyone, a patient with AIDS named Jeff Getty personified the promise and problems of cross-species transplants (called xenografts or xenotransplants, from the Greek work *xeno*, meaning *foreign* or *strange*). In December 1995, the 38-year-old Getty underwent an experimental xenotransplant at San Francisco General Hospital, receiving bone marrow from a baboon. It was a risky procedure aimed at saving or at least extending the life of Getty, who had tried all other available AIDS treatments without success. Bone marrow from a healthy donor contains cells capable of reconstituting the immune system, which is impaired in patients with AIDS.

Some doctors believed Getty's transplant had a chance of success, because baboon bone marrow cells resist becoming infected with the most common strain of HIV, the virus that causes AIDS. They hoped that the baboon's bone marrow cells infused into Getty's bloodstream would proliferate, revive his weakened immune system, and prevent a worsening of his condition. Prior to the transplant, Getty had undergone radiation treatments designed to further suppress his already impaired immune system to keep it from attacking the baboon cells.

Three weeks after the procedure, Getty was well enough to leave the hospital. In February 1996, however, doctors said that laboratory tests had detected no sign of baboon DNA (deoxyribonucleic acid, the molecule genes are made of) in Getty's blood, indicating that the transplanted baboon cells had failed to take hold. Nevertheless, for reasons that were not understood, Getty showed signs of improvement: He had gained about 4½ kilograms (10 pounds) and he had nearly three times the pre-transplant number of a type of disease-fighting white blood cell called CD4. Researchers were talking about fine-tuning the procedure and trying it again in other AIDS patients.

Many researchers and patients alike are counting on progress in cross-species transplants, particularly those involving organs that could save thousands of human lives a year. Medical experts estimate that about 40,000 people are currently on national waiting lists in the United States to receive transplanted organs, and that number is increasing. Many of those on waiting lists die every year before the organ they need becomes available. By one estimate, 20 to 30 percent of patients needing a new liver, for example, die before a donor organ becomes available.

Researchers have been working on xenotransplants for years. In a widely reported experimental treatment in 1984, doctors at Loma Linda University Hospital in Los Angeles transplanted a baboon heart into a 15-day-old infant known as "Baby Fae," who had been born with a devastating heart defect. Twenty days after the operation, however, the baby died when her immune system rejected the animal organ.

Although cross-species transplants are appealing because of their potential to alleviate the shortage of suitable organs for transplant, scientists face a number of challenges in turning this hope into reality. Rejection of an organ by the recipient's immune system remains one of the major problems with xenotransplants. Cells of the immune system may identify transplanted tissue as "foreign," and attack and destroy it—sometimes within minutes or hours. To minimize this danger, physicians must give the recipient drugs that suppress the immune system.

Scientists are also concerned about the risk that viruses or bacteria harbored by animals could present if the microorganisms make the leap from the animals to humans during transplants, perhaps posing a serious threat to public health. They note the potentially devastating nature of these microbes as they bridge species. For examples, they point to HIV and to the Ebola virus, a deadly microorganism that kills up to 90 percent of those it infects, both of which may have originated in African monkeys. Even viruses that are harmless in animals can turn lethal once they are transmitted to humans. In fact, when plans were being made for Getty's procedure, the U.S. Food and Drug Administration requested that a new baboon replace the original candidate, which carried numerous viruses.

Baboons had already been used by other transplant surgeons not long before Getty's procedure. In June 1992 and January 1993, at the University of Pittsburgh Medical Center in Pennsylvania, baboon livers were transplanted into two men who were gravely ill with severe viral hepatitis, but both patients died.

Some scientists are turning their attention to the use of pigs as potential organ donors. They believe that if viruses are present in donor pigs, those microbes would be less likely to thrive in

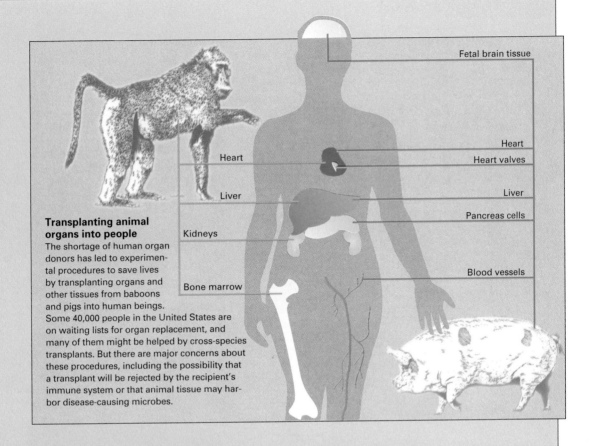

Transplanting animal organs into people

The shortage of human organ donors has led to experimental procedures to save lives by transplanting organs and other tissues from baboons and pigs into human beings. Some 40,000 people in the United States are on waiting lists for organ replacement, and many of them might be helped by cross-species transplants. But there are major concerns about these procedures, including the possibility that a transplant will be rejected by the recipient's immune system or that animal tissue may harbor disease-causing microbes.

Fetal brain tissue

Heart
Heart valves
Liver
Pancreas cells

Blood vessels

Heart
Liver
Kidneys
Bone marrow

human beings than viruses harbored by baboons or other primates, which are genetically closer to human beings. Pigs have other advantages as well: They are easier to breed than primates, and their organs are similar in size to human organs.

To further improve the likelihood of success, several teams of researchers have created genetically altered strains of pigs with organs that are less likely to be rejected by the human immune system. At the Duke University Medical Center in Durham, North Carolina, for example, researchers have injected human DNA into pig embryos. The pigs that develop from the embryos have both pig and human DNA in their cells. Presumably, organs from such pigs would be less likely to be rejected by the human immune system.

In 1995, to test this approach in animal transplant recipients, the Duke investigators implanted the hearts of three genetically altered pigs into baboons. The baboons survived for longer than would normally have been expected.

Scientists are also using pigs in other organ transplant studies. In Sweden, for example, specialized cells from the pancreases of pigs have been transplanted into humans with diabetes, a disorder in which the body fails to produce or

properly use the hormone insulin to regulate the level of sugar in the blood. The hope is that the pig cells will secrete insulin and help the patients maintain normal blood-sugar levels.

Researchers are also exploring the transplantation of brain tissue from pig fetuses into the brains of humans with serious brain disorders such as Parkinson's disease. Although human cells from the brains of aborted fetuses can also be used for these procedures, there is controversy, particularly in the United States, about the use of fetal tissue in medical procedures.

But xenotransplants have raised controversies of their own. Animal-rights activists have decried the use of animal organs for transplants, insisting that breeding animals for this purpose is cruel. Opponents of xenotransplants argue that the money used for these experiments would be better spent on public education to help prevent the diseases that the transplants are designed to treat.

As the debate continued, some analysts were predicting in 1996 that some pig-to-human transplants could begin later in the year. Xenotransplants with pig kidneys, they said, could move beyond the experimental stage by the year 2000.

[Richard Trubo]

actually increase the risk of heart attack and death. Calcium-channel blockers are a popular class of drugs used for the treatment of high blood pressure, or hypertension, as well as coronary artery disease and heart-rhythm irregularities.

The August study, led by Bruce M. Psaty of the University of Washington in Seattle, evaluated 2,655 patients who had been medicated for hypertension; 623 of the group had experienced heart attacks. The researchers found that the incidence of heart attacks was 60 percent greater in patients taking high doses of short-acting nifedipine rather than other antihypertensive drugs, such as diuretics or beta-blockers.

In September 1995, researchers directed by Curt Furberg at the Bowman Gray School of Medicine in Winston-Salem, North Carolina, pooled data from 16 earlier studies comparing 8,350 heart-disease patients, of whom part took nifedipine and part were given placebos. The researchers concluded that high doses of nifedipine increased the risk of death nearly three-fold. It was theorized that the risks associated with

the short-acting nifedipine stem from the drug's ability to produce rapid changes in blood pressure—a problem less common in long-acting versions of the drug.

Controversy raged around the conclusions of this research. As early as August 1995, the National Heart, Lung and Blood Institute advised physicians to prescribe the short-acting form of the drug "with great caution, if at all," particularly at higher doses. Nevertheless, in January 1996, an advisory committee to the U.S. Food and Drug Administration declared that calcium-channel blockers remain safe for hypertensive patients. Experts urged patients not to stop taking these medications, nor to adjust their dosages, without their doctor's guidance.

Diabetes advances. Researchers at the University of Massachusetts in Cambridge and Dartmouth Medical School in Hanover, New Hampshire, announced in October 1995 that they had halted diabetes in mice by successfully transplanting insulin-producing pancreatic cells from unrelated healthy donor

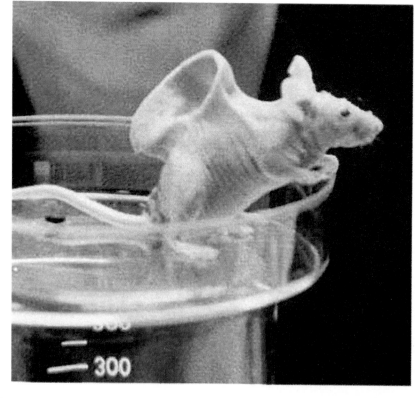

A laboratory mouse with a human ear growing under its skin provides a dramatic demonstration of progress in tissue engineering. The ear was made by seeding a biodegradable mold with human cartilage cells and then implanting the structure under the mouse's skin. The research, reported in October 1995, was conducted by scientists at the University of Massachusetts and the Massachusetts Institute of Technology. The ultimate aim is to replace lost body parts by stimulating the body into regenerating what is missing.

A previously obese mouse that was given injections of a newly discovered protein called leptin looks down at a still-fat mouse that did not get the protein. The mice have a flawed gene—called *ob*, for obese—that produces a faulty version of the protein. Discovery of the protein in July 1995 raised hopes that it could be used to control weight in people. But clinical research reported in February 1996 indicated that leptin would not become a "magic bullet" against fat.

mice. Antirejection drugs (used to suppress the immune system) were not employed in the procedure, thanks to a technique used to deceive the immune system of the mice into accepting the transplanted foreign tissue. The research was considered an important step toward a cure for diabetes. While some people have received transplants of insulin-producing cells, strong antirejection drugs, which produce significant side effects, have been needed.

The recipient mice were incapable of producing insulin because their pancreases had been incapacitated. The immune systems of some of the mice were then "trained" to accept transplanted pancreatic cells through injections of white blood cells from donor mice. They were also given an antibody (disease-fighting molecule), called anti-CD40L, that sufficiently disrupted the mice's immune systems to keep them from rejecting the transplanted material. A second group of mice was not given this treatment.

After seven weeks of the injections, the transplants were performed in both

groups of mice. Among those in the treatment group, 90 percent did not reject the new cells. The cells began making insulin, providing effective control of the diabetes. In contrast, the immune systems of the mice in the untreated group rejected the transplants.

Diabetes drugs. On another front in the control of diabetes, years of clinical trials have resulted in the approval of new oral medications for the treatment of Type II (noninsulin-dependent) diabetes. For the past two decades, the only oral drugs available for Type II patients belonged to a class of compounds called sulfonylureas. These drugs work by stimulating the pancreas to manufacture more insulin. Two new classes of medications have now been sanctioned for use by these patients.

In September 1995, the U.S. Food and Drug Administration (FDA) approved the production of acarbose, designed to slow the digestion of carbohydrates. This effect minimizes sharp increases in blood *glucose* (sugar) levels, which take place after diabetics ingest carbohydrates and certain other foods.

Another new drug, metformin, which received FDA approval in December 1994, works by preventing the liver from producing excessive amounts of sugar. In August 1995, two studies of metformin, performed by the Multicenter Metformin Study, were published showing that the drug—whether given alone or in combination with sulfonylureas—significantly improved blood-sugar control in moderately obese, Type II patients.

In one of the trials, 289 people who were unable to control their diabetes with diet alone took either metformin or a placebo. After 29 weeks of treatment, the patients on metformin had glucose levels that were almost 25 percent lower than the placebo group.

In the second study, 632 patients were assigned to one of three treatment groups: metformin plus glyburide (a sulfonylurea drug); metformin alone; or glyburide alone. After 29 weeks, the patients who were taking the metformin-glyburide combination had glucose levels significantly lower than patients in the other two groups.

Hemoglobin function. In March 1995, cell biologist Jonathan Stamler of the Duke University Medical Center reported the discovery of another function of the protein hemoglobin, which gives blood its characteristic red color. As well as transporting oxygen from the lungs to body tissues and removing carbon dioxide on the return journey, hemoglobin was found to carry a third gas—an unusual form of nitric oxide, which is synthesized in the lungs.

According to the Duke study, hemoglobin, with its cargo of nitric oxide—in a form that Stamler and his colleagues called super nitric oxide—plays a key role in regulating blood pressure. It does this by delivering nitric oxide to cells surrounding blood vessels, causing them to expand or contract.

The findings of the Duke study have totally revised the scientific view and study of the human respiratory cycle. The findings may also lead to significant changes in the treatments of blood pressure, heart attack, stroke, and sickle-cell anemia. Scientists believe the discovery might also lead to the creation of an effective blood substitute.

A boost for folic acid. A California study published in the British medical journal *Lancet* in August 1995 concluded that women who take multivitamins containing folic acid from very early in pregnancy reduced the risk of giving birth to a baby with a cleft lip or palate by 25 to 50 percent. Researchers suggested that this vitamin helps *DNA* (deoxyribonucleic acid, the molecule genes are made of) develop in a normal manner. Earlier studies had shown that folic acid and other vitamins could reduce the risk of *neural-tube birth defects* (birth defects, such as spina bifida and anencephaly, associated with the development of the brain and spinal cord).

Scientists at the University of Utah in Salt Lake City reported in September 1995 that individuals could lower blood levels of homocysteine, an amino acid considered a risk factor for heart disease when found in high amounts, by consuming more folic acid.

In a separate study at the University of Washington in Seattle, reported in October 1995, researchers analyzed the findings of 38 studies of folic acid and concluded that elevated homocysteine is responsible for 10 percent of heart-disease deaths of American men over age 45. Reductions in homocysteine were linked to increased levels of folic acid in the diet. Folic acid is found in such foods as spinach, peas, beans, and orange juice. (See also PUBLIC HEALTH.)

Cross-species sperm production. Veterinarian Ralph Brinster of the University of Pennsylvania in Philadelphia reported in May 1996 that sperm stem cells, from which all sperm cells arise, could be frozen, stored for an indefinite period, thawed, and then transplanted into the testes of an animal of another species. Brinster successfully generated rat sperm from stem cells of a rat transplanted into the testes of a mouse.

Sperm stem cells, unlike mature sperm cells, can reproduce themselves, providing a continuing source of a man's or animal's sperm. Brinster said that applications of his research might be limited, for the time being, to animal husbandry. A racehorse might, for example, gain immortality through its endlessly dividing stem cells that have been transplanted into the testes of a lesser horse or even of a laboratory mouse. [Richard Trubo]

See also DRUGS; GENETICS. In WORLD BOOK, see AIDS; DIABETES.

Beta-carotene supplements, widely touted as an anticancer agent, provide no protection against lung cancer and heart disease, according to two major studies reported in late 1995 and early 1996. One of the studies found that beta-carotene supplements may actually increase the risk of those diseases. A 1994 study by Finnish researchers had reported similar results.

Beta-carotene, found naturally in fruits and vegetables, is converted into Vitamin A (also known as retinol) by the body. Beta-carotene became the focus of both scientific research and a nutritional fad because of its antioxidant properties. Antioxidants are compounds capable of blocking the destructive effects of molecules called free radicals. In the body, free radicals can cause genetic damage to cells that may lead to cancer and can increase the heart-damaging effects of the fatty substance cholesterol.

In the first study, a 12-year trial called the Physicians' Health Study, 22,071 male doctors took either 50 milligrams of beta-carotene or a *placebo* (inactive substance) daily. The study ended in December 1995 with researchers reporting that beta-carotene supplements did not reduce the risk of cancer, heart disease, or death among the trial's participants. When presenting the findings, study director Charles Hennekens of Brigham and Women's Hospital in Boston concluded, "Beta-carotene can neither substitute for a good diet or compensate for a bad one."

The second study, the Beta-Carotene and Retinol Efficacy Trial—known as CARET—involved 14,254 long-time current or former smokers and 4,060 people who had been exposed to asbestos, a powerful cancer-causing substance, most of whom smoked. The participants in the four-year study took either beta-carotene, retinol, both substances, or a placebo.

The CARET researchers halted their study in January 1996—21 months early—because of their negative findings. They reported that the rate of lung cancer was 28 percent higher, and that of heart disease 26 percent higher, among participants who took beta-carotene or retinol supplements than among those

Olestra, a substitute for fat

A substance called olestra that can be used in food as a replacement for fat received federal government approval in January 1996. Olestra was designed to have the flavor of fat without having any calories. Although olestra is made from vegetable oil, the oil molecules have been altered so that they cannot be digested by the body.

Fat

A fat molecule contains fatty acids, which are broken away from the core of the molecule by digestive enzymes in the small intestine and used by the body as energy.

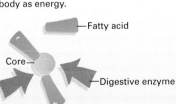

Fatty acid

Core—

Digestive enzyme

Olestra

An olestra molecule has so many fatty acids crowded around the molecule's core that the enzymes cannot break into the structure.

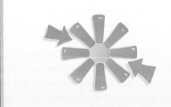

taking a placebo. In addition, participants who took the supplements had a 17-percent-higher death rate.

Nutrition and viruses. Scientists in 1996 continued to investigate pioneering research reported in May 1995 that a harmless virus can be *mutated* (genetically changed) into a disease-causing form by nutritional deficiencies in the host it infects. The research also found that the mutated virus can produce serious illness in well-nourished hosts. The study was the first to find that a dietary deficiency can change a virus's genes.

The focus of the research was the Coxsackie B3 virus, which has been found in people with a heart condition called Keshan disease. Keshan disease once was common in China among women and children living in areas where the soil is deficient in the trace element selenium. The disease has been largely eliminated by the use of selenium supplements.

In 1995, immunologist Melinda A. Beck of the University of North Carolina in Chapel Hill and her colleagues exposed two groups of mice to the Coxsackie B3 virus, which is usually harmless to mice. One group of mice was fed a diet deficient in selenium. The other group received adequate levels of the trace element. The researchers found that within 7 to 10 days, the selenium-deficient mice developed serious heart damage, while the other mice remained healthy.

When well-nourished mice were exposed to samples of the virus taken from the selenium-deficient mice, they also developed heart damage. This result suggested that the once-harmless virus had mutated permanently into a more virulent form.

In February 1996, Beck reported on new research suggesting that selenium deficiencies can also cause influenza viruses to become more deadly. And other researchers in 1996 speculated that dietary deficiencies may play a major role in the evolution of new and more virulent strains of other viruses.

Investigators are unsure how a selenium deficiency changes a virus's genes. They speculated that some viruses, such as the Coxsackie virus, may be vulnerable to mutation because their genes are made of RNA (ribonucleic acid) rather than DNA (deoxyribonucleic acid). Un-

like DNA viruses, RNA viruses do not have an internal mechanism for recognizing and correcting mutations that occur during reproduction. Beck said that because selenium has antioxidant properties—a protection against mutations—its absence may promote these changes in RNA viruses.

Birth defect risk with vitamin A. Women who take excessive amounts of vitamin A during the first three months of pregnancy greatly increase the risk of birth defects in their baby. That conclusion, reported in October 1995, came from the first major study linking specific levels of vitamin A to human birth defects. Previous studies had demonstrated the negative effect of high doses of the vitamin on pregnant laboratory animals.

Nutritional researcher Kenneth Rothman and his colleagues at Boston University studied the dietary histories of 22,784 women during the first trimester of their pregnancies. They found that the greater the amount of vitamin A taken the higher the risk of birth defects. Women who consumed more than 15,000 international units (IU's) of vitamin A daily, either in supplements or food, in the first seven weeks of pregnancy were 3.5 times more likely to give birth to a baby with birth defects than women who took 5,000 IU's. (The recommended daily allowance of vitamin A is 4,000 IU's.)

The birth defects associated with excessive consumption of vitamin A involved the head, brain, spinal cord, and heart. Laboratory studies have shown that in developing embryos, vitamin A influences the development of embryonic cells from which some brain, spinal and nerve cells arise and the action of genes that regulate the growth of *axons,* the long extensions of nerve cells that carry impulses away from the cell.

Experts recommended that women who are or might become pregnant should avoid taking supplements with more than 8,000 IU's of vitamin A. They also recommended moderation in the consumption of liver and liver products, which are rich in vitamin A. The researchers noted that their study did not reveal any danger associated with eating fruits and vegetables that are rich in beta-carotene, which the body converts to vitamin A.   [Phylis B. Moser-Veillon]

In World Book, see Nutrition.

A vastly improved map of the sea floor was released by scientists in the United States in October 1995. The researchers relied heavily on declassified data from a U.S. Navy satellite to make the map.

The new map reveals hundreds of undersea features that had been undetected and will almost certainly force scientists to revise their understanding of geological processes that occur in deep ocean basins. The map's publication immediately doubled the known number of undersea volcanoes, for instance, and scientists saw scores of trenches, fissures, plains, and *seamounts* (undersea hills or mountains) for the first time. The map is expected to aid oil and mineral exploration and research into climate change and *volcanology* (the study of volcanoes).

Traditional undersea mapping relies on shipboard equipment that bounces sound waves off the ocean floor and measures the time they take to return. (See pictorial feature on page 254.) Shorter return times signal shallower regions, and longer return times signal deeper areas. This method produces accurate maps, but it is time consuming and expensive. Scientists estimate that standard techniques would require 100 years to map the entire sea floor in detail and cost about $2 billion. The satellite map took 18 months and cost about $80 million, according to researchers.

Because of the time and expense required to produce standard undersea maps, sections of the ocean floor as large as Kansas were unexplored. The satellite map, in contrast, detected every undersea feature larger than 10 kilometers (6 miles) across.

Marine geophysicist David Sandwell of the Scripps Institution of Oceanography in San Diego and oceanographer Walter Smith of the U.S. National Oceanic and Atmospheric Administration produced the new map. They combined data from a U.S. Navy satellite called Geosat that was launched in March 1985 with similar but less extensive data from a European satellite and traditional sea-floor maps.

Geosat produced the enhanced map by measuring gravitational influences on sea-surface heights exerted by varying features of the sea floor. Since an object's *mass* (the property that gives an object weight) determines the strength of gravity around it, large objects such as volcanoes exert greater gravitational pull than smaller objects.

The enhanced gravitational pull gathers extra water around large objects, and this effect is mirrored in a bulge of water at the sea surface. The opposite effect occurs around deep trenches and large depressions in the bottom, where less mass produces a dip in sea-surface levels. A typical seamount 3,000 meters (10,000 feet) high causes the sea surface to bulge 3 meters (10 feet), for instance. Yet because such large undersea features spread over many kilometers, the change they produce in sea-surface heights is undetectable from ships.

Such changes can be measured precisely with radar beams from space, however. Geosat bounced radar signals off the ocean surface and measured how long the beams took to return. Since radar waves travel at the speed of light (299,792 kilometers [186,282 miles] per second), ground-based computers factored in that speed to calculate the distances based on the round trip time. Scientists determined that the satellite, even at orbital heights of nearly 800 kilometers (500 miles), measured changes in sea-surface level to within 2.5 centimeters (1 inch). With repeated measurements, the scientists averaged away changes due to waves.

Making the sea bloom. Scientists have long been puzzled by the shortage of *phytoplankton* (microscopic plants that float with ocean currents) in three large areas of the global ocean—the northern North Pacific Ocean, the equatorial Pacific, and the Southern Ocean around Antarctica. The puzzle stems from the fact that surface waters in these areas consistently contain high levels of nutrients such as nitrate and phosphate that support phytoplankton.

In June 1996, marine biologist Kenneth Coale of the Moss Landing Marine Laboratories in Moss Landing, California, revealed results from an experiment showing that low levels of dissolved iron in seawater can limit the phytoplankton growth even when other nutrients are abundant. The announcement followed ocean experiments a year earlier to test the hypothesis. Oceanographers had also tested the theory in October 1993.

Phytoplankton exist in vast numbers

New sea-floor images reveal continental shelf features

New images of the continental shelf off the United States were released in January 1996 by scientists at the Lamont-Doherty Earth Observatory in Palisades, New York. Ships with advanced *sonar* (sound-wave) equipment produced the images, which revealed unknown cliffs, canyons, ridges, and ravines.

A sheer cliff made up of the shells of dead marine organisms rises 1.6 kilometers (1 mile) above the sea floor from Fort Myers to Sarasota, Florida, *top*. A massive plateau stretches northeast along the Louisiana coast, *right*. According to scientists, compressed salt deposits beneath the ocean floor pushed up sediment in the area to form the plateau. Ridges formed from the pile-up of sea-floor sediment at the intersection of two *tectonic plates* (huge, rigid pieces of rock that make up Earth's crust) extend south along the Oregon coast, *below*.

near the surface. When nutrients are abundant, the microorganisms reproduce rapidly. As they multiply, the phytoplankton rapidly consume most of the nutrients. Consequently, the surface waters of the ocean normally contain far fewer nutrients than deep waters, except in the three curious regions that Coale and his colleagues investigated.

Coale's team investigated the iron hypothesis near the Galapagos Islands in the eastern equatorial Pacific. Seawater in the region contains little dissolved iron, primarily because winds do not transport dust from large land masses to that region of the ocean, eliminating the main source of iron for most surface waters. Deeper ocean currents in the area also lack significant amounts of iron.

Three times during an eight-day period, the scientists added iron to a square patch of the ocean measuring 64 square kilometers (25 square miles). Each addition of iron caused a rapid increase in phytoplankton, which finally reached levels 10 times greater than their original concentration. More dramatically, concentrations of chlorophyll, the substance within phytoplankton that converts sunlight to energy during photosynthesis, increased 30-fold.

El Niño's southern reach. In April 1996, oceanographers reported evidence that an ocean phenomenon known as El Niño plays a major role in regulating atmospheric and ocean conditions in the southern seas surrounding Antarctica. Warren White and Ray Peterson at the Scripps Institution of Oceanography reported the finding. El Niño may even control the extent of Antarctic ice fields, according to the scientists. The report was the first clear evidence that El Niño's effects reach so far south.

El Niño is the occasional appearance of abnormally warm water off the coasts of Peru and Ecuador. This water originates around Indonesia, and it travels in an immense pool about the size of the United States east along the equator to South America, where it forms warm currents. El Niños occur about every 4 to 5 years, and abnormally cool currents replace the warm ones in other years. These swings in temperature affect much of Earth's climate, but such effects have been difficult to see in the Southern Ocean that rings Antarctica.

Using data collected from satellites since the late-1970's, the researchers found a connection between swings of air and water temperature at the equator that are associated with El Niño and similar, but opposite, changes north of New Zealand. They believe that rising air currents over the warm pool of water at the equator are matched by descending air north of New Zealand that cools the ocean in that area. When the warm pool of water at the equator cools, the air currents change direction, and the water off New Zealand becomes warmer two or three years later.

The two researchers found that the changes in temperature north of New Zealand spread south into ocean currents that carry them east around the globe. The warm and cool pools expand as they travel east and greatly affect weather and water conditions in the Southern Ocean.

It takes 8 to 10 years for a pool of water to be carried all the way around Antarctica. During this time, other large pools of water, both warm and cool, form near the equator and move into the Southern Ocean. The timing of El Niño cycles along the equator combined with the speed of ocean currents produce a surprisingly simple pattern around Antarctica, the researchers said—two warm pools on opposite sides of the globe with a pair of cooler regions between them.

The changes in temperature from a warm pool to a cool one are only about 1 to 1.5 Celsius degrees (1.8 to 2.7 Fahrenheit degrees). Yet this difference is enough to produce two distinct weather patterns in the Southern Hemisphere.

One of the most dramatic effects of this climate system can be seen in Antarctic ice fields, according to Peterson and White. Pools of cool water cause ice fields to extend up to 160 kilometers (100 miles) farther north than normal, and ice retreats a similar distance during the passage of warm pools. Such changes in water temperatures may explain fluctuations in populations of *krill* (small shrimplike animals) and other marine organisms near the Antarctic coast, the researchers said.

[Ray G. Peterson]

See also ATMOSPHERIC SCIENCE. In WORLD BOOK, see OCEAN.

A long-sought new state of matter, the Bose-Einstein condensate (BEC), was created in 1995 by three research teams in the United States. A BEC is a kind of "superatom" formed when certain atoms are made to merge with each other under conditions of extreme cold.

The first observation of a BEC was made in July by a team of physicists at the National Institute of Standards and Technology (NIST), the University of Colorado, and the Joint Institute for Laboratory Astrophysics, all located in Boulder. Research teams at Rice University in Houston and the Massachusetts Institute of Technology (MIT) in Cambridge soon duplicated the accomplishment.

Bose-Einstein condensation was first postulated by Albert Einstein in a 1924 paper developing ideas of the Indian physicist Satyendranath Bose. But the condensate, named in their honor, remained only a theoretical possibility until the early 1990's, when scientists first became able to approach the extremely low temperatures needed to form a BEC. Scientists denote such low temperatures, which are not found in nature, in degrees Kelvin, also called kelvins. Zero degrees Kelvin, or absolute zero—the lowest temperature possible—is about −273 °C (−460 °F). Bose-Einstein condensation occurs only at temperatures of less than one millionth of a kelvin. At these temperatures, little heat energy is available to maintain an atom's velocity, and atoms slow almost to a complete stop.

The peculiar behavior of a BEC is explained by quantum theory, a branch of physics that deals with the behavior of atoms and subatomic particles. Quantum theory states that atoms, though they are physical objects, also behave somewhat like waves. The frequency of a wave associated with an atom represents the atom's energy level, or "quantum state." Normally, atoms can occupy any of numerous quantum states. But when they are confined to a limited space, the number of quantum states they can fall into shrinks.

Normally, an atom rarely occupies the same quantum state as one of its neighbors. But at temperatures close to absolute zero, as atoms slow to nearly zero velocity, a large fraction of atoms fall into the lowest possible state. If these very cold atoms are crowded so close together that their waves overlap, they lose their individual identities and merge into a single entity, the BEC. Although the atoms are barely moving, it is impossible to pinpoint where in the BEC any individual atom is located.

Producing a BEC requires great skill not only in cooling atoms to extremely low temperatures but also in confining them so they form a dense concentration. The three research teams that produced BEC's in 1995 achieved concentrations of a few trillion atoms per cubic centimeter (0.06 cubic inch).

All three teams worked with atoms of metals called alkalis—rubidium for the NIST team, lithium at Rice, and sodium at MIT. Alkali atoms act like tiny magnets, enabling them to be captured in a magnetic "trap." By surrounding atoms with overlapping magnetic fields, the researchers were able to confine the atoms to a region 1 millimeter (0.04 inch) or so in diameter. The scientists then cooled the atoms through various means, including the use of laser beams that reduced the atoms' motion.

Once the temperature of the atoms had fallen below that needed for condensation, the Boulder and MIT scientists turned off their magnets and flashed a laser beam into their traps. The light scattered from the trapped atoms, producing an image of the condensate on a video screen. The images revealed a bright spot in the center of the trap, where atoms were densely packed and hardly moving. That bright spot was a BEC.

Because the Rice team used permanent magnets for their trap, the trap could not be turned off. As a result, conclusive evidence for a BEC at Rice was lacking. For this and other reasons, some researchers remain unconvinced that the Rice experiment produced a true BEC.

Although the Boulder team reached the finish line first in this very close race, the MIT team may have gotten there with the most. The MIT investigators trapped more than 30 times as many atoms as the Boulder group, making further research on the properties of a BEC much easier.

The type of BEC produced in the 1995 work is unlikely to have much practical value. However, it does open a

Researchers in Japan in late 1995 inspect a huge neutrino detector being constructed in a lead mine shortly before the detector was to be filled with water. Neutrinos—tiny particles that have little or no mass and travel at or near the speed of light (299,792 kilometers [186,282 miles] a second)—interact so feebly with other matter that trillions zip unimpeded through the Earth each second. The detector was designed to record the rare collisions of neutrinos with atoms in water molecules. Scientists hope data from the detector will enable them to determine if neutrinos have any mass.

new window on the peculiar world of quantum physics—a world that underlies much of the technology of our time.

A "heavenly accelerator." Supernovae, or exploding stars, account for at least part of the solution to an 80-year-old mystery, the origin of cosmic rays. This was the November 1995 finding of a team of scientists at Japan's Kyoto University and the National Aeronautics and Space Administration's (NASA) Goddard Space Flight Center in Greenbelt, Maryland.

Physicists have known about cosmic rays—high energy radiation that bombards the Earth from all directions—since 1912. Cosmic rays consist of subatomic particles—primarily nuclei, along with some electrons—that are moving at nearly the speed of light (299,792 kilometers [186,282 miles] per second). Physicists often refer to the mysterious mechanisms required to produce them as "heavenly accelerators."

The bulk of cosmic rays have energies of a few billion electronvolts, and a few reach energies of up to a billion trillion electronvolts—an energy level equivalent to that of a major league fast ball, carried in a single particle. (An electronvolt, or eV, is the energy acquired by an electron propelled through a one-volt battery.) The most powerful particle accelerator on Earth—at Fermilab in Batavia, Illinois—can reach less than 1 trillion eV (1 TeV).

Because hydrogen and helium make up more than 98 percent of the matter in the universe, the nuclei of these elements form most cosmic rays. Showing where the radiation originates, however, has been difficult, because our galaxy is filled with magnetic fields—including those of the sun and Earth—that deflect electrically charged particles from their courses. As a result, by the time cosmic rays reach Earth no connection remains between the direction they are moving in and where they came from.

The scientists did not observe cosmic rays directly. Rather, they analyzed X rays that were created as a by-product of the process that generated cosmic rays. X rays, like visible light (but unlike cosmic rays), are a form of electromagnetic radiation, but with very short wavelengths. Like light, X rays are not deflected by magnetic fields and therefore can be traced back to their sources.

Antiatoms' Fleeting Debut

To physicists who study electrons and the other particles that make up atoms, antimatter is neither new nor mysterious. The existence of subatomic particles that have an electrical charge opposite that of ordinary particles was predicted by the British theorist Paul A. M. Dirac in 1930. Antielectrons, also called positrons, were discovered in 1932, antiprotons in 1955, and antineutrons in 1956. (Although neutrons have no charge, they —like protons—are composed of smaller charged particles called quarks. An antineutron is made of oppositely charged antiquarks.)

For years, physicists have routinely produced antiparticles by the trillions in high-energy *particle accelerators* (huge machines that boost subatomic particles to tremendous speeds). Not until September 1995, however, were physicists able to combine positrons and antiprotons to produce the first complete atoms of antimatter ever seen. In a three-week experiment, a team of Italian, German, and Swiss physicists created 11 atoms of antihydrogen, the simplest atomic form of antimatter. The antiatoms lasted only 37 nanoseconds (billionths of a second) before being destroyed in collisions with particles of ordinary matter.

The European scientists, headed by physicist Walter Oelert of the Julich Institute for Nuclear Physics Research in Germany, produced the antiatoms at the European Laboratory for Particle Physics—also known by the initials of its former French name, CERN—in Switzerland. They announced their achievement in January 1996. Oelert acknowledged that a share of the credit should go to physicist Charles Munger of the University of California at Irvine, who in 1992 invented the tricky process that produced the antiatoms.

According to the laws of physics, when matter arises from energy, as it did during the explosion that created the universe, antimatter is created simultaneously. That means that each particle of ordinary matter has a corresponding antiparticle with the same mass and other characteristics except for its electrical charge, which is reversed. Thus, a hydrogen atom, the simplest atomic form of matter, is made up of a negatively charged electron orbiting a positively charged proton. In contrast, an antihydrogen atom consists of a positively charged positron (antielectron) orbiting a negatively charged antiproton.

But years of astronomical observations have failed to detect concentrations of naturally occurring antimatter anywhere in the universe. Many physicists believe the apparent absence of natural antimatter is the result of a process that took place in the early moments of the universe that resulted in a slight imbalance of matter over antimatter.

This imbalance doomed antimatter, because when an ordinary particle and antiparticle collide, they annihilate each other in a violent burst of

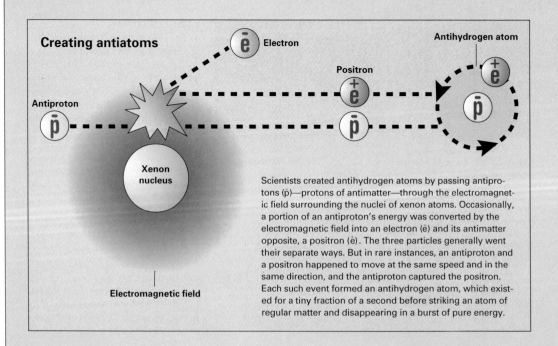

Creating antiatoms

Antihydrogen atom

Electron

Positron

Antiproton

Xenon nucleus

Electromagnetic field

Scientists created antihydrogen atoms by passing antiprotons (p̄)—protons of antimatter—through the electromagnetic field surrounding the nuclei of xenon atoms. Occasionally, a portion of an antiproton's energy was converted by the electromagnetic field into an electron (ē) and its antimatter opposite, a positron (ė). The three particles generally went their separate ways. But in rare instances, an antiproton and a positron happened to move at the same speed and in the same direction, and the antiproton captured the positron. Each such event formed an antihydrogen atom, which existed for a tiny fraction of a second before striking an atom of regular matter and disappearing in a burst of pure energy.

energy. Repeated collisions of matter and anti-matter destroyed all the antimatter, leaving only the remaining matter, from which the universe was made.

The incompatibility between matter and anti-matter complicates scientists' ability to study anti-matter. Although particle accelerators produce an abundance of antiparticles, these bits of anti-matter are still vastly outnumbered by ordinary particles in their vicinity. As a result, it is nearly impossible for antiparticles to find each other and form antiatoms before they meet up with ordinary particles and annihilate.

Munger's proposal for dealing with this prob-lem was to let antiprotons generate their own positrons. Accordingly, the CERN physicists took antiprotons from one of their laboratory's particle accelerators and passed them about 3 million times per second through a puff of xenon gas in a near vacuum. Some antiprotons passed through the strong electromagnetic field near the xenon nuclei, and, occasionally, some of an antiproton's energy was converted into an electron and a positron.

Most of the time, each antiproton and its off-spring electron and positron went their separate ways. But in rare instances, a positron was moving at the same speed and in the same direction as the antiproton and was captured by the antipro-ton. When the two combined, they formed an antihydrogen atom.

Each of the antihydrogen atoms lasted just long enough to travel 10 meters (33 feet) to an array of particle detectors. Inside the detectors, positrons met electrons and annihilated, producing two gamma rays of a particular energy. Measurements of the gamma rays confirmed that they had been produced by matter-antimatter annihilations.

Physicists would like to study antihydrogen to learn whether antimatter behaves according to the laws that govern matter. For example, do an-tiatoms absorb and emit light in exactly the same way that regular atoms do?

Interestingly, however, antiatoms' most signifi-cant use might be for the study of gravity, the least understood of the four fundamental forces of nature. If it were discovered, for example, that an-tihydrogen atoms are less affected by the pull of gravity than hydrogen atoms, physicists would have to significantly revise the general theory of relativity, the widely accepted theory of gravitation proposed in 1915 by German-born physicist Al-bert Einstein.

For these kinds of investigations, however, physicists will need to devise ways of producing antiatoms in volume. And they must find methods of slowing down the fast-moving antiatoms and confining them in antimatter traps away from or-dinary matter.   [Robert H. March]

Physics continued

Because X rays cannot penetrate Earth's atmosphere, the researchers studied them using an X-ray telescope aboard a Japanese-American satellite named ASCA, for *Advanced Satellite for Cosmology and Astrophysics.* The tele-scope was trained on SN1006, the rem-nant of a supernova explosion whose light reached Earth in the year 1006, when astronomers described it as being as bright as the moon. The shock wave from the explosion is still strong and traveling outward, heating any gas or dust it encounters to a glow. The Ameri-can and Japanese observers found that two regions of the shock front are in-tense sources of X rays.

X rays and cosmic radiation. In 1949, the Italian-born American physicist En-rico Fermi suggested that a shock wave moving through the thin gas of interstel-lar space could trap particles so that they continually bounce between the wave and a magnetic field at the shock front. The particles would gain energy at each encounter until they reach the energies of cosmic rays. If some of the trapped particles were electrons, they would shed some of this energy in the form of X rays through a phenomenon called synchrotron radiation. This form of radiation, which is produced when electrons moving at high speeds pass through a magnetic field, owes its name to the fact that it was first observed when electrons were accelerated in machines known as synchrotrons.

The American and Japanese research-ers observed X rays from the outer edge of the SN1006 shock wave with energies of up to 8,000 eV (8 KeV). The X rays were in a smooth spectrum, meaning that they exhibited a continuous range of wavelengths. This spectrum was what would be expected from synchrotron radiation.

To produce 8 KeV X rays in the weak magnetic fields of interstellar space, electrons must be accelerated to as much as 200 TeV. The electrons ob-served by the researchers had presum-ably been produced by being stripped loose from nuclei. So if they were being accelerated to such high energies, the nuclei must have been accelerated as well. The nuclei became cosmic rays.

Researchers know of several other young supernova remnants like SN1006, and there are now plans to investigate whether similar X rays are being emitted from these sources. However, it is likely that shock wave acceleration is not the sole source of cosmic rays. The energy from SN1006 is under 1,000 TeV, which marks a point called the knee in the cosmic-ray spectrum. Above 1,000 TeV, the number of cosmic rays drops rapidly as their energy increases. Physicists have long suspected that cosmic rays beyond the knee are produced by a different mechanism than those below, but no one yet knows what that mechanism might be.

Quantum oddities. Demonstrations of the peculiarity of the quantum world have become common. Two recent examples of "quantum weirdness" may be of practical importance.

In December 1995, two teams of researchers showed how computers might exploit some of the strange features of the quantum world. A quantum computer would be vastly more powerful than conventional computers. In 1985, a researcher at Oxford University in the United Kingdom worked out a theory of how a quantum computer might oper-ate. But no one had been able to figure out how to make one of the key parts of such a computer, a component called a gate.

The two teams that announced their results in December 1995 successfully demonstrated two different kinds of quantum gates. One team worked at the California Institute of Technology (Caltech) in Pasadena, California. The other was at the NIST laboratory in Boulder.

A gate is a device that can assume either of two states, which correspond to the two binary digits, 0 and 1. (Digital computers store and manipulate information by encoding it in the binary numeration system.) The gate must be able to switch electronically from one state to the other. A computer contains a large number of gates—typically several million in the newest computer chips—that are electronically linked.

In most computers, tiny components called transistors serve as the gates, and the two states correspond to two different voltages. Each transistor is always in one state or the other. In a computer based on quantum theory, the gates

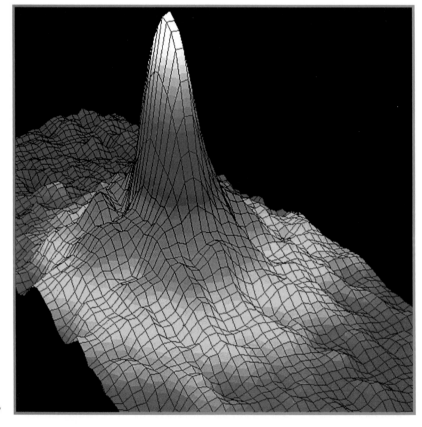

A spike on a computer-generated image made in July 1995 by reseachers in Boulder, Colorado, shows the presence of a new state of matter called a Bose-Einstein condensate. The condensate was created by confining rubidium atoms to a small volume and cooling them to an extremely low temperature, thereby causing them to merge into a sort of "superatom."

would be atomic particles, and the two states would correspond to two different energy levels of the particles.

What makes this technology potentially so powerful is that in a quantum system, particles that remain undisturbed do not always exist in a single definite state. They can hover in a combination of both states until something forces them to assume one state or the other.

If many such quantum gates were linked together in a computer, the computer could simultaneously assume a huge number of possible states—and thus perform a huge number of calculations. A computer with 100 gates, for instance, could be in as many as 2^{100} states at the same time, or about 1 followed by 30 zeros. To achieve the computing speed of such a device using conventional circuits would require that many computers working in parallel.

Making quantum gates. To create their gate, the NIST researchers used radio waves to trap a single beryllium ion (a beryllium atom with one electron removed). They then cooled the ion so it could occupy only two possible quantum states. Those states—0 and 1—depended on whether the outermost electron on the ion had a spin parallel to or opposite the spin of the beryllium nucleus. ("Spin," a property of subatomic particles, is unrelated to the spinning of an object such as a top.) The gate could be flipped from one state to another by a carefully timed radio signal tuned to the energy level of one of the two states.

The Caltech team produced their gate using *photons* (particles of light). Two photons were trapped between mirrors spaced 0.053 millimeters (0.002 inch) apart. The digits 0 and 1 corresponded to two possible states of *polarization*, the plane in which the photons vibrated. The gate was set at 0 or 1 according to the polarization of one of the two photons between the mirrors at a given time. That photon carried the *qubit*, or binary information. (In ordinary computing, the information carried by a 0 or 1 is known as a *bit*, giving rise to the term *qubit* for quantum bit.) The other photon, at a slightly different wavelength, operated the gate, altering the polarization of the qubit photon. Because interactions between photons are weak, the second photon acted by modifying the spin of a cesium atom passing between the mirrors at the same time. The cesium atom then changed the polarization of the qubit photon.

As yet, neither the NIST nor the Caltech gate is reliable enough to serve in an actual computer. And as experts point out, a quantum computer would require gates that are far more reliable than those in a conventional computer. In an ordinary computer gate, the voltage levels that differentiate 0's from 1's need not be exact. If a signal arrives somewhat off the correct value, the circuits are designed to respond as if it were perfect, correcting the error.

In a quantum computer, however, no such self-correcting mechanism would exist. To the contrary, any error would be preserved and passed along to the next gate. After many such steps, the signal would be completely distorted. And a quantum computer would be highly vulnerable to error, since even a single wayward particle could throw its delicate operations off track.

Still, some computer operations require very few steps, and for those a quantum computer might be suitable. One of them is the encoding of sensitive messages, such as those tranmitted by financial institutions. Because a quantum computer could perform vast numbers of computations at great speed, experts believe a message coded by such a computer would be indecipherable. Moreover, any attempt to intercept the message would leave telltale signs warning users of the presence of an eavesdropper. Given the present state of the technology, however, any such application will probably be far in the future.

In May 1996, a team at the NIST Boulder laboratory reported an even more peculiar "mixed" quantum state. In this case, an ion of beryllium was in a mixture of states in different locations. It was literally in two places at once. The two states were not very far apart—only about 80 *nanometers* (billionths of an inch). Still, the separation was more than 100 times the diameter of the ion. Although this experiment did not have the potential practical application of quantum gates, it was yet another vivid demonstration of the strangeness of the quantum world.   [Robert H. March]

In the Science Studies section, see THE COMPUTER COMES OF AGE. In WORLD BOOK, see PHYSICS.

Research suggesting a genetic influence on an individual's tendency to engage in adventurous or risk-taking behavior was reported in January 1996 by independent research teams at the Laboratory of Clinical Science at the National Institute of Mental Health in Bethesda, Maryland, and the Sarah Herzog Memorial Hospital in Jerusalem. If confirmed, the findings would be the first evidence linking a normal personality trait and a gene involved in *neurotransmission* (the transmission of nerve impulses).

The researchers reported that the gene is responsible for 10 percent of behavior associated with a basic personality trait known as novelty-seeking. Individuals who score high in novelty-seeking on psychological tests tend to be more excitable, exploratory, fickle, extravagant, and quick-tempered than individuals with lower scores.

Both studies were designed to test the theory that novelty-seeking is influenced by the way in which the brain processes a chemical messenger called dopamine. Dopamine relays signals between nerve cells in the brain. Previous studies have

also shown that dopamine is involved in the "high" that results from narcotics.

The two teams of researchers gave their subjects personality tests and conducted a genetic analysis of their blood cells. They found that individuals who scored highest in novelty-seeking had a variation of a gene called D4DR containing extra-long repeated sequences of DNA (deoxyribonucleic acid, the molecule genes are made of). The gene determines the way in which dopamine is transmitted by controlling the formation of molecules on nerve cells to which dopamine attaches. The subjects who had low scores for novelty-seeking had a shorter version of the gene.

Caution for Alzheimer's test. An increasingly widespread genetic test for Alzheimer's disease is not sensitive or specific enough to predict who will develop the devastating brain disorder, a task force of geneticists reported in November 1995. The group concluded that although the test may identify an important risk factor for Alzheimer's disease, its use could lead to misdiagnosis, anguish, and even discrimination.

Laboratory mice lacking an important chemical messenger in the brain are ferocious and sexually aggressive and attack another mouse. Researchers at Johns Hopkins University in Baltimore and Massachusetts General Hospital in Boston reported in November 1995 that the violent mice lacked a gene responsible for the production of nitric oxide, which they theorize may help regulate social behavior in mice—and human beings.

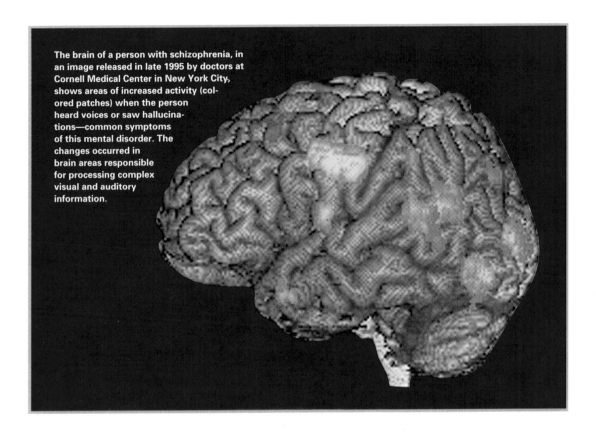

The brain of a person with schizophrenia, in an image released in late 1995 by doctors at Cornell Medical Center in New York City, shows areas of increased activity (colored patches) when the person heard voices or saw hallucinations—common symptoms of this mental disorder. The changes occurred in brain areas responsible for processing complex visual and auditory information.

Alzheimer's disease is an incurable disease characterized by a progressive loss of memory and reasoning power. The fourth most common cause of death among the elderly, the disorder affects at least 2.5 million and perhaps as many as 6.8 million Americans.

Alzheimer's is difficult to diagnose. The physiological signs of the disease— tangled fibers within nerve cells and dense deposits of proteins and degenerated nerve endings called plaques—can be detected only by examining the brain after death. Physicians diagnose the disorder by evaluating a patient's condition and eliminating other possible conditions, such as strokes and thyroid disease, that could cause similar symptoms.

Since 1993, research studies have shown a compelling association between Alzheimer's and a protein that plays a role in transporting the fatty substance cholesterol from the blood into body cells. According to the studies, people with one variant of this protein, called apolipoprotein-4 (APOE-4), are significantly more likely to develop Alzheimer's. Early reports suggested that near-ly all individuals who inherit two copies of the gene for APOE-4 will develop Alzheimer's by age 80. From 25 to 50 percent of people who inherit one copy of the gene will develop the disease.

The task force concluded, however, that the presence of the APOE-4 gene is only one of several factors that may increase the risk of Alzheimer's. The geneticists noted that a large proportion of individuals with one copy of the gene never develop Alzheimer's disease, and even the presence of two copies of the gene is not as predictive of the disease as had been thought. In addition, they pointed out that at least 35 to 50 percent of individuals with Alzheimer's disease do not carry the APOE-4 gene. Thus, a positive test for the gene could result in inaccurate predictions. In addition, as there are no treatments to halt or reverse the disease, a positive finding could cause distress and create possibilities for discrimination without affecting the course of the disease.

Does psychotherapy help? An unusual evaluation of the usefulness of psychotherapy published by *Consumer*

Reports magazine in November 1995 concluded that it can provide substantial benefits over time. Psychotherapy is the treatment of mental and emotional problems by verbal communication between a client and therapist. The evaluation attracted a notable amount of academic and clinical attention because of the large group of patients who reported their impressions of psychotherapy.

The usefulness of psychotherapy has increasingly become the focus of scientific study. However, a randomized controlled trial, in which patients are arbitrarily assigned to receive either treatment or a *placebo* (inactive substance), is poorly suited to the study of long-term psychotherapy. Patients in psychotherapy usually have multiple problems, rather than a single symptom that can be measured in a research study. Improvement over the course of therapy can occur in many areas, including personal relationships, work, and internal feelings. Finally, the treatment differs between each therapist and patient.

Consumer Reports asked its 180,000 subscribers to complete a survey if they had sought help for stress and emotional problems in the previous year. Of approximately 7,000 respondents, about 3,000 had talked with friends, family, or clergy, and 4,000 saw a mental health professional or family doctor or attended a support group. Respondents who received professional help were asked to describe the mode of therapy, the type and severity of their original mental or emotional problems, their perception of improvement due to therapy, and their satisfaction with the therapy.

Most respondents reported substantial improvement over the course of therapy. They reported greater improvement from long-term therapy than from short-term treatment. Psychiatrists, psychologists, and social workers were judged equally effective, but marriage counselors less so, and family doctors reportedly achieved less improvement in long-term cases. No specific mode of psychotherapy resulted in greater improvement than any other, according to the respondents. Readers who reported that their insurance coverage affected the type, frequency, or duration of therapy reported showing less improvement.

The study had many limitations. For example, the absence of a *control group* (a group that, for comparison purposes, does not receive a treatment being evaluated) could mean that the passage of time rather than the therapy produced the noted improvement. Nonetheless, the study provided a useful assessment of the effectiveness of treatment as actually delivered in clinical practice.

Panic disorder may have a greater effect on health and well-being than that of other chronic mental and medical conditions, according to a February 1996 report by researchers at the University of California at Los Angeles and the Rand Corporation of Santa Monica, California. Panic disorder consists of recurrent sudden episodes of intense fear or apprehension, accompanied by such bodily sensations as a pounding heart, shortness of breath, sweating, and dizziness. The attacks occur in the absence of underlying medical conditions. The condition affects more than 1 in 30 Americans over their lifetime.

The researchers found that patients with panic disorder rated their current health, mental functioning, general well-being, and ability to carry out day-to-day activities consistently lower than did members of the general population. Patients with panic disorder had limitations in everyday functioning comparable to those observed in patients suffering from depression. Moreover, their limitations were worse than those of patients with many other chronic medical illnesses, including diabetes, heart disease, and arthritis. They rated their social functioning as comparable to or worse than that of individuals with other chronic medical conditions.

Patients with panic disorder can be substantially limited in their ability to function normally. They often develop anxiety about having panic attacks and so avoid places or situations that can induce attacks, such as being in crowded or enclosed areas or driving an automobile.

Controlled trials and clinical experience have identified several effective treatments for panic disorder. Certain drugs can reduce the frequency and intensity of panic attacks and the associated avoidance behavior. In addition, a program of gradual exposure to dreaded situations can reduce panic, anxiety, and avoidance.   [Richard C. Hermann]

In WORLD BOOK, see PSYCHOLOGY.

Fearing a link between so-called mad-cow disease, a deadly neurological disease in cattle, and a fatal human brain disorder, the United Kingdom in May 1996 began killing 4.7 million cattle most likely to be infected. The slaughter followed an admission by the British government on March 20 that eating beef contaminated with bovine spongiform encephalopathy was "the most likely explanation" for the appearance of a new strain of the human disorder, Creutzfeldt-Jakob disease. Researchers have no direct scientific evidence linking the two diseases, whose causes are unknown, and British officials had previously denied a connection.

Creutzfeldt-Jakob disease causes severe mental deterioration and death. The disease, which strikes about one person in a million worldwide, takes decades to develop and usually affects middle-aged and elderly people. Between 1985 and 1996, however, the number of British cases grew from 28 to 55. And since 1986, 10 people under age 42 in Britain have fallen ill with what researchers believe is a new strain

of the disease. In April 1996, health officials in France reported that the new strain was probably responsible for the death of a 26-year-old Frenchman.

On March 27, the European Union, an organization of 15 Western European governments, banned all imports of British beef and beef products. The United States had imposed a similar ban in 1989, when a British scientific panel concluded that mad-cow disease resulted when livestock were given feed containing sheep parts contaminated with scrapie, a disease that attacks the nervous system of sheep. In response to that report, the British government forbade the addition of sheep parts to feed. In April 1996, the World Health Organization (WHO), an agency of the United Nations, recommended a worldwide ban on animal tissue in livestock feed.

Mad-cow disease had affected about 162,000 cattle in Britain since it was first identified in 1986. (France and Switzerland also reported cases.) In April 1996, the U.S. Department of Agriculture reported that mad-cow disease had not appeared in U.S. cattle. Nevertheless, in

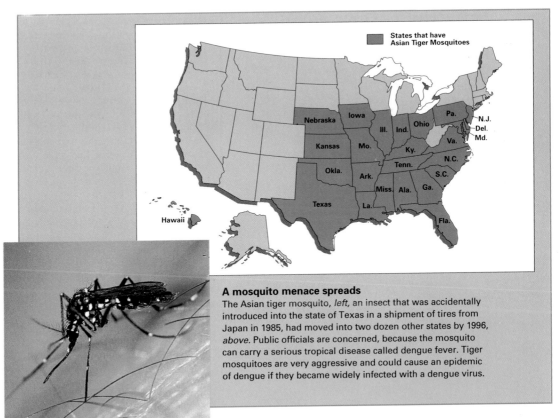

A mosquito menace spreads
The Asian tiger mosquito, *left,* an insect that was accidentally introduced into the state of Texas in a shipment of tires from Japan in 1985, had moved into two dozen other states by 1996, *above.* Public officials are concerned, because the mosquito can carry a serious tropical disease called dengue fever. Tiger mosquitoes are very aggressive and could cause an epidemic of dengue if they became widely infected with a dengue virus.

It's Just Not Cool.

Smoking is an addiction that kills

More than 400,000 people die every
year from smoking-related diseases.
That's more than from alcohol,
cocaine, crack, heroin, murders, suicide,
car accidents, and AIDS *combined.*

Great American
SMOKEOUT

AMERICAN
CANCER
SOCIETY

November 16, 1995

A poster publicizes the Great American Smokeout on Nov. 16,
1995. The annual event, sponsored by the American Cancer Society, included various activities aimed at discouraging smoking
among young people. The previous month, the society launched a
television advertising campaign aimed at preventing youths from
becoming cigarette smokers.

that month at least 20 states ordered
the slaughter of cattle that had been imported from Britain before 1989. U.S.
officials also announced increased precautions against the importation of
products made from boiled beef carcasses, including gelatins, jelly beans, and
cosmetics. In April, however, WHO concluded that beef-derived gelatin posed
no threat to human health.

Tobacco suit. A huge class-action lawsuit against major U.S. tobacco companies and a tobacco lobbying group was
dismissed by a federal appeals court in
New Orleans, Louisiana, in May 1996.
The court said the suit, which could
have covered up to 50 million American
smokers, was too complex to manage.

The lawsuit was originally filed in
1994 by three smokers and by the husband of a smoker who died of lung cancer. It accused the tobacco industry of
concealing knowledge that smoking is
addictive and of manipulating nicotine
levels in cigarettes to keep smokers ad-
dicted. The tobacco companies have denied the charges. In February 1995, a
federal judge had ruled that an alliance
of nearly 60 law firms representing almost every U.S. smoker could participate in the suit. The appeals court ruled
that the original four plaintiffs in the
case could proceed with their suit.

In March 1996, the smallest defen-
dant in the suit, the Liggett Group of
Durham, North Carolina, agreed to a
separate settlement in the case. Liggett
controls about 2 percent of the U.S.
cigarette market. In return for being ex-
cluded from the lawsuit, Liggett announced that it would contribute up to
5 percent of its annual pretax income
over the next 25 years to programs
aimed at helping people stop smoking.
Liggett also agreed to comply with certain federal regulations intended to
discourage cigarette sales to children.
In August 1995, President Bill Clinton
authorized the Food and Drug Administration (FDA) to begin a new program to stop the sale and marketing
of cigarettes to children.

Gun injuries. A report on the dangers
of BB and pellet guns and other guns
that do not use gunpowder was released
in December 1995 by the Centers for
Disease Control and Prevention (CDC)
in Atlanta, Georgia. Each year, about
30,000 people, more than 80 percent of

them under age 19, seek emergency care for injuries caused by such guns.

According to the report, almost 90 percent of the injuries each year are accidental. The typical victim is a boy who either has shot himself or was shot by a friend, acquaintance, or relative while using a gun or playing with one at home. Nearly one-third of the injuries involve the eyes, face, head, or neck.

The CDC noted that although most nonpowder guns are used by people aged 8 to 18 years, the government has not established safety standards. Eighty percent of the guns have muzzle velocities greater than 105 meters (350 feet) per second; 50 percent have velocities from 150 to 280 meters (500 to 930 feet) per second. Such guns can cause tissue damage similar to that caused by conventional firearms. The CDC recommended that users of such guns should be supervised by an adult, wear protective eyewear, and learn about gun safety.

Folic acid supplements. In an effort to prevent thousands of birth defects annually, the FDA on Feb. 29, 1996, ordered that enriched foods, including flour, pasta, corn meals and rice, be fortified with folic acid. (Enriched foods have added vitamins and minerals.) The rule, which takes effect on Jan. 1, 1998, is the first new government-ordered fortification since 1943.

Folic acid is found naturally in dark-green leafy vegetables, beans, and peas. The supplementation was intended to boost to 400 milligrams the average daily intake of folic acid for pregnant women who do not obtain adequate amounts from their diet.

Research studies have shown that folic acid supplementation could reduce by one-half to three-fourths the number of infants born with spina bifida and anencephaly, two of the most common severe birth defects. Spina bifida is a condition in which the spinal cord is not completely enclosed. Varying degrees of paralysis may result. Anencephaly is the absence or near absence of brain matter in the cranium. Infants with anencephaly generally die soon after birth.   [Richard A. Goodman and Deborah Kowal]

In WORLD BOOK, see PUBLIC HEALTH.

Science and Society

The conservative 104th Congress made many changes in science and technology policy in 1995 and 1996 and passed a controversial law aimed at limiting the availability of "indecent" materials on the Internet, a worldwide computer network. Meanwhile scientists continued to debate ethical issues, including research on the link between genetics and human behavior, and misconduct in scientific research.

Congress reshapes science policy. Disagreements between Congress and President Bill Clinton on how to balance the federal budget had a major impact on scientific research. The annual budget resolution passed by Congress in June 1995 called for a 33-percent cut in spending on nonmilitary research and development by the year 2002. The budget process became a battleground between advocates for science funding and congressional "deficit hawks."

The lengthy budget stalemate led to two government shutdowns, which took their toll on government and university researchers. Laboratories were closed, field experiments (such as the tracking of endangered species in wilderness areas) were halted, and the processing of grants and proposals was suspended.

Congress made sharp reductions in environmental research, including eliminating the National Biological Service, formed by President Clinton to consolidate ecological research in the Interior Department. It also shut down or cut back several programs intended to help develop partnerships between government and industry in support of commercial technology development. But it made only minor reductions in the National Science Foundation's budget and provided a surprising 6-percent increase for medical research at the National Institutes of Health.

OTA falls victim to budget ax. On Sept. 29, 1995, the Congressional Office of Technology Assessment (OTA) shut down. Several weeks earlier, Congress had voted to close the small but important agency. OTA had been established in 1972 as a "think tank" to advise Congress on complex scientific and technological issues. During its 23-year life, OTA's small staff of about 200 people produced some 750 reports on subjects such as telecommunications, space, energy, agriculture, and education. It provided congressional committees with access to the nation's top experts in those areas, assisting lawmakers in understanding the technical dimensions of issues facing the country.

OTA studies in 1994 and 1995 covered topics including antibiotic-resistant bacteria, U.S.-Russian cooperation in space, and sanitation in Alaskan villages. The audience for OTA's work included not only Congress but also the press and individuals in the federal and state governments, universities, and industry.

OTA served both parties in Congress, but some critics felt that it had closer ties to the Democrats and that its reports often supported their positions. Others also noted that OTA's style and pace—it often took over a year to complete a study—were not in tune with Congress's needs.

Through the efforts of several OTA staff members, copies of all OTA reports will be available to the public on a set of CD-ROM's, on the Internet's World Wide Web, and in several university libraries.

Pornography and the Internet. On Feb. 8, 1996, President Clinton signed the controversial Communications Decency Act. This law makes it a crime to transmit "patently offensive" material, or allow such material to be transmitted, over public computer networks where it might become available to children. The law was immediately challenged in the courts. Critics argued that it was an unworkable law and an unwarranted intrusion on free speech.

The speed with which the Communications Decency Act was passed and the amount of attention it received demonstrated how awareness of the Internet, known mainly to scientists until 1994, had exploded in just two years. But many observers noted a significant lag between the advance of computer network technology and the ability of policymakers to deal with that technology.

A study published in June 1995 had helped focus public attention on the kinds of material being offered on the Internet. The study, entitled "Marketing Pornography on the Information Superhighway," was conducted by an undergraduate student at Carnegie Mellon University in Pittsburgh, Pennsylvania. The study contended that a great deal of pornography was readily available to children. But critics disputed the study's methods and findings, persuading many people that the problem—if, indeed, there was one—had been grossly exaggerated. The study also sparked debates that took place on the Internet itself. Nevertheless, the law passed with large majorities in both houses of Congress.

President Clinton signed the bill but expressed reservations about the constitutionality of some of its provisions. Within days, a group of some 20 organizations—including the American Civil Liberties Union, the Electronic Frontier Foundation, Planned Parenthood, and Human Rights Watch—filed suit in federal court to have the law overturned. The Clinton Administration announced that it would not enforce the law pending a ruling by the court, expected in summer 1996. Regardless of the decision, the ruling was likely to be appealed all the way to the Supreme Court.

Misconduct in science. Prospects for agreement on a system for handling cases of scientific misconduct were uncertain in 1995 and 1996, as several individuals with misconduct complaints filed suit under the False Claims Act. This law was enacted in 1863 to help the government prosecute defense contractors who sold shoddy goods to the Union Army. The law allows private citizens who believe they have evidence of wrongdoing to sue for fraud on behalf of the government.

The law was modified in 1986 and now allows those who sue to collect up to 30 percent of the fine ordered by the court if the suit is successful. In the past, most such lawsuits have been brought against defense contractors. More recently, however, several scientific researchers, frustrated with university and government procedures for dealing with accusations of misconduct, have turned to the False Claims Act.

In May 1995, an epidemiologist who had sued researchers at the University of Alabama at Birmingham for using her work without giving her credit was awarded nearly a third of a $1.6-million settlement. But in October 1995, a federal judge in Maryland dismissed a suit by a former researcher at the University of California at San Francisco. That scientist had claimed that her inability to duplicate the research results of several other investigators at that institution indicated fraud.

Advocates of the False Claims Act see it as a way to "level the playing field" for *whistleblowers* (people who expose misconduct). These individuals claim that they are often mistreated in universities' internal review processes and that government follow-up takes too long. Opponents claim that the law invites frivolous lawsuits motivated by greed, that it could cause problems for honest researchers, and that the courts are not an appropriate place to resolve scientific disputes. The fate of several cases currently making their way through the courts should determine whether the False Claims Act becomes a major weapon in the fight to maintain integrity in scientific research.

Radiation experiment victims. At a White House ceremony on Oct. 3, 1995, the president issued a formal apology to all the unwitting subjects of secret radiation experiments conducted in the United States from 1945 to 1975. He was responding to a report by the Advisory Committee on Human Radiation Experiments, which he had formed in January 1994.

The committee included experts from ethics, law, history, and medicine, as well as a citizen representative. Its 925-page report recommended that the government apologize to the subjects of radiation experiments or their surviving family members and provide financial compensation to those who were physically or emotionally harmed. A bill to provide compensation was introduced in Congress a week after the release of the committee's report, but no action had been taken on it by mid-1996.

The committee urged that in the future there should be no exceptions to the requirement that experimenters obtain informed consent from the subjects of their experiments. In response to the committee's concerns, the president announced the establishment of a National Bioethics Advisory Commission. He ordered all federal agencies to review their policies governing human experiments, taking account of the recommendations of the Advisory Committee on Human Radiation Experiments, and to report back to the new commission.

Genetics and crime. Is the tendency toward violence and criminal behavior inherited? Or do these behaviors stem from social causes such as poverty, unemployment, and racism? In September 1995, the National Institutes of Health in Bethesda, Maryland, sponsored a conference to seek answers to those questions.

The meeting had many critics, including minority political leaders who charged that the results of research on genetics and crime would likely be used to victimize minority groups. Although the conference was held at a remote location in Maryland, it was disrupted by protesters who burst into the auditorium accusing the participants of racism and genocide.

A number of studies presented at the conference seemed to suggest that some types of antisocial behavior are inherited. One researcher found similarities between criminal records of identical twins who had been raised separately. Others reported chemical changes in the brains of children with attention deficit hyperactivity disorder, suggesting genetic links for that type of behavior, which may lead to antisocial tendencies. Such findings were countered by other studies that pointed to the strong environmental influences on behavior.

Several participants noted the dangers inherent in conducting research on genetics and behavior, reminding their fellow scientists that once their studies are completed, scientists have little control over how the studies might be used. For example, government officials could try to link high crime rates among minorities to genetic causes. They could then seek to reduce crime by medicating people instead of improving the conditions under which those people live. The specter of research on *eugenics* (attempts to genetically improve the human species), conducted in the early 1900's and later used by Nazi Germany to support policies that led to mass murder, hung over the meeting.

Scientists attending the conference agreed that it had been a "wake-up call," sensitizing participants to the potential misuses of genetic research. But most participants felt that the research was potentially very important and, with appropriate safeguards, should continue.

[Albert H. Teich]

A new era in human space flight was inaugurated in 1995, as American astronauts and Russian cosmonauts began routinely flying on each other's spacecraft. By mid-1996, the United States space shuttle Atlantis had docked with Russia's space station Mir three times—all while workers on the ground were busy building components for a new, international space station to be assembled in orbit in the late 1990's.

Atlantis visits Mir. The first U.S. orbiter to dock with Mir was Atlantis, on June 29, 1995. After chasing Mir in orbit for two days, the shuttle commander, U.S. Navy Captain Robert L. "Hoot" Gibson, guided Atlantis the final few feet to the Russian station. A ring on the docking system in the shuttle's cargo bay was gently pushed onto a similar ring on Mir's Kristall module. After checking the seal between the two spacecraft and then equalizing the air pressure, the crews opened the hatches for a historic meeting.

Two cosmonauts, Anatoly Y. Solovyev and Nikolai M. Budarin, flew to Mir with the Atlantis crew. They remained on the space station, replacing the previous Mir crew: Vladimir N. Dezhurov, Gennady M. Strekalov, and Norman E. Thagard, who returned to Earth with the Atlantis. Thagard, an American astronaut and physician who was a guest researcher on Mir, had spent 115 days in space—a U.S. record—by the time the Atlantis landed on July 7, 1995.

There was one hitch at the end of the mission. Solovyev and Budarin had flown from Mir in a Soyuz spacecraft to photograph the shuttle and Mir linked together. After Atlantis left Mir, a computer controlling Mir's *attitude* (position in space) lost part of its memory, and the Russian station began to drift. Solovyev and Budarin hurried back in their Soyuz to correct the problem.

The next time Atlantis flew to Mir, on November 12, 1995, it carried a new module for the Russian station. The purpose of the module was to make it easier for U.S. shuttles to dock by giving the two spacecraft a longer connecting tunnel and therefore more clearance.

Delivering the new module presented Atlantis's commander, U.S. Marine

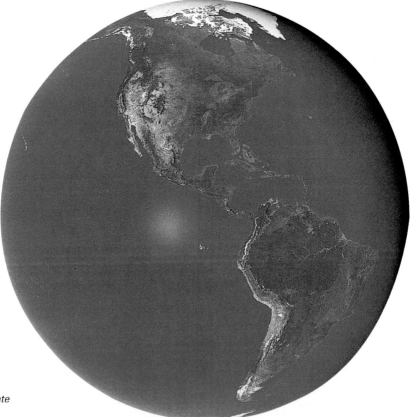

A new technique developed by ARC Science Simulations of Loveland, Colorado, produced an image of a cloudless Earth. The picture, released in December 1995, combines data from global weather satellite images and photographs taken from space. Although the Earth as a whole is never without clouds, there are always areas that are cloud-free. A computer sorted through all the data and pulled out images from every point on Earth taken on clear days. The data was then combined into an image of a cloudless Earth.

Partners in space

A new era in space began in 1995 as American astronauts and Russian cosmonauts began to routinely fly and work on each other's spacecraft. On June 29, 1995, the U.S. space shuttle Atlantis became the first American space vehicle to dock with the Russian space station Mir. Atlantis brought food and other supplies to Mir, as well as the two cosmonauts sent to replace Mir's crew. As Atlantis prepared to return to Earth on July 4, 1995, *right,* cosmonauts aboard a Soyuz spacecraft photographed the historic moment. The antenna of the Soyuz can be seen slightly below Atlantis. The six astronauts and four cosmonauts aboard Mir, *below,* made up the largest group of people in orbit in the same spacecraft up to that date.

Corps Colonel Kenneth D. Cameron, with a challenging task. When the new docking module was mounted atop the orbiter's regular docking system, it created a stack 8 meters (25 feet) high sticking out of Atlantis's cargo bay. Cameron and his four crew mates could not see the docking ring on top when they looked out the shuttle's windows. They had to rely on information from television cameras, radar, and laser-operated range-finding equipment to help them dock the shuttle.

The two spacecrafts' crews worked together for three days, creating one of the most diverse groups ever to fly in space. In addition to Russians and Americans, the crew included Canadian Air Force Major Chris A. Hadfield from the Atlantis and Thomas Reiter of Germany, a European Space Agency astronaut on board Mir.

On the shuttle's third mission to Mir, launched March 22, 1996, the crew included a U.S. astronaut, biochemist Shannon W. Lucid, who then remained on the station. She was scheduled to stay on Mir for 4½ months, which would break the record set by Thagard. Before Atlantis left Mir, astronauts Linda M. Godwin and Army Lieutenant Colonel M. Richard Clifford performed a spacewalk to attach U.S. experiments to the exterior of Mir.

According to the original agreement between Russia and the United States, NASA was to fly a total of seven shuttle missions to Mir, carrying food, water, supplies, astronauts, and experiments. Because of its dire financial situation, however, Russia could not afford to both continue working on Mir and contribute to the construction of the planned international space station. The United States agreed to fly two more shuttle visits to Mir than had been planned. In April 1996, the Russians added the last module, called Priroda, to Mir.

Other shuttle flights. On July 13, 1995, after Atlantis landed at the end of its first mission to Mir, NASA launched the shuttle Discovery. That mission followed the Atlantis flight by just six days—more closely in time than any previous mission. The Discovery's crew of five deployed a large communication satellite, one of five Tracking and Data Relay Satellites now orbiting Earth.

The shuttle Endeavour went into orbit on September 7, 1995, but that flight encountered several problems. Troubles with the Wake Shield Facility, a satellite designed to provide a vacuum for growing semiconductor crystals in space, prompted controllers to cut short its mission. And when the shuttle moved in to capture a Spartan satellite, which had been studying the *solar wind* (a stream of charged particles emitted by the sun), they found it in the wrong position and rotating. But the crew of five managed to snare the satellite and the mission was capped by a successful spacewalk to test new tools that had been designed for space station assembly.

The space shuttle Columbia lifted off on Oct. 20, 1995, with a crew of seven, including two scientists who were not career astronauts but specialists in areas of experimentation planned for the flight. For 16 days, they worked in the Spacelab module, carried in the payload bay and connected to the crew cabin. The mission, designated the second U.S. Microgravity Laboratory, involved low-gravity research in fluid physics, materials science, and biotechnology.

Columbia was launched again on Feb. 22, 1996, to attempt an experiment with a space tether. By dragging a spherical satellite supplied by the Italian Space Agency tethered to the shuttle with a cable, scientists hoped to generate electricity. The tether experiment had been attempted in 1992 by the crew of the shuttle Atlantis. But on that flight, the reel jammed after the tether had barely started to unfurl.

The retest in 1996 proved to be just as disappointing. The tether, just 2.5 millimeters (0.1 inch) thick and 20 kilometers (12.4 miles) long, had been unwound almost as far as intended when it snapped and the satellite drifted away. It fell toward Earth less than a month later and burned up when it entered the atmosphere.

A panel that investigated the failure of the experiment determined that the tether insulation had been punctured. The puncture allowed electricity to jump from the copper wire in the tether to a circuit in the shuttle's payload bay. The resulting short circuit burned through the tether in just nine seconds, severing it.

On May 19, 1996, the shuttle Endeav-

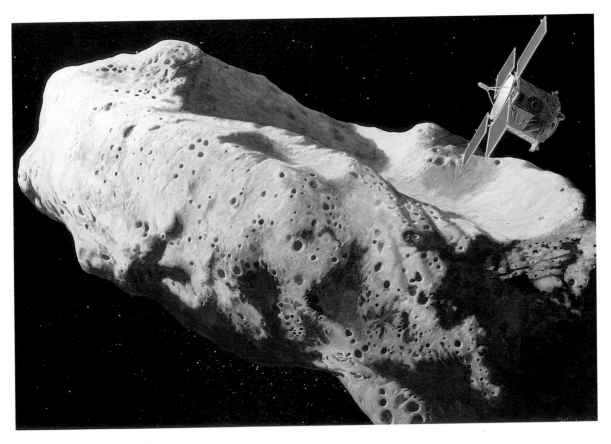

A spacecraft called NEAR (for Near Earth Asteroid Rendezvous), shown in an artist's conception, was launched from the Kennedy Space Center in Florida in February 1996 on a mission to the asteroid Eros, a rocky body about 40 kilometers (25 miles) long. NEAR, the first spacecraft ever sent to orbit an asteroid, was scheduled to reach Eros in early 1999. It will circle the asteroid for about a year and radio back photographs and data.

our was launched on a mission to test new space technology. The crew of five U.S. and one Canadian astronaut also performed biology and materials science experiments. A highlight of the flight was the testing of a huge inflatable antenna on a satellite that Endeavour carried into orbit and released. Scientists wanted to study the possibility of using inflatable structures in space, because they are lighter, cheaper, and less complicated than their solid counterparts.

Planetary spacecraft. One of the most important space-exploration missions of 1995 was the voyage of the Galileo spacecraft to Jupiter. Launched by the United States in 1989, Galileo traveled 3.7 billion kilometers (2.3 billion miles) to gather data about the solar system's largest planet. Despite damage to an antenna and a tape recorder that threatened to ruin the mission, Galileo neared Jupiter in July 1995 and released a 340-kilogram (750-pound) probe carrying six instruments to plumb the planet's atmosphere.

Both spacecraft arrived at Jupiter on

Dec. 7, 1995, becoming the first artificial objects to orbit one of the solar system's outer planets. Galileo will remain in orbit around Jupiter until 1997—when its fuel is expected to be exhausted—sending photographs and data about the planet and its moons back to Earth.

The probe's mission, however, ended in less than an hour. It fell through Jupiter's atmosphere, collecting data and sending it back to Galileo. It finally disintegrated in the extreme temperature and pressure of the planet.

The probe, a cone-shaped object just 1.3 meters (4.2 feet) in diameter, was built to withstand Jupiter's atmospheric conditions for as long as possible. As it decelerated from 170,500 kilometers (106,000 miles) per hour, the probe encountered heat far greater than that endured by any other spacecraft. The heat was twice as high as that on the surface of the sun. Its aerodynamic design, engineers determined, would create a *bow shock* (shock wave) ahead of it as it plowed through the atmosphere. Although the temperature in the bow shock reached 15,500 °C (28,000 °F), the shock wave kept the temperature on the probe itself to about half that. Most of the 15-centimeter- (6 inch-) thick heat shield covering the cone wore away from friction with Jupiter's atmosphere.

The probe withstood the blazing entry, its parachute opened, and, for nearly an hour, it radioed data to the orbiter for relay to Earth. Finally, the probe was crushed by the ever-increasing pressure it encountered. It was a dramatic start to a mission that is expected to produce a wealth of information about the solar system's largest planet and its moons. (See also ASTRONOMY.)

Asteroid mission. The first spacecraft ever sent on a mission to orbit an asteroid was launched from the Kennedy Space Center in Florida on Feb. 17, 1996. Called NEAR, for Near Earth Asteroid Rendezvous, the 805-kilogram (1,775-pound) spacecraft is expected to reach its target, an oblong asteroid called Eros, early in 1999. Eros, discovered in 1898, is barely 40 kilometers (25 miles) long.

Astronomers once regarded asteroids as uninteresting debris in the solar system. But in recent decades, asteroids have captured the imagination of scientists and lay people alike. Astronomers believe that some asteroids are made up of matter unchanged since the formation of the solar system. Once the planets formed, asteroids had an impact— literally—on the larger bodies, including Earth. An asteroid collision with Earth may have led to the extinction of dinosaurs and many other species. And though the odds are low that an asteroid large enough to wreak similar havoc will strike again any time soon, such a catastrophe is not impossible. That adds to the fascination with asteroids.

On its way to Eros, NEAR is to fly by a larger asteroid, Mathilde, taking pictures and chemical readings of it in June 1997. When it arrives at Eros, NEAR will orbit the asteroid for about a year at a height of 40 kilometers (25 miles) or less and study it with a camera and other instruments.

European spacecraft. The European Space Agency launched two major science spacecraft in the fall of 1995. The Infrared Space Observatory (ISO) was launched into Earth orbit on November 16, 1995, from Kourou, French Guiana.

ISO is a telescope, like NASA's Hubble Space Telescope. However, ISO allows astronomers to look at objects in the infrared portion of the spectrum, instead of in visible light.

Soon after its launch, ISO began examining cool objects that cannot be seen with conventional visible-light telescopes or instruments on Earth. Scientists plan to use ISO to look for so-called cold dark matter, which many astronomers and astrophysicists think makes up most of the mass of the universe. For example, they began searching for brown dwarfs, clouds of contracting gas and dust too large to be planets but too small to become stars.

To explore this hidden universe, the telescope had to be cooled to −270 °C (−454 °F), a temperature just above absolute zero. To keep it cold, ISO is enclosed in a *dewar*, a container similar to a thermos that is filled with liquid helium, and is shielded from the sun.

The other European spacecraft, the Solar and Heliospheric Observatory (SOHO), is a joint project with NASA. SOHO was launched on Dec. 2, 1995, from Florida and flew to a point in space between Earth and the sun called the L1 "Lagrangian" or "libration" point. At that spot, the gravitational pulls of the two bodies are equal, thus in effect canceling each other out. From this relatively stable point about 1.6 million kilometers (1 million miles) away, SOHO's 12 telescopes and other instruments began to study the structure and dynamics of the sun. Astronomers hope to learn more about the sun's surface, its internal heating system, its atmosphere, and the solar wind.

Scientists have long known that the sun's cycle of activity averages 11 years, and they timed the SOHO mission for a *solar minimum* (the point in the cycle in which massive sunspots and huge eruptions called solar flares are least likely). However, pictures and data from SOHO show that the sun is surprisingly active even in these relatively quiet times. Scientists have been startled to find ceaseless turmoil everywhere on the sun. SOHO will remain at the Lagrangian point for two or more years, providing astronomers with a new look at the center of our solar system. [James R. Asker]

In WORLD BOOK, see SPACE EXPLORATION; SPACE TRAVEL.

Science You Can Use

In areas selected for their current interest, *Science Year* presents information that the reader as a consumer can use in understanding everyday technology or in making decisions—from buying products to caring for personal health and well-being.

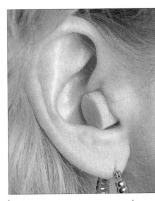

Loud Music's Assault on Your Hearing

While many people feel that the music of such rock-and-roll legends as Rod Stewart and The Who's Pete Townshend has held up fairly well over the years, the performers themselves admit that they—or at least their ears—are somewhat the worse for wear. As with other well-known rock musicians, including heavy-metal star Ted Nugent and the Talking Heads' Jerry Harrison, years of playing music amplified to ground-shaking levels left them with impaired hearing and a persistent buzzing or ringing in their ears called *tinnitus*.

Their difficulties underscore what hearing experts have known for years:

Excessive levels of noise can gradually, painlessly—and permanently—damage your hearing, making your ears old before their time.

Although many people suffer from a gradual hearing loss attributed to normal aging, age-related hearing impairment apparently isn't inevitable. In one study, scientists tested the hearing of members of a tribe living in a remote area of Sudan, free of the noises of industrialized societies, and found little hearing loss in older tribal members, even those in their 70's and 80's.

On the other hand, some 28 million people in the United States have im-

How loud is too loud?

The louder a noise is, the greater the risk it poses to your hearing. And as the volume escalates, sound, measured in decibels (dB), needs less time to cause harm. Sounds of about 80 dB or softer are harmless; those of 85 to 110 dB can damage hearing over time; and those of 120 dB or more can cause more immediate hearing loss.

Decibels	Noise
Safe Range	
20	Leaves rustling
40	quiet street noise
60	normal conversation
80	heavy traffic
Risk Range	
85–90	motorcycle; snowmobile
85–110	rock concert
Injury Range	
120	jackhammer 3 feet away
130	jet engine 100 feet away
140	shotgun blast

Sources: *Mayo Clinic Family Health Book; The American Medical Association Family Health Guide.*

paired hearing. For more than one-third of them, ear damage caused by loud noise is at least partly responsible, according to the National Institutes of Health (NIH) in Bethesda, Maryland. And in today's world, there's no shortage of loud noises to assault our ears, from screeching subway cars to pounding factory machinery to wailing ambulance sirens. According to NIH estimates, more than 20 million Americans are exposed on a regular basis to hazardous noise levels that could impair their hearing.

Many people, including fire fighters, police officers, construction and factory workers, musicians, and farmers, are bombarded with hazardous levels of noise on the job. Even our amusements—roaring across wintry landscapes on snowmobiles; hunting and target shooting; playing in a rock band; or listening to loud music at rock concerts, dance clubs, or through headphones—can immerse us in sound levels that are hazardous to our ears.

The ear is a complex and delicate mechanism. It consists of three main parts: the outer ear, the middle ear, and the inner ear. When a musician plucks the strings of a guitar or a baseball player solidly connects wood with horsehide, the sound waves that are produced enter the outer ear and are funneled through a passageway called the external auditory canal. Vibrations are generated when these sound waves strike the eardrum. The vibrations are transmitted from the eardrum to the key components of the middle ear, three tiny *ossicles* (bones) commonly known as the hammer, anvil, and stirrup.

The ossicles, in turn, amplify these vibrations and pass them along to the inner ear, which contains structures that help us maintain our balance as well as hear. The amplified vibrations finally pass into a bony, snail-shaped, fluid-filled structure called the *cochlea*. There, microscopic sensory cells called *hair cells* perform a remarkable feat: They convert the energy of the sound waves into electrical nerve impulses.

The delicate hair cells are so named because each is topped with several rows of hairlike projections called *stereocilia*. The sound waves cause the stereocilia to bend, triggering chemical changes in the cells that result in electrical signals

that race along the auditory nerve to the brain. The brain, which interprets these signals, generally is able to distinguish one kind of sound from another, because sounds that differ in pitch and loudness move the hair cells in slightly different ways.

It is the 16,000 hair cells in each cochlea that appear to be the structures most vulnerable to noise-induced hearing loss. Loud noises can destroy large numbers of hair cells by twisting, bending, or fusing their stereocilia or by altering the structures that normally anchor the stereocilia. Once destroyed, hair cells are not replaced.

We're all vulnerable to this kind of damage. A panel of experts who gathered in 1990 at the NIH to examine the issue of noise-induced hearing loss concluded that people of any age can suffer temporary or permanent hearing loss if they're exposed for long enough to loud sounds.

A unit called the decibel (dB) is used to denote the intensity of a sound, which roughly translates to how loud it is. Each 10-unit increase in decibel level indicates a tenfold increase in intensity. For example, the sound of normal conversation or birdsong (60 dB) is 10,000 times louder than rustling leaves or a ticking watch (about 20 dB). A noisy restaurant (70 dB) is 100,000 times louder, and heavy traffic (80 dB) 1,000,000 times louder.

Experts say that sounds with levels less than about 80 dB are unlikely to cause hearing loss, even when people are regularly exposed to them for hours at a time. But studies reveal that prolonged, repeated exposure to noise above 85 to 90 dB—a level not uncommon in many factories or other workplaces—can lead to permanent hearing loss.

In general, the louder the noise, the greater the risk to your hearing and the faster damage can occur. Thus, the average person's ears can tolerate the noise from a lawnmower (90 dB) for about eight hours before damage occurs. But increase that lawnmower's noise level another 5 dB, and the time it could take to injure the ears is halved, to four hours.

Pump up the volume to 110 dB—a level found at many rock concerts, particularly near the loudspeakers—and if

How we hear

The outer ear funnels sound waves to the eardrum, making it vibrate. The vibrations pass to three tiny bones in the middle ear called the ossicles, which amplify the vibrations and send them to the inner ear. There, in a fluid-filled structure called the cochlea, the sound waves are converted into electrical impulses. The auditory nerve carries these signals to the brain, which recognizes them as sound.

When damage occurs

The cochlea contains specialized cells called hair cells. When loud noise bombards the ear, it can destroy many hair cells. Once destroyed, the hair cells do not grow back. Without them, the inner ear cannot convert sound waves into electrical impulses.

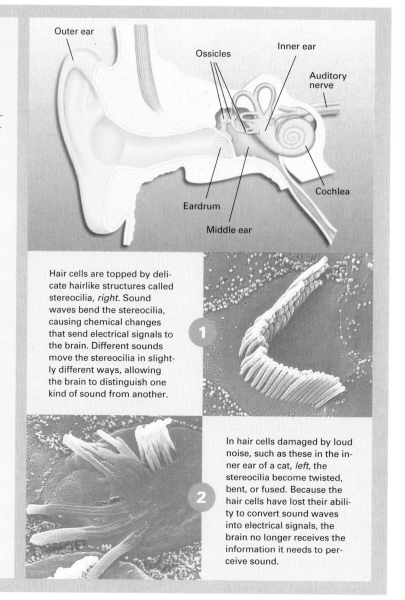

Outer ear

Ossicles

Inner ear

Auditory nerve

Cochlea

Eardrum

Middle ear

Hair cells are topped by delicate hairlike structures called stereocilia, *right*. Sound waves bend the stereocilia, causing chemical changes that send electrical signals to the brain. Different sounds move the stereocilia in slightly different ways, allowing the brain to distinguish one kind of sound from another.

In hair cells damaged by loud noise, such as these in the inner ear of a cat, *left,* the stereocilia become twisted, bent, or fused. Because the hair cells have lost their ability to convert sound waves into electrical signals, the brain no longer receives the information it needs to perceive sound.

your ears could talk, they'd plead for mercy after 30 minutes. Most hazardous of all are sudden, very high-decibel noises, such as close-proximity gunshots (140 dB), which can cause immediate hearing damage.

When the ears are blitzed with such a sudden burst of exceptionally loud noise, even brief exposure can cause pain and severe, permanent hearing loss. Such damage is particularly likely if the noise occurs without warning. This element of surprise is important

because muscles attached to the ossicles in the middle ear normally help protect hearing amid prolonged loud noise by tensing up, reducing the bones' ability to transmit sound vibrations.

But with noises such as an explosion or a rifle fired at close range, the inner ear is assaulted by the full force of the vibrations before this protective response can occur. This kind of injury, called *acoustic trauma,* can damage all the structures in the inner ear.

Noise-related hearing loss was once

thought to be mostly an on-the-job hazard for people who worked in noisy surroundings such as factories or construction sites. But in 1969, *audiologist* (hearing expert) David Lipscomb, then at the University of Tennessee in Knoxville, tested the hearing of incoming freshmen and made some startling discoveries.

Lipscomb found that about 60 percent of the students had significant hearing loss, and that about 1 in 7 of the male students had hearing comparable to men in their 60's. Since only 4 percent of a group of sixth-graders tested had hearing loss, it seemed likely that something—most likely exposure to loud noises—had damaged the college students' hearing as teen-agers.

Many audiologists came to suspect that the cause of this unexpected hearing loss was loud music from concerts, clubs, car radios, and "boom boxes." A number of studies found that people attending rock concerts or dance clubs are routinely exposed to sound levels above 100 to 120 dB—the latter being the volume of a jackhammer in full throttle only 1 meter (1 yard) away.

Adding to the risk, personal stereos with earphones hit the market, providing an opportunity to pour high-decibel noise directly into the ears. Researchers found that these devices can produce sounds in the 120-dB range. Customized, souped-up car stereos with huge amplifiers expose people to similar sound levels.

Later research lent further support to suspicions that excessively loud music poses a threat to listeners. In one study reported in 1990, British researchers tested the hearing of 60 students. They discovered that students who had commonly been exposed to loud music at rock concerts and clubs and through the headphones of their personal stereos had a reduced ability to hear high-pitched sounds. They also had trouble distinguishing between sounds that differed slightly in pitch.

People are much more likely, however, to suffer damage to their hearing gradually, after prolonged exposure to high-decibel noises. Initially, exposure to noises above safe levels—say, after a loud concert or riding on a snowmobile—can cause a temporary loss of hearing, called *temporary threshold shift* or TTS. Sounds are muffled, or the ears buzz or feel full. Scientists do not know exactly why this happens. They suspect

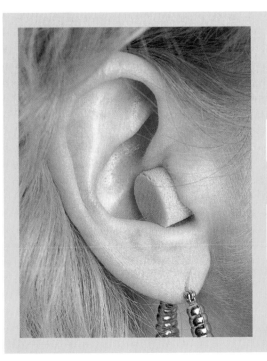

Preventing hearing loss

Rather than being the inevitable result of aging, experts say, hearing loss is an avoidable injury inflicted by a noise-drenched world. Because hearing loss is permanent, it is particularly important to protect ears while they're healthy.

- When you have to shout to make yourself heard, dangerous levels of sound are afflicting your ears. Turn down the volume.

- If you cannot control the volume of sound surrounding you, move as far as possible from the sound source, such as stereo speakers.

- Muffle noise by wearing earmuffs, foam or fitted earplugs, or a combination of earmuffs and earplugs. Avoid cotton balls, which are too porous to block dangerously loud sound.

- Protect your ears from sudden noises, such as a wailing siren, by covering them with your hands. This deflects some sound waves, giving muscles inside your ears time to tense up and inhibit the transmission of the noise to the inner ear.

that loud noise subtly alters the inner ear's hair cells and makes its nerve endings swell, distorting the electrical signals that travel to the brain.

Although TTS fades away after a number of hours, it's a sign that you're already on your way to damaging your ears. Experts warn that repeated exposure to sounds that cause TTS may gradually increase the number of irreversibly damaged hair cells and permanently impair hearing.

The damage first causes the ears to become less sensitive to certain high-pitched sounds. Although most of the sounds of normal speech are pitched below this range, women's and children's voices become more difficult to understand.

Consonant sounds, which tend to be higher in pitch than vowel sounds, also become harder to distinguish. This is particularly true in a setting with background noise, where it may seem that the people one is conversing with are mumbling. Eventually, the ability to make out lower tones is also affected. The persistent ringing or buzzing in the ears that is a hallmark of tinnitus is another sign of damage, and, like the loss in sensitivity to sounds, can become permanent.

People vary greatly in their susceptibility to noise-induced damage, perhaps because of differences in their genetic makeup, personal illnesses, or differing exposures to various environmental factors. Certain drugs, such as some antibiotics, also appear to increase the damaging effects of noise, so doctors who prescribe such medications should advise patients to take precautions to avoid loud noise. For the most part, however, doctors can't predict who will be most vulnerable to loud noises.

What is certain is that, all other factors being equal, repeated exposure to loud noises substantially increases one's likelihood of suffering hearing loss. The good news for those who are exposed to high-volume noise is that in nearly all cases—with the exception of accidental exposures, such as sudden explosions—noise-induced hearing loss is preventable.

Hearing experts say that if you have to shout to make yourself heard, or if you're playing music through headphones loud enough for other people to hear, you're being exposed to noise levels that could damage your hearing. If that's the case, you need to take steps to shield your ears from injury.

Simple strategies include putting some distance between yourself and the source of noise or turning down the volume of the television or stereo (particularly if you're listening through headphones). In situations where you can't avoid hazardous levels of noise, earplugs or earmuffs can be earsavers.

Earplugs reduce the noise levels reaching the inner ear by about 20 to 30 dB and vary widely in design. These range from inexpensive foam plugs (sold by drugstores, hardware stores, and gun shops) that are rolled and inserted into the external ear canal, to much more costly custom-fitted models made from impressions of an individual's ear canal.

One home remedy, cotton balls, does not offer adequate protection. Damaging sound waves can move through cotton balls because they are made of a porous substance and fit the ear canal poorly. Cotton balls muffle sound by about 7 dB.

Some people prefer to use earmuffs, which, like some models of stereo headphones, are designed to cover the ear completely. Although they are slightly less effective than foam earplugs, they reduce most loud noises to acceptable levels, and many people find them more comfortable and easier to use. In really loud situations, you can wear both earmuffs and earplugs.

On those occasions when you find yourself unexpectedly bombarded with noise, such as the wailing siren of a passing fire engine or ambulance, covering your ears with your hands can help reduce the high-decibel sound reaching your ears.

Although noise-related hearing loss is presently irreversible, scientists hope that someday this might change. Researchers have found that some animals can replace destroyed hair cells. It may be possible, they say, to promote this kind of regeneration in the human ear.

But for now, prevention is the only tool we have. For the majority of us who live in a too-noisy world, our best strategy is to turn down the volume and shield our ears to head off hearing loss.

[Joan Stephenson]

Water in a Bottle vs. Tap: Is It Any Tastier or Safer?

Americans have a growing thirst for bottled water. In the mid-1990's, they were drinking more than 10 billion liters (2.6 billion gallons) of bottled water a year, about five times as much as they consumed in 1980.

Most consumers opt for bottled water because they think it tastes better than tap water, according to the International Bottled Water Association (IBWA), an industry trade group. Many others choose bottled water because they're concerned about the safety of tap water from municipal water supplies. But do those who pay a premium for bottled water really get a safer, better-tasting thirst-quencher? Or are they simply falling prey to clever advertisements depicting bottled water as a magically healthful elixir?

For years, buyers of bottled water were pretty much flying blind. The sheer variety of bottled water—about 700 brands are sold in the United States—made comparison shopping difficult. Adding to the confusion was the fact that labels on bottled water could legally carry a number of misleading claims.

But consumers recently got a helping hand from the U.S. Food and Drug Administration (FDA). In November 1995, the FDA—which regulates bottled water in the United States because it is classed as a food—issued new regulations to clear the waters, so to speak. These regulations became law in May 1996.

The new regulations provide standard definitions for different types of bottled water, such as spring water and mineral water. They also require that labels on bottled water, except distilled and purified water, state the source of the water. For example, spring water must really come from a spring, and its label must specify whether the water flows from a natural opening in the ground or is extracted from a bore hole at the spring's source.

This is an important distinction, because about 25 percent of bottled water comes from public water supplies, the same source as tap water, though it may be processed further afterward. In the past, unscrupulous manufacturers could legally sell bottled tap water as spring water. But under the new FDA regulations, water bottled from public water supplies must say so on the label.

The regulations define *mineral water* as water obtained from geologically and physically protected underground sources. Previously, the term *mineral water* was misleading because all water, except distilled and purified water, contains minerals. Also, in the past manufacturers could simply filter ordinary water, add or remove minerals for taste,

An ocean of choices

Making an educated choice among bottled waters was difficult in the past, considering how many varieties and brands of water there are and the fact that labels could legally carry a number of misleading claims. In 1996, a new federal law aimed to clear the confusion by setting standard definitions for every kind of bottled water.

and call the end result "mineral water."

Other kinds of bottled water are also strictly defined in the regulations. *Distilled water* must have all its dissolved minerals removed by vaporization. In vaporization, the water is heated so that it turns into a vapor, leaving behind the dissolved minerals. The vapor is then condensed back into a liquid. *Purified water* is water that has been treated by chemical or physical processes, such as filtration or a process called ion exchange, to remove dissolved minerals. And only water that is naturally fizzy because it absorbed carbon dioxide gas from an underground source can be called *naturally sparkling water*.

Some drinks that consumers regard as bottled water have long been classified as soft drinks by the FDA. For example, in some cases manufacturers add carbon dioxide to water drawn from municipal systems. The result, products labeled *carbonated water, seltzer water,* and *soda water,* will continue to be defined as soft drinks. In addition, naturally sparkling water is considered a soft drink if *fructose* (fruit sugar) and fruit juices are added for flavoring.

Because these waters are classified as soft drinks, their labels need not specify the source of the water. But because the source for virtually all such products is a municipal water system, the water has passed federal purity standards.

The new regulations assure that consumers of bottled water will know exactly what they're buying. But that still leaves the question of whether their purchase represents a better deal—in taste and safety, if not cost—than tap water.

As for taste, it's true that some minerals found in tap water, such as sulfur and sodium, can give the water an unpleasant flavor. A high sulfur content can make water taste like rotten eggs, for example, while too much sodium makes it taste salty. And chlorine, commonly used to disinfect public water supplies, can make tap water taste as though it came from a swimming pool. Sulfur and chlorine can also give water an unpleasant odor.

Bottled water, on the other hand, generally is low in sodium. Depending on its source, however, it may contain sulfur. Spring water, for example, is more likely to contain sulfur than other kinds of bottled water. Most bottled-water plants shy away from chlorine and instead disinfect their products with *ozone,* a form of oxygen. Unlike chlorine, ozone gives water no flavor or odor. In some cases, therefore, bottled water may taste better than tap water.

But what about safety? Some consumers opt for bottled water because they believe tap water may be tainted. Such fears are not groundless. Contaminants such as industrial pollutants, disease-causing bacteria and viruses, and pesticides can, and sometimes do, end up in public water supplies.

In 1974, to protect the public from such pollutants, Congress passed the Safe Drinking Water Act. The act authorized the Environmental Protection Agency (EPA) to ensure that public water systems meet minimum health standards.

The Safe Drinking Water Act sets maximum contaminant levels (MCL's) for municipal tap water, limiting its content of bacteria, pesticides and other synthetic chemicals, nitrates, and some harmful metals, such as lead, arsenic, and mercury. The law requires water systems to test water for those substances, keep all pollutants below their MCL's, and alert consumers when a contaminant cannot be reduced to an acceptable level.

Nonetheless, many Americans continue to be uneasy about the safety of tap water. Their anxieties are fed by studies of municipal water supplies, such as one carried out in 1993 by the U.S. General Accounting Office (GAO), the investigative arm of Congress. The GAO reported that about half of the nation's 59,000 large public water systems and 20 percent of its 139,000 small systems were not being adequately monitored. The problems reported included failing to inspect water systems as often as required by law, a lack of formal training among inspectors, and neglecting to verify that faults found during inspections were corrected.

Another problem with some tap water, especially in older homes and apartments, is that it contains the toxic metal lead, leached from lead pipes or lead solder in pipe joints. If absorbed by the body, lead can interfere with the production of red blood cells and damage the brain.

As if these concerns weren't enough to worry about, studies have found that some of the measures taken to make tap water safe may themselves create potentially harmful substances. For example, the chlorine used to kill disease-causing microorganisms also produces chemicals called trihalomethanes (THM's) when it reacts with certain naturally oc-

curring compounds in water. Some studies have linked THM's with an increased cancer risk. To minimize that risk, the EPA limits THM's in drinking water to 100 parts per billion.

While such reports are likely to spur the sales of bottled water, consumers should be aware that bottled water is just as vulnerable to contamination as tap water. That's because all water—whether in a municipal reservoir or a tinted bottle with a designer label—originates from the same sources: lakes, rivers, springs, or *aquifers* (underground rock formations saturated with water).

The new FDA standards for bottled water require bottlers to meet or exceed the EPA's purity and safety requirements for municipal drinking water. But the FDA inspects bottled-water plants less frequently than municipal water systems. So, while bottled water is subject to the same purity standards as tap water, those standards are less likely to be enforced in the case of bottled water.

Certainly bottled water is not immune to reports of contamination. In 1987, a survey by the Massachusetts Department of Public Health found excessive levels of such contaminants as ar-

How bottled, tap water line up

Bottled water costs more than tap water, but many consumers think it is tastier and safer to drink. In areas where tap water is high in sulfur or sodium, bottled water may indeed taste better—though it, too, may contain sulfur. While bottled and tap water must meet the same safety standards, both have sometimes been found to be contaminated.

	Bottled Water	Tap Water
Cost	25 cents to more than $2 a liter	A fraction of a cent per liter
Portability	Very portable	Not portable unless poured into a special container.
Taste	Varies greatly; many bottled waters are very tasty. But may have chlorine taste if made from tap water. Some contain sulfur, giving a rotten-egg taste. Generally low in sodium.	Treated with chlorine, which can make it taste like swimming-pool water. May also contain sulfur, giving it a rotten-egg taste, or sodium, which is salty.
Additives	May contain chlorine if made from tap water. Occasionally, high levels of naturally occurring fluoride, which can discolor teeth.	Disinfected with chlorine; fluoride often added to prevent dental cavities.
Regulations	Subject to the same standards as tap water, but they are less likely to be enforced.	Must limit levels of bacteria, pesticides and other chemicals, nitrates, harmful metals.
Odor	Sulfur may give a rotten-egg odor.	Sulfur may give rotten-egg odor, chlorine a swimming-pool odor.

What's in the water

Despite legal limits on the amount of pesticides, heavy metals, nitrates, and bacteria, many consumers fear the health effects of substances found in tap and bottled water.

- **Lead** may leach into tap water from lead pipes or solder in pipe joints. Can damage the brain, liver, and other organs.

- **THM's,** which occur when chlorine reacts with naturally occurring compounds in water, may raise the risk of cancer. Limited by law to 100 parts per billion of water. May be present in tap water or in bottled water made from tap water.

- **Fluoride,** added to tap water to prevent cavities and naturally present in some bottled water, may stain the teeth if present in levels above 1.2 parts per billion.

- **Minerals,** such as iron, magnesium, and calcium may be naturally present in bottled water or "hard" tap water. Such minerals may help protect us against some chronic diseases, but large amounts of minerals can harm some people.

senic, radioactive particles, and bacteria in 32 of the 57 bottled waters sold in the state. And in 1990, traces of the cancer-causing chemical benzene were found in Perrier, one of the most prestigious bottled waters on the market. Perrier recalled 150 million bottles of its water.

Some bottled waters also have been found to contain THM's, despite the prevailing practice among bottlers of killing microbes with ozone rather than chlorine. In 1992, *Consumer Reports* magazine found that several bottled carbonated waters made from municipal water exceeded the EPA limit of THM's.

Fluoride, too, can be a problem in bottled water. Fluoride is often added to tap water to prevent dental cavities. But the concentration of fluoride in water supplies is closely monitored, because excessive amounts can discolor teeth or give them white spots. The legal limit of fluoride in tap water varies from 0.7 to 1.2 parts per million. Some bottled water, particularly spring water, may contain concentrations of naturally occurring fluoride that significantly exceed those limits.

Bottled mineral water and "hard" tap water may contain such minerals as iron, calcium, or magnesium, depending on the mineral content of soil around the water's source. These substances are often a selling point for bottled mineral water, because scientific evidence indicates that the calcium and magnesium in such water may have a protective effect against some chronic diseases, such as cardiovascular disease.

But drinking too much mineral-laden water may be harmful to some people. Studies have found that 1 American in 10 has the ability to over-absorb iron, which can cause liver damage and may increase the risk of heart disease. And some people who absorb too much calcium may develop painful stones in their kidneys. Consumers who enjoy mineral water, therefore, should drink only moderate amounts.

Finally, there's the matter of price. Compared to tap water, bottled water is quite expensive. A liter (0.26 gallon) of bottled water can cost from 25 cents to more than $2, compared to a fraction of a cent for a liter of tap water.

Sometimes, bottled water may be a safer choice than tap water, and so to some consumers it is worth the added

expense. It certainly would be worth it where local water systems have failed to meet EPA standards. In most cases, however, consumers of bottled water are paying for little more than a difference in taste.   [Phylis Moser-Vellion]

If you are concerned about the possible presence of lead in your tap water, the EPA has a Safe Drinking Water Hotline at 800-426-4791. The hotline can put you in contact with a state-certified testing laboratory that, for a small price, will test your water for lead. Most lead in tap water comes from the pipes carrying the water, including the pipes in many older houses and apartment buildings. People living in older homes can lower the amount of lead in their tap water by letting the water run for a few minutes before using it. This flushes out the water that has been in contact with lead in the pipe for the longest time. Also, it is a good idea to use cold tap water, rather than warm, for cooking purposes, because warm water picks up more lead from pipes.

If you frequently use an office drinking fountain or other public water source and want to know the purity of the water, contact your city or state public health department. It will have test records, listing the amounts of all major contaminants, for that water source.

If your tap water comes from a well and you are concerned about its safety, your local public health department or the EPA Safe Drinking Water Hotline can put you in contact with a state-certified laboratory to test your water.

If you have questions about your favorite brand of bottled water, try calling the International Bottled Water Association (IBWA). This industry trade group, which represents about 90 percent of domestic bottled-water makers and many imported brands, can be reached at 703-683-5213.

Lessening the Hazards of Home Pesticides

We have all heard disturbing reports about the potential health hazards of traces of pesticides in our food and water. Some scientists believe that pesticide residues in the environment may increase the rates of cancer, birth defects, and other disorders in human beings and wildlife. In most cases, though, the concentrations of these contaminants in food and water are quite small—in the parts-per-million or even parts-per-billion range. (A concentration of one part per billion is roughly equivalent to adding a few grains of salt to the water of an Olympic-size swimming pool.)

But many of us are exposed every day to pesticide levels hundreds or thousands of times higher than that. These hazardous amounts of poison come from the chemical sprays, powders, and liquids we use to control insects around our homes.

While many household pests can be controlled by nonchemical methods such as installing window screens or keeping the house clean, some infestations may seem serious enough to justify chemical control agents. When used as directed, most experts say, these products can be effective, at least temporarily, and their *toxicity* (poisonous effects) to people and pets can be minimized. Unfortunately, many people apply such products without first reading the directions and warnings on the labels. As a result, they may spread high levels of potentially dangerous chemicals around their homes.

Pesticides, which include any preparation designed to repel or destroy unwanted insects, weeds, rodents, or other pests, come in a wide array of formulations and packaging. They are available in the form of aerosol sprays, dusts, granules, liquids, fogs, and baited traps.

Pesticides intended for homes and gardens generally contain one or more active ingredients combined with *inert* (inactive) ingredients, which carry or disperse the active chemicals. But inert does not necessarily mean harmless. Although these inactive substances don't take part in the pesticide's main mission—to kill a pest—they may include hazardous compounds such as kerosene. The inert ingredients in a pesticide may irritate eyes and skin or cause headaches, drowsiness, and nausea if used in an unventilated room.

The largest-selling consumer pesticides are insect-control agents, known as insecticides. The active ingredients in commercial insecticides differ in the way they are absorbed by insects. Some, called contact poisons, are absorbed through the surfaces of insects' bodies. Others, called stomach poisons, are absorbed after being ingested.

Insecticides fall into several chemical categories. One large group, *organophosphates*, are compounds of carbon, phosphorus, oxygen, and hydrogen. Another important category, the *carbamates*, contain carbon, nitrogen, oxygen, and hydrogen. *Pyrethroids* are the synthetic versions of natural plant-derived insecticides called pyrethrins; they contain carbon, hydrogen, and oxygen.

One group of insecticides still common on farms but less so in homes are the *organochlorines*, which are made of carbon, chlorine, hydrogen, and sometimes oxygen. One of the earliest organochlorines was DDT, which used to be widely used on crops in the United

States. DDT decays slowly and is absorbed by the body tissues of people who eat foods containing DDT residues. Moreover, DDT kills useful as well as harmful insects and may endanger birds and fish. The United States banned almost all uses of DDT in 1972, but it is still used in many other countries.

Most insecticides kill by paralyzing the nervous system of insects that absorb them. Organophosphates and carbamates, for example, interfere with the the transmission of nerve impulses.

Insecticides vary widely in potency and usually target insects with similar habits or habitats. Some, for example, are designed to kill pests that fly (flies and mosquitoes) or crawl (ants and cockroaches), while others are aimed at insects that infest gardens (aphids and caterpillars).

To broaden insecticides' uses, manufacturers often combine two or more active ingredients in their products. Such mixtures can have another advantage: They sometimes have greater potency than an equal concentration of any one of the ingredients used by itself.

There are several things to take into account before deciding which pesticide to use for a particular problem. The type of pest you're combating, the location of the infestation, and the degree to which humans and pets in the household might be sensitive or allergic to particular pesticide ingredients are all important considerations.

Several insecticides are available for the control of flying or crawling creatures in your home. They include products with such generic names as propoxur, resmethrin, and propetamphos.

Propoxur, sold under a number of trade names, including Baygon, Unden, and Suncide, is a broad-spectrum carbamate that kills flies, mosquitoes, ants, and cockroaches. It is also effective against fleas and ticks on pets. Propoxur is available in aerosol sprays, ready-to-use liquids, powdered concentrates, and impregnated pet collars and strips. This insecticide is moderately toxic to humans and highly toxic to birds and fish.

Resmethrin is a pyrethroid that is used to control flying and crawling insects in homes and backyards. The com-

Using pesticides

To lessen the hazards of pesticides, follow all directions on the label. Mix and dilute outdoors or in a well-ventilated room. Inside, remove pets, dishes, and toys from the area to be treated. Apply only where needed, such as cracks, and use plenty of ventilation. Outdoors, spray only on a calm day. Wash hands and equipment afterward. Check label for instructions on disposal of rinsewater.

Product	Target	Hazards
Propoxur	Flies, mosquitoes, ants, cockroaches, fleas, ticks.	Moderately toxic to humans; highly toxic to birds and fish.
Resmethrin	Flying and crawling insects.	Moderately toxic to humans, mammals, and birds; highly toxic to fish.
Propetamphos	Cockroaches, flies, ants, ticks, moths, fleas, mosquitoes.	Moderately toxic to humans, mammals, and birds; highly toxic to fish.
Acephate	Aphids, leaf miners, caterpillars, sawflies.	Moderately toxic to humans, mammals, and birds; harmless to fish.
Methoxychlor	Chewing insects, mosquitoes, ticks, flies.	Slightly toxic to humans, mammals, fish, birds.
Rotenone	Lice, ticks, insects that feed on garden plants.	Toxic to humans and wildlife, especially fish.
Diazinon	Fleas, ticks, aphids, leafhoppers, cutworms, sawflies, cockroaches, ants, silverfish, carpet beetles.	Toxic to humans and wildlife, especially birds.
Carbaryl	Parasites on pets, army worms, cutworms, squash bugs, leafhoppers.	Moderately toxic to humans and wildlife; lethal to many helpful insects, such as honeybees.

pound, which is available in solutions and sprays, is added to many pet sprays and shampoos. Common trade names for resmethrin include Raid Flying Insect Killer, Chrysron, and Crossfire. Resmethrin is moderately toxic to humans, mammals, and birds, and very harmful to fish.

Propetamphos, sold under such trade names as Safrotin and Blotic, is an organophosphate designed to rid homes of cockroaches, flies, ants, ticks, moths, fleas, and mosquitoes. It is available in aerosols, emulsified concentrates, liquids, and powders. The compound is moderately toxic to humans, mammals, and birds and highly toxic to fish.

Several chemicals are effective at keeping chewing, sucking, and biting garden pests at bay. They include such preparations as acephate, methoxychlor, and rotenone.

Acephate, sold under such names as Orthene, Ortran, and Pillarthene, is an organophosphate that destroys flower-devouring aphids as well as such vegetable garden scourges as leaf miners, caterpillars, and sawflies. Acephate comes in aerosol sprays, soluble powders, and granules. The chemical is moderately toxic to humans, mammals and birds, but relatively nontoxic to fish.

Methoxychlor is a contact and stomach pesticide that controls chewing insects that attack ornamental flowers, vegetables, shade trees, and shrubs. It is also effective against mosquitoes, ticks, and flies. Methoxychlor is available in aerosol sprays, powders, emulsifiable concentrates, and dusts. Methoxychlor brand names include Marlate, Methoxychlor 25, and Chemform. This compound has relatively low toxicity to humans, mammals, birds, and fish.

Rotenone is a concentrated natural extract from the roots, seeds, and leaves of certain plants belonging to the pea family. Because of its origin, it is classified as a "botanical" pesticide, as are the pyrethrins and pyrethroids. Available under such brand names as Derrin, Cenol Garden Dust, and Chem-Mite, rotenone kills lice and ticks on dogs and many insects that feed on garden plants. Rotenone is often combined with other pesticides.

Rotenone in its concentrated form is quite toxic to humans and wildlife and must be handled with care. It is so lethal to fish that it is sometimes used to thin out fish populations for game-control purposes.

Some pesticides are particularly effective at eradicating the parasites that infest the skin and hair of dogs and cats. Among them are the compounds diazinon and carbaryl.

Diazinon, an organophosphate, is potent against fleas and ticks and is often used in pest strips. The compound also kills aphids, leafhoppers, cutworms, and sawflies in the garden. Inside the house, it eradicates cockroaches, ants, silverfish, and carpet beetles. Diazinon is marketed under such names as Spectracide, Basudin, and Knox-Out in the form of aerosol sprays, powders, granules, and concentrates.

Diazinon is quite toxic to humans and wildlife, particularly birds. When sprayed into the air, diazinon can be broken down by the sun's rays into more toxic compounds. In most pest strips, however, the compound is enclosed in microscopic capsules that slowly release their contents, minimizing the danger of increased toxicity.

Carbaryl, a carbamate, destroys parasites that infest domestic pets and livestock. It also acts against such garden pests as army worms, cutworms, squash bugs, and leafhoppers. Trade names for carbaryl include Sevin, Carbamine, and Hexavin. The chemical is marketed as a dust, spray, or liquid concentrate. Carbaryl is moderately to highly toxic to humans and wildlife and should be handled cautiously. The chemical is also lethal to many helpful insects, particularly honeybees.

Once you have decided which pesticide is most appropriate for your particular problem, follow the safety advice offered by poison experts. Their first recommendation is to always read the entire label for such information as the active ingredients, directions for use, special precautions, environmental hazards, first-aid instructions, and directions for storage and disposal. If you plan to use a product in the kitchen, be sure the label says that it is safe to be applied in food-preparation areas.

Follow all instructions completely, including those for mixing and diluting the product. All mixing and dilution should be done outdoors or in a well-ventilated room. While mixing (and lat-

Less hazardous alternatives

Pesticides, while effective, are not the only way to kill or repel pests. Alternative, nontoxic methods of pest control can also work.

To control	Try
Ants	Boric acid; planting mint or onions outside house.
Roaches	Borax; mixture of borax and diatomaceous earth; bay leaves; mixture of flour, borax, cocoa.
Fleas, ticks	Spray or sponge pet with rinse made from half a cup of dried or fresh rosemary that has been steeped in boiling water for 20 minutes and then strained and cooled. Inside the house, use flea traps made of lights suspended a few inches above dishes filled with soapy water.
Flies	Flypaper.
Moths	Cotton bags filled with cedar shavings, dried lavender, equal parts dried rosemary and mint.

Source: Greenpeace.

er applying) the product, wear any protective clothing or goggles the label recommends. If a spill occurs, don't wash it away, which can contaminate nearby areas. Instead, wipe it up completely with an absorbent material such as sawdust or kitty litter.

Before applying the pesticide, remove all pets (including birds and fish), dishes, and toys from the area being treated. Apply surface sprays only to the limited areas where they are needed, such as cracks or crevices. And always use plenty of ventilation when applying pesticides indoors.

If you plan to use a spray pesticide outdoors, wait for a calm day—wind makes it difficult to control an airborne poison. Close the windows and doors of your house while spraying, and keep the pesticide away from birds and other wildlife and from plants you do not want to treat.

Always store pesticides in their original containers. Never pour them into food jars or soft-drink bottles, which can attract children.

Be sure to wash your hands thoroughly after using a pesticide. Also, wash all pesticide sprayers and other application equipment. Check the product label for instructions regarding disposal of the rinsewater. Simply letting poison-laced water run down the drain can be hazardous to the environment.

If you worry about the long-term effects of pesticides on you, your family, and wildlife, you might consider nonchemical pest controls. Such approaches can be highly effective, according to the Environmental Protection Agency.

One nonchemical route is to spread commercially available bacteria, fungi, and viruses that infect and kill particular pests. An example is *Bacillus thuringiensis*, a strain of soil bacteria that attack gypsy moths, black flies, mosquitoes, midges, and cabbage loopers. A number of beneficial microorganisms can be ordered through garden-supply catalogs.

Many larger predators are also available from garden-supply companies. For example, you can obtain parasitic wasps that lay eggs inside the eggs or larvae of such pests as tomato hornworms. Once the wasp eggs hatch, the offspring kill their insect hosts and eat them. Ladybugs and their larvae eat aphids, mealy bugs, white flies, and mites. Other helpful predators that kill harmful insects include spiders, centipedes, dragonflies, ground beetles, and certain ants.

Some birds, such as the purple martin, are particularly helpful at ridding yards and gardens of insects. To attract such birds, try building a birdhouse.

Biochemical agents such as *pheromones* and *juvenile hormones* can also be effective against house and garden pests. Pheromones are chemical substances released by many insects to attract mates. Synthetic versions of these compounds are effective at luring harmful insects into traps. Juvenile hormones are substances that guide a creature's early development. Applied to insect larvae, the hormones keep the larvae immature, thereby preventing them from growing and reproducing.

No matter how much we try to control them, however, insects and other pests will always be with us. In some cases, the best solution may be to learn to live with them. Ask yourself, for example, whether every tomato and flower in your garden must be blemish-free.

But when Japanese beetles are devouring your prize roses or roaches are scampering across the kitchen counter, it is hard to resist reaching for the bug spray. Just be sure when you do so that you know what you're using, how much to apply, and how to protect your family and pets.   [Gordon Graff]

Bad Hair Days: a Case of Bad Chemistry

If you think chemistry has nothing to do with your everyday life, take a look in the mirror and think again. Specifically, look at your hair.

Chemistry has everything to do with whether your hair is straight or curly; blond, red, or brown; easily shaped into your favorite style; or a difficult-to-manage unruly mop. In fact, a chemist probably can provide as much—if not more—insight as your hair stylist on what makes the difference between a bad hair day and a good hair day.

Given the time and money most of us lavish upon our crowning glory, it's hard to believe that hair is merely dead skin. As skin cells in a cell layer known as the hair matrix die, they produce a tough protein called *keratin*. The pressure of new cells packs the dead cells and keratin together and pushes them to the surface of the scalp, where they emerge as strands of hair.

The average human head has between 100,000 and 150,000 strands of hair. From a chemist's viewpoint, that hair is virtually the same as bird feathers, horse hooves, cat claws, sheep's wool, and even snake scales—all of which are made primarily of keratin. Like all proteins, keratin is constructed from building blocks called amino acids. Much of keratin's strength is attributed to its high content of the amino acid cystine, which has particularly strong chemical bonds between sulfur atoms.

The physical structure of a human hair can be seen through a microscope. It consists of three layers of dead skin cells: the *cuticle,* a smooth, outer covering fashioned from cells that overlap like fish scales; the *cortex,* a thick, middle layer made of spindle-shaped cells filled with keratin and hair color; and the *medulla,* a relatively narrow central column containing cube-shaped cells and pockets of air.

Hair's chemical structure cannot be seen under a microscope. Like all matter, hair is made up of tiny units called atoms. The outer part of an atom consists of even smaller particles called electrons that whirl around the atom's center region. When two or more atoms join to form molecules—combinations of atoms—they do so by exchanging or sharing electrons.

At the molecular level, hair is composed mostly of chains of keratin molecules. These chains are cross-linked by chemical bonds in much the same way that the sides of a ladder are held together by rungs.

The bonds include very strong links between sulfur atoms found in cystine and much weaker electrical attractions between hydrogen atoms in other parts of the keratin molecules.

What's in a hair?

Hair is made of long chains of a tough protein called keratin. The chains of keratin are held together by chemical bonds between the hair's sulfur atoms and electrical bonds between hydrogen atoms.

Why hair lies straight

In straight hair, bonds form between atoms at approximately the same site on neighboring keratin chains. Because the bonded atoms lie side by side, the hair hangs smoothly.

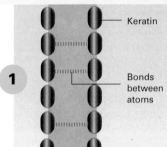

Keratin

Bonds between atoms

1

Why hair curls

In curly hair, bonds form between atoms that are not adjacent on neighboring keratin chains. Because the bonded atoms do not lie side by side, the hair is pulled into loops.

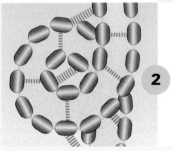

2

In straight hair, bonds form between atoms located at approximately the same sites on neighboring keratin chains. This creates relatively level "rungs" that allow the sides of the "ladder" to remain straight. In wavy or curly hair, molecules from different sites along adjacent keratin chains are attracted to each other, forming arching bonds that cause the sides of the keratin ladder to bend or loop around.

As for color, the shade of your hair is determined by natural pigments called *melanins* that are produced by skin cells. Surprising as it may seem, just one melanin—a black pigment called eumelanin—is responsible for most hair shades, from blond to black. The formula is simple: the greater the eumelanin level, the darker the hair. However, eumelanin cannot take credit for red hair, which owes its unique hue to a rarer, reddish type of melanin called pheomelanin. When skin cells grow old and stop producing eumelanin or pheomelanin, a person's hair turns gray or white.

Our genes determine the color and texture of our hair, but there are ways of getting around genetics. As the one-third of American women who color their hair and the half who perm or relax their locks can attest, hair chemistry can be easily changed. Perms, relaxers, dyes, shampoos, conditioners, and even curling irons and blow dryers all work their magic by tinkering with hair's normal chemical structure.

In fact, every time you wash your hair or go swimming, you generate a small chemical reaction. Hydrogen-rich water molecules snap the weak hydrogen bonds between your hair's keratin chains, prompting even the curliest of locks to straighten temporarily when wet. As the hair dries, the hydrogen bonds are reestablished, and waves or curls return.

The opposite occurs with straight hair that is dampened and then wound around pins or rollers so that different parts of the keratin chains are adjacent to one another. As the hair dries, it forms new hydrogen bonds and is temporarily transformed from straight to curly or wavy. Blow dryers, electric rollers, and curling irons act along the same principle, but use heat energy to reinforce the new bonding pattern.

But as people whose hair style depends on a curling iron or a blow dryer know, their efforts can be undone in minutes. All it takes is a little water in the form of a sprinkling of rain or a moist sea breeze to send your hair's hydrogen bonds scrambling back into their normal alignments.

For more lasting changes to your hair style—and your hair chemistry—you must turn to permanent waving (perming) or straightening. These processes not only alter hair's hydrogen bonds but also split apart stronger chemical bonds that are unaffected by water. Although waving and straightening (also called relaxing) produce opposite results, the two procedures employ the same chemical tricks.

Whether hair is permed or relaxed, the first step, called softening, involves *reduction*. Reduction is a chemical reaction that adds hydrogen to a chemical compound. In the perming or straightening process, reducing agents, sometimes together with heat, break the hair's water-stable bonds—primarily the sulfur-to-sulfur links in cystine.

In the next step of the process, called

rearrangement, the keratin chains are molded into the desired configuration. This is accomplished by winding the softened hair on rods to produce curls or holding it flat to straighten it.

The final step, hardening, makes the rearrangement permanent by rebuilding the sulfur-to-sulfur bonds and other water-stable molecular links that hold hair strands together. This is accomplished through *oxidation*—a chemical reaction that reverses reduction by adding oxygen to a compound. For perms and relaxers, the chemicals that initiate oxidation are either sodium bromate or hydrogen peroxide solutions.

Although perming and straightening are called "permanent," perms and relaxants do not change the hair matrix. Thus, their effects eventually disappear as hair grows out.

When properly formulated and used according to directions, products that perm or relax hair should not change its color or significantly weaken it. But both hair and scalp can be damaged if such products are carelessly manufactured or applied. In 1995, for example, the U.S. Food and Drug Administration (FDA) warned against the use of two hair relaxers sold under the name of Rio Hair Naturalizer System. The FDA took that action after more than 1,800 consumers complained that the products had irritated their scalp, caused their hair to break off, or turned it green. FDA investigators found that the products contained too much acid and were improperly labeled.

Another process that must be carefully controlled to avoid unpleasant results is bleaching. Hair is usually bleached with hydrogen peroxide, a chemical that lightens hair by oxidizing its melanin pigment.

The greater the concentration of hydrogen peroxide and the longer it is left on, the lighter the hair becomes until it approaches the harsh yellow-white of the stereotypical "bleached blonde." The bleaching process is halted by rinsing the hair with very hot water or a

The secret of hair color: melanins

Hair color depends on the kind, and amount, of natural pigments produced by skin cells. These pigments, called melanins, are responsible for all shades of color, from blond to raven black. Red hair results from a reddish melanin called pheomelanin; other colors result from a black melanin called eumelanin. The declining production of these pigments causes hair to turn gray or white.

Blond hair
Blond hair gets its flaxen hue thanks to low levels of eumelanin.

Brown hair
Brown hair is darker than blond hair because it has more eumelanin.

Black hair
The dark beauty of black hair comes from its high levels of eumelanin.

Red hair
Red hair owes its distinctive tint to the presence of pheomelanin, which is much rarer than eumelanin.

Gray or white hair
Hair loses its natural color and turns white or gray when aging skin cells stop producing eumelanin or pheomelanin.

mild acid solution, such as pyruvic acid.

The results achieved by bleaching are also determined by how much ammonium hydroxide, a chemical that activates oxidation, is added to the peroxide solution. Too much of this ammonia compound can produce unattractive reddish tints.

Hair tinting, which is capable of producing a rainbow of natural-looking hues from ginger gold to chestnut brown, also relies on oxidation. Colorants are a complex brew of chemicals. Oxidation is provided by a *developer*, usually hydrogen peroxide or another oxidizing agent. The developer acts on an *intermediate*. Intermediates are synthetic compounds, often derived from coal tar, that develop into dyes when they are oxidized.

Other components of hair color include *modifiers*, compounds that enhance or stabilize certain shades of color; *antioxidants*, which prevent the intermediates from oxidizing before they are applied to hair; and *alkalizers*, chemicals that improve the absorption of dye by softening the hair.

Like other hair treatments, coloring does not alter the cells that produce hair or its pigment. Thus, people who tint their hair must touch up their natural roots periodically if they want their growing tresses to retain an even color between complete dye treatments.

In recent years, many women have experimented with semipermanent and temporary dyes. Semipermanent colors use lower concentrations of oxidizing agents and wash out in four to six shampoos. Temporary colors, or rinses, are acid dyes that coat only the surface of the hair and readily wash out in the next shampoo. Because they simply add a tint to the surface of hair, rinses can be used only to produce a darker hair color.

Perming, relaxing, and coloring are the harshest things you can do to your hair from a chemist's viewpoint. But shampoos and conditioners also take advantage of chemistry to get their work done.

The job of shampoo is to clean the hair, so it's not surprising that the main ingredient in nearly all shampoos is detergent. Detergents create an *anionic*, or

Hair change through chemistry

All hair products, from shampoos to perms, rely on chemistry to change the appearance of hair. Because none of the products affect the cells that produce hair, however, their effects are temporary.

Process or Product	Action	Result
Setting hair with damp rollers	Rearranges hydrogen bonds between hair's keratin chains.	Hair curls.
Setting hair with hot rollers, curling iron, blow dryer	Heat energy rearranges hydrogen bonds between hair's keratin chains.	Hair curls or straightens, depending on how appliance is used.
Permanent waving and straightening (relaxing)	Hair is chemically softened to break its sulfur-to-sulfur bonds, then molded around rods or held flat. Chemicals are used to harden the hair's new sulfur bonds.	Hair curls or straightens, depending on how it is molded.
Bleaching	Hydrogen peroxide is applied, adding oxygen to the melanin pigment that gives hair color.	Hair lightens.
Coloring	Dyes and chemicals change the tint of hair's natural pigment.	Hair lightens or darkens.
Shampoo	Detergent creates a negatively charged solution.	Dirt and oil are stripped from hair; hair's outer surface ruffles.
Conditioner	Creates a positively charged solution.	Smooths hair.

negatively charged, solution when combined with water. Such a formula is good for cleaning hair by attracting positively charged ions, such as oil. But it also tends to ruffle hair's outer cuticle, explaining why just-washed hair is often flyaway, unmanageable, and rather dull.

To counteract these undesirable effects and smooth down the hair cuticle, people often follow a shampoo with a rinse of a *cationic*, or positively charged, solution. In years past, people used vinegar, lemon juice, or beer for this purpose. Such rinses made hair glossier and easier to comb, but they could leave hair smelling like a tossed salad or a brewery. Modern conditioners achieve the same results and also have a pleasant fragrance more appropriate for hair.

One of the most important classes of conditioning agents is the quaternary ammonium compounds. These cationic substances help counteract static electricity and flyaway hair by binding to the anionic strands of shampooed hair. Because hair that has been permed, relaxed, or colored is considerably more anionic than normal hair, manufacturers design special conditioners packed with cationic ingredients for hair that has undergone a strong chemical treatment. Some formulas can even temporarily repair or strengthen chemically processed hair through the use of cationic proteins that cling to the hair's weakened keratin chains through hydrogen bonds.

Of course, it would be best to avoid damaging your hair in the first place. Experts have a few tips to offer on how to keep your hair from looking like the result of a failed chemistry experiment.

First, they caution, do everything in moderation. Don't test the limits of your hair's ability to form and re-form chemical bonds by subjecting it to repeated perming, coloring, or straightening over a short time.

Second, don't begin any treatment until you have thought it over and know for sure what look you want to achieve. If you impulsively decide to put a poodle perm in your stick-straight hair or bleach your raven locks to platinum blond, it will be weeks or months before you can change your look again without seriously damaging your hair.

Third, follow all instructions on hair-care products to the letter. And before

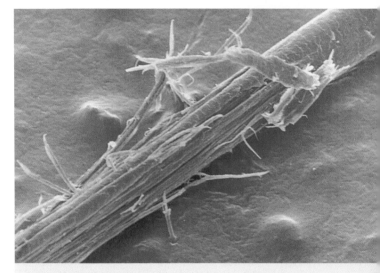

Avoiding hair damage

Experts offer these tips for protecting your crowning glory.

- Avoid perming, coloring, and straightening hair in rapid succession—this strains the hair's ability to form and re-form chemical bonds.
- Follow all instructions on hair-care products.
- Before home perming, straightening, or coloring, go through all steps of the process in your mind. Gather all materials you will need before beginning the process.
- In case of disaster, turn to a hair-care professional for help—don't apply more chemicals in an attempt to put matters right yourself.

starting any time-sensitive chemical process, such as coloring or a perm, do a dry run—go through the whole process in your mind and set out all the items you will need.

Lastly, if you end up creating a hair disaster, see a hair-care professional. Don't try to fix the problem yourself with home remedies or other chemical products. A professional may be able to salvage your hair, provide you with products to repair the damage, or at least cut your hair so that it looks reasonably attractive while you wait for your mangled tresses to grow out.

And here's one final tip: Consider being content with the hair you were born with, be it kinky or straight, dishwater blond or carrot red. You'll save a lot of energy—both chemical and personal—if you develop a sense of style that emphasizes your hair's natural beauty rather than an artificial look that requires you to constantly beat your hair into submission.   [Rebecca Kolberg]

Recycling Used Motor Oil

Someone changes the oil in his or her car. Instead of taking the old oil to a filling station to be recycled, he or she lets it drain onto the ground or pours it down a storm drain. Is it convenient? Yes. Is it harmless? Definitely not.

Sooner or later, that discarded oil will find its way into a stream that feeds a lake or reservoir, or into underground water supplies that are tapped by wells. In the meantime, it can contaminate the soil, kill or sicken wildlife, and destroy vegetation.

Each year in the United States, do-it-yourselfers dump an estimated 750 million liters (200 million gallons) of used oil where they should not. An additional 375 million liters (100 million gallons) ends up in unlined landfills, where it can leak into underground *aquifers* and contaminate them. (An aquifer is an underground layer of earth or porous rock containing water that can be pumped to the surface.)

These combined amounts are equivalent to about 30 times the notorious *Exxon Valdez* oil spill in Alaska in 1989—and they exclude the equally large amount that businesses and industries improperly discard. A further 67 million liters (17.8 million gallons) of used motor oil is tossed into landfills in the form of used oil filters—more than 300 million of them each year in the United States.

When you consider that 1 liter (2.5 pints) of oil spilled onto water can create an oil slick covering 1 hectare (2.5 acres), the potential for damage becomes very clear. In fact, about 40 percent of all pollution in our waterways is estimated to come from used motor oil.

It doesn't take much oil to make water undrinkable. According to the Environmental Protection Agency (EPA), 1 liter of oil can make 1 million liters (264,000 gallons) of water unfit for human consumption. At this concentra-

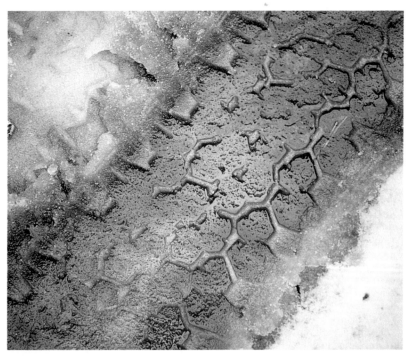

tion—just 1 part per million—oil makes the water taste and smell so unpleasant that most people would not want to drink it.

Nor should they if they value their health. Used oil contains a number of *toxic* (poisonous) substances. These include compounds called polycyclic aromatics, which have been shown to cause cancer in laboratory rats. So serious do experts consider the health risks from exposure to used motor oil that oil containers manufactured for the consumer market now carry health warnings. The warnings advise consumers who change their own oil to avoid prolonged skin contact with dirty oil and to wash their hands and other exposed skin areas with soap and water.

Waste oil can harm wildlife even more than it hurts people. Some of the lighter components of oil dissolve in water, damaging fish and other organisms. Researchers have found cancerous growths in fish that live in oil-polluted waters. Scientists are still debating how much oil must be present in water before fish are poisoned. The EPA says a concentration of 310 parts per million of dissolved oil harms freshwater fish, and 1 part per million can poison saltwater fish and other marine organisms.

Some scientists, however, believe that fish are even more sensitive to oil. Basing their views on data gathered after large oil spills, they say concentrations of oil as low as 2 to 10 parts per billion can kill microscopic fish larvae, and that adult fish may die when concentrations reach 300 or more parts per billion.

Moreover, a film of oil on top of water interferes with sunlight, making it difficult for aquatic plants to carry out *photosynthesis* (use of the sun's energy to make food and oxygen). It also blocks the absorption of oxygen from the air, choking off the aquatic life below.

That's not all. At the level of 50 parts per million, oil can interfere with the operation of sewage plants. And even if the spilled oil remains in the soil, its lighter, more *volatile* (evaporating easily) components may dissipate into the air. Rain or snow can bring them down again, to reenter the soil or pollute bodies of water.

Improperly discarded oil is also a tremendous economic waste. If all the used motor oil in the United States

Why recycle used oil?

Recycling motor oil offers a number of advantages, both environmental and economic, over refining new oil.

- Recycling motor oil helps prevent the contamination of drinking water by discarded oil. One liter of oil can render 1 million liters of water unsafe for humans to drink.

- By recycling motor oil, we reduce the chances of poisoning aquatic life. Used oil contains many *toxic* (poisonous) compounds that are very hazardous to wildlife. Some scientists believe that as little as 2 to 10 parts of oil per billion may kill fish larvae, while 300 parts per billion may kill adult fish. Aquatic plants can also be harmed by oil.

- Oil is a resource that, once taken from the ground, is not renewed. Recycling allows the same oil to be used again and again.

- Recycling motor oil saves energy. Recycling uses only one-third of the energy needed to refine new oil.

could be collected and burned to produce electricity, it would supply enough energy for nearly 900,000 homes a year. But a better idea is to clean the oil and reuse it.

In fact, a considerable amount of oil is being recycled. Service stations in Massachusetts, New Jersey, New York, Minnesota, and Wisconsin are required by law to accept used motor oil for recycling. Other states and communities have established drop-off centers for do-it-yourselfers' oil.

Businesses have sprung up to collect used oil from these and other sources, such as quick-lube shops and factories. These collectors sell the oil to companies that remove impurities from it so it can be reused.

In 1995, about 3 billion liters (800 million gallons) of used oil from all sources was recycled, according to industry estimates. Of this, about 2.6 billion liters (700 million gallons) was *reprocessed* and 375 million liters (100 million gallons) was *re-refined*.

Reprocessing, which is simpler and cheaper than re-refining, consists of removing water and dirt from the oil. The end product is used as a fuel in industrial plants.

A process similar to reprocessing, called *reclaiming*, is used by some companies that use large amounts of motor oil, such as automobile manufacturers. The end product, however, is lubricating oil rather than industrial fuel. Companies that reclaim oil do so on their own premises, and only reclaim oil that they themselves have used. Thus, this oil is not included in the totals of recycled oil.

Re-refining is an elaborate and expensive process that returns oil to its original condition so that it can be reused as an engine lubricant. Re-refining involves a number of steps. First, each batch is tested for contaminants. The most common contaminants are dirt, metal particles from engine wear, and phosphorus and silicon from additives that manufacturers add to improve the oil's performance. From additives also come zinc, boron, and calcium. (Although additives improve motor oil's performance, they become degraded when the oil is used. Because there currently is no practical way to measure how degraded the additives in used oil have become, they must be removed and added again later.)

Used oil may also contain chlorine, picked up from degreasing solvents used in service stations, repair shops, and industry. For example, a mechanic may use a solvent to clean an engine's carburetor, then dump the used solvent into a container of used motor oil instead of paying to have the solvent collected as hazardous waste.

Oil that contains excessive chlorine may be rejected for re-refining because it corrodes the refinery equipment. Reprocessors making fuel out of used oil with a chlorine content above 1,000 parts per million may be required by EPA regulations to handle the oil separately from batches with a lower chlorine content.

Polycyclic aromatics are another hazardous component of used oil. These cancer-causing compounds form when oil is partly burned in the engine cylinders. Polycyclic aromatics are rendered harmless by most re-refining methods.

Gasoline, which leaks down into the crankcase past the piston rings in internal combustion engines, is always present in used motor oil. In diesel engines, diesel fuel may enter the oil when some uncombusted fuel blows by the pistons. Also, experts say, unscrupulous service people sometimes dump gasoline and diesel fuel into collection tanks designed for used oil. Some used oil also contains contaminants that are similar to heating oil.

Occasionally, recycling plants receive oil from worn-out electric-utility transformers. This oil may contain toxic chemicals called polychlorinated biphenyls (PCB's). Oil containing PCB's should not be reprocessed into fuel, because the PCB's, which contain chlorine, form other poisons called dioxins when they are burned. But PCB-containing oil can often be re-refined into lubricating oil.

Once used oil has been tested for all these contaminants, it is pumped into large storage tanks, where it sits for several days to separate out water and solid particles. The water and particles sink to the bottom of the tank and are removed periodically. Filtration may also be used to remove solid particles.

Next, the oil is pumped into an apparatus called a flash evaporator tower, where it is heated to between 121 °C and 149 °C (250 °F and 300 °F) at atmospheric pressure. The high temperature of this processing step, called dehydration, causes gasoline and other volatile contaminants, as well as any remaining water, to vaporize. The vapors are drawn off and returned to liquid form by cooling. The water is sent to a wastewater treatment plant; the mixture of volatile contaminants is used as fuel at the re-refining plant.

In the next step, called fuel stripping, other fuels are distilled off at their respective boiling points, ranging from 205 °C to 340 °C (400 °F to 650 °F). A moderate vacuum is used to aid the vaporization of this material. The fuels are

Two kinds of oil recycling

Most used motor oil is recycled in two ways: through reprocessing or re-refining. In 1995, about 2.6 billion liters (690 million gallons) of used oil were reprocessed and 380 million liters (100 million gallons) were re-refined.

Used
motor oil

Reprocessing

Reprocessing is the simplest and least expensive recycling method. It simply separates water and dirt from the used motor oil, which then is sold as industrial fuel.

Settling or filtration
(or both)

Industrial
fuel

Re-refining

Re-refining is more elaborate and involves the removal of a number of contaminants, including fuels, that have accumulated in the oil. First, used motor oil from which dirt and other solid contaminants have been taken out is subjected to a dehydration process that separates water and light fuels from the oil. Then a fuel-stripping step removes other fuels, including gasoline. Next, the oil is vaporized in an extreme vacuum and then condensed into oil of differing weights. Finally, in a process called hydrotreating, hydrogen is added to the oil, along with a catalyst. The catalyst causes the remaining impurities in the oil to chemically combine with hydrogen, converting them into compounds that become part of the oil. After the remaining hydrogen is removed, the final product is high-grade motor oil.

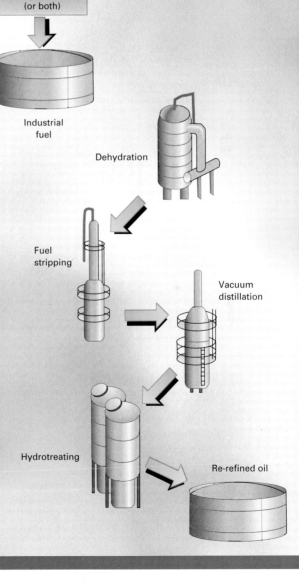

Dehydration

Fuel
stripping

Vacuum
distillation

Hydrotreating

Re-refined oil

either used at the re-refinery or sold to industries.

Next comes distillation in a device called a thin-film evaporator, at between 260 °C and 399 °C (500 °F and 750 °F) and under an extreme vacuum. The oil is condensed into two or three fractions of differing *viscosities* (thicknesses). The primary by-product of this stage is a thick, gooey black substance called asphalt flux or asphalt extender. This material is used in making tar paper and roofing shingles, or mixed with asphalt for paving streets.

In the final step, called hydrotreating or hydrofinishing, sulfur, nitrogen, chlorine, PCB's, and oxidized compounds are removed from the oil, along with phosphorus, silicon, and the remaining heavy metals. In hydrotreating, hydrogen is added to the the oil at a high temperature and pressure. With the aid of a *catalyst* (a substance that causes a chemical reaction while remaining unchanged itself), the hydrogen reacts with the contaminants, converting them into compounds that become part of the oil. Any remaining hydrogen is then separated from the oil under high pressure, cleaned, and recycled.

The end product of the re-refining process is pure lubricating oil that meets all industry and government standards. With the addition of new engine-protection additives, the oil can be reused in automobiles, even high-performance models. And with re-refining, nothing goes to waste. Even the spent catalyst is usually sent back to the manufacturer to be regenerated and used again.

Re-refining, if done properly, releases no toxic substances, though oil can leak or spill from collecting tanks. Some communities require that tanks be placed on a liquid-tight surface and surrounded by a *berm* (raised rim) to contain any oil that escapes.

The uncontrolled burning of reprocessed oil, environmentalists say, can harm the environment. The lead and other heavy metals that oil contains are released into the atmosphere in the form of ash—and then come down again to enter the soil and water. Reprocessing experts insist, however, that the oil is safe if it is burned in furnaces equipped with smokestack scrubbers that remove the toxic ash.

In many states, companies that burn reprocessed oil are required to register their use of the oil and equip their furnaces with scrubbers, especially if the used-oil fuel does not meet specifications set by the EPA. But, say experts, some smaller companies may be unaware of this requirement and burn the oil without using scrubbers.

Thus, with a few safeguards, both reprocessing and re-refining are environmentally sound. Moreover, these processes help conserve a natural resource—petroleum—that cannot be renewed. Reprocessing allows us to use motor oil twice—once as a lubricant and once as a fuel—while re-refining allows us to use it many times over. What's more, re-refining requires only one-third the energy that refining crude oil does.

Still, the success of the oil recycling business is dependent on several factors. First of all, recyclers must be able to compete on price. When crude oil is priced low, it can be made inexpensively into new motor oil. Currently, re-refined oil costs about the same as, or slightly less than, new oil. Recyclers also need a steady supply of used oil, which requires a willingness on the part of do-it-yourselfers and others to turn in their used oil for collection.

Recycling also depends on people's willingness to buy re-refined motor oil, especially when they are not getting a major break on the price. But there are a growing number of buyers, especially in government. The U.S. Postal Service and the military now purchase recycled oil for their vehicles, as do many cities and towns.

Re-refined oil is sold in containers marked with either the American Petroleum Institute's "doughnut" or its "starburst" symbol. The symbols mean that the oil meets all of the highest industry standards. The oil may be 100 percent recycled or a mixture of recycled and new oil. Manufacturers are not required to disclose what percentage of a can of oil is recycled. But if the label also carries a Green Seal symbol, the oil contains a minimum of 25 percent re-refined oil.

You and your family can look for these symbols when you buy oil. By purchasing re-refined oil, you will help conserve energy and vital natural resources, boost the economy, and preserve the environment.   [Peter R. Limburg]

World Book *Supplement*

Nine new or revised articles reprinted
from the 1996 edition of
The World Book Encyclopedia

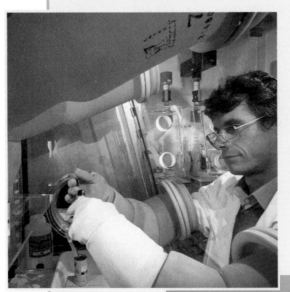

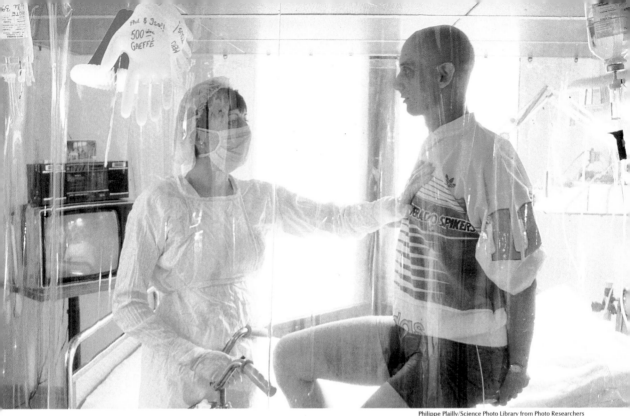

A patient without a working immune system is kept in a sterile environment to guard against disease, *above*. Normally, the immune system defends the body against disease-causing organisms. But without the protection of this system, infections that typically are not serious can be fatal.

Immune system

Immune system is a group of cells, molecules, and tissues that help defend the body against diseases and other harmful invaders. The immune system provides protection against a variety of potentially damaging substances that can invade the body. These substances include disease-causing organisms, such as bacteria, fungi, parasites, and viruses. The body's ability to resist these invaders is called *immunity.*

A key feature of the immune system is its ability to destroy foreign invaders while leaving the body's own healthy tissues alone. Sometimes, however, the immune system attacks and damages these healthy tissues. This reaction is called an *autoimmune response* or *autoimmunity.*

The immune system cannot protect the body from all diseases by itself. Sometimes it needs help. Physicians give their patients vaccines to help protect them from certain severe, life-threatening infections. Vaccines and serums boost the body's ability to defend itself against particular types of viruses or bacteria. The process of administering vaccines and serums is known as *immunization.*

The scientific study of the immune system, known as *immunology,* dates from about the late 1800's. Until then, scientists knew little about how the immune sys-

tem works. Today, *immunologists*—that is, the doctors and scientists who study the immune system—are making great advances in their knowledge of how this disease-fighting system works.

Parts of the immune system

The immune system is composed of many parts that work together to fight infections when *pathogens* or poisons invade the human body. Pathogens are disease-causing organisms such as bacteria and viruses. The immune system reacts to foreign substances through a series of steps known as the *immune response.* The substances that trigger an immune response are called *antigens* (pronounced *AN tuh juhnz).* Several types of cells may be involved in the immune response to antigens. They include *lymphocytes (LIHM fuh sytz)* and *antigen-presenting cells.*

Lymphocytes are special types of white blood cells. Like other white blood cells, lymphocytes originate in the bone marrow, the blood-forming tissue in the center of many bones. Some lymphocytes mature in the bone marrow and become *B lymphocytes,* also known as *B cells.* The *B* stands for *bone marrow derived.* Some of these cells develop into *plasma cells,* which produce *antibodies.* Antibodies are proteins that attack antigens. They are carried in the blood, in tears, and in secretions of the nose and the intestines.

Other lymphocytes do not mature in the bone marrow. Instead, they travel through the bloodstream to the *thymus,* an organ in the upper chest. In the thymus, the immature lymphocytes develop into *T lymphocytes,* also known as *T cells.* The *T* stands for *thymus derived.*

G. Wendell Richmond, the contributor of this article, is Assistant Professor of Immunology/Microbiology at Rush-Presbyterian-St. Luke's Medical Center in Chicago.

Large numbers of lymphocytes are stored in tissues called the *primary lymphoid organs* and *secondary lymphoid organs.* The primary lymphoid organs are the bone marrow and the thymus, the places where lymphocytes develop. Secondary lymphoid organs include the lymph nodes, the tonsils, and the spleen. Lymph nodes are small bean-shaped organs. They are bunched in certain areas, especially the neck and armpits. Lymph nodes filter out harmful particles and bacteria from a network of vessels called the *lymphatic system.* When the body is fighting an infection, the lymph nodes may swell and become painful. See **Lymphatic system.**

Antigen-presenting cells surround foreign substances and digest them in a process called *phagocytosis* (pronounced *FAG uh sy TOH sihs*). Through phagocytosis, antigen-presenting cells engulf foreign substances and break them up into smaller pieces. The cells then *present* the fragments—which include antigen pieces—to nearby T cells. Presenting the fragments involves moving them to the surface of the antigen-presenting cells. There, the T cells can come into contact with the fragments. In some cases, an immune response will then be triggered.

The chief antigen-presenting cells include B lymphocytes, *dendritic (dehn DRIHT ihk) cells,* and *macrophages (MAK ruh fayj uhz).* Dendritic cells, which have many long armlike projections, are found throughout the body, though they are concentrated in lymphoid tissues. Macrophages are found throughout the body.

Other white blood cells that are important in fighting infections include *eosinophils (EE uh SIHN uh fihlz),* *monocytes (MAHN uh sytz),* and *neutrophils (NOO truh fihlz).* These cells, like antigen-presenting cells, are phagocytes *(FAG uh sytz)*—that is, they can *phagocytize* (engulf and digest) pathogens. Eosinophils play an important role in killing parasites and are associated with allergic reactions.

The immune response

There are two forms of the immune response, (1) the humoral immune response and (2) the cell-mediated immune response. They differ mainly in the parts of the immune system that are involved. Many antigens trigger both forms of the immune response.

Immune system terms

Antibody is a protein that attacks foreign invaders in the body.
Antigen is a virus or other foreign substance in the body that triggers an immune response.
Autoimmune response occurs when the immune system attacks the body's own healthy tissues.
Immune response includes all the steps the immune system takes to destroy foreign invaders.
Immunity is the body's ability to resist certain diseases and poisons.
Immunization is the process of protecting the body against diseases by means of vaccines or serums.
Immunology is the scientific study of the immune system.
Lymphocyte is a type of white blood cell. There are two main types of lymphocytes, B lymphocytes and T lymphocytes.
Pathogen is a disease-causing organism, such as a bacterium or virus.
Phagocytosis is the process by which a macrophage or other cell engulfs a foreign substance and digests it, breaking it down into smaller pieces.

The human immune system

The immune system consists of many organs and tissues that work together to fight infection. Important parts of the system include the *bone marrow,* a spongy filling inside certain bones; the *thymus,* an organ in the chest; a network of vessels called *lymphatic vessels;* and small masses of tissue called *lymph nodes.* The tonsils and the spleen also play a role in immunity.

WORLD BOOK diagram by Mark Swindle

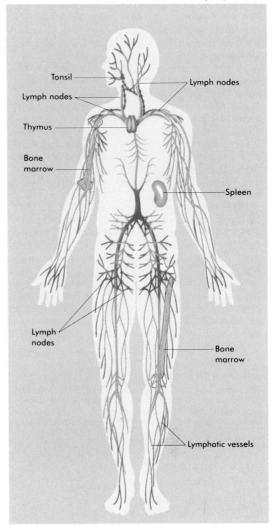

Tonsil
Lymph nodes
Lymph nodes
Thymus
Bone marrow
Spleen
Lymph nodes
Bone marrow
Lymphatic vessels

The humoral immune response, sometimes called the *antibody immune response,* uses antibodies to fight infection. The word *humoral* refers to the bodily fluids that carry the antibodies. Antibodies, also known as *immunoglobulins (ih MYOO noh GLAHB yuh lihnz),* are protein molecules produced by B lymphocytes and plasma cells. They protect the body from infection and from the *toxins* (poisons) secreted by some bacteria.

The first step in the humoral response involves the detection of an antigen by a B lymphocyte. Each B lymphocyte is highly *specific*—that is, it responds to only one particular antigen. When a B lymphocyte comes into contact with the right antigen, it attaches itself to the antigen. Then, the B cell divides into a number of identical cells. These cells mature into either plasma cells or *memory B lymphocytes.* Plasma cells produce a large quantity of antibodies, which circulate through the lymphatic vessels and the bloodstream to fight infection. Memory B lymphocytes enable the immune system to respond more rapidly to infection if the same type of antigen is encountered at a later time. These lymphocytes are stored in the lymphoid organs until needed.

Antibodies fight infection in several ways. For example, some antibodies coat antigens to make them more easily phagocytized by macrophages and neutrophils. Antibodies also neutralize toxins from bacteria.

A number of antibodies defend the body against infection by activating a group of proteins called *complement.* Complement is found in the clear part of blood, known as *serum.* When activated, complement can assist in reactions that kill bacteria, viruses, or cells. For example, complement helps the process of phagocytosis. A bacterium is much more effectively phagocytized if it is coated with both antibody and complement rather than with just one or the other. Complement proteins can also attract disease-fighting white blood cells to an area of infection.

Like B lymphocytes, antibodies are highly specific, and each one acts effectively against only a particular antigen. For example, each type of influenza virus causes the body to produce a different antibody. The antibody that fights one influenza virus is not effective against another.

The effects of antigens on the body vary. In some cases, when foreign antigens enter the body, the body produces enough antibodies to prevent symptoms from developing. In other cases, the body does not manufacture enough antibodies to prevent symptoms, but the antibodies help the victim recover.

People's immune systems differ, largely due to heredity. As a result, individuals respond to antigens differently. For example, the immune systems of most people are not affected by pollen. But in sufferers of the allergy known as hay fever, pollen acts as an antigen and triggers an immune response.

The cell-mediated immune response occurs through the action of T lymphocytes and their chemical products. Like B lymphocytes and antibodies, T lymphocytes are highly specific and respond only to particular antigens. Two specialized proteins, the *major histocompatibility complex* (MHC) *proteins* and the *T cell receptor proteins,* help determine whether a T lymphocyte reacts to a certain antigen. MHC proteins are found on the outside surface of almost all cells. T cell receptor proteins lie on the surface of T lymphocytes.

The first step in a cell-mediated immune response involves action by macrophages or other antigen-presenting cells. After an antigen enters the body, antigen-presenting cells phagocytize the antigen and digest it into pieces called *antigen peptides.* MHC proteins bind to the peptides to form *peptide-MHC complexes,* also known as *antigen-MHC complexes.* Only certain MHC proteins can combine with specific peptides. The peptide-MHC complexes are then displayed on the surface of the antigen-presenting cells.

Next, T cell receptors on nearby T lymphocytes sample the peptide-MHC complexes to determine if the T lymphocytes can bind to them. Only certain peptide-MHC complexes fit particular T cell receptors, much as certain keys fit only particular locks. A proper fit of MHC complexes and T cell receptors sends the first signal for the T lymphocytes to be activated.

Activation of T lymphocytes also requires a second signal from *accessory molecules* on the surface of

The humoral immune response

The humoral immune response begins with the detection of an antigen by a B lymphocyte. B lymphocytes originate and mature in bone marrow. Each B lymphocyte responds to a particular antigen. After it attaches to an antigen, the B cells divide into many identical cells. Some of these cells mature into plasma cells. Plasma cells produce antibodies, which fight infection.

WORLD BOOK diagram by Mark Swindle

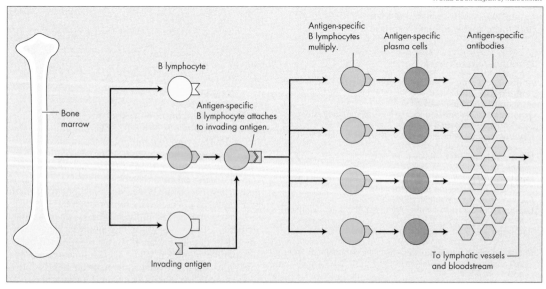

The cell-mediated immune response

The cell-mediated immune response involves T lymphocytes, which originate in bone marrow but mature in the thymus. First, an antigen-presenting cell digests an antigen into smaller *antigen peptides*. The peptides attach to major histocompatibility complex (MHC) proteins to form *peptide-MHC complexes*. Binding of a peptide-MHC complex to a T cell receptor begins T cell activation.

WORLD BOOK diagram by Mark Swindle

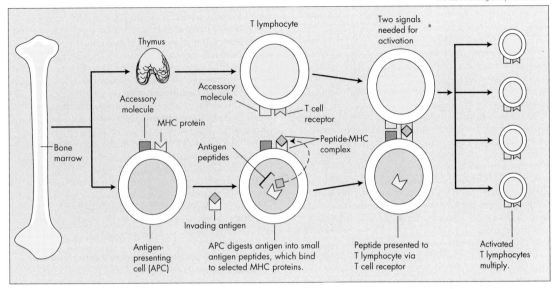

antigen-presenting cells and T cells. These molecules come into contact as the T cell receptors sample the peptide-MHC complexes. Only T lymphocytes that receive two proper signals—one through their T cell receptors and the other through their accessory molecules—will be activated. Upon activation, the proper T lymphocytes begin to multiply, and large numbers are released from the lymphoid organs into the bloodstream and lymphatic vessels. The lymphocytes then circulate through the body to fight the infection.

The kind of T cell that participates in a cell-mediated immune response depends on the type of antigen involved. Antigens in virus-infected cells often activate *cytotoxic T lymphocytes*, which kill the infected cell. Other antigens activate *T helper lymphocytes*, which secrete chemicals called *lymphokines (LIHM fuh kynz)*. Lymphokines belong to a group of chemicals called *cytokines (SY tuh kynz)*. One kind of lymphokine stimulates the production and growth of cytotoxic T lymphocytes, which kill the infected cell. Other lymphokines cause macrophages to accumulate at the infected area and help them destroy the invading organisms.

Another group of lymphocytes that defend the body against viruses and tumors are *natural killer* (NK) *cells*. NK cells differ from other lymphocytes in several ways. For example, they do not require the help of T cell receptors and peptide-MHC complexes to be activated. Instead, NK cells kill cells containing foreign substances on their own.

After the immune system has cured an infection, T cells secrete lymphokines that suppress or help shut down the immune response, and the production of the appropriate T lymphocytes stops. Many of the activated T cells die, but some are stored in the lymphoid organs, ready to fight a similar infection when needed.

The cell-mediated immune response plays an important role in the success or failure of organ transplants. Except in cases involving identical twins, who have the same genetic makeup, organ donors and recipients are genetically different. As a result, the immune system of a transplant recipient interprets the donated organ as foreign. The foreignness of the organ triggers a cell-mediated immune response, which can damage, or even cause the rejection of, the transplanted organ. To reduce the likelihood of organ rejection, therefore, physicians try to identify donors and recipients who are genetically similar. They also use drugs called *immunosuppressant drugs* that prevent an immune response from occurring or limit its activity. See **Transplant**.

How the body develops immunity

There are two kinds of immunity. They are (1) *active immunity* and (2) *passive immunity.*

Active immunity is acquired after a certain antigen enters the body either through infection or vaccination. Memory B cells and T cells will react to a later attack by such an antigen much more quickly than they did the first time. The immune response they trigger is stronger and lasts longer than the first response.

Immunity to some diseases lasts longer than immunity to others. For example, one attack of the yellow fever virus protects a person permanently from another attack. This disease is caused by a single kind of virus. On the other hand, the common cold is caused by many different kinds of viruses. Immunity to the common cold is not permanent because the body is constantly exposed to new and different kinds of cold viruses. An attack by one kind of cold virus does not provide protection against an attack by another cold virus.

Many people have an active immunity without knowing it. At some time, they have had a mild form of a disease. The infection may not have made them feel ill, but the body produced antibodies to fight it.

Vaccination, sometimes called *active immunization,* produces active immunity to a disease. A vaccine contains bacteria or viruses that have been killed or weakened so they produce only mild symptoms of the disease or no symptoms at all. However, the killed or weakened organisms have antigens that trigger an immune response so that the immune system will rapidly react to later attacks by the same disease-producing organisms. In some cases, a person needs a booster dose of vaccine after a time to maintain protection against the disease.

Passive immunity is generally acquired by receiving one or more injections of serum that contains antibodies for fighting a particular disease. Physicians obtain such serum—usually called an *antiserum*—from the blood of a person or an animal who has recovered from the disease or has been immunized against it. Instead of using the entire serum, doctors often use only a part of it known as *gamma globulin,* which contains most of the blood's antibodies. Gamma globulin obtained from a mixture of blood from many donors has a variety of antibodies. Physicians give gamma globulin injections to patients who cannot produce enough antibodies. Doctors also use gamma globulin to prevent such diseases as measles and viral hepatitis if a person who has not been vaccinated is exposed to the infection.

The body soon breaks down antibodies provided by passive immunization and does not replace them. As a result, passive immunity is short-lived, lasting only a few weeks to a few months. Active immunity lasts for years.

A fetus acquires passive immunity against certain diseases by receiving antibodies from the mother. These antibodies protect the baby for several months after birth. Breast-fed babies receive additional antibodies in mother's milk.

The autoimmune response

The immune response is typically directed at substances that are foreign to the body and not at the body's own tissues. Sometimes, however, the immune system attacks the body's tissues as though they were foreign. This reaction is known as an autoimmune response or autoimmunity. The autoimmune response causes several disorders that can result in severe tissue damage.

Everyone has the ability to produce *autoantibodies—* that is, antibodies that can attack their own tissues—and T lymphocytes that can do the same. However, these lymphocytes and autoantibodies are usually kept in check by cytokines produced by T cells, the failure to provide a second activating signal to T cells, and, in some cases, antibodies. As a result, most individuals do not actually develop an autoimmune disease. Scientists do not know why some people get such a disease and others do not. But they have found evidence that some people may inherit a tendency to develop an autoimmune disease.

There are two main groups of disorders caused by the autoimmune response. They are (1) organ-specific autoimmune diseases and (2) systemic autoimmune diseases.

Organ-specific autoimmune diseases involve tissue damage to individual organs, such as the thyroid gland, skin, or pancreas. For example, the autoimmune disorder Graves' disease involves the thyroid and causes the gland to become overactive. In most people with this disease, antibodies in the bloodstream react with thyroid tissue, stimulating it to grow and to produce extra amounts of thyroid hormone. The excess hormone causes a number of symptoms, including nervousness and an irregular or rapid heartbeat. The disease is commonly treated with drugs that decrease the secretion of thyroid hormone. See **Graves' disease.**

Systemic autoimmune diseases involve several organs. One of the most serious is systemic lupus erythematosus (SLE), pronounced *sihs TEHM ihk LOO puhs ЕHR uh ТНЕHM uh TOH sihs.* It is a systemic autoimmune disease that can result in damage to the skin, kidneys, nervous system, joints, and heart. SLE involves the production of autoantibodies that combine with tissue and circulating antigens to activate complement. The activated complement produces inflammation, which damages tissues. Physicians treat SLE with aspirin, cortisone, and other drugs. See **Lupus.**

Disorders of the immune system

The immune system is subject to a number of disorders that disrupt its operation. Some of these conditions, such as allergies, cause great discomfort. Much more serious are the disorders called *immunodeficiency diseases,* such as AIDS (acquired immunodeficiency syndrome). These diseases can lead to death.

Allergies are mistaken and harmful responses of the body's immune system to substances that are harmless to most people. The substances that provoke an allergic reaction are called *allergens.* They include pollen, dust, mold, and feathers. Among the common allergic diseases are asthma, *eczema* (itchy red swellings of the skin), hay fever, and hives.

An allergic reaction takes place in several steps. Allergens bind to antibodies that are attached to *mast cells.* Mast cells are large cells in certain tissues of the respiratory system, the skin, and the stomach and intestines. Mast cells become activated when allergens bind to allergen-specific antibodies on their surface. When activated during an allergic reaction, mast cells are stimulated to release *histamine* and other chemicals. White blood cells called *basophils (BAY suh fihlz)* also release histamine. Histamine produces many of the symptoms normally associated with allergic reactions, such as sneezing, nasal congestion, itching, and wheezing. Consequently, physicians prescribe drugs called *antihistamines,* which counteract the effects of histamine, to reduce the symptoms of many allergic disorders. See **Allergy.**

Immunodeficiency diseases, also called *immune deficiency diseases,* include AIDS and severe combined immunodeficiency disease (SCID). Immunodeficiency diseases are among the most severe disorders of the immune system. People afflicted with such conditions lack some basic feature or function of their immune system. As a result, their immune system fails to respond adequately to harmful invaders. For this reason, people with immune deficiency diseases suffer frequent, and, in many cases, life-threatening, infections.

AIDS is a deadly immune deficiency disease caused by the human immunodeficiency virus (HIV). Infection with HIV results in the progressive loss of immune function. As the immune system weakens over time, individuals infected with HIV become more likely to develop illnesses that do not usually occur or that are usually not serious. These illnesses are called *opportunistic infections* because they take advantage of the weakened immune system. Eventually, the breakdown of the immune system leads to death. See **AIDS**.

Severe combined immunodeficiency disease is an immune deficiency disorder that is present at birth. It is caused by a defective gene. Infants with this condition have insufficient numbers of functioning B cells and T lymphocytes. Therefore, they lack both cell-mediated and humoral immunity. Victims of SCID develop severe infections early in life, and most die before the age of 2.

Physicians have had some success transplanting healthy bone marrow into SCID patients to supply them with normal disease-fighting blood cells. With the discovery of one of the gene defects that causes some cases of SCID, doctors hope that *gene therapy* may prove to be a way of combating the disorder. Gene therapy involves replacing the defective gene that causes SCID with a normal one. See **Bone marrow transplant; Gene therapy.**

Other problems of the immune system include deficiencies of complement proteins. These deficiencies are typically associated with an autoimmune disease, such as systemic lupus erythematosus, or with repeated cases of pneumonia, meningitis, or other bacterial infections. Physicians use antibiotics to treat the infections that occur in patients with complement deficiency.

Chemotherapy—that is, the medications used in the treatment of cancers—can also have significant effects on the immune system. In many cases, these medications diminish cell-mediated immunity as well as antibody responses. Chemotherapy may also dramatically decrease the number of white blood cells, leaving the patient vulnerable to infection.

Extensive burns or other injuries can also have severe effects on immunity, as can malnutrition. Some studies have suggested that stress can weaken the immune response and make an individual more likely to fall ill.

The study of the immune system

Early discoveries. In 1796, the British physician Edward Jenner administered the first vaccination. Jenner conducted an experiment in which he vaccinated a child with a cowpox virus to try to protect the youngster from the deadly smallpox virus. The cowpox virus and the smallpox virus are similar. Jenner's experiment worked, and vaccination against smallpox became common.

Although scientists recognized that Jenner's vaccine worked, they did not know why. They had little understanding of the immune system until the late 1800's. At that time, the French scientist Louis Pasteur showed that vaccination could be used for other diseases besides smallpox. He developed a number of vaccines, including ones for rabies and for anthrax, which is a disease that attacks livestock.

In 1883, the Russian biologist Élie Metchnikoff discovered phagocytes. In 1890, two bacteriologists, Emil A. von Behring of Germany and Shibasaburo Kitasato of

Japan, identified chemicals in serum that neutralize certain toxins secreted by bacteria. They called these chemicals *antitoxins.* Antitoxins are now known to be the same as antibodies or immunoglobulins. Also during the late 1800's, the German bacteriologist Paul Ehrlich discovered that vaccines work by stimulating an antibody response in the body.

Further breakthroughs in immunology came in the early and mid-1900's. In the early 1900's, for example, the Austrian-born scientist Karl Landsteiner learned how antibodies interact with antigens. During the 1930's, Arne W. K. Tiselius, a Swedish chemist, and Elvin A. Kabat, an American biochemist, classified the proteins found in serum. They concluded that antibodies belonged to the class of serum proteins known as gamma globulin. In the mid-1960's, the American scientist Henry N. Claman and his colleagues at the University of Colorado described B lymphocytes and T cells.

In 1975, two scientists, Cesar Milstein of Argentina and Georges J. F. Köhler of Germany, reported a technique for producing *monoclonal antibodies* in the laboratory. Monoclonal antibodies are groups of identical antibodies that act against specific antigens. They can be manufactured in large quantities and have proved greatly useful in the study of immunity. They have also helped physicians diagnose certain diseases and have been used to slow the rejection of transplanted organs. See **Monoclonal antibody.**

The discovery of AIDS led to increased research on the immune system. The first cases of this deadly disease were identified in the United States in 1981, and HIV was discovered in 1983. Since then, scientists have sought to learn how HIV works against the immune system. They have also tried to develop a vaccine against the virus. These efforts have resulted in a greater knowledge of the immune system.

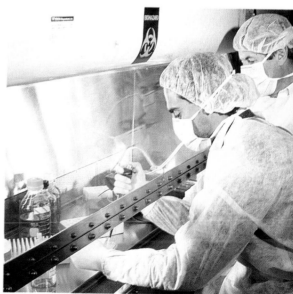

Will & Deni McIntyre, Photo Researchers

AIDS researchers work under a glass hood and wear protective clothing to guard against infection, *above*. AIDS research has led to an increased understanding of the immune system.

Recent advances in immunology include the identification of the genes responsible for certain immune functions and the discovery of T cell receptors and cytokines. For example, genetic research has uncovered the genes involved in the production of immunoglobulins. Because each antibody binds to a specific antigen, the immune system produces millions of different antibodies. Identifying the genes responsible for the production of antibodies means that gene therapy may be used someday to help individuals who lack certain needed antibodies.

The discovery of the T cell receptor has helped scientists understand T cell activation. This research has created interest among people who work with organ transplants. The ability to control the interaction between T cell receptors and T cells could lead to a greater survival rate for people with transplanted organs by preventing the immune system from rejecting the organs.

Identifying various cytokines and learning how they affect the immune response has led to possible new treatments for various conditions. For example, some researchers believe that cytokines may help fight cancers. Some studies have also indicated that certain cytokines influence the function of other organ systems besides the immune system. As a result, researchers have begun to study the relationship of the immune system to other systems of the body.   G. Wendell Richmond

Ice age is a period in the earth's history when ice sheets cover vast regions of land. Ice ages alternate with *interglacial periods,* when the ice sheets mostly disappear. An ice age generally lasts about 100,000 years; an interglacial period, from 10,000 to 20,000 years. The most recent ice age ended about 11,500 years ago. Most earth scientists expect that another ice age will follow the interglacial period in which we now live.

Ice ages occur during times known as *glacial epochs.* The earth has had several glacial epochs. Each lasted from 20 million to 50 million years. The earliest known ice ages occurred as long as 2.3 billion years ago. Three major glacial epochs took place between about 900 million and 600 million years ago. There were two more about 450 million and 300 million years ago.

The most recent glacial epoch occurred mainly during the Pleistocene Epoch, a time that began around 2 million years ago and ended about 11,500 years ago. The term *Ice Age,* if capitalized, usually refers to the Pleistocene glacial epoch, when numerous separate ice ages occurred.

Development of the Pleistocene glaciers. About 55 million years ago, the earth's atmosphere began to cool. Glaciers started to form in Antarctica about 38 million years ago. They grew rapidly about 13 million years ago, forming the Antarctic ice sheet. This sheet has buried almost all of Antarctica for the last 5 million years. About 7 million years ago, ice sheets began to form in North America, Europe, and Asia. By 2.5 million years ago, they covered vast areas.

Extent of the Pleistocene glaciers. Scientists have determined the shape and size of the ice sheets mainly from traces left by the ice as it flowed outward under the pressure of its own weight. On rocks over which the ice moved, it left *striae* (scratches). Valley glaciers gouged out U-shaped gorges in former river valleys. When glaciers melted, they left behind soil and rocks, often in mounds and ridges, called *moraines.* Low places that had been scoured out by the ice filled up with water, forming lakes and fiords.

Scientists have also measured changes in the level of the ground to determine the extent of the glaciers. The great pressure of the ice in the center of the sheets pushed the underlying rock down. Rock along the edges of the sheets reacted by bending upward. As the ice melted, rock under the center rose, and rock along the edges sank. Some of this adjustment is still occurring.

The most recent Pleistocene glaciers reached a depth of about 10,000 feet (3,000 meters). When they were at

The last ice age

In the most recent ice age, which ended about 11,500 years ago, ice sheets covered vast areas in the Northern Hemisphere. During its farthest advance, *right,* the ice cap covered what are now the Scandinavian countries and other northern parts of Europe, and most of Canada. An ice sheet also covered Antarctica, but the ice cap was less extensive in the Southern Hemisphere.

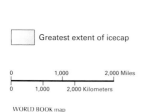
Greatest extent of icecap

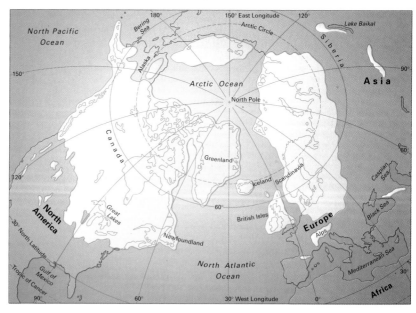

WORLD BOOK map

their greatest extent, so much water was frozen in them that the sea level was at least 330 feet (100 meters) lower than it is now.

The center of the main ice sheet in North America was near Hudson Bay in Canada. This sheet covered large parts of North America, south to about the present valleys of the Missouri and Ohio rivers.

The Scandinavian Peninsula was the center of the main sheet in Europe. This sheet reached into northern Germany and almost to Moscow. It was about half the size of the North American sheet.

The glaciers last began to retreat less than 20,000 years ago. Today, only Antarctica and Greenland are almost completely covered by glaciers.

Evidence of ice ages and their climates. During the Pleistocene Epoch, as many as 18 ice ages may have occurred. Each ice age consisted of many warmer and colder times of varying length and intensity. The amount of ice also varied. Sources of evidence of the various ice ages and their climates include *sediments* (deposits of mud and other matter) on land and in the oceans, and today's glaciers and ice sheets.

Evidence from land was the basis of the earliest descriptions of Pleistocene ice ages. This evidence included striae on rocks and some huge boulders deposited far from their place of origin. By the mid-1800's, many scientists believed that the evidence resulted from the movement of glaciers that had covered vast areas of Europe and North America. By the late 1800's, researchers concluded that certain moraines and other material left behind by glaciers in North America resulted from four ice ages. They named these ages the *Nebraskan, Kansan, Illinoian,* and *Wisconsin.*

An analysis of river terraces on the north slope of the Alps mountain system in Europe led to the identification of four ice ages in Europe. The terraces are composed of layers of gravel. Scientists concluded that rivers had deposited the gravel when the climate was cold. At such times, the action of frost readily breaks up rock, forming gravel. Also, there is not much vegetation, so there are relatively few plant roots to hold broken rock in place. As a result, runoff from rainfall carries much gravel to streams and rivers.

Scientists named the ice ages the Günz, Mindel, Riss, and Würm, after four rivers in the area that had been studied. No one knows exactly how the older ice ages fit into the sequence of about 18 Pleistocene ice ages.

Further evidence of ice ages occurs in sediment near the mouths of rivers. Researchers discovered that, in some river mouths, sediment had built up at least four different times. Before each build-up, the rivers had washed away most of the older sediment.

The researchers concluded that the times of sediment build-up were interglacial periods. The sea level was high during those times due to runoff from melted glaciers, and the sea flooded the mouths of river valleys. The flow at the river mouths therefore was slow. As a result, sand, silt, and other material in the water sank to the river beds, building interglacial sediments. The times of sediment washout were ice ages. The sea level was low. The rivers therefore flowed swiftly, scrubbing out the sediment.

The record of river deposits is valuable but incomplete. The sediments represent only a small fraction of

Rich Reid, Earth Scenes

Remnants of the last ice age still exist in Alaska in the form of glaciers, *above.* These large, slow-moving bodies of ice flow from mountaintops and merge like rivers. As they creep to the sea, the glaciers scour out deep valleys.

the time in which glacial epochs have occurred. Furthermore, due to erosion, little or nothing remains of the oldest deposits.

Information on ice age climate also comes from deposits of *loess* (fine, wind-blown dust), lake sediments, and *bogs* (wetlands containing partially decayed plant and animal matter). Scientists examine a deposit for pollen and remnants of plants and animals. They then analyze their specimens according to two factors: (1) the depth at which they found the specimens, and (2) the climate in which the same species grow today.

The depths at which specimens are found indicate when the specimens were deposited. In general, deeper material was deposited earlier. The comparison with present growth patterns indicates what the climatic conditions were when the specimens were deposited.

Evidence from oceans comes from *cores* (cylindrical samples) drilled out of sediment in the ocean floor. For example, researchers count the shells of different kinds of tiny ocean-dwelling animals called *foraminifera* found at various depths in the cores. Some of these species grow well in warm water, while others grow well in cold water. By comparing the numbers of the species at a given depth, researchers estimate the temperature of the water when the specimens were deposited.

Scientists determine how much ice was locked in glaciers and ice sheets by measuring the *isotopes* (forms) of oxygen in foraminifera shells. Two isotopes of oxygen occur most often in nature. One of them, known as O-18, is heavier and much rarer than the other, O-16.

A water molecule (H_2O) consists of two atoms of hydrogen (H) and one atom of oxygen (O). Water molecules with O-16 evaporate more readily than do water molecules that have O-18. The O-16 isotope therefore accumulates in snow and ice sheets, while O-18 stays more in the ocean. Thus, during ice ages, when the sea level was low, the ocean had a higher percentage of O-18 than during interglacial periods.

The shells of foraminifera contain carbonate (CO_3), which consists of one atom of carbon (C) and three atoms of oxygen (O). Foraminifera obtain the oxygen for their carbonate from the ocean water. Thus, foraminifera that lived during ice ages accumulated a higher percentage of O-18 in their shells than did foraminifera that lived during interglacial periods.

Evidence from today's glaciers. The best and most detailed evidence of ice age climate comes from cores of ice drilled in Greenland and Antarctica. Scientists drilled two cores in Greenland to a depth of about 10,000 feet (3,000 meters). The cores provide a reliable record of the temperature, chemical activity, dust concentration, and gas composition of the atmosphere for the last 100,000 years.

The evidence indicates that large variations in the climate of Greenland occurred frequently during the last ice age. The climate changed rapidly—often in a few decades, sometimes in a few years. Ocean processes may have caused these changes. For example, warm currents in the Atlantic Ocean may have shifted, causing ice sheets to decay.   Pieter M. Grootes

Uranium is a silvery-white, radioactive metal. It is the source of energy used to generate electric energy at all large commercial nuclear power plants. A chunk of uranium the size of a softball can release more energy than a trainload of coal that weighs 3 million times as much. Uranium also produces the tremendous explosions of certain nuclear weapons.

Uranium is the second heaviest element found in nature. Only plutonium is heavier. Engineers put the heaviness of uranium to use in a number of applications. They use uranium in gyrocompasses for aircraft, as a counterweight for ailerons and other control surfaces of aircraft and spacecraft, and as a radiation shield. The uranium used in these applications has an extremely low level of radioactivity. Scientists also use uranium to determine the age of rocks and ground water, and of deposits of *travertine* (a form of limestone) at archaeological sites.

Uranium occurs chiefly in rocks, usually in extremely small concentrations. On average, uranium accounts for only 2.6 pounds of every million pounds of the earth's crust. Uranium occurs in even smaller concentrations in rivers, lakes, the oceans, and other bodies of water. On average, uranium accounts for only 0.1 to 10 pounds of every billion pounds of the water and the other substances in the water.

In 1789, German chemist Martin H. Klaproth discovered uranium. He found it in pitchblende, a dark, bluish-black mineral. Klaproth named uranium after the planet Uranus, which had been discovered in 1781. In 1841, French chemist Eugène Péligot separated pure uranium from pitchblende.

Sources of uranium

Pitchblende, the first uranium ore discovered, is the most important variety of uraninite. Other major ores include uranophane, coffinite, and carnotite. Sandstone, shale, and phosphate may contain deposits of uranium ores. Granite usually has small amounts of uranium.

In the early 1990's, the world had about 1,800,000 short tons (1,600,000 metric tons) of uranium ore that could be mined at a reasonable cost. World production

of uranium is about 36,000 short tons (32,500 metric tons) a year. Canada leads all countries in the production of uranium. More than half of Canada's uranium comes from Saskatchewan. The chief deposits of uranium ore in the United States are in Arizona, Colorado, New Mexico, Texas, Utah, and Wyoming. There are smaller deposits in Florida, Nebraska, and Washington.

Uranium isotopes

In nature, uranium occurs in three *isotopes* (forms). Each has an *atomic number* (number of protons in the nucleus) of 92. Each isotope, however, has a different number of neutrons and so differs in its *atomic mass number* (total number of protons and neutrons in the nucleus). The lightest natural isotope has 92 protons and 142 neutrons, for a total of 234 nuclear particles. The name of this isotope, U-234, comes from the chemical symbol for uranium—U—and the atomic mass number. The other two natural isotopes of uranium are U-235 and U-238. These isotopes have 143 and 146 neutrons, respectively.

U-238 makes up about 99.28 percent of all natural uranium. U-235 accounts for approximately 0.71 percent of all natural uranium; U-234, only about 0.006 percent.

U-235 is the only natural isotope of uranium whose nucleus can easily be made to undergo *fission*—that is, to split into two parts. The fission process releases the nuclear energy used in power plants and weapons.

Properties of uranium

Uranium has an atomic weight of 238.029. At 25°C, its density is 19.05 grams per cubic centimeter (see **Density.** Uranium melts at 1132 °C and boils at 3818 °C. It belongs to the group of elements known as the *actinide series* (see **Element, Chemical** [Periodic table]).

Uranium combines readily with other elements. In nature, uranium always occurs in chemical compounds with oxygen. In most surface and ground waters, uranium is combined with oxygen, carbon dioxide, phosphate, fluoride, or sulfate. In addition, uranium reacts with acids to form compounds called *uranyl salts.* All uranium compounds are highly poisonous.

Radioactivity. All isotopes of uranium are radioactive. Their nuclei *decay* (break apart), releasing particles and energy, chiefly *alpha particles, beta particles,* and *gamma rays* (see **Radiation** [diagram: Radioactive decay]). When an isotope decays, it turns into another

Leading uranium-producing countries

Tons of uranium concentrate produced in a year	
Canada	●●●●●●●●●●●●●●
	10,690 short tons (9,690 metric tons)
Niger	●●●●◖
	3,280 short tons (2,980 metric tons)
Russia	●●●●◖
	3,270 short tons (2,970 metric tons)
Australia	●●●◖
	2,510 short tons (2,280 metric tons)
Kazakhstan	●●●◖
	2,470 short tons (2,240 metric tons)

Figures are for 1994.
Source: The Uranium Institute, London.

isotope. A succession of decays eventually changes uranium into a lead isotope that is not radioactive.

Scientists measure the rate at which an isotope decays in terms of its *half-life*. The half-life of an isotope is the length of time after which only half the atoms of what began as a sample of that isotope would still be atoms of that isotope.

Uranium isotopes have long half-lives. The half-life of U-238 is about $4\frac{1}{2}$ billion years. U-235 has a half-life of about 700 million years; U-234, about 250,000 years. Much of the internal heat of the earth is thought to be a result of radiation given off by uranium.

Fissionability. A U-235 nucleus can split into two fragments when struck by a neutron. When this nucleus splits, it releases energy. It also releases two or more neutrons. These neutrons, in turn, can cause other U-235 nuclei to break apart. When the other nuclei undergo fission, they also release energy and neutrons. Under certain circumstances, this process can continue in a self-sustaining series of fission events called a *chain reaction.*

A U-238 nucleus rarely breaks apart when struck by a neutron. Usually, U-238 nuclei merely absorb neutrons that strike them.

How uranium is mined and processed

Mining uranium. Mining companies use three chief methods to remove uranium from the ground: (1) *in situ solution mining,* (2) *open-pit mining,* and (3) *underground mining.*

In situ solution mining begins with the pumping of a special solution through holes drilled into the earth. The solution dissolves oxides of uranium. The solution containing the oxides is then pumped into tanks at the surface.

In almost all cases, the holes used for in situ solution mining have already been drilled as part of an effort to locate rich deposits of uranium. During the exploratory process, prospectors lowered radiation detectors into the holes.

Open-pit mining uses explosives to break up rock and soils that cover uranium deposits near the surface of the earth. Miners dig blast holes, then fill them with the explosives. After the explosions, huge power shovels clear away the rubble. Smaller shovels then dig out the uranium ore.

Underground mining is used if the uranium ore lies far beneath the surface. Mining companies dig tunnels into the deposits. The miners drill into the tunnel walls to install explosives that loosen the ore. The miners then load the ore into buckets, which are hoisted to the surface.

Refining and processing uranium ore. The ore from the mine goes to a *mill,* where the uranium is concentrated. At the mill, workers use sulfuric acid or carbonate solutions to produce a uranium salt called *yellowcake.* The salt is purified to an oxide, also called yellowcake, which has the chemical symbol U_3O_8. At a *conversion plant,* the oxide undergoes a chemical reaction with fluorine. This reaction produces uranium hexafluoride (UF_6).

The uranium hexafluoride goes to an *enrichment plant,* where U-235 and U-238 are separated from each other. This separation produces *enriched uranium,* which has a higher percentage of U-235 than does natural uranium. Most nuclear reactors at power plants in the United States use fuel that contains about 2 to 4 percent U-235. Nuclear weapons and the reactors for nuclear-powered ships require uranium with much higher concentrations of U-235.

Enriched uranium for reactors goes to a *fuel-fabrication plant,* where the uranium hexafluoride is converted to uranium dioxide (UO_2). The uranium dioxide is compressed into cylindrical pellets that are used as fuel.

Separating uranium isotopes. Scientists have invented several methods for separating uranium isotopes. Enrichment plants use two of these methods, *gaseous diffusion* and *centrifugal enrichment.* A third method, *laser isotope separation,* is still experimental.

The gaseous diffusion method is used in the United States. In this process, a pump forces molecules of uranium hexafluoride gas through barrierlike structures. These structures have millions of tiny holes in them.

Lighter gas molecules pass through the holes in the barriers more rapidly than do heavier molecules. The lighter molecules contain U-235 atoms. As a result, gas that passes through the barrier contains a higher percentage of U-235 than did the original gas. The increase in concentration is extremely small, however. The gas must pass through the barrier several thousand times to produce enriched uranium for a power plant.

The centrifugal method is used in several plants in Europe and Japan. The centrifuge in this process consists of vertical cylinders that spin rapidly. Pumps force uranium hexafluoride gas into each cylinder through a stationary vertical tube in the center of the cylinder.

The spinning of a cylinder forces almost all the gas outward to the curved walls. In addition, a scoop connected to the bottom of the stationary tube helps create

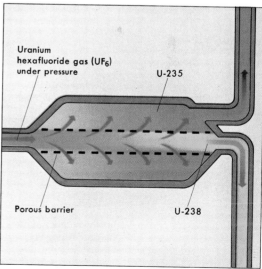

WORLD BOOK diagram by James Magine

The gaseous diffusion method of isotope separation, shown in the diagram above, uses porous barriers to separate uranium isotopes. Separation occurs because the molecules of uranium hexafluoride gas containing the isotope U-235 pass through the barriers faster than those containing U-238.

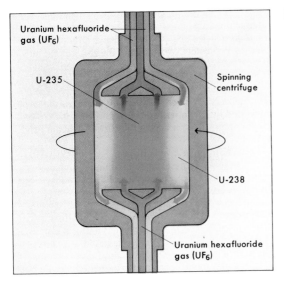

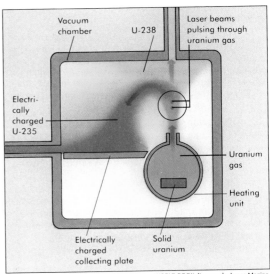

WORLD BOOK diagrams by James Magine

The centrifugal method of separating isotopes uses a spinning cylinder. The rotation of the cylinder forces uranium hexafluoride gas outward. Gas that contains U-238 is relatively heavy, and so it crowds against the walls. As a result, lighter gas, which contains U-235, is concentrated near the center.

Laser isotope separation uses one or more beams of laser light (two beams shown above). This light causes only U-235 atoms in a uranium gas to acquire an electric charge. An oppositely charged plate attracts these atoms, but does not affect the U-238 atoms. Thus, the gas separates into two streams.

a vertical flow in the gas. Differences in temperature within the cylinder also contribute to the flow of the gas.

Due to these three influences—the spinning of the cylinder, the action of the scoop, and the temperature differences—the gas flows in a complex pattern. As a result, the gas near the bottom of the cylinder becomes more concentrated in U-238 than does the gas at the top.

The scoop at the bottom removes waste gas, which has a relatively high concentration of U-238. A scoop at the top removes enriched gas, which has a relatively high concentration of U-235. The process repeats until the desired concentration of U-235 is obtained.

Laser isotope separation uses a combination of laser light and electric charge to separate uranium isotopes. A laser produces a thin beam of light that has a very narrow range of *frequency* (rate of vibration of the light waves).

In *atomic vapor laser isotope separation* (AVLIS), a beam of electrons heats a piece of uranium at the bottom of a closed container. The heat changes the uranium into *vapor* (gas). A laser beam then pulses into the vapor. The frequency of the beam is tuned so that electrons in atoms of U-235 can absorb the light, but U-238 electrons cannot.

When a U-235 electron absorbs this light, it gains enough energy to leave the atom. This process changes the electrical balance of the atom. An electron carries a negative electric charge. A nucleus carries one or more positive charges. In a normal atom, the number of positve charges is the same as the number of negative charges. Thus, when an electron leaves an atom, the atom acquires a positive charge. Scientists say that the atom becomes a *positive ion*. Thus, the laser light ionizes U-235 atoms, but not U-238 atoms.

The hot vapor rises. Negatively charged collector plates near the top of the container attract the positive U-235 ions. Because the collector plates are cooler than

the gas, the U-235 *condenses* (changes from a gas to a liquid) on them. The U-235 liquid drips off the collector plates into special containers, forming a solid mass called a *splat*. The splats are collected, then purified and oxidized for use as nuclear fuel.

Meanwhile, the electrically neutral U-238 travels past the charged plates. It then condenses on a waste plate near the top of the container.

In another laser technique, an electric unit heats a piece of uranium, producing a vapor. Two laser beams work together to ionize U-235 atoms in the vapor. A positively charged plate collects U-235 ions, while a vapor of U-238 atoms exits through an opening in the top of the container.

Laser isotope separation uses much less electric energy than does gaseous diffusion. In addition, the separation equipment costs much less than centrifuge equipment. Government-sponsored companies in France, Japan, and the United States are experimenting with laser isotope separation.

History of the use of uranium

People have used uranium and its compounds for almost 2,000 years. Colored glass produced for a mosaic mural about A.D. 79 contains uranium oxide, and glass manufacturers continued to use this compound as a pigment until the 1800's. People who painted or glazed china also employed uranium as a pigment. In addition, the metal was used in the processing of photographs.

In 1896, French physicist Antoine Henri Becquerel discovered that uranium is radioactive. His achievement marked the first time that any element had been found to be radioactive.

In 1935, Arthur J. Dempster, a Canadian-born physicist, discovered U-235. German chemists Otto Hahn and Fritz Strassman used uranium to produce the first artificial nuclear fission in 1938. In 1942, Italian-born physicist

Enrico Fermi and his co-workers at the University of Chicago produced the first artificial chain reaction. They used U-235 as the fissioning material. Fermi's work led to the development of the atomic bomb.

Scientific research also led to peacetime uses of uranium. In 1954, the U.S. Navy launched the *Nautilus,* the first submarine powered by nuclear fuel. In 1957, the first nuclear power plant in the United States began to operate in Shippingport, Pennsylvania, near Pittsburgh.

Since the early 1970's, uranium-fueled nuclear power plants have been an important source of energy. About 30 countries now have such plants. Several of these countries continue to build them. In the United States, however, new plants are no longer built. Reasons for the halt include public concerns over safety; government regulations relating to safety; and the high costs of building and operating new plants, relative to the costs of new power plants that use energy from the burning of coal or natural gas.   Anne Lewis-Russ and Harold R. Roberts

See also **Atom** (diagram: How atoms compare); **Isotope; Nuclear energy; Nuclear weapon; Radiation** (Naturally radioactive substances).

Uranus, *YUR uh nuhs* or *yu RAY nuhs,* is the seventh planet from the sun. Only Neptune and Pluto are farther away. Uranus is the farthest planet that can be seen without a telescope. Its mean distance from the sun is about 1,786,400,000 miles (2,875,000,000 kilometers), a distance

that takes light about 2 hours 40 minutes to travel.

Uranus is a giant ball of gas and liquid. Its diameter is 31,763 miles (51,118 kilometers), more than four times the diameter of Earth. The surface of Uranus is composed of blue-green clouds made up of tiny crystals of methane. Far below the visible clouds are probably thicker cloud layers made up of liquid water and crystals of ammonia ice. Deeper still—about 4,700 miles (7,500 kilometers) below the visible cloud tops—may be an ocean of liquid water containing dissolved ammonia. At the very center of the planet may be a small, rocky core about the size of Earth. Scientists doubt that Uranus has any form of life.

Uranus was the first planet discovered since ancient times. British astronomer William Herschel discovered it in 1781. It was named after a sky god in Greek mythology. Most of our information about Uranus comes from the flight of the United States spacecraft Voyager 2. In 1986, that craft flew within 67,000 miles (107,000 kilometers) of Uranus.

Orbit and rotation. Uranus travels around the sun in an *elliptical* (oval-shaped) orbit, which it completes in 30,685 earth-days, or just over 84 earth-years. As it orbits the sun, Uranus also rotates on its *axis,* an imaginary line through its center. The planet's *interior* (ocean and core) takes 17 hours 14 minutes to spin around once on its axis. However, much of the *atmosphere* (the cloud layers) rotates faster than that. Winds near the poles blow

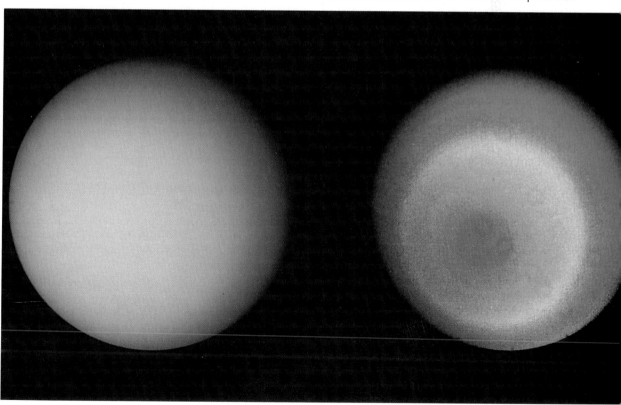

Jet Propulsion Laboratory

Uranus appears above in true colors, left, and false colors, right, in images produced by combining numerous pictures taken by the Voyager 2 spacecraft. The false colors emphasize bands of smog around the planet's south pole. The small spots are shadows of dust specks in the camera.

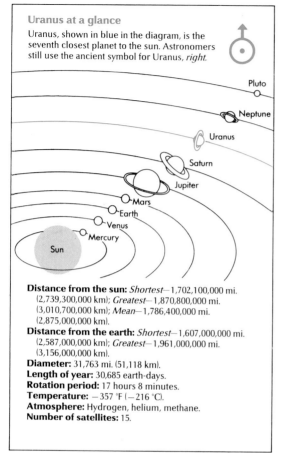

Uranus at a glance

Uranus, shown in blue in the diagram, is the seventh closest planet to the sun. Astronomers still use the ancient symbol for Uranus, *right.*

Pluto

Neptune

Uranus

Saturn

Jupiter

Mars

Earth

Venus

Mercury

Sun

Distance from the sun: *Shortest*—1,702,100,000 mi. (2,739,300,000 km); *Greatest*—1,870,800,000 mi. (3,010,700,000 km); *Mean*—1,786,400,000 mi. (2,875,000,000 km).
Distance from the earth: *Shortest*—1,607,000,000 mi. (2,587,000,000 km); *Greatest*—1,961,000,000 mi. (3,156,000,000 km).
Diameter: 31,763 mi. (51,118 km).
Length of year: 30,685 earth-days.
Rotation period: 17 hours 8 minutes.
Temperature: −357 °F (−216 °C).
Atmosphere: Hydrogen, helium, methane.
Number of satellites: 15.

mospheric pressure beneath the methane cloud layer is about 19 pounds per square inch (130 kilopascals), or about 1.3 times the atmospheric pressure at the surface of Earth. Atmospheric pressure is the pressure exerted by the gases of a planet's atmosphere due to their weight.

The visible clouds of Uranus look almost the same all over the surface of the planet. Images of Uranus taken by Voyager 2 show very faint bands of various shades of blue-green parallel to the equator. These bands are made up of different concentrations of smog produced as sunlight breaks down methane gas. In addition, there are a few small spots on the planet's surface. These spots probably are violently swirling masses of gas resembling a hurricane.

The temperature of the atmosphere is about −355 °F (−215 °C). In the interior, the temperature rises rapidly, reaching perhaps 4200 °F (2300 °C) in the ocean and 12,600 °F (7000 °C) in the rocky core. Uranus seems to radiate as much heat into space as it receives from the sun.

Because Uranus is tilted 98° on its axis, its poles receive more sunlight during a Uranian year than does its equator. However, the weather system seems to distribute the extra heat fairly evenly over the planet.

Satellites. Uranus has 15 known satellites. Astronomers discovered the 5 largest satellites between 1787 and 1948. Photographs taken by Voyager 2 in 1986 revealed the other 10. The largest is Titania, with a diameter of 980 miles (1,580 kilometers). The smallest is Cordelia, only 16 miles (26 kilometers) across.

Miranda, the smallest of the five large satellites, has certain surface features that are unlike any other formation in the solar system. These are three oddly shaped regions called *ovoids.* Each ovoid is 120 to 180 miles (190 to 290 kilometers) across. The outer areas of each ovoid resemble a race track, with parallel ridges and canyons wrapped about the center. In the center, however, ridges and canyons crisscross one another randomly. Scientists have not determined how the ovoids formed.

at more than 340 miles per hour (545 kilometers per hour). Thus, areas near the poles make one complete rotation every 14 hours.

Uranus is tilted so far on its side that its axis lies nearly level with its path around the sun. Scientists measure the tilt of a planet relative to a line at a right angle to the *orbital plane,* an imaginary surface touching all points of the orbit. Most planets' axes tilt less than 30°. For example, the tilt of Earth's axis is about $23\frac{1}{2}$°. But Uranus's axis tilts 98°, so that the axis lies almost in the orbital plane.

Mass and density. Uranus has a *mass* (quantity of matter) $14\frac{1}{2}$ times larger than that of Earth. However, the mass of Uranus is only about $\frac{1}{20}$ as large as that of the largest planet, Jupiter.

Uranus has an average *density* of 1.27 grams per cubic centimeter, or about $1\frac{1}{4}$ times the density of water. Density is the amount of mass in a substance divided by the volume of the substance. The density of Uranus is $\frac{1}{4}$ that of Earth, and is similar to that of Jupiter.

The force of gravity at the surface of Uranus is about 90 percent of that at the surface of Earth. Thus, an object that weighs 100 pounds on Earth would weigh about 90 pounds on Uranus.

The atmosphere of Uranus is composed of about 83 percent hydrogen, 15 percent helium, 2 percent methane, and tiny amounts of ethane and other gases. The *at-*

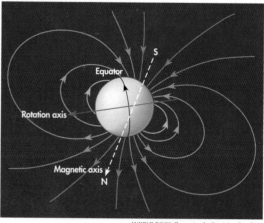

WORLD BOOK illustration by Precision Graphics

The axis of rotation of Uranus is greatly offset from the planet's magnetic axis. The diagram above shows how those axes are oriented when the sun is directly to the left. The curved lines indicate the direction of the magnetic field of Uranus.

Rings. Uranus has 10 dark, narrow rings around it. They range in width from less than 3 miles (5 kilometers) to 60 miles (100 kilometers). They are no more than 33 feet (10 meters) thick. The rings are probably composed of chunks of ice about 20 inches (50 centimeters) across, and covered by a layer of material containing carbon.

Magnetic field. Uranus has a strong magnetic field. The *axis* of the field (an imaginary line connecting its north and south poles) is tilted 59° from the planet's axis of rotation. The magnetic field has trapped high-energy, electrically charged particles—mostly electrons and protons—in *radiation belts* around the planet.

Peter J. Gierasch and Philip D. Nicholson

Internet is a vast network of computers that connects many of the world's businesses, institutions, and individuals. The Internet, which means *interconnected network of networks,* links tens of thousands of smaller computer networks. These networks transmit huge amounts of information in the form of words, images, and sounds.

The Internet has information on virtually every topic. Network users can search through sources ranging from vast databases to small electronic "bulletin boards," where users form discussion groups around common interests. Much of the Internet's traffic consists of messages sent from one computer user to another. These messages are called *electronic mail* or *e-mail.* Internet users have electronic addresses that allow them to send and receive e-mail.

Other uses of the network include obtaining news, joining electronic debates, and playing electronic games. One feature of the Internet, known as the World Wide Web, provides graphics, audio, and video to enhance the information in its documents. These documents cover a vast number of topics.

People usually access the Internet with a device called a *modem.* Modems connect computers to the network through telephone lines. Much of the Internet operates through worldwide telephone networks of *fiber-optic cables.* These cables contain hair-thin strands of glass that carry data as pulses of light. They can transmit thousands of times more data than local phone lines, most of which consist of copper wires.

The history of the Internet began in the 1960's. At that time, the Advanced Research Projects Agency (ARPA) of the United States Department of Defense developed a network of computers called *ARPAnet.* Originally, ARPAnet connected only military and government computer systems. Its purpose was to make these systems secure in the event of a disaster or war. Soon after the creation of ARPAnet, universities and other institutions developed their own computer networks. These networks eventually were merged with ARPAnet to form the Internet. By the 1990's, anyone with a computer, modem, and Internet software could link up to the Internet.

In the future, the Internet will probably grow more sophisticated as computer technology becomes more powerful. Many experts believe the Internet may become part of a larger network called the *information superhighway.* This network, still under development, would link computers with telephone companies, cable television stations, and other communication systems. People could bank, shop, watch TV, and perform many other activities through the network.   Keith Ferrell

Element, Chemical, is any substance that contains only one kind of atom. All chemical substances are elements or *compounds* (combinations of elements). For example, hydrogen and oxygen are elements, and water is a compound of hydrogen and oxygen. Oxygen and silicon are the most plentiful elements in the earth's crust, accounting for about 47 percent and 28 percent of the crust's weight, respectively.

The International Union of Pure and Applied Chemistry (IUPAC) recognizes the existence of 109 elements. Scientists have claimed the discovery of two additional elements, known as *element 110* and *element 111.*

The IUPAC is the recognized authority in crediting the discovery of elements and assigning names to them. For a discovery to be recognized by the IUPAC, scientists must produce a sample of the element and measure some of its characteristic properties. In addition, it is desirable that another experiment confirm the discovery.

Names of elements. The names of some elements come from Greek or Latin words. *Bromine,* for example, comes from the Greek word for *stench* (foul odor). Many artificially produced elements are named after a place or an individual. Scientists at the University of California at Berkeley produced an element and named it berkelium in honor of that city. The element einsteinium was named after the German-born physicist Albert Einstein.

Traditionally, the scientific community has granted the discoverer of an element the right to name it, subject to acceptance by the IUPAC. Recently, however, the IUPAC has not always accepted names proposed by discoverers. As a result, controversy has surrounded the naming of several artificially produced elements. By mid-1995, disagreements still delayed a naming of six elements (see **Element 104** through **Element 109**).

Symbols of elements. Each officially named element has a chemical symbol consisting of one or two letters. In some cases, the symbol is the first letter of the name. For example, C is the symbol for carbon. If the first letter is already the symbol for another element, another letter of the name is combined with the first. For instance, calcium has the symbol Ca. Some symbols come from an old name of the element. The symbol for lead, Pb, comes from *plumbum,* the Latin word for *lead.* Chemists use the symbols to write formulas for compounds. The formulas tell which elements and how many atoms of each are in a compound. See **Compound.**

Discovery of elements. Ancient people recognized the unique properties of a few substances that were later determined to be elements. Among the first known were gold, copper, carbon, and sulfur. Small amounts of these elements occur naturally in pure—or nearly pure—form. As people discovered how to obtain pure metals from compounds, iron, lead, silver, tin, and other elements came to be known.

Experimenters discovered a few elements from the 1500's to the early 1700's. The number of known elements began to increase rapidly in the mid-1700's. But even then, scientists had difficulty determining whether certain substances were elements or compounds. In the late 1700's, French chemist Antoine Lavoisier, who is regarded as the founder of modern chemistry, created a system for classifying the known elements. But his list still included many compounds. Since 1940, almost all discoveries of elements have been made by researchers

Periodic table of the elements

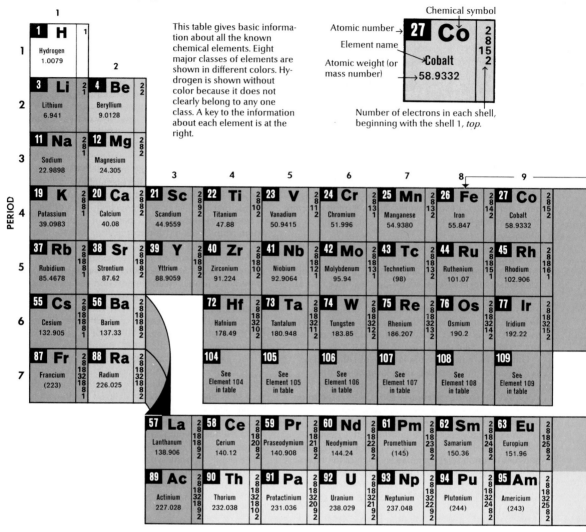

This table gives basic information about all the known chemical elements. Eight major classes of elements are shown in different colors. Hydrogen is shown without color because it does not clearly belong to any one class. A key to the information about each element is at the right.

Chemical symbol

Atomic number →
Element name
Atomic weight (or mass number)

27   Co
Cobalt
58.9332

Number of electrons in each shell, beginning with the shell 1, *top.*

Table of the elements and their discoverers

Name	Symbol	Atomic number	Atomic weight*	Discoverer	Country of discovery	Date of discovery
Element 105	—	105	[263]	Joint Institute for Nuclear Research	Russia†	1970-
				Lawrence Berkeley Laboratory ‡	United States	1971
Element 106	—	106	[266]	Lawrence Berkeley Laboratory‡	United States	1974
				Lawrence Livermore National Laboratory§		
Element 107	—	107	[264]	Heavy Ion Research Center	Germany	1981
Element 108	—	108	[267]	Heavy Ion Research Center	Germany	1984
Element 109	—	109	[268]	Heavy Ion Research Center	Germany	1982
Erbium	Er	68	167.26	Carl Mosander	Sweden	1843
Europium	Eu	63	151.96	Eugène Demarçay	France	1901
Fermium	Fm	100	[257]	Argonne; Los Alamos; U. of Calif.	United States	1953
Fluorine	F	9	18.9984	Henri Moissan	France	1886
Francium	Fr	87	[223]	Marguerite Perey	France	1939
Gadolinium	Gd	64	157.25	Jean de Marignac	Switzerland	1880
Gallium	Ga	31	69.72	Paul Émile Lecoq de Boisbaudran	France	1875
Germanium	Ge	32	72.59	Clemens Winkler	Germany	1886
Gold	Au	79	196.967		Known to ancients	
Hafnium	Hf	72	178.49	Dirk Coster; Georg von Hevesy	Denmark	1923

*A number in brackets indicates the atomic mass number of the most stable isotope.   †Then part of the Soviet Union.   ‡Then Lawrence Radiation Laboratory.   §Then Lawrence Livermore Laboratory.

Legend:

- Alkali metals
- Actinide series
- Alkaline earth metals
- Other metals
- Transition metals
- Nonmetals
- Lanthanide series (rare earths)
- Noble gases

Periodic table (portion shown), with group numbers, atomic number, symbol, name, atomic weight, and electron shell configuration:

Groups: 10, 11, 12, 13, 14, 15, 16, 17, 18

Z	Symbol	Name	Atomic weight	Shells
2	He	Helium	4.00260	2
5	B	Boron	10.81	2,3
6	C	Carbon	12.011	2,4
7	N	Nitrogen	14.0067	2,5
8	O	Oxygen	15.9994	2,6
9	F	Fluorine	18.9984	2,7
10	Ne	Neon	20.179	2,8
13	Al	Aluminum	26.9815	2,8,3
14	Si	Silicon	28.0855	2,8,4
15	P	Phosphorus	30.9738	2,8,5
16	S	Sulfur	32.06	2,8,6
17	Cl	Chlorine	35.453	2,8,7
18	Ar	Argon	39.948	2,8,8
28	Ni	Nickel	58.69	2,8,16,2
29	Cu	Copper	63.546	2,8,18,1
30	Zn	Zinc	65.39	2,8,18,2
31	Ga	Gallium	69.72	2,8,18,3
32	Ge	Germanium	72.59	2,8,18,4
33	As	Arsenic	74.9216	2,8,18,5
34	Se	Selenium	78.96	2,8,18,6
35	Br	Bromine	79.904	2,8,18,7
36	Kr	Krypton	83.80	2,8,18,8
46	Pd	Palladium	106.42	2,8,18,18,0
47	Ag	Silver	107.868	2,8,18,18,1
48	Cd	Cadmium	112.41	2,8,18,18,2
49	In	Indium	114.82	2,8,18,18,3
50	Sn	Tin	118.71	2,8,18,18,4
51	Sb	Antimony	121.75	2,8,18,18,5
52	Te	Tellurium	127.60	2,8,18,18,6
53	I	Iodine	126.905	2,8,18,18,7
54	Xe	Xenon	131.29	2,8,18,18,8
78	Pt	Platinum	195.08	2,8,18,32,17,1
79	Au	Gold	196.967	2,8,18,32,18,1
80	Hg	Mercury	200.59	2,8,18,32,18,2
81	Tl	Thallium	204.383	2,8,18,32,18,3
82	Pb	Lead	207.2	2,8,18,32,18,4
83	Bi	Bismuth	208.980	2,8,18,32,18,5
84	Po	Polonium	(209)	2,8,18,32,18,6
85	At	Astatine	(210)	2,8,18,32,18,7
86	Rn	Radon	(222)	2,8,18,32,18,8

Lanthanide and actinide series:

Z	Symbol	Name	Atomic weight	Shells
64	Gd	Gadolinium	157.25	2,8,18,25,9,2
65	Tb	Terbium	158.925	2,8,18,27,8,2
66	Dy	Dysprosium	162.50	2,8,18,28,8,2
67	Ho	Holmium	164.930	2,8,18,29,8,2
68	Er	Erbium	167.26	2,8,18,30,8,2
69	Tm	Thulium	168.934	2,8,18,31,8,2
70	Yb	Ytterbium	173.04	2,8,18,32,8,2
71	Lu	Lutetium	174.967	2,8,18,32,9,2
96	Cm	Curium	(247)	2,8,18,32,25,9,2
97	Bk	Berkelium	(247)	2,8,18,32,26,9,2
98	Cf	Californium	(251)	2,8,18,32,28,8,2
99	Es	Einsteinium	(252)	2,8,18,32,29,8,2
100	Fm	Fermium	(257)	2,8,18,32,30,8,2
101	Md	Mendelevium	(258)	2,8,18,32,31,8,2
102	No	Nobelium	(259)	2,8,18,32,32,8,2
103	Lr	Lawrencium	(260)	2,8,18,32,32,9,2

Table of the elements and their discoverers

Name	Symbol	Atomic number	Atomic weight*	Discoverer	Country of discovery	Date of discovery
Helium	He	2	4.00260	Sir William Ramsay; Nils Langlet; P. T. Cleve	Britain; Sweden	1895
Holmium	Ho	67	164.930	J. L. Soret	Switzerland	1878
Hydrogen	H	1	1.0079	Henry Cavendish	Britain	1766
Indium	In	49	114.82	Ferdinand Reich; H. Richter	Germany	1863
Iodine	I	53	126.905	Bernard Courtois	France	1811
Iridium	Ir	77	192.22	Smithson Tennant	Britain	1804
Iron	Fe	26	55.847		Known to ancients	
Krypton	Kr	36	83.80	Sir William Ramsay; M. W. Travers	Britain	1898
Lanthanum	La	57	138.906	Carl Mosander	Sweden	1839
Lawrencium	Lr	103	262	Joint Institute for Nuclear Research	Russia†	1961-
				Lawrence Berkeley Laboratory‡	United States	1971
Lead	Pb	82	207.2		Known to ancients	
Lithium	Li	3	6.941	Johann Arfvedson	Sweden	1817
Lutetium	Lu	71	174.967	Georges Urbain	France	1907
Magnesium	Mg	12	24.305	Sir Humphry Davy	Britain	1808
Manganese	Mn	25	54.9380	Johan Gahn	Sweden	1774
Mendelevium	Md	101	[258]	Lawrence Berkeley Laboratory‡	United States	1958

*A number in brackets indicates the atomic mass number of the most stable isotope.   †Then part of the Soviet Union.   ‡Then Lawrence Radiation Laboratory.

who produced previously unknown radioactive elements in particle accelerators or nuclear reactors.

The periodic table lists the elements in rows, called *periods,* in order of increasing *atomic number.* Elements that have similar properties lie in vertical columns called *groups.* The table also lists *atomic mass numbers, atomic weights,* and numbers of electrons in *electron shells;* and indicates major *classes* of elements.

Atomic number is the number of *protons* (positively charged particles) in an atom's nucleus. All the atoms of an element have the same number of protons. All atoms except those of the simplest form of hydrogen also have particles with no electric charge, called *neutrons,* in their nucleus.

Some forms of an element have a different number of neutrons than do other forms of that element. Each form of an element with a different number of neutrons is known as an *isotope* of that element.

The numbers of protons and neutrons in some atoms change in a process known as *radioactive decay.* Because the number of protons distinguishes one element from another, any change in the number of protons produces a different element. The change is called a *transmutation.*

Atomic mass number is the total number of protons and neutrons in an isotope. The periodic table lists atomic mass numbers for elements that have only radioactive isotopes. In each case, the number listed is the atomic mass number of the most *stable* isotope—that is, the one that takes the most time to decay.

Atomic weight. The atomic weight of an isotope is its weight relative to that of the isotope of carbon whose atomic mass number is 12. This carbon isotope has been assigned an atomic weight of exactly 12 *atomic mass units* (amu). Another term for atomic weight is *relative atomic mass.*

If only one isotope of an element occurs in nature, the atomic weight of that isotope appears in the periodic table. If an element has more than one natural isotope, an average atomic weight appears in the table. Scientists calculate this average from the atomic weights of the isotopes and the proportions in which they occur in nature.

Groups and electron shells. Each column in the table lists a group of elements that behave somewhat alike in forming compounds. Each group has a number from 1 to 18. The groups were formerly numbered from 1A to 8A and from 1B to 8B.

The similarity in the behavior of the elements in a group results from a similarity in the structure of the atoms of those elements. All atoms have one or more *electrons* (negatively charged particles) surrounding the nucleus. An electrically balanced atom has the same number of electrons as there are protons in the atomic nucleus. The electrons are arranged in levels called *electron shells,* according to how much energy the electrons have. Generally, those closest to the nucleus have the least energy. The electrons in an atom's outer shells require the least energy to remove from the atom, and thus control the chemical behavior of the atom. In most groups, the elements have the same number of electrons in their outer shells.

Each electron shell has a number. The shell closest to the nucleus is *shell 1.* Each shell can hold only a certain

Table of the elements and their discoverers

Name	Symbol	Atomic number	Atomic weight*	Discoverer	Country of discovery	Date of discovery
Actinium	Ac	89	227.028	André Debierne	France	1899
Aluminum	Al	13	26.9815	Hans Christian Oersted	Denmark	1825
Americium	Am	95	[243]	G. T. Seaborg; R. A. James; L. O. Morgan; A. Ghiorso	United States	1945
Antimony	Sb	51	121.75	Unknown; name applied to pure element in France in 1787		
Argon	Ar	18	39.948	Sir William Ramsay; Baron Rayleigh	Britain	1894
Arsenic	As	33	74.9216	Uncertain; often credited to Albertus Magnus in Germany about 1250		
Astatine	At	85	[210]	D. R. Corson; K. R. MacKenzie; E. Segrè	United States	1940
Barium	Ba	56	137.33	Sir Humphry Davy	Britain	1808
Berkelium	Bk	97	[247]	G. T. Seaborg; S. G. Thompson; A. Ghiorso	United States	1949
Beryllium	Be	4	9.0128	Friedrich Wöhler; A. A. Bussy	Germany; France	1828
Bismuth	Bi	83	208.980	Unknown; preparation described in Germany in 1556		
Boron	B	5	10.81	H. Davy; J. L. Gay-Lussac; L. J. Thenard	Britain; France	1808
Bromine	Br	35	79.904	Antoine J. Balard; Carl J. Löwig	France; Germany	1826
Cadmium	Cd	48	112.41	Friedrich Stromeyer	Germany	1817
Calcium	Ca	20	40.08	Sir Humphry Davy	Britain	1808
Californium	Cf	98	[251]	G. T. Seaborg; S. G. Thompson; A. Ghiorso; K. Street, Jr.	United States	1950
Carbon	C	6	12.011		Known to ancients	
Cerium	Ce	58	140.12	W. von Hisinger; J. Berzelius; M. Klaproth	Sweden; Germany	1803
Cesium	Cs	55	132.905	Gustav Kirchhoff, Robert Bunsen	Germany	1860
Chlorine	Cl	17	35.453	Carl Wilhelm Scheele	Sweden	1774
Chromium	Cr	24	51.996	Louis Vauquelin	France	1797
Cobalt	Co	27	58.9332	Georg Brandt	Sweden	Late 1730's
Copper	Cu	29	63.546		Known to ancients	
Curium	Cm	96	[247]	G. T. Seaborg; R. A. James; A. Ghiorso	United States	1944
Dysprosium	Dy	66	162.50	Paul Émile Lecoq de Boisbaudran	France	1886
Einsteinium	Es	99	[252]	Argonne; Los Alamos; Berkeley	United States	1952
Element 104	___	104	[261]	Joint Institute for Nuclear Research	Russia†	1969-
				Lawrence Berkeley Laboratory‡	United States	1970

*A number in brackets indicates the atomic mass number of the most stable isotope. †Then part of the Soviet Union. ‡Then Lawrence Radiation Laboratory.

Table of the elements and their discoverers

Name	Symbol	Atomic number	Atomic weight*	Discoverer	Country of discovery	Date of discovery
Mercury	Hg	80	200.59			Known to ancients
Molybdenum	Mo	42	95.94	Carl Wilhelm Scheele	Sweden	1778
Neodymium	Nd	60	144.24	C. F. Auer von Welsbach	Austria	1885
Neon	Ne	10	20.179	Sir William Ramsay; M. W. Travers	Britain	1898
Neptunium	Np	93	237.048	E. M. McMillan; P. H. Abelson	United States	1940
Nickel	Ni	28	58.69	Axel Cronstedt	Sweden	1751
Niobium	Nb	41	92.9064	Charles Hatchett	Britain	1801
Nitrogen	N	7	14.0067	Daniel Rutherford	Britain	1772
Nobelium	No	102	[259]	Joint Institute for Nuclear Research	Russia†	1966
Osmium	Os	76	190.2	Smithson Tennant	Britain	1804
Oxygen	O	8	15.9994	Joseph Priestley; Carl Wilhelm Scheele	Britain; Sweden	1774
Palladium	Pd	46	106.42	William Wollaston	Britain	1803
Phosphorus	P	15	30.9738	Hennig Brand	Germany	1669
Platinum	Pt	78	195.08	Julius Scaliger	Italy	1557
Plutonium	Pu	94	[244]	G. T. Seaborg; J. W. Kennedy; E. M. McMillan; A. C. Wahl	United States	1940
Polonium	Po	84	[209]	Pierre and Marie Curie	France	1898
Potassium	K	19	39.0983	Sir Humphry Davy	Britain	1807
Praseodymium	Pr	59	140.908	C. F. Auer von Welsbach	Austria	1885
Promethium	Pm	61	[145]	J. A. Marinsky; Lawrence E. Glendenin; Charles D. Coryell	United States	1945
Protactinium	Pa	91	231.036	Otto Hahn; Lise Meitner; Frederick Soddy; John Cranston	Germany; Britain	1917
Radium	Ra	88	226.025	Pierre and Marie Curie	France	1898
Radon	Rn	86	[222]	Friedrich Ernst Dorn	Germany	1900
Rhenium	Re	75	186.207	Walter Noddack; Ida Tacke; Otto Berg	Germany	1925
Rhodium	Rh	45	102.906	William Wollaston	Britain	1803
Rubidium	Rb	37	85.4678	R. Bunsen; G. Kirchhoff	Germany	1861
Ruthenium	Ru	44	101.07	Karl Klaus	Russia	1844
Samarium	Sm	62	150.36	Paul Émile Lecoq de Boisbaudran	France	1879
Scandium	Sc	21	44.9559	Lars Nilson	Sweden	1879
Selenium	Se	34	78.96	Jöns Berzelius	Sweden	1817
Silicon	Si	14	28.0855	Jöns Berzelius	Sweden	1823
Silver	Ag	47	107.868			Known to ancients
Sodium	Na	11	22.9898	Sir Humphry Davy	Britain	1807
Strontium	Sr	38	87.62	A. Crawford	Britain	1790
Sulfur	S	16	32.06			Known to ancients
Tantalum	Ta	73	180.948	Anders Ekeberg	Sweden	1802
Technetium	Tc	43	[98]	Carlo Perrier; Émilio Segrè	Italy	1937
Tellurium	Te	52	127.60	Franz Müller von Reichenstein	Romania	1782
Terbium	Tb	65	158.925	Carl Mosander	Sweden	1843
Thallium	Tl	81	204.383	Sir William Crookes	Britain	1861
Thorium	Th	90	232.038	Jöns Berzelius	Sweden	1828
Thulium	Tm	69	168.934	Per Theodor Cleve	Sweden	1879
Tin	Sn	50	118.71			Known to ancients
Titanium	Ti	22	47.88	William Gregor	Britain	1791
Tungsten	W	74	183.85	Fausto and Juan José de Elhuyar	Spain	1783
Uranium	U	92	238.029	Martin Klaproth	Germany	1789
Vanadium	V	23	50.9415	Nils Sefström	Sweden	1830
Xenon	Xe	54	131.29	Sir William Ramsay; M. W. Travers	Britain	1898
Ytterbium	Yb	70	173.04	Jean de Marignac	Switzerland	1878
Yttrium	Y	39	88.9059	Johann Gadolin	Finland	1794
Zinc	Zn	30	65.39	Andreas Marggraf	Germany	1746
Zirconium	Zr	40	91.224	Martin Klaproth	Germany	1789

*A number in brackets indicates the atomic mass number of the most stable isotope.   †Then part of the Soviet Union.

quantity of electrons. The maximum numbers of electrons that shells 1, 2, 3, 4, 5, 6, and 7 can hold are, respectively, 2, 8, 18, 32, 50, 72, and 98. However, no element has even five full shells because electrons tend to go into the outermost shells before the inner shells are full. The seven shells are sometimes called the K, L, M, N, O, P, and Q shells.

The rule that the behavior of elements may be predicted from their positions on the table is known as the *periodic law.* Russian chemist Dmitri Mendeleev announced his discovery of this law in 1869.

Classes. The periodic table uses colors to indicate classes of elements that have similar properties. For example, the periodic table in this article uses a medium blue to indicate the *noble gases.* These are gases that do not combine readily with other elements. For information about classes of elements, see **Alkali; Metal; Noble gas;** and **Rare earth.**   Richard L. Hahn

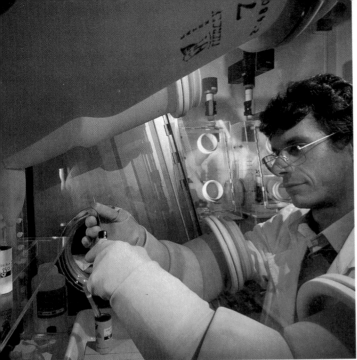
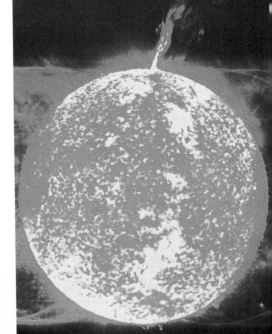

Philippe Plailly/SPL, Photo Researchers

NASA

Radiation is a vital form of energy. Artificially produced radiation has many uses in medicine and other fields. A medical worker handles radioactive iodine, *left*, with special gloves through a protective shield. All life on earth depends on natural radiation from the sun, *right*.

Radiation

Radiation is energy given off in the form of waves or small particles of matter. Radiation is found throughout the universe and comes in many forms. Most people have heard of X rays, gamma rays, and radiation from nuclear reactors. These types of radiation are often mentioned as possible health hazards, though X rays and gamma rays also have valuable uses in medicine. But there are many other forms of radiation as well. The most familiar is probably the light we see, such as the light from the sun or a flashlight. The sun's ultraviolet rays, which cause suntan and sunburn, are another form of radiation. Heat from a fireplace, radio signals bringing music, the intense light from a laser, and the microwaves used to cook food are still others.

Radiation is present whenever energy moves from one place to another. Atoms and molecules give off radiation to dispose of excess energy. When the radiation strikes a substance, it may transfer some or all of its energy to the substance. Often, the energy takes the form of heat, raising the temperature of the material. Except for light, most kinds of radiation are invisible.

There are two chief types of radiation. One type, called *electromagnetic radiation,* consists only of energy. The other type, known as *particle radiation* or *particulate radiation,* consists of tiny bits of matter.

There are many sources of electromagnetic radiation. All materials that have been heated act as sources of

---

Douglas John Crawford-Brown, the contributor of this article, is Professor of Radiation Physics in the Department of Environmental Science and Engineering, University of North Carolina.

such radiation. The sun produces electromagnetic radiation from nuclear reactions in its core. This energy heats the sun's outer layer until the hot gases glow, giving off light and other radiation. This solar radiation travels through space to the earth and other planets.

Particle radiation comes from radioactive substances. Radium, uranium, and many other heavy elements found in rocks and soil are naturally radioactive. In addition, scientists can create radioactive forms of any element in a laboratory by bombarding the element with *atomic particles,* the tiny bits of matter that make up atoms.

All life on earth depends on radiation, but some forms of radiation can be dangerous if not handled properly. X rays, for example, allow doctors to locate and diagnose hidden diseases. But X rays also can damage cells, causing them to become cancerous or die. Light from the sun enables plants to grow and warms the earth, but it also causes sunburn and skin cancer. Gamma radiation is used to treat disease by killing cancer cells, but it also can cause birth defects. Nuclear power plants produce electric energy, but the same facilities create radioactive waste that can kill living things.

Uses of radiation

In medicine, radiation and radioactive substances are used for diagnosis, treatment, and research. X rays, for example, pass through muscles and other soft tissue but are stopped by dense materials. This property of X rays enables doctors to find broken bones and to locate cancers that might be growing in the body. Doctors also find certain diseases by injecting a radioactive substance and monitoring the radiation given off as the substance moves through the body.

In communication. All modern communication systems use forms of electromagnetic radiation. Variations in the intensity of the radiation represent changes in the sound, pictures, or other information being transmitted. For example, a human voice can be sent as a radio wave or microwave by making the wave vary to correspond to variations in the voice.

In science, researchers use radioactive atoms to determine the age of materials that were once part of a living organism. The age of such materials can be estimated by measuring the amount of radioactive carbon they contain in a process called *radiocarbon dating.* Environmental scientists use radioactive atoms known as *tracer atoms* to identify the pathways taken by pollutants through the environment.

Radiation is used to determine the composition of materials in a process called *neutron activation analysis.* In this process, scientists bombard a sample of a substance with particles called *neutrons.* Some of the atoms in the sample absorb neutrons and become radioactive. The scientists can identify the elements in the sample by studying the radiation given off.

In industry, radiation has many uses. Food processing plants employ low doses of radiation to kill bacteria on certain foods, thus preserving the food. Radiation is used to make plastics because it causes molecules to link together and harden. Industry also uses radiation to look for flaws in manufactured materials in a process called *industrial radiography.*

Nuclear power plants obtain energy from *nuclear fission,* the splitting of the nucleus of an atom into the nuclei of two lighter elements. Fission releases large amounts of radiation, including infrared radiation that is used to turn water into steam. This steam then runs a turbine that produces electric energy.

The opposite process, *nuclear fusion,* occurs when the nuclei of two lighter elements join to form the nucleus of a heavier one. Fusion, like fission, releases vast amounts of radiation. Fusion creates the heat and light of the sun and other stars, and the explosive force of the hydrogen bomb. Scientists are learning how to harness fusion to produce electric energy.

In military operations, radio waves are used in radar systems to locate aircraft and ships. Microwaves and the light from lasers have been used both for communication and to guide "smart" missiles to their targets. Heat-sensing devices for night detection rely on the infrared radiation given off by living bodies.

Radiation and radioactivity

Scientists distinguish radiation from *radioactivity,* which is a property of some types of matter. Radioactivity causes matter to release certain forms of radiation as the result of changes in the nuclei of the atoms that make up the matter.

To understand radiation and radioactivity, it is necessary to understand how an atom is constructed and how it can change. An atom consists of tiny particles of negative electric charge called *electrons* surrounding a heavy, positively charged nucleus. Opposite electric charges attract each other, and like charges *repel* (push away) each other. The positively charged nucleus therefore attracts the negatively charged electrons and so keeps them within the atom.

The nucleus of every element except the most common form of hydrogen consists of particles called *protons* and *neutrons.* (A normal hydrogen nucleus is made up of a single proton and no neutrons.) Protons carry a positive charge, and neutrons have no charge. The most common form of helium, for example, has two protons and two neutrons in the nucleus and two electrons outside the nucleus. Protons and neutrons consist of even smaller particles called *quarks.*

Within the nucleus, the positively charged protons repel one another because they have like charges. The protons and neutrons remain together in the nucleus only because an extremely powerful force holds them together. This force is called the *strong nuclear force* or the *strong interaction.* See **Atom** (Forces in the nucleus).

An atom can change the number of protons and neutrons in its nucleus by giving off or taking in atomic particles or bursts of energy—that is, by giving off or taking in radiation. But any change in the number of protons in the nucleus produces an atom of a different element. Radioactive atoms spontaneously release radiation to take on a more stable form. The process of giving off atomic particles is called *radioactive decay.* As radioactive elements decay, they change into different forms of the same element or into other elements until they finally become stable and nonradioactive.

Radioactive decay takes place at different rates in different elements or different forms of the same element. The rate of decay is measured by the *half-life,* the length of time needed for half the atoms in a sample to decay. For example, the half-life of cesium 137, a radioactive form of the metal cesium, is about 30 years. After about 60 years, approximately a fourth of the original cesium 137 remains. After another 30 years, only an eighth remains, and so on. The half-life of radon 222 is about 3.8 days. Half-lives vary from fractions of a second to billions of years.

Electromagnetic radiation

Electromagnetic radiation consists of electric and magnetic energy. Every electrically charged body is surrounded by an *electric field,* a region where the body's electric force can be felt. Every magnetic body is surrounded by a similar region known as a *magnetic field.* An electric current or a changing electric field creates a magnetic field, and a changing magnetic field creates an electric field. Electric and magnetic fields act together to produce electromagnetic radiation.

Electromagnetic radiation moves through space as a wave, but it also has properties of particles. Atoms release electromagnetic radiation in the form of a tiny packet of energy called a *photon.* Like a particle, a photon occupies a fixed amount of space. Like waves, however, photons have a definite frequency and wavelength, which can be measured. The number of times each second that a wave passes through one cycle is called its *frequency.* The distance a wave travels in the time it takes to pass through one cycle is called the *wavelength.* The energy of a photon of electromagnetic radiation varies according to the frequency and wavelength. If the radiation has a high frequency and a short wavelength, its photons have high energy. If the radiation has a low frequency and a long wavelength, its photons have low energy.

In a vacuum, all electromagnetic radiation moves at the speed of light—186,282 miles (299,792 kilometers)

Kinds of electromagnetic radiation

Electromagnetic radiation travels through space in waves, which vary in *frequency* (how quickly a wave passes through a cycle) and *wavelength* (how far the wave travels during one cycle). The kinds of radiation range in wavelength from short gamma rays to long radio waves.

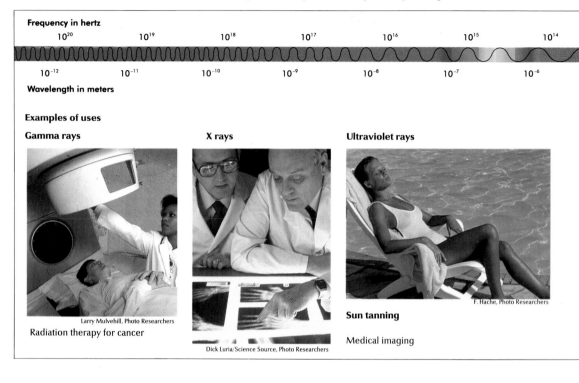

Frequency in hertz
10^{20} 10^{19} 10^{18} 10^{17} 10^{16} 10^{15} 10^{14}

10^{-12} 10^{-11} 10^{-10} 10^{-9} 10^{-8} 10^{-7} 10^{-6}
Wavelength in meters

Examples of uses

Gamma rays

Larry Mulvehill, Photo Researchers
Radiation therapy for cancer

X rays

Dick Luria/Science Source, Photo Researchers
Medical imaging

Ultraviolet rays

F. Hache, Photo Researchers
Sun tanning

per second. The various kinds of radiation differ, however, in their frequency and wavelength. They are classified according to an arrangement called the *electromagnetic spectrum.* In order of increasing wavelength, the kinds of electromagnetic radiation are gamma rays, X rays, ultraviolet rays, visible light, infrared (pronounced *IHN fruh REHD*) rays, microwaves, and radio waves. Gamma rays and X rays are high-energy forms of radiation. Radio waves, on the other end of the spectrum, have relatively low energy.

Particle radiation

Particle radiation consists of protons, neutrons, and electrons, the tiny particles that are the building blocks of an atom. All types of particle radiation have both mass and energy. Most such radiation travels at high speeds but slower than the speed of light. A type of particle called a *neutrino,* however, has an undetermined mass and travels at or near the speed of light.

Scientists have discovered that protons, neutrons, and electrons, which we usually think of as particles, also behave like waves. These waves, called *matter waves,* have wavelengths. The faster a particle is moving, the shorter its wavelength. This means that particle radiation, like electromagnetic radiation, has characteristics of both particles and waves. There are four common types of particle radiation: (1) alpha particles, (2) beta particles, (3) protons, and (4) neutrons.

Alpha particles consist of two protons and two neutrons and are identical with the nuclei of helium atoms. Alpha particles have a positive electric charge. The mass of an alpha is about 7,300 times larger than the mass of an electron. Alpha particles are given off by the nuclei of some radioactive atoms. Most alpha particles eventually gain two electrons and become atoms of helium gas.

Beta particles are electrons. Most beta particles are produced when a radioactive nucleus creates and releases an electron. In the process, a neutron in the nucleus changes into a proton and a beta is released.

Most beta particles are negatively charged, but some are positively charged particles called *positrons* produced when an atom changes a proton into a neutron. Positrons are a form of *antimatter,* matter which resembles ordinary matter except that its electric charge is reversed. When a positron collides with a negatively charged electron, the two particles destroy each other, and two or three gamma ray photons are produced. This collision is called *pair annihilation* (pronounced *uh NY uh LAY shuhn*).

Two other small particles, *neutrinos* and *antineutrinos,* accompany beta radiation. When a nucleus produces a positron, it also releases a neutrino, which has no charge and an undetermined mass. When a nucleus creates and releases a negatively charged beta particle, it also gives off an antineutrino, the antimatter form of a neutrino.

Protons and neutrons can also be released from some radioactive nuclei. Each has a mass about 1,850 times larger than the mass of an electron. The mass of a neutron is slightly larger than the mass of a proton. Neutron radiation is more common than proton radiation, which rarely is produced naturally on earth.

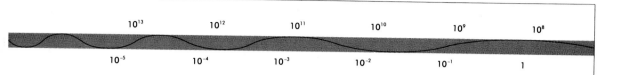

Infrared rays

Aaron Haupt, Frazier Photolibrary

Heating and cooking

Microwaves

H. Gans, The Image Works

Microwave cooking

Radio waves

David R. Frazier

Television broadcasting

WORLD BOOK illustrations by Hans & Cassady, Inc.

Sources of radiation

Natural sources of radiation include the sun and other stars, and naturally radioactive elements. There are also many artificial sources of radiation.

The sun and other stars give off both electromagnetic and particle radiation. This radiation results from the fusion of hydrogen nuclei in the star. The hydrogen changes into helium and releases a large amount of energy, producing electromagnetic radiation across the entire spectrum. Besides visible light, a star gives off everything from radio waves to high-energy gamma radiation. However, the gamma radiation, which is produced when new elements form deep in the core of the star, does not reach earth directly.

Stars also produce alpha and beta particles, protons, neutrons, and other forms of radiation. The high-energy particles released by stars are called *cosmic rays*. Even the sun puts on brief displays called *solar flares,* bathing the earth in cosmic rays strong enough to interfere with communications.

Naturally radioactive substances. Most naturally radioactive substances belong to one of three sequences of change called *radioactive decay series:* (1) the uranium series, (2) the thorium series, and (3) the actinium series. In each of these series, heavy *isotopes* (forms of the same element that have different numbers of neutrons) decay into various lighter isotopes by giving off radiation until they eventually become stable.

The uranium series begins with uranium 238, the heaviest isotope of uranium, which has 92 protons and 146 neutrons. After losing an alpha particle, which consists of 2 protons and 2 neutrons, the nucleus has 90 protons and 144 neutrons. It is no longer uranium but a radioactive isotope of thorium. Scientists call this process of changing into another element *transmutation.* The thorium, in turn, breaks down in several steps to radium 226. The radium 226 decays into radon, a naturally occurring radioactive gas. Radon may become a health hazard if it accumulates in certain buildings, especially poorly ventilated ones. The series continues until the isotope becomes a stable form of lead.

The thorium series begins with thorium 232, an isotope of thorium. The actinium series begins with uranium 235, also called U-235, another isotope of uranium. These two series also end with lead.

A fourth group of naturally radioactive substances includes a wide variety of materials that do not belong to a radioactive series. Many of these elements, including carbon 14, potassium 40, and samarium 146, are produced by cosmic radiation striking the earth's atmosphere. Carbon 14 and potassium 40 are also present in the human body.

Artificial radioactive substances are made by human activities, such as the fission that takes place in nuclear weapons and nuclear reactors, or in laboratories. When fission splits a nucleus, it releases several types of radiation, including neutrons, gamma radiation, and beta particles. Fission also produces new radioactive atoms called *fission products.* For example, atomic bomb tests in the 1950's and 1960's covered the earth with a fission product called cesium 137, a radioactive

Particles given off by radioactive atoms

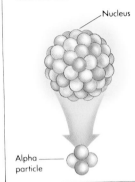

Alpha particles consist of two protons and two neutrons that act as one particle. When the nucleus of a radioactive atom emits an alpha particle, it thus loses two protons and two neutrons.

Nucleus

Alpha particle

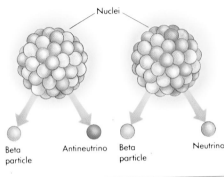

Beta particles are high-speed electrons emitted from the nuclei of certain radioactive elements. Beta particles can be either negative or positive. When a nucleus emits a negatively charged beta particle, it also gives off an antineutrino. When a nucleus emits a positively charged beta particle, called a *positron,* it also gives off a neutrino.

Nuclei

Beta particle   Antineutrino   Beta particle   Neutrino

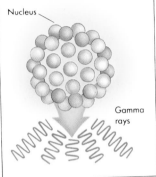

Gamma rays are particles of electromagnetic energy called *photons.* Gamma rays are released when a nucleus, after radioactive decay, is in a high-energy state. The rays travel at the speed of light.

Nucleus

Gamma rays

WORLD BOOK illustration by Sarah Woodward

isotope of cesium. Used fuel from nuclear power plants also contains many fission products, such as plutonium 239, strontium 90, and barium 140. This used fuel, called nuclear waste, remains radioactive and dangerous for thousands of years.

In addition, nuclear plants create new radioactive elements known as *activation products.* Activation products form when the pipes and other materials in a nuclear reactor absorb neutrons and other types of radiation, becoming radioactive.

Many other types of radiation are created by human activities. Physicists use powerful devices called *particle accelerators* to speed up the movement of electrically charged particles, including electrons, protons, and entire nuclei. The physicists then bombard stable, nonradioactive atoms with beams of these high-speed particles. The resulting collisions produce new radioactive

atoms and help scientists learn more about the structure and properties of atoms.

Causes of radiation

Within an atom, electrons are confined to regions called *electron shells* at various distances from the nucleus according to how much energy they have. Electrons with less energy travel in inner shells, and those with more energy are in outer shells. Protons and neutrons in the nucleus are also arranged according to their energy levels in layers known as *nuclear shells.* All the protons, neutrons, or electrons in a shell have almost the same amount of energy.

Just as water always seeks its lowest possible level, electrons seek the state of lowest energy. When an electron shifts from an outer shell to one closer to the nucleus, the electron releases a packet of energy called a

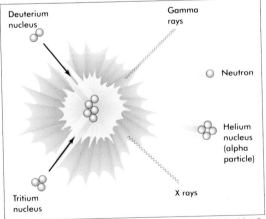

Deuterium nucleus

Gamma rays

Neutron

Helium nucleus (alpha particle)

Tritium nucleus

X rays

WORLD BOOK illustration by Mark Swindle

Nuclear fusion releases large amounts of radiation. Fusion occurs when the nuclei of two lightweight elements join to form the nucleus of a heavier one. In the example above, nuclei of deuterium and tritium unite and form a helium nucleus.

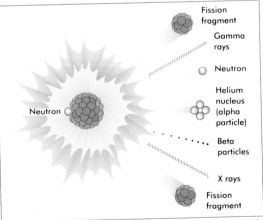

Fission fragment

Gamma rays

Neutron

Helium nucleus (alpha particle)

Beta particles

X rays

Fission fragment

Neutron

WORLD BOOK illustration by Mark Swindle

Nuclear fission releases several types of radiation, including neutrons, alpha and beta particles, gamma rays, and X rays. Fission involves using a neutron to split a nucleus of a heavy element, such as uranium, into two fission fragments.

photon, which escapes from the atom. The energy of the photon equals the difference in energy between the original shell of the electron and the new one. If the energy difference is small, as in a light bulb, the atom will give off visible light, infrared radiation, or both. If the difference is large, the atom might produce X rays.

When a proton or neutron moves from one nuclear shell to another, the nucleus releases gamma radiation. Most atoms that release particle radiation in the course of radioactive decay also produce gamma radiation because their protons and neutrons are shifting into new shells. The radiation produced by nuclear reactions also results from protons, neutrons, and electrons moving to new shells. In nuclear fission, for example, the particles are moving to the shells of new nuclei created when a nucleus splits into two smaller nuclei.

Electromagnetic radiation also is produced if an electrically charged particle changes direction, speed, or both. A particle that enters an electric or magnetic field, for example, slows down and changes course. As a result, the particle releases radiation. X rays are produced whenever electrons suddenly decelerate, such as when they collide with atoms of metal to create the X rays in an X-ray machine. Electrons also produce X rays if they pass near a large nucleus. The negatively charged electrons are attracted by the positively charged nucleus. As the electrons change direction, they produce X rays called *bremsstrahlung* (pronounced *BREHM shtrah lung*), a German word that means *braking radiation.*

Effects of radiation

Radiation produces two main effects in atoms or molecules: (1) excitation and (2) ionization. In *excitation,* an atom or molecule absorbs energy from radiation. Its electrons move to higher-energy shells. In most cases, the excited atom can hold the extra energy for only a fraction of a second before it releases the energy as a photon and falls back to a state of lower energy. In *ionization,* the radiation transfers enough energy to the electrons in an atom that they leave the atom and move through space. Atoms that have lost electrons become positively charged particles called *positive ions.* The electrons may then join other atoms.

Excitation and ionization also affect living tissues. The body's cells contain molecules, many of which are held together by electrons. When radiation excites or ionizes the molecules in cells, chemical bonds may be broken and the shape of a molecule may be changed. These changes disrupt the normal chemical processes of the cells, causing the cells to become abnormal or die.

If radiation affects molecules of DNA (deoxyribonucleic acid), the hereditary material in living cells, it may cause a permanent change called a *mutation.* In rare cases, mutations caused by radiation may pass on undesirable traits to offspring. Even low-energy photons, particularly ultraviolet light from the sun, may produce damage by excitation. If the injury is severe, the cell becomes cancerous or dies while trying to divide. The effect produced depends on the radiation's ionizing ability, the dose received, and the type of tissue involved.

Ionizing ability. Radiation may be classified as *ionizing* or *non-ionizing.* Ionizing radiation is the most dangerous. Some types of ionizing radiation have enough energy to directly strip electrons from any atoms near their path. Such radiation includes alpha and beta particles and protons. Other types of ionizing radiation, including X rays, gamma radiation, and neutron radiation, must first transfer energy to an atom. The added energy then causes the atom to lose an electron.

Non-ionizing radiation consists of photons with too little energy to cause ionization. Radio waves, microwaves, infrared radiation, and visible light are all non-ionizing radiation. Each will cause only excitation.

Dose. Scientists use two systems for measuring the amount, or *dose,* of radiation absorbed by a substance. The older system, still commonly used, measures doses in units called *rads. Rad* stands for *radiation absorbed dose.* One rad is produced when 1 gram of material absorbs 100 ergs. (An *erg* is an extremely small unit of energy.) The newer system, introduced in 1975, measures dosage in units called *grays,* named after Louis H. Gray, a British radiation biologist. One gray is equal to 100 rads or 1 joule per kilogram of material. A *joule* is a unit of energy equal to 10 million ergs. A typical dental X ray, for example, exposes the patient to about 0.25 rad (0.0025 gray).

Radioactive decay

A radioactive decay series is the process by which a radioactive atom releases radiation and changes into different forms of the same element or into other elements. The uranium series, shown at the right, begins with uranium 238. Losing an alpha particle, the atom changes into radioactive thorium 234. The series continues through many more steps of decay until the atom becomes a stable form of lead.

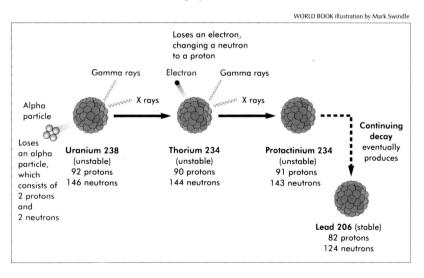

WORLD BOOK illustration by Mark Swindle

Loses an electron, changing a neutron to a proton

Gamma rays   Electron   Gamma rays

Alpha particle   X rays   X rays

Loses an alpha particle, which consists of 2 protons and 2 neutrons

Uranium 238
(unstable)
92 protons
146 neutrons

Thorium 234
(unstable)
90 protons
144 neutrons

Protactinium 234
(unstable)
91 protons
143 neutrons

Continuing decay eventually produces

Lead 206 (stable)
82 protons
124 neutrons

Different types of radiation produce different effects at the same dose. To account for this, scientists have developed the *quality factor*. The quality factor indicates how much the radiation damages living tissue compared with an equal dose of X rays. For example, a dose of alpha particles causes about 10 times as much damage as the same dose of X rays, so alpha particles have a quality factor of 10. X rays, gamma radiation, and beta particles have a factor of 1. Neutrons range from 2 to 11.

Multiplying the dose by the quality factor gives a measure of damage called the *dose equivalent.* If the dose is given in rads, the dose equivalent will be in *rems.* A rem, which stands for *r*oentgen *e*quivalent in *m*an, is the amount of radiation necessary to cause the same effect on a human being as 1 rad of X rays. If the dose is reported in grays, the dose equivalent will be in *sieverts,* named for Swedish radiologist Rolf M. Sievert. Grays and sieverts are part of the metric system of measurement, officially called the Système International d'Unités (International System of Units).

Large doses cause a combination of effects called *radiation sickness.* Doses above 100 rems damage red and white blood cells. This damage is known as the *hematopoietic effect.* At doses above 300 rems, death may follow in several weeks. Above 1,000 rems, the cells lining the digestive tract die and bacteria from the intestines invade the bloodstream. This effect, known as the *gastrointestinal effect,* may lead to death from infection within a week. At doses of several thousand rems, the brain is injured and death can come within hours.

Deaths from radiation sickness are extremely rare. People have only suffered such large doses in reactor accidents, in a few cases where radioactive material was mishandled, and in the 1945 bombings of Hiroshima and Nagasaki, Japan, during World War II. The worst reactor accident in history was a 1986 explosion and fire at the Chernobyl nuclear power plant in Ukraine, then part of the Soviet Union. Thirty-one workers died.

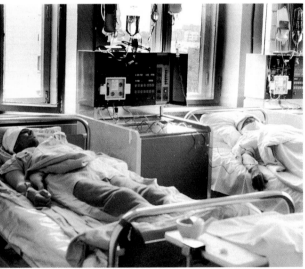

Robert Gale, Sygma

The worst radiation accident in history was a 1986 explosion and fire at the Chernobyl plant in Ukraine. Hundreds of workers suffered radiation sickness, *above,* and 31 died.

Small doses. The doses received in daily life, sometimes called *background doses,* are much smaller. Some scientists believe that the average background dose is 0.3 to 0.4 rem per year. About half of this amount comes from breathing radon gas released by radioactive rocks and soil. Medical and dental X rays add another 0.04 rem per year. Other sources, such as nuclear power plants and waste disposal sites, typically account for less than 0.01 rem per year. Smokers take in much higher doses from radioactive isotopes in smoke.

An accumulation of small doses of radiation increases the risk of developing a condition, but not the severity of the condition. The chief effects of repeated small doses of radiation are cancer and birth defects.

To protect people from the effects of radiation, the International Commission on Radiological Protection, a panel of experts from many countries, sets guidelines for exposure. This group recommends that nuclear workers receive a maximum permissible dose (MPD) of no more than 5 rems per year. The commission also urges that the general public receive no more than 0.5 rem in any year. Other agencies, including the National Council on Radiation Protection and Measurements in the United States and the Atomic Energy Control Board in Canada, set similar guidelines.

History

Early theories and discoveries. Scientists have studied radiation since ancient times. In the 300's and 200's B.C., the Greek philosopher Epicurus wrote of particles "streaming off" from the surface of bodies. Euclid, a Greek mathematician of the same time, thought the eye sent out radiation to allow an object to be seen.

Robert Grosseteste, an English bishop and scholar of the 1200's, thought of light as the root of all knowledge. He believed that understanding the laws controlling light would uncover all the laws of nature.

The composition of light was debated in the 1600's by the followers of the English scientist Sir Isaac Newton and the Dutch physicist Christiaan Huygens. Newton insisted that light consisted of tiny particles, while Huygens suggested it was composed of waves. Scientists argued about these two theories for more than 100 years. Then, in the early 1800's, the British physicist Thomas Young showed that light had properties similar to those of sound and water waves. A few years later, the French physicist Augustin Fresnel provided more evidence. By 1850, most scientists accepted Young's and Fresnel's findings as proof of the wave nature of light.

In 1864, the British scientist James Clerk Maxwell suggested that light consisted of electromagnetic waves. Maxwell also predicted that other, invisible forms of electromagnetic radiation would be discovered. Maxwell's predictions came true with the work of two German physicists, Heinrich R. Hertz and Wilhelm C. Roentgen. Hertz discovered radio waves in the late 1880's, and Roentgen discovered X rays in 1895.

Discovery of radioactivity. In 1896, the French physicist Antoine Henri Becquerel discovered that crystals of a uranium compound would darken photographic plates even if the plates were not exposed to light. He proposed that uranium gave off energy in the form of radiation. Later experiments by the British physicist Ernest Rutherford showed that this radiation consisted of particles he named *alphas* and *betas*.

In 1898, the French physicists Marie and Pierre Curie found other substances that produced radiation, naming them *polonium* and *radium*. A few years later, Rutherford showed that radioactive substances could change into new elements in the process of transmutation.

The work of Rutherford and the Curies led to great interest in the structure of the atom. Rutherford, his colleagues, and other scientists soon proved that the atom had a nucleus of high mass and positive electric charge surrounded by negatively charged electrons.

The quantum theory. In 1900, the German physicist Max Planck studied radiation from hot objects. He suggested that objects could only emit and absorb this radiation in packets of energy called *quanta,* a name later changed to *photons.* Another German physicist, Albert Einstein, used Planck's theory in 1905 to explain a phenomenon known as the *photoelectric effect.* Earlier scientists had discovered this effect, in which a bright beam of light striking a metal causes the metal to release electrons. Einstein proposed that the energy supplied by a single photon could free an electron from an atom in the metal. To produce the photoelectric effect, photons act in a localized manner characteristic of particles rather than as waves. Thus, Einstein's ideas revived the particle theory of light. Scientists now know that radiation has features of both particles and waves.

The Danish physicist Niels Bohr used the quantum theory in 1913 to explain the structure of the hydrogen atom. Bohr proposed that electrons can have only certain values of energy. He showed that atoms release photons of radiation when their electrons drop from a high-energy level to a lower one. In 1924, the French physicist Louis de Broglie predicted that electrons themselves might act as waves, called matter waves.

The nuclear age began in 1942, when Italian-born physicist Enrico Fermi and his co-workers at the University of Chicago produced the first artificial nuclear chain reaction. Since then, many scientists have turned their attention from understanding what causes radioactivity and radiation to finding uses for them. Nuclear weapons based on fission—the atomic bomb—and fusion—the hydrogen bomb—were developed. The first full-scale nuclear power plant began operation in 1956. Radiation from across the entire electromagnetic spectrum was harnessed for communication, medicine, industry, and research.   Douglas John Crawford-Brown

Related articles in *World Book* include:

Kinds of radiation

Alpha particle	Gamma rays	Radio (How radio
Beta particle	Infrared rays	works)
Cosmic rays	Light (The nature	Sun (Solar radia-
Electromagnetic	of light)	tion)
waves	Microwave	Ultraviolet rays
		X rays

Radioactive substances

Actinium	Curium	Element 107	Fermium
Americium	Einsteinium	Element 108	Francium
Astatine	Element 104	Element 109	Lawrencium
Berkelium	Element 105	Element 110	Mendelevium
Californium	Element 106	Element 111	Neptunium

Nobelium	Promethium	Radon	nium
Pitchblende	Protactinium	Technetium	element
Plutonium	Radiocarbon	Thorium	U-235
Polonium	Radium	Transura-	Uranium

Other related articles

Atom	Nuclear physics
Cancer (Carcinogens;	Nuclear weapon
Radiation therapy)	Particle accelerator
Energy	Particle detector
Environmental pollution	Phosphorescence
(Hazardous waste)	Photon
Fallout	Plasma (physics)
Fluorescence	Quantum electrodynamics
Geiger counter	Quantum mechanics
Ion	Radiochemistry
Irradiation	Radiogeology
Isotope	Radiology
Luminescence	Subatomic particle
Nuclear energy	Transmutation of elements

Outline

Questions

What is radioactivity?
How does ionizing radiation damage living cells?
What is the final product of uranium decay?
How are positive ions produced?
What are some natural sources of radiation?
How do physicists create radioactive forms of elements?
Who first suggested that radiation came in packets of energy called *quanta* or *photons*?
Why do atoms give off gamma radiation?
What are the chief health risks caused by repeated low doses of radiation?
What is the difference between electromagnetic radiation and particle radiation?
What are the chief types of electromagnetic radiation?

Additional resources

Caufield, Catherine. *Multiple Exposures: Chronicles of the Radiation Age.* 1989. Reprint. Univ. of Chicago Pr., 1990.
Lillie, David W. *Our Radiant World.* Ia. State Univ. Pr., 1986.
Murphy, Wendy and Jack. *Nuclear Medicine.* Chelsea Hse., 1994.
Pringle, Laurence. *Radiation.* Enslow, 1983.
Tucker, Wallace, and Giacconi, Riccardo. *The X-Ray Universe.* Harvard Univ. Pr., 1985.
Wolfson, Richard. *Nuclear Choices: A Citizen's Guide to Nuclear Technology.* Rev. ed. MIT Pr., 1993.

Electricity is a fundamental force of the universe. It reveals its power during a lightning storm, *above,* when huge electric charges jump between clouds or from the clouds to the ground.

Electricity

Electricity is a basic feature of the matter that makes up everything in the universe. When most people hear the word *electricity,* they think of lights, television, microwave ovens, computers, air conditioners, and other electrically powered devices. Electricity makes these and many other useful things possible. But electricity is much more important than that. Electricity and magnetism together make up a force called *electromagnetism,* one of the fundamental forces of the universe. Electrical force is responsible for holding together the atoms and molecules from which matter is composed. In this way, electricity determines the structure of every object that exists.

Electricity is also associated with many biological processes. In the human body, electrical signals travel along nerves, carrying information to and from the brain. Electrical signals tell the brain what the eyes see,

Richard Wolfson, the contributor of this article, is Professor of Physics at Middlebury College.

what the ears hear, and what the fingers feel. Electrical signals from the brain tell muscles to move. Electrical signals even tell the heart when to beat.

One of the most important properties of electricity is *electric energy.* During the 1800's, people learned to harness electricity to do work. This new source of energy had so many practical applications that it greatly changed the way people lived. Inventors and scientists learned how to generate electric energy in large quantities. They found ways to use that energy to produce light, heat, and motion. They developed electric devices that enabled people to communicate across great distances and to process information quickly. The demand for electric energy grew steadily during the 1900's. Today, most people cannot imagine life without electric energy.

Uses of electric energy

Many aspects of our daily lives depend on electric energy. People living in the United States, Canada, and other developed nations use numerous electrically powered devices every day. One of the most important is the computer, which uses electric energy to process information. Computers have changed our lives at home, in school, and in the workplace.

In homes. Electric appliances, such as dishwashers, toasters, vacuum cleaners, and washing machines, save hours of labor. Electric ranges, microwave ovens, and food processors help us prepare meals quickly and easily. Refrigerators and freezers preserve food. Air conditioners and electric fans cool our homes, while electric heaters provide warmth and hot water. Television, radio, video games, compact disc players, and videocassette recorders furnish entertainment. Electric lights let us make use of the nighttime hours.

In industry. Modern industry would be impossible without electric energy. Factories produce many products on assembly lines using electrically operated conveyor belts and equipment. Manufacturers use electric instruments to ensure correct product sizes and quality. Drills, saws, and many other small tools run on electric energy. Electric motors run elevators, cranes, and most other large machinery.

In communication. Electric energy powers almost every device people use to communicate. Telephones, TV's, radios, fax machines, and computer modems all run on electric energy. Communications satellites use electric energy from devices called *solar cells* to relay information around the world. TV and radio signals are partly electrical, as are telephone, computer, and fax signals that travel along wires or thin strands of glass called *optical fibers.*

In transportation. Electric energy supplies power to subways, trolleys, and trains that carry millions of people to and from work. Most cars use electric sparks to ignite the gasoline that powers the engine. Electric devices help reduce fuel consumption and air pollution in gasoline engines. Many controls in airplanes and ships are electrically powered.

In medicine and science. Health care workers use numerous electric instruments to examine patients and perform medical tests. For example, X-ray machines and magnetic resonance imagers enable doctors to see inside our bodies. Electrocardiograph machines record tiny electrical signals from the heart, helping doctors to diagnose heart disease.

Scientists from every field use electric devices to conduct research. Microbiologists, for example, use powerful instruments called *scanning electron microscopes* to learn the secrets of living cells. Physicists use electrically operated particle accelerators to probe the interiors of atoms. Huge telescopes with electric motors help astronomers study planets, stars, and galaxies.

Electric charge

All matter in the universe, from the human body to the distant stars, is made from two kinds of tiny particles called *electrons* and *quarks.* Quarks, in turn, make up larger particles known as *protons* and *neutrons.* Electrons and quarks have a property called *electric charge.* Electrons have one kind of charge, called *negative.* Quarks have either negative charge or the opposite kind of charge, called *positive.* Protons have a positive charge the same size as an electron's negative charge because each proton contains two quarks with $\frac{2}{3}$ unit of positive charge each and one quark with $\frac{1}{3}$ unit of negative charge. Neutrons, in contrast, contain two quarks with $\frac{1}{3}$ unit of negative charge each and one quark with $\frac{2}{3}$ unit of positive charge. The charges cancel each other out, leaving the neutron electrically *neutral,* meaning it has no overall electric charge.

Opposite charges, also called *unlike charges*—negative and positive—attract one another. *Like* charges—positive and positive, or negative and negative—*repel* (push away) one another. The power to attract and repel other charges is caused by invisible influences called *electric fields* that surround each charged particle. Because of the fields, particles attract or repel one another even when they are not touching.

Atoms. Quarks combine to form protons and neutrons. Protons and neutrons, in turn, combine with elec-

David R. Frazier   David R. Frazier   Michael Newman, PhotoEdit

Electric energy can be harnessed to produce heat, motion, and light. Three useful applications of this form of energy are the electric oven, motorized shopping cart, and halogen lamp, *above.*

Terms used in electricity

Ampere is the unit used to measure the rate of flow of an electric current.

Conductor is a material through which electric current flows easily.

Electric charge is a basic feature of certain particles of matter that causes them to attract or repel other charged particles.

Electric circuit is the path that an electric current follows.

Electric current is the flow of electric charges.

Electric field is the influence a charged body has on the space around it that causes other charged bodies in that space to experience electric forces.

Electrode is a piece of metal or other conductor through which current enters or leaves an electric device.

Electromagnetism is a basic force in the universe that involves both electricity and magnetism.

Electron is a subatomic particle with a negative electric charge.

Insulator is a material that opposes the flow of electric current.

Ion is an atom or group of atoms that has either gained or lost electrons, and so has an electric charge.

Kilowatt-hour is the amount of electric energy a 1,000-watt device uses in one hour.

Neutron is a subatomic particle that has no electric charge.

Ohm is the unit used to measure a material's resistance to the flow of electric current.

Proton is a subatomic particle with a positive electric charge.

Resistance is a material's opposition to the flow of electric current.

Static electricity is electric charge that is not moving.

Voltage is a type of "pressure" that drives electric charges through a circuit.

Watt is the unit used to measure the rate of energy consumption, including electric energy.

---

trons to make up atoms. In an atom, protons and neutrons join to form a tiny core, called the *nucleus.*

The positively charged nucleus of an atom attracts negatively charged electrons. The nucleus has a positive charge because it contains protons but no electrons. The negative electrons whirl around the positive nucleus in somewhat the same way planets orbit the sun.

Each type of atom has a different number of protons in its nucleus. For example, hydrogen, the simplest atom, has only 1 proton in its nucleus. An oxygen atom has 8 protons. Iron has 26. Uranium has 92. Normally, an atom has an equal number of protons and electrons. As a result, the negative charges of the electrons exactly balance the positive charges of the protons. The atom is, therefore, electrically neutral.

Ions. Sometimes an atom loses or gains one or more electrons. If it gains an electron, the atom takes on a negative charge. If it loses an electron, the atom takes on a positive charge. Atoms that carry an electric charge are called *ions.* Most ions are positive, and the word *ion* used alone usually means an atom that has lost one or more electrons. Positive and negative ions attract one another and can combine to form solid materials. Ordinary table salt, for example, consists of sodium and chlorine. Each sodium atom gives up one electron to form a positive sodium ion. The chlorine takes on this electron to become a negative chloride ion. The strong electrical attraction between the ions makes salt a solid material with a high melting point.

Molecules. Neutral atoms often share electrons with other atoms. Atoms that share electrons become electrically attracted to one another. The attraction causes the

atoms to join and form *molecules.* For example, two hydrogen atoms can share electrons with one oxygen atom to make a water molecule. The electrons tend to spend more time near the oxygen atom, giving it a slightly negative charge. The two hydrogen atoms take on slightly positive charges. The electric attraction between these charged atoms holds the water molecule together.

Static electricity. Sometimes, a large number of atoms in an object gain or lose electrons. When such a gain or loss happens, the entire object takes on an electric charge. The term *static electricity* describes situations where objects carry electric charge.

Static electricity occurs, for example, when you rub a balloon on your shirt. The friction between the cloth and the balloon causes electrons to transfer from your shirt to the balloon. The shirt then has an overall positive charge because it has more protons than electrons. The balloon takes on a negative charge because it has extra electrons. The balloon will then stick to the shirt or to another surface, such as a wall.

Similarly, when you walk across a rug on a dry day, friction between your shoes and the rug transfers electrons from your body to the rug, giving your body a positive charge. If you touch a doorknob or other metal object, electrons may jump from the object to your body. You may see a spark and feel a slight shock.

Lightning results from static electricity. Scientists believe that raindrops tossed in the winds of thunderclouds build up electric charge. Parts of the cloud become positively charged, while other parts become negatively charged. Charge may jump between different parts of the cloud, or from the cloud to the ground. The result is the huge electric spark we call lightning.

Static electricity has many uses in homes, businesses, and industries. For example, the copying machines found in most offices are *electrostatic copiers.* They make duplicates of printed or written material by attracting negatively charged particles of *toner* (powdered ink) to positively charged paper. Static electricity is also used in air cleaners called *electrostatic precipitators.* These devices put a positive electric charge on particles

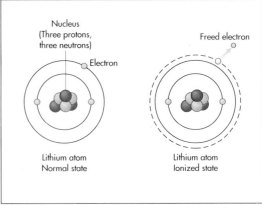

WORLD BOOK diagram by Tom Brucker, Precision Graphics

An atom becomes an ion when it gains or loses an electron and so acquires an electric charge. A normal atom, *left,* has an equal number of positive protons and negative electrons. If it loses an electron, *right,* it becomes a positively charged ion.

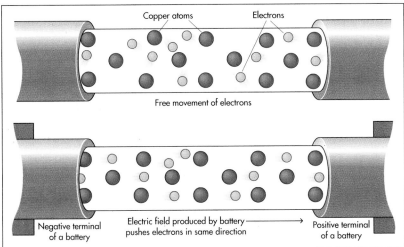

Copper atoms   Electrons

Free movement of electrons

Negative terminal
of a battery

Electric field produced by battery
pushes electrons in same direction

Positive terminal
of a battery

**Electric current
in metals**

Metals, such as copper wire, are good conductors because they have a large number of free electrons. If a copper wire is connected between the terminals of a battery, free electrons in the wire move from the negative to the positive terminal. This movement is defined as a flow of current.

WORLD BOOK diagram by Tom Brucker, Precision Graphics

of dust, smoke, bacteria, or pollen in the air. Negatively charged collector plates attract the positive particles out of the air.

Conductors and insulators

Electric charge moves through some materials better than others. Charge moves easily through substances called *conductors*. Materials known as *insulators* resist the movement of electric charge.

Conductors. Materials that conduct electricity contain charged particles that are free to move throughout the material. If extra electric charge is applied to a conductor, the charged particles will not stay in place but will spread over the material's surface. In most conductors, the free particles are electrons that are not attached to atoms. In some conductors, the free particles are ions.

Metals are good conductors because they contain a large number of free electrons. Most wires used to carry electric energy are made of metal, usually copper. Some liquids are also conductors. Salt water, for example, is a conductor because it contains sodium and chloride ions that are free to move about.

Some gases are also conductors. If a gas is extremely hot, its atoms move so fast that they collide hard enough to tear electrons free. Then the gas becomes a type of electric conductor called *plasma*. The hot, glowing gas inside a fluorescent light is one example of plasma. The hot gases that make up the sun and other stars are also plasma.

In most conductors, moving electrons continuously collide with atoms and lose energy. But in some materials, called *superconductors,* electrons move perfectly freely without losing energy. Superconductors only work at very cold temperatures. Because they require extreme cold, superconductors are only used in special situations. Someday, however, superconductors may be used to make highly efficient motors, generators, and power lines.

Insulators. In materials called insulators, electrons are tightly bound to atoms and are not free to move around. If extra electric charge is applied to an insulator, the charge will stay in place and will not move through

the material. Glass, rubber, plastic, dry wood, and ordinary dry air are good insulators.

Insulators are important for electrical safety. Most electrical cords are made from a conducting material covered with an insulating material, such as rubber or plastic. The insulator makes the cords safe to touch, even when they are plugged into an outlet.

Semiconductors. Some materials conduct electric charge better than insulators but not as well as conductors. These materials are called *semiconductors*. Silicon is the most commonly used semiconductor. By adding small amounts of other substances to a semiconductor, engineers can adjust its capacity to conduct electric charge. Semiconductors are essential to the operation of computers, calculators, radios, television sets, video games, and many other devices.

Resistance refers to a material's opposition to the passage of electric charges through it. Resistance occurs when electrons moving in the material collide with atoms and give up energy. The energy the electrons give up is converted into heat. A good conductor, such as copper, has low resistance. The semiconductor silicon has higher resistance. Insulators, such as glass or wood, have such high resistance that it is nearly impossible for electric charges to flow through them. Superconductors offer no resistance to the flow of electric charges.

Resistance depends not only on the type of material but also on its size and shape. For example, a thin copper wire has more resistance than a thick one. A long wire has greater resistance than a short one. A material's resistance may also vary with temperature.

Electric current

A flow of electric charge through a conductor is called *electric current*. Energy is associated with the flow of current. As current flows through electric devices, this energy may be converted to useful forms. For example, electric energy is converted into heat by an electric range and into light by a light bulb.

Direct and alternating current. Current that flows steadily in one direction is called *direct current* (DC). A battery produces direct current. Sometimes current flows back and forth, changing direction rapidly. It is then called *alternating current* (AC). The current in household wiring is alternating current. In the United States and Canada, household current reverses direction 120 times per second, completing 60 full cycles.

Sources of current. By itself, a conductor does not have electric current flowing in it. But if a positive charge is applied to one end of the conductor, and a negative charge to the other end, then electric charge will flow through the conductor. Because positive and negative charges attract, some type of energy must be supplied to separate the charges and keep them at opposite ends of the conductor. The energy may come from chemical action, motion, sunlight, or heat.

Batteries produce electric energy by means of chemical action. A battery has two structures called *electrodes,* each made from a different chemically active material. Between the electrodes, the battery contains a liquid or paste called an *electrolyte,* which conducts electric current. The electrolyte helps promote chemical reactions at each electrode. As a result of the chemical reactions, a positive charge builds up at one electrode and a negative charge builds up at the other. Electric current will then flow from the positive electrode, through a conductor, to the negative electrode.

In a flashlight battery, the flat end is the negative electrode. The end with a bump connects to the positive electrode. When a wire links the electrodes, a current flows. The electric energy is converted to light if it passes through a flashlight bulb. Chemical reactions in the electrolyte keep the electrodes oppositely charged and so keep the current flowing.

Eventually, the chemical energy runs out and the battery can no longer produce electric energy. Some worn-out batteries must be discarded. Others, called *rechargeable batteries,* can be charged again by passing electric current through them.

Generators change mechanical energy into electric energy. In a generator, a source of mechanical energy spins coils of wire near a magnet to produce electric current. A generator works because moving a conductor near a magnet produces a current in the conductor. Most generators produce alternating current.

Generators furnish most of the electric energy people use. In a car, a small generator called an *alternator* is turned by the engine and produces electric energy that recharges the car's battery. A large generator in an electric power plant can provide enough electric energy for a city of 2 million people. Electric current from the generator reaches homes, factories, and offices through vast networks of power lines.

Solar cells, also called *photovoltaic cells,* convert sunlight into electric energy. Solar cells power most artificial satellites and other spacecraft as well as many handheld calculators. Photovoltaic cells are made from semiconducting materials, usually specially treated silicon. Energy from the sun forces negative and positive charges in the semiconductor to separate. The charges will then flow through a conductor.

Piezoelectric crystals are nonmetallic minerals that develop electric charge along their surfaces when stretched or compressed. Quartz is the most common piezoelectric crystal. Some microphones use piezoelectric crystals to convert sound energy into electric energy

for recording or radio broadcasting. Modern gas ranges have piezoelectric crystals instead of pilot lights. The crystals produce electric sparks that ignite the gas.

Electric circuits

To use electric energy, an electric device must be connected to an energy source. A complete path must be provided for electric current to flow from the energy source to the device and back again. Such a path is called an *electric circuit.*

A simple circuit. Suppose you want to make a battery-powered light bulb shine. Electric current will only flow if there is a complete circuit that leads from the battery to the bulb and back to the battery. To make the circuit, connect a wire from the positive terminal of the battery to the light bulb. Then, connect another wire from the bulb back to the negative terminal. Electric current will then flow from the battery's positive terminal, through the light bulb, to the battery's negative terminal.

Inside the bulb is a thin wire called a *filament.* The filament is made from a material with greater resistance than the wires linking the battery and bulb. The moving electrons that make up the current collide with atoms in the filament and give up most of their energy. The released energy heats the filament, which glows and gives off light.

Series and parallel circuits. A single battery or generator often powers more than one electric device. In such cases, circuit designs called *series circuits* and *parallel circuits* are necessary.

A series circuit has only one path. The same current flows through all parts of the path and all electric devices connected to it. Flashlights, some Christmas tree lights, and other simple devices use series circuits. In a parallel circuit, the current splits to flow through two or more paths. Parallel circuits enable a single energy source to provide current to more electric devices than a series circuit could. Household lights and appliances are connected in parallel circuits.

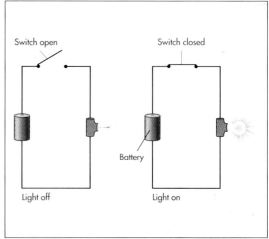

WORLD BOOK diagram by Tom Brucker, Precision Graphics

An electric circuit is a path that electric current can follow between a device, such as a light bulb, and an energy source, such as a battery. With the switch open, a gap separates the connecting wires so that the current cannot complete its path.

Many circuits include some parts that are series and some that are parallel. An extremely complex circuit, like that in a computer or TV, has millions of parts connected in various series and parallel combinations.

Electric and magnetic fields. When most people think of an electric current, they think of moving electrons carrying charges through a wire. Actually, most of the energy flows in electric and magnetic fields surrounding the wire. Energy from the fields enters the wires and replaces energy the electrons lose through resistance. The battery, generator, or other energy source continually restores energy lost from the fields.

In DC circuits, electrons flow from one battery terminal, through the circuit, to the other terminal. But the energy of the electric and magnetic fields flows at the same time from both terminals to the electric device. In AC circuits, individual electrons move back and forth in the wires and do not travel the entire circuit. Nevertheless, electric energy flows from the energy source to the device in the form of the fields.

Controlling electric current. The simplest way to stop a current flowing through a circuit is with a *switch.* A basic switch consists of two electric conductors that can be moved apart to create a gap in a circuit. When the switch is off, the gap is open, and no current flows. When the switch is on, the conductors are connected, and current flows.

Wires and electric devices become dangerously hot if too much current flows through them. Switches called *fuses* and *circuit breakers* protect the wiring in most buildings. If too many electric devices are plugged into an outlet, a fuse or circuit breaker will shut off the current. Many individual electric devices also contain fuses.

Sometimes people need to vary the strength of current, rather than merely turn it on or off. One way to adjust current strength is to vary resistance within the circuit. For example, turning the volume knob on a radio operates a *variable resistor.* This device adjusts resistance to the flow of current through the radio, making the sound louder or softer.

Switches and variable resistors cannot change currents quickly. Tiny semiconductor devices called *transistors* can be used to adjust current more rapidly. Transistors act as high-speed switches that turn on and off billions of times each second. Some devices contain millions of transistors on a single tiny chip of silicon, called an *integrated circuit* or simply a *chip.* Integrated circuits form the heart of computers, calculators, video games, and many other devices.

Electrically powered devices are said to be *electronic* if they carry electrical signals that can be varied in some way to represent information. Electronic devices include transistors, diodes, capacitors, inductors, and integrated circuits. Signals may represent sounds, pictures, numbers, letters, computer instructions, or other information. In the amplifier of a compact disc player, for example, transistors provide a continuous range of currents that strengthen electrical signals representing the sounds being played.

Electrical safety

Most people know that electricity can be dangerous. Understanding why can help you avoid electrical injury and use electric energy safely.

Electric shock is caused by an electric current passing through the body. The body's own electrical signals normally travel along nerves, carrying information to and from the brain. These electrical signals regulate the beating of the heart and other vital functions. Currents flowing through the body can disrupt these signals, causing muscle contractions, heart and respiratory failure, and death. Electric current can also burn skin and other body tissues.

Voltage measures the "push" that a source of electric energy supplies to move a charge through a circuit. The voltage of a flashlight or radio battery is usually too

Safety with electricity

Electricity can be dangerous. But following certain precautions can help you avoid electrical injury.

WORLD BOOK illustrations by Yoshi Miyake

Do not touch electric devices when you are in a shower or bathtub or when you are wet.

Dry your hands thoroughly before using a hairdryer, electric shaver, or other electric appliance.

Do not overload electrical outlets. Never plug in an electric device that has a damaged cord.

Insert safety plugs into unused electrical outlets within reach of children.

Do not fly kites or climb trees near power lines. Never go near fallen power lines after a storm.

Find shelter indoors during a lightning storm. Use the telephone only in emergencies.

small to cause serious injury. But the 120 volts available at most household outlets could severely injure or even kill a person. The danger of electric shock is much greater when a person's skin is wet because water, mixed with salt from the skin, lowers the body's electrical resistance. A given voltage can then pass a greater current through the body. For information about first aid for electric shock, see **First aid.**

Most electric devices have safety features to help prevent shock. Many appliances and tools have plugs with a third prong that connects the metal parts of the device to a wire leading to the ground. If the wiring inside the device becomes defective, the third prong usually causes the current to flow harmlessly to the ground.

Electrical dangers outdoors. If you climb a tree near an electric power line, you may get a shock if the tree touches the line. Storms sometimes knock down electric power lines. You could be injured or killed if you touch a fallen line when the power is still on.

Lightning discharges involve about 100 million volts. This voltage is more than enough to drive a current through the body that can kill a person. You can avoid being struck by lightning by staying indoors during a storm. If you get caught outdoors, stay away from open fields and high places. A forest is safer than open land. But do not stand under a tall or isolated tree, which is more likely to be struck. One of the safest places during a lightning storm is inside a car. If the vehicle is struck by lightning, its metal body will conduct the electric charge around the outside of the car, leaving the interior unharmed.

Electrical fire is another danger. When an electric current passes through a conductor, resistance causes the conductor to become hot. Sometimes the heat is desirable. For example, the wires in a toaster heat up to brown bread. But overheating in electrical cords or in household wiring can cause a fire. Electrical fires destroy many homes every year. To avoid fires, do not plug too many devices into the same outlet, and never use electric devices with worn or frayed cords.

Electricity and magnetism

The magnet you stick to your refrigerator may not seem related to electricity. But magnetism and electricity are actually closely related. Just as an electric field surrounds an electric charge and produces a force that affects other charges, so a *magnetic field* surrounds a magnet and produces forces that act on other magnets. Like an electric charge, a magnet will attract or repel another magnet. Moreover, magnetism is the result of electric currents. In materials called *permanent magnets,* the currents come from the motions of electrons in some of the atoms. The electrons spin on their axes like tops, and they also circle the atomic nuclei.

Together, magnetism and electricity make a fundamental force of the universe called electromagnetism. Electromagnetism is based on the fact that the motion of electric charges can produce magnetic fields, and changing magnetic fields can produce electric currents.

For example, passing an electric current through a coil of wire makes the coil a temporary magnet called an *electromagnet.* The electric current creates a magnetic field around the coiled wire. As long as the current flows, the coil will be a magnet.

Magnetism can, in turn, produce an electric current by means of *electromagnetic induction.* In this process, a coil of wire moves near a magnet. This action causes an electric current to flow in the wire. The current flows as long as the movement continues. Generators produce electric current through this process.

Together, changing electric and magnetic fields make *electromagnetic waves,* also called *electromagnetic radiation.* These waves carry energy known as *electromagnetic energy* at the speed of light. Light, radio and TV signals, and microwaves all consist of electromagnetic waves. So do the infrared rays that you feel as heat when you stand near a hot stove, and the ultraviolet rays that cause sunburn. The X rays that doctors use to see inside your body are electromagnetic waves. The gamma rays that come from nuclear reactors and from outer space are also electromagnetic waves.

History

Early discoveries. Several thousand years ago, the ancient Greeks observed that a substance called *amber* attracted bits of lightweight material, such as feathers or straw, after it was rubbed with cloth. Amber is fossilized pitch from pine trees that lived millions of years ago. Amber is a good electric insulator, so it easily holds electric charge. Although the Greeks did not know about electric charge, they were actually experimenting with static electricity when they rubbed amber. The Greek word for amber is *elektron.* The English words *electricity* and *electron* come from this word.

Other peoples, including the ancient Greeks and Chinese, knew of another substance that could attract things. It was a black rock called *lodestone* or *magnetite.* Today we know that it is a natural magnet. Lodestone attracts iron objects, which tend to be heavy. In contrast, amber attracts only light things, like straw. In 1551, the Italian mathematician Girolamo Cardano, also known as Jerome Cardan, realized that the attracting effects of amber and of magnetite must be different. Cardano was the first to note the difference between electricity and magnetism.

In 1600, the English physician William Gilbert reported that such materials as glass, sulfur, and wax behaved like amber. When rubbed with cloth, they too attracted light objects. Gilbert called these materials *electrics.* He studied the behavior of electrics and concluded that their effects must be due to some kind of fluid. Today, we know that what Gilbert called electrics are materials that are good insulators.

Experiments with electric charge. In the 1730's, the French scientist Charles Dufay found that charged pieces of glass attracted amberlike substances but repelled other glasslike substances. Dufay decided that there must be two kinds of electricities. He called them *vitreous* (for glasslike substances) and *resinous* (for amberlike substances). Dufay had found negative and positive electric charge, though he thought of them as two kinds of "electric fluid."

The American scientist and statesman Benjamin Franklin began to experiment with electricity in 1746. Franklin thought that there was only one kind of electric fluid. He theorized that objects with too much fluid would repel each other, but they would attract objects with too little fluid. If an object with an excess of fluid touched an object deficient in fluid, the fluid would be shared. Franklin's idea explained how opposite charges cancel each other out when they come in contact.

Franklin used the term *positive* for what he thought was an excess of electric fluid. He used the term *negative* for a deficiency of fluid. Franklin did not know that electricity is not a fluid. Rather, electricity is associated with the charges of electrons and protons. Today, we know that most positively charged objects actually have a deficiency of electrons, while negatively charged objects have an excess of electrons.

In 1752, Franklin performed his famous experiment of flying a kite during a thunderstorm. When the kite and string became electrically charged, Franklin concluded that the storm clouds were themselves charged. He became convinced that lightning was a huge electric spark Fortunately, lightning did not strike Franklin's kite. If it had, he probably would have been killed.

In 1767, the English scientist Joseph Priestley described the mathematical law that shows how attraction weakens as the distance between oppositely charged objects increases. In 1785, the French scientist Charles Augustin de Coulomb confirmed Priestley's law. Coulomb showed that the law also held true for the repulsive force between objects with the same charge. Today, the principle is known as *Coulomb's law.*

In 1771, Luigi Galvani, an Italian anatomy professor, found that the leg of a recently killed frog would twitch when touched with two different metals at the same time. Galvani's work attracted much attention. In the late 1790's, Alessandro Volta, an Italian physicist, offered an explanation. Volta showed that chemical action occurs in a moist material in contact with two different metals. The chemical action results in an electric current. The flow of current had made Galvani's frog twitch. Volta gathered pairs of disks, consisting of one silver and one zinc disk. He separated the pairs with paper or cloth moistened with salt water. By piling up a stack of such disks, Volta constructed the first battery, called a *voltaic pile.*

Many experiments with Volta's battery and electric circuits followed. The German physicist Georg S. Ohm devised a mathematical law to describe the relationship between current, voltage, and resistance for certain materials. According to Ohm's law, published in 1827, a larger voltage can push a larger current through a given resistance. In addition, a given voltage can push a larger current through a smaller resistance.

Electricity and magnetism. In 1820, the Danish physicist Hans C. Oersted found that an electric current flowing near a compass needle will cause the needle to move. Oersted was the first to show a definite connection between electricity and magnetism. During the 1820's, André Marie Ampère discovered the mathematical relationship between currents and magnetic fields. That relationship, called Ampère's law, is one of the basic laws of electromagnetism.

In the early 1830's, the English scientist Michael Faraday and the American physicist Joseph Henry independently discovered that moving a magnet near a coil of wire produced an electric current in the wire. Further experiments showed that electrical effects occur any time a magnetic field changes. Audio and videotape recording, computer disks, and electric generators are based on this principle.

The Scottish physicist James Clerk Maxwell combined all the known laws covering electricity and magnetism into a single set of four equations. Maxwell's equations, published in 1865, describe completely how electric and magnetic fields arise and interact. Maxwell made a new prediction that a changing electric field would produce a magnetic field. That prediction led him to propose the existence of electromagnetic waves, which we now know include light, radio waves, and X rays. In the later 1880's, the German physicist Heinrich R. Hertz showed how to generate and detect radio waves, proving Maxwell correct. In 1901, the Italian inventor Guglielmo Marconi transmitted electromagnetic waves across the Atlantic Ocean, setting the stage for radio, TV, satellite communications, and cellular telephones.

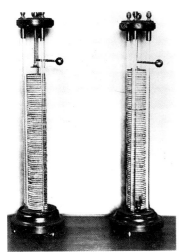

The voltaic pile, invented in the late 1790's, was the first battery. It provided the first source of steady electric current.

The dynamo was the first efficient electric generator. It used an electromagnet to produce current, instead of the permanent magnets previously employed. The German inventor Ernst Werner von Siemens discovered the principle of the dynamo in 1866.

The electronic age. The Irish physicist G. Johnstone Stoney believed that electric current was actually the movement of extremely small, electrically charged particles. In 1891, he suggested that these particles be called *electrons.* In 1897, the English physicist Joseph John Thomson proved the existence of electrons and showed that all atoms contain them. In research published in 1913, the American physicist Robert A. Millikan accurately measured the electron's charge.

In the late 1800's, scientists discovered that electrons can be dislodged from a metal surface in a *vacuum tube.* A vacuum tube is a glass tube with most of the air removed. The tube contains electrodes with wires that extend through the glass. Linking batteries to the electrodes causes a current of electrons to flow within the tube. The current can be modified by adjusting the voltage. Vacuum tubes can amplify, combine, and separate weak electric currents. This invention helped make radio, TV, and other technologies possible.

In 1947, the American physicists John Bardeen, Walter H. Brattain, and William Shockley invented the transistor. Transistors do the same jobs as vacuum tubes, but they are smaller and more durable, and they use far less energy. By the 1960's, transistors had replaced vacuum tubes in most electronic equipment. Since then, electronics companies have developed ever smaller transistors. Today, millions of interconnected transistors fit on a single chip called an integrated circuit.

Recent developments. Every year, the worldwide demand for electric energy increases. Most of the electric energy we use comes from power plants that burn fossil fuels, such as coal, oil, or natural gas. Some electric energy comes from nuclear and *hydroelectric* (water power) plants. Smaller amounts come from solar cells, windmills, and other sources.

Many people are concerned that the earth's supply of fossil fuel is limited and will someday run out. Another problem is that present methods of generating electric energy may harm the environment. In response, scientists, engineers, and power companies are trying to develop alternative sources of electric energy. Such sources may include solar, geothermal, wind, and tidal energy. See **Energy supply** (Problems; Challenges).

Many scientists hope that new electric devices will actually help curb the growing demand for electric energy. Computers, for example, can control the lights, air conditioning, and heating in buildings to reduce energy use. Compact fluorescent lamps, using miniature electronic circuits, provide the same light as ordinary light bulbs but use only one-fifth as much electric energy. Computers and modern communication systems enable people to work at home and save energy they would have used for transportation.   Richard Wolfson

Additional resources

Level I
Ardley, Neil. *The Science Book of Electricity.* Harcourt, 1991.
Clemence, John and Janet. *Electricity.* Garrett Educational, 1991.
Glover, David. *Batteries, Bulbs, and Wires.* Kingfisher Bks., 1993.
Parker, Steve. *Electricity.* Dorling Kindersley, 1992.

Level II
Hall, Dorothea, ed. *Electricity: A Step-by-Step Guide.* Smithmark, 1993.
Middleton, Robert G. *Practical Electricity.* 4th ed. Ed. by L. Donald Meyers and J. A. Tedesco. Macmillan, 1988.
Nye, David E. *Electrifying America.* MIT Pr., 1990.
Wong, Ovid K. *Experimenting with Electricity and Magnetism.* Watts, 1993.

Seven Natural Wonders of the World is a listing of outstanding natural features of the earth. Teachers use such listings to introduce students to the study of earth science. Listings of wonders also help us appreciate the great variety of the earth's landscape. Factors considered in making up a list include a feature's geographic character and geological importance, and its popularity with tourists. Various listings include different features. However, a majority of earth scientists probably would cite most of the following as worthy of inclusion on such a list.

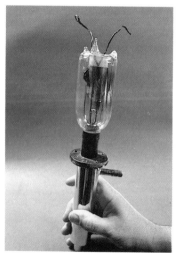

David R. Frazier

The vacuum tube led to the development of radio and television. This large early tube was made about 1922.

Fermilab Visual Media Services

A particle accelerator helps scientists study electricity and other natural forces. The accelerator at the Fermi National Accelerator Laboratory near Batavia, Illinois, accelerates protons to almost the speed of light in an underground tunnel, *above.*

Seven Natural Wonders of the World

Remarkable features of the earth's surface have been listed as natural wonders because they are imposing to the eye and are striking examples of how natural forces shape the landscape. The photographs on this page and the following page show seven features that are commonly listed as natural wonders.

The Grand Canyon is a valley that is about 1 mile (1.6 kilometers) deep.

Mount Everest is the world's highest mountain.

Ayers Rock is the largest single stone on earth.

Chris Bonington, Bruce Coleman Ltd.

The Matterhorn is known for its pyramidal shape.

Meteor Crater Enterprises

Meteor Crater formed when a meteorite fell to earth.

© Mark Boulton, Bruce Coleman Inc.

Victoria Falls is about 1 mile (1.6 kilometers) wide.

Andrew N. Drake

The Great Barrier Reef is the longest group of coral reefs.

The Grand Canyon, in the United States, is a breathtaking feature created by the *erosion* (wearing away) of rock by the Colorado River over a period of about 6 million years. The canyon extends across northwestern Arizona for 277 miles (446 kilometers), and is about 1 mile (1.6 kilometers) deep. The erosion exposed rock formations that represent 1¾ billion years of earth's history. The flow of the river, and thus the rate of erosion, has been reduced by the construction of the Glen Canyon Dam upstream from the Grand Canyon.

Mount Everest, rising 29,028 feet (8,848 meters) above sea level, is the world's highest mountain. It stands on the border of Nepal and Tibet in a massive range called the Himalaya. This range formed in a gradual collision of 2 of the approximately 30 *tectonic plates* that make up the earth's outer shell. One plate folded like a tablecloth that is pushed across a table. The highest "wrinkle" is the Himalaya. The range is still rising about 1 centimeter each year.

Ayers Rock is the world's largest *monolith* (single large stone). It rises 1,142 feet (348 meters) above the desert floor in central Australia. The rock is loaf-shaped and has a circumference of about 5½ miles (9 kilometers). It is composed of red sandstone. Its name is *Uluru* in the language of Australia's Aborigine people.

The Matterhorn is one of the most beautiful mountains on earth. Its base is in Switzerland and Italy. Its peak, in Switzerland, is 14,692 feet (4,478 meters) above sea level. The Matterhorn is known for its extraordinary pyramidal shape, called a *horn* by earth scientists. Glaciers formed the horn by eroding rock from a mountain as they pushed inward from opposite sides.

Victoria Falls is a waterfall on the Zambezi River in southern Africa, between Zimbabwe and Zambia. At the falls, the river is about 1 mile (1.6 kilometers) wide. The falls plunges 355 feet (108 meters) into a gorge. The local name of the falls, *Mosi oa Tunya* (smoke that thunders), describes its tremendous sound and the water vapor that rises from the falls.

Meteor Crater, also known as Barringer Crater, is a huge circular depression in the ground near Winslow, Arizona. It formed when a meteorite struck the earth about 50,000 years ago—a recent event in geological history. The crater is 570 feet (175 meters) deep and 4,180 feet (1,275 meters) wide. Scientists consider it the best crater of its kind on earth because it was created so recently. It is in almost perfect condition.

The Great Barrier Reef is the world's longest group of coral reefs. It follows the coast of Australia for about 1,250 miles (2,010 kilometers). The reef consists of small islands of solid coral, patches of coral sand, and submerged coral. Coral is made up of hardened skeletons of water animals called *polyps* that have died. But billions of live polyps are attached to submerged coral. Living polyps and other animals give undersea parts of the Great Barrier Reef a brilliant coloring. Many people are concerned about possible damage to the reef by the large numbers of tourists who visit it. Paul D. McDermott

Related articles in *World Book.* For information on other outstanding natural features, see *Related articles* Desert, Lake, **Mountain, River,** and **Waterfall.** See also:

Grand Canyon	Matterhorn	Victoria Falls
Great Barrier Reef	Mount Everest	

Index
• • • • • • • • • • • • •

How to use the index

This index covers the contents of the 1995, 1996, and 1997 editions of *Science Year*, the World Book Science Annual.

Each entry gives the last two digits of the edition year, followed by the colon and the page number or numbers. For example, this entry that information on propoxur may be found on page 286 of the 1997 *Science Year*.

When there are many references to a topic, they are grouped alphabetically by clue words under the main topic. For example, the clue words under **Proteins** group the references to that topic under the main heading and at least one subtopic.

An entry in all capital letters indicates that there is a Science News Update article with that name in at least one of the three volumes covered by this index. References to the topic in other articles may also be listed in the entry.

The "see" and "see also" cross-references indicate that references to a topic are listed under another entry in the index.

An entry that only begins with a capital letter indicates that there are no Science News Update articles with that title but that information on this topic may be found in the editions and on the pages listed.

The indication (il.) after a page number means that the reference is to an illustration only.

An entry followed by *WBE* refers to a new or revised *World Book Encyclopedia* article in the *Science Year* supplement section. This entry means that there is a *World Book Encyclopedia* article on radiation on pages 318-325 of the 1997 *Science Year*.

Index

A

Index

Cosmology, **97:** 198
  see also **Astronomy; Universe**
Costa Rica, 96: 188
Cotton, 96: 199
Cougars, 97: 68-70
Cough suppressants, 95: 324
Courts, Science in, 95: 298-299
Coxsackie B3 (virus), **97:** 252, **96:** 277-278
Coyotes, 97: 66-67, 69 (il.)
Cranes (birds), **97:** 211 (il.), **95:** 254
Craters, 97: 242-243, **96:** 21
Crayons, Soybean, 96: 196 (il.)
Cretaceous Period, 97: 232, **96:** 264-265, **95:** 89
Creutzfeldt-Jakob disease, 97: 164, 265
Crew resource management (program), **97:** 139
Crichton, Michael, 95: 77, 92
Crime, 97: 269, **96:** 159-171
Criminology, 96: 159-171
Crixivan (drug), **97:** 216
Crocodiles, 95: 83-84, 89 (il.)
Cro-Magnons, 96: 204
Crozo de Gentillo (France), **97:** 17 (il.)
Crustaceans, 96: 261
Crutzen, Paul, 97: 188
Cryolophosaurus ellioti (dinosaur), **95:** 269
Cubic-Crete System, 97: 224
Currents, Ocean, 97: 113
Cyanoacrylate (chemical), **96:** 168
Cyclones, 96: 32-33
Cygnus Loop (nebula), **97:** 122 (il.)
Cygnus X-1 (black hole), **95:** 26

D

Dams, 95: 62, 69 (il.), 71, 185-187, 263-264
Dante II (robot), **96:** 275 (il.)
Dark matter, 97: 179, 274, **95:** 224-225
David, House of, 95: 213 (il.)
DC-X (rocket), **95:** 306 (il.), 308
DDT (pesticide), **97:** 79, 81, 84, 228, 285-286
Dead Sea Scrolls, 95: 220 (il.)
Deafness. See Hearing loss
Death, Causes of. See Public health; Risk assessment
DEATHS OF SCIENTISTS, 97: 214-215, **96:** 248-249, **95:** 256-257
Decibels, 97: 277-279
Decongestants, 95: 324
Deep biosphere, 96: 230-231
Deep Blue (computer), **97:** 159 (il.), 161
Deer, 97: 65 (il.), 67-70, 195 (il.), **96:** 246-247
Deer mice, 95: 280
Dehydration, 95: 315
Deltadromeus (dinosaur), **97:** 232
Delusions, 95: 292
Dementia, 95: 132
Dendrimers (molecules), **97:** 200-201
Deoxyribonucleic acid. See DNA
Depression (illness), **95:** 295
Deserts, 96: 247
Deuterium, 95: 291
Developing nations, 96: 188, **95:** 201-203

Dextromethorphan (drug), **95:** 324
Diabetes, 97: 217, 247-250, **96:** 251, **95:** 258, 281-282
Diademed sifakas, 97: 212 (il.)
Diamonds, Synthetic, 97: 226
Diarrhea, 97: 166
Diatoms, 96: 251-252
Diazinon (pesticide), **97:** 287
Diet. See Nutrition
Digestive system, 97: 230-233
Digital code. See Binary system
Digital compression, 95: 167, 173
Digital Satellite System, 97: 205 (il.)
Digital videodiscs, 97: 149-150, 208-209
Dikes, 95: 67
Dinosaurs
  bird evolution, **97:** 234, **95:** 269-271
  cloning, **95:** 92, 101, 103 (il.)
  extinction, **95:** 178, **96:** 179, **95:** 119
  fossil discoveries, **97:** 232-234, **96:** 261-263, **95:** 269
  Jurassic Period, **95:** 77, 81-89
Dioxin, 96: 259-260, **95:** 268
Diphtheria, 96: 293
Diplodicus (dinosaur), *WBE,* **95:** 352
Direct broadcast satellite, 96: 304
Diring (site), **97:** 171-172
Disc-operating systems, 97: 152-153
Discovery (space shuttle), **97:** 272, **96:** 298, 300-301, **95:** 306
Disease, 95: 51-56, 208
  see also **Medical research; Nutrition; Public health**
Distilled water, 97: 282
DNA
  Alzheimer's disease, **97:** 237
  amphibian deaths, **95:** 253-254
  cancer research, **96:** 76-85, **95:** 272
  chromosome map, **95:** 274
  cloning, **95:** 92-93, 101
  computers of future, **97:** 161
  forensic science, **96:** 159-166
  fossils, **96:** 265
  lichen origins, **97:** 196-197
  Nobel Prize research, **95:** 234
  origin of life, **97:** 47-54
  plant photoreceptivity, **95:** 241
  radiation effects, **96:** 125-127
  retroviruses, **95:** 124-130, 136-137
  see also **Gene therapy; Genes; Genetic engineering; Genetics**
DNA fingerprinting, 96: 161-164
Dopamine, 96: 280
Doppler effect, 97: 31
DOS. See Disc-operating systems
Dos Pilas (city), **95:** 217
Draper Prize, 95: 266
Dredging, of rivers, 95: 70-71
Drought, 95: 211-213
Drug abuse, 96: 291
DRUGS, 97: 216-217, **96:** 250-251, **95:** 258-259
  biodiversity benefits, **96:** 182-183
  chemistry advances, **97:** 202-203
  see also **Medical research** and specific diseases
Dryopithecus laietanus (ape) **97:** 168-169
DVD's. See Digital videodiscs
Dwarfism, 96: 269
Dwarfs (space objects), **97:** 179, **95:** 221-222, 224
Dwingeloo 1 (galaxy), **96:** 216 (il.)

Dyes, Hair, 97: 292-293
D-Zero (particle detector), **96:** 140-143

E

Eagle Nebula, 97: 117 (il.), 181
Eagles, 96: 246
Earplugs, 97: 280
Ears, 97: 248 (il.), 276-280
Earth
  collision with space objects, **96:** 21-27, **95:** 119
  origin of life, **97:** 43-57
  space image, **97:** 270 (il.)
  see also **Atmosphere; Ecology; Environmental pollution; Geology; Oceanography**
Earth Summit, 96: 188
Earthquakes
  Kobe, Japan, **96:** 271 (il.)
  measurement, **96:** 272-273
  New Madrid, **96:** 270-271
  ocean, **96:** 285-286
  smart materials, **95:** 265
  western U.S., **96:** 271-275, **95:** 278-279, 298
Ebola virus, 96: 293
ECOLOGY, 97: 219-221, **96:** 251-253, **95:** 259-261
  see also **Ecosystems; Environmental pollution**
Ecosystems
  cave, **96:** 97-103
  Jurassic, **95:** 85
  Lake Erie, **97:** 72
  river, **95:** 62-75
  threatened species, **96:** 183-184, 189-192
Eemian Period, 95: 233
Eggs, Dinosaur, 97: 234, **96:** 261-263
Egypt, Ancient, 96: 203, **95:** 219 (il.)
Einstein, Albert, 97: 41, 256, **95:** 15-18, 21, 27
Electricity, *WBE,* **97:** 326-333
Electrolytes, 95: 317
Electromagnets, 96: 289
Electron guns, 97: 202
Electronics, *WBE,* **96:** 330-340
  see also **Computers and electronics**
Electrons, 97: 259, **96:** 121, 132, **95:** 290
  see also **Superconductivity**
Electronvolt (measurement), **96:** 133
Element 106, 95: 244-245
Element 110, 96: 288-289
Element 111, 96: 288-289
Element 112, 97: 201
Elements, Chemical, *WBE,* **97:** 313-317
Elevators (aviation), **97:** 133
El Niño, 97: 186, 255, **96:** 220, 283, **95:** 230-232
El Pital (city), **95:** 213-214
Embedded computing, 97: 150
Embryos
  cloning, **95:** 92-105
  dinosaur, **96:** 261-263
  genes and development, **97:** 189, **95:** 238-239
  research guidelines, **96:** 296
Emissions. See Air pollution;

Index

217, **95:** 226-227

formation, **97:** 181 (il.), 184, **96:** 217-219

Hubble Space Telescope photos, **97:** 124-127 (ils.), **96:** 215 (il.), **95:** 14, 25 (il.), 223, 227 (il.), 305 (il.)

low-density, **95:** 223 (il.)

mergers, **95:** 223-226

see also **Astronomy; Milky Way Galaxy**

Galileo (spacecraft), **97:** 175-176, 177, 273-274, **96:** 18, **95:** 228

Gallo, Robert C., 97: 243, **95:** 302

Gamma Ray Observatory, 95: 222-223

Gamma rays, 96: 121, 123 (il.), **95:** 222

Garbage. See Recycling; Waste

Gasification, 95: 190

Gasohol, 96: 53

Gasoline, 97: 296, **95:** 266-267, 318-321

Gasoline engines. See Internal-combustion engines

Gates (electronics), **97:** 260-261

Gates, Bill, 95: 252

Gatorade (drink), **95:** 315

Geese, Canada. See Canada geese

Gene expression, 95: 93

Gene regulation, 95: 93

Gene therapy, 96: 85, 270, **95:** 132-136, 274-275

Genes

Alzheimer's disease, **97:** 236-238, 262-263

ataxia telangiectasia, **97:** 238

cancer, **97:** 238, 239, 244, **96:** 75-85, 266, **95:** 272

cheetah genetic variation, **95:** 44-59

cloning, **95:** 92, 96-101

DNA testing, **96:** 164

embryo growth, **95:** 238-239

mapping, **97:** 238, **96:** 269, **95:** 208, 273-274

obesity, **97:** 244-245, 249 (il.), **96:** 282

patents, **95:** 298

plant development, **97:** 193-194, **96:** 232-233, **95:** 240-241

premature aging, **97:** 239

retrovirus, **95:** 124-130, 136-137

risk-taking behavior, **97:** 262

see also **DNA; Drugs; Gene therapy; Genetic engineering; Genetics; Medical research**

Genetic engineering

agriculture, **97:** 165-166, **96:** 198-199, **95:** 206-208

extinction problem, **96:** 182

global warming solutions, **96:** 152

Medfly control, **97:** 238-239

medical research, **96:** 276-278

see also **Cloning; Gene therapy; Genes**

Genetic medicine. See Gene therapy; Genetic engineering

Genetic variation, 95: 46, 50-58

GENETICS, 97: 236-239, **96:** 266-270, **95:** 272-275

criminal behavior, **97:** 269

Nobel Prizes, **97:** 189, **95:** 234-235

see also **Genes; Human Genome**

Project

Geoengineering, 96: 145-157

GEOLOGY, 97: 240-243, **96:** 270-276, **95:** 276-279

books, **96:** 235, **95:** 243

see also **Caves; Earthquakes; Fossil studies; Oceanography; Plate tectonics; Volcanoes**

Geopressured energy, 95: 191

Geosat (satellite), **97:** 253

Geothermal energy, 95: 191-193, 201, 202

Gershwin (software), **97:** 153

Getty, Jeff, 97: 246

Geysers, 95: 191

Gibberellin (chemical), **97:** 201 (il.)

Giganotosaurus (dinosaur), **97:** 232-233

Gilbert, Hurricane, 96: 34 (il.)

Gilman, Alfred, 96: 224

GL 229 (space object), **97:** 179-180

Glaciers, 97: 114, **96:** 91 (il.)

Glass, 97: 226, **96:** 324-328

Glass cockpit, 97: 132

Glimepiride (drug), **97:** 217

Global Positioning System, 95: 308

Global warming, 96: 220-221

Antarctica studies, **97:** 108-111, 113

ecological evidence, **96:** 251-252

fossil fuels, **95:** 180-181

geoengineering, **96:** 145-155, **95:** 259

ocean effects, **96:** 283-284

refrigerants, **96:** 317

scientific consensus, **97:** 185-186

volcano effects, **95:** 118

see also **Climate; Greenhouse effect**

Globular star clusters, 97: 39

Glucose, 97: 217, **95:** 258, 281-282, 315, 316

Glucose polymers, 95: 316

Glutamic acid decarboxylase, 95: 282

Glyphs, 95: 216

Goldin, Daniel, 97: 97-98

Gondwanaland (land mass), **97:** 103

Goodall, Jane, 96: 105-117

Gorillas, Mountain, 97: 210-211

Go-teams (aviation), **97:** 130-131

Graham, Matthew David, 97: 192

Grand Awards, 97: 191

Grand Canyon National Park, 97: 213

Grass, 97: 201 (il.)

Gravitation

antimatter research, **97:** 259

black holes, **95:** 14-27

expansion of universe, **97:** 41

lenses, **97:** 40, 179, **95:** 224-225

waves, **95:** 23 (il.), 27, 234

Gravity. See Gravitation

Gray wolves, 96: 244-245

Great Lakes, 97: 72, 75 (il.)

Great Lakes Water Quality Guidance Regulations (1995), **97:** 83-84

Greenhouse effect, 97: 108, 185, **96:** 145-146, 220, 317, **95:** 118

see also **Global warming**

Greenland Ice Core Project, 95: 233

Greenpeace, 96: 188 (il.)

Grissom, Virgil I. (Gus), 97: 92

Growth factors (cancer), **96:** 78-79

Guano, 96: 100, 102

Guns. See Firearms

H

Habitats, 97: 211-213, 220-221, **96:** 191

see also **Ecology**

Hadrons, 96: 286

Hair, 97: 289-293

Hair cells, 97: 277, 278 (il.), 280

Haise, Fred W., Jr., 97: 87, 90, 91

Hale-Bopp, Comet, 97: 177-178

Halley, Comet, 96: 14-16

Hallucinations, 95: 292-293

Halo (space object), **97:** 179

Handwriting recognition technology, 95: 249

Hanford, William E., 97: 214

Hanks, Tom, 97: 87, 95

Hantavirus, 95: 280, 283 (il.)

Hares, 97: 219-220

Hawaii wildlife, 96: 174

Hawkes, Jacquetta, 97: 214

Hawking, Stephen, 95: 24-25

Hawking radiation, 95: 23 (il.), 25

Head-mounted displays, 95: 32 (il.), 35-37, 40-43

Headphones, 97: 279, 280

Health, Public. See Public health

Hearing loss, 97: 276-280

Heart attacks. See Heart disease

Heart disease, 97: 245-248, 250-252, 251-252, **96:** 270, 277-278, **95:** 259, 285

Heart failure, Congestive, 97: 228-229

Heart surgery, 96: 250-251

Heart transplants, 97: 247

Heat energy. See Geothermal energy

Heat loss, and windows, 96: 324-328

Helictites (formations), **96:** 96

Heliostats, 97: 221, **95:** 194

Helsingius, Johan, 96: 295

Hemoglobin, 97: 250, **96:** 236

Hepatitis, 95: 258

Herbivores, 96: 85

Heredity, WBE, 96: 341-350

see also **Genes; Genetics**

Heterosexual AIDS transmission, 95: 298

Higgs boson, 96: 288, **95:** 289

Higgs field, 96: 145

High blood pressure. See Hypertension

Hildoceras (animal), **95:** 78, 80

Hill, Julian W., 97: 214

Hippocampus, 95: 239-240

HIV. See AIDS

Hominids. See Prehistoric people

Homo erectus (hominid), **96:** 201, **95:** 208-209

Homo habilis (hominid), **96:** 201-202, 208

Homo sapiens, **95:** 209, 211, 220

Homocysteine (amino acid), **97:** 250

Honey bees, 97: 220 (il.)

Horites, 97: 172-174

Hormones, 95: 206-207

Hornets, 97: 220 (il.)

Horses, 97: 166, 195 (il.), **96:** 279-280, **95:** 219

Hot springs, 95: 191

Housing construction, 97: 161, 224

Hubble constant, 97: 30-31, 34, **96:**

Index

205 (il.), **95:** 218-219
Muons (subatomic particles), **97:** 107
Mushrooms, 97: 165 (il.)
Music, and hearing loss, 97: 276-280
Mutation, 96: 77-85, 125, **95:** 234
Myosin (protein), **97:** 197
Myst (software), **95:** 250-251
Myxomatosis, 97: 209

N

Nanotechnology, 97: 161
Nanotubes, 97: 201-202, **95:** 245-246
NASA. See **National Aeronautics and Space Administration**
Nathaniel B. Palmer (ship), **97:** 101, 102
National Aeronautics and Space Administration, 97: 272-274, **96:** 298-302, **95:** 303-308
comet threat to Earth, **96:** 14, 25
extrasolar planets, **97:** 183
Lovell interview, **97:** 90-99
origin of life studies, **97:** 57
virtual reality systems, **95:** 39, 41 (il.), 42 (il.)
see also **Hubble Space Telescope; Space probes**
National Biological Service, 96: 190
National High Magnetic Field Laboratory, 96: 289-291
National Ignition Facility, 96: 254
National Institutes of Health, 95: 298
National Science and Technology Council, 95: 299
National Transportation Safety Board, U.S., 97: 129-141
Nationwide Rivers Inventory, 95: 74
Native Americans, 97: 169-170, 174-175, **96:** 208-211, **95:** 215-218
see also **Archaeology; Maya**
Natural gas, 96: 54-55, **95:** 180, 184, 202
Natural history, 97: 199, **96:** 235, **95:** 243
see also **Prehistoric animals; Prehistoric people**
Natural selection. See **Evolution**
Naturally sparkling water, 97: 282
Navigator (computer), **97:** 147 (il.), 150
NEAR (spacecraft), **97:** 273 (il.), 274
Near-Earth objects, 96: 25
Nebulae, 97: 117 (il.), 121-124 (ils.)
NEC Corp., 95: 40-41
Neolithic Age, 95: 218
Neptune, 96: 214-215
Nerve cells. See **Neurons**
Net, The. See **Internet**
Netscape (software), **97:** 153-154, 204
Network computers, 97: 205
Networks, Computer. See **Computer networks**
Neurons, 95: 239-240
Neuroscience. see **Brain; Neurons**
Neutrino detectors, 97: 257 (il.)
Neutrinos, 97: 106-107, **96:** 136, **95:** 141, 142
Neutron stars, 95: 20-22
see also **Pulsars**
Neutrons, 96: 121, 132, 136, 223-224, **95:** 292

New Madrid earthquakes, 96: 270-271
Newton, Sir Isaac, 95: 15
Newton MessagePad (computer), **95:** 249
NGC 4258 (galaxy), **96:** 219
NGC 4261 (galaxy), **97:** 180 (il.), **95:** 25 (il.)
NGC 4571 (galaxy), **97:** 36
NGC 7252 (galaxy), **95:** 223-226
Nifedipine (drug), **97:** 245-248
Nighthawks, 97: 64
Nintendo of America, Inc., 97: 209, **96:** 241, **95:** 41-42
Nitric oxide, 97: 250, **96:** 261
Nitrogen dioxide, 96: 260, 261
NOAA-13 (satellite), **95:** 307
Nobel Prizes, 97: 188-189, **96:** 223-224, **95:** 141, 146, 234-235
Noble gases, 96: 326
Norvir (drug), **97:** 216
Novae, 95: 221-222
see also **Supernovae**
Nuclear energy, 95: 159, 161-163, 163, 181-182, 202
see also **Fusion, Nuclear**
Nuclear magnetic resonance imaging, 96: 291
Nuclear reactors. See **Nuclear energy**
Nuclear transfer, 97: 194-196
Nuclear weapons, 96: 119-120, 127-128, 296-297, **95:** 299, 300
Nucleic acids, 97: 47-52
Nucleotides, 97: 47, 48 (il.), 52, 161
Nüesslein-Volhard, Christiane, 97: 189, 190 (il.)
NUTRITION, 97: 251-252, **96:** 282-283, **95:** 284-285
gene-altered food, **95:** 207-208
mad-cow disease, **97:** 164, 265-266
sports drinks, **95:** 315-317

O

Obesity, 97: 244-245, 249 (il.), **96:** 267-268, 282
Object-oriented programs, 97: 154
OCEANOGRAPHY, 97: 253-255, **96:** 283-285, **95:** 286-287
Antarctica studies, **97:** 113
comet collision with Earth, **96:** 22-25
deep-sea life, **96:** 230-231
energy sources, **97:** 223, **96:** 255
iron fertilization, **97:** 253-255, **96:** 145-149, 151-152, **95:** 259
origin of life, **97:** 54-56
sea-level rise, **96:** 275, **95:** 286
seafloor volcanoes, **95:** 116
submarine canyons, **95:** 277
see also **El Niño; Oil spills**
Oceans. See **Oceanography**
Octane rating, 95: 319
Office of Technology Assessment, 97: 267-268
Oil. See **Motor oil; Petroleum**
Oil pipelines, 96: 259, **95:** 267
Oil spills, 97: 229, 294, **96:** 259, **95:** 267
Oil wells, 95: 286-287
Olah, George A., 96: 223
Olestra, 97: 251 (il.)

Olive oil, 96: 283
Olivine, 97: 240
Olympiads. See **Science student awards**
Oncogenes, 96: 78-79, 82, **95:** 127, 284
see also **Cancer**
On-line computer services. See **Computer networks**
Oort Cloud, 97: 177, 178, **96:** 15 (il.), 16, 18
Operating systems (computer), **97:** 151-153, 206
Opossums, 97: 62 (il.)
Oppenheimer, J. Robert, 95: 20-21
Optical computing, 97: 159
Optical digital recording. See **CD-ROM**
Optical fibers. See **Fiber optics**
Optics, 97: 36, 226
Oracle Corp., 97: 150, 205
Oral tolerization, 95: 280-281
Organ transplants. See **Transplants**
Organochlorines (compounds), **97:** 79-81, 228, 285-286
Organophosphates (compounds), **97:** 228, 285, 286
Orion Nebula, 97: 121 (il.), 122 (il.), **95:** 226 (il.)
Orthograde posture, 97: 167-168
Osiris (deity), **96:** 203
Ossicles, 97: 277, 278
Osteoporosis, 97: 216-217, **95:** 272-273
Ovarian cancer, 96: 84
Oviraptor (dinosaur), **97:** 234, **96:** 263
Owls, Spotted, 97: 213, **96:** 190
Oxidation, 97: 291, 292
Oxygen, 95: 238
Oxygenates, 95: 320-321
Ozone layer depletion, 96: 146, 155-157
amphibian deaths, **95:** 253
Antarctic, **97:** 111-112, 186-188, **96:** 222, 317, **95:** 233
Arctic, **96:** 317
Nobel Prize, **97:** 188
refrigerants, **96:** 315-324
Ozone pollution, 96: 46, 261, **95:** 318, 321

P

p53 (protein), **96:** 81, 85
Pacific Ocean, 96: 145, 174, 283-284, **95:** 277
Packard, David, 97: 215
Paleo-Indians, 97: 174-175
Paleolithic era, 96: 204, 206-207
Paleontology, 95: 178, 78
see also **Dinosaurs; Fossil studies**
Paleozoic Era, 95: 178
Pancreatic cancer, 97: 239, **96:** 84
Pancreatic transplants, 97: 247, 248-249
Pangaea (continent), **97:** 233, **96:** 276, **95:** 276
Panic disorder, 97: 264
Panthers, Florida, 97: 213
Paper, 95: 314, 325-328
Parallel processing, 97: 149
Paranthropus robustus (hominid), **96:** 201-202
Parkinson's disease, 97: 247, **96:** 280

Index

Index

Acknowledgments

The publishers of *Science Year* gratefully acknowledge the courtesy of the following artists, photographers, publishers, institutions, agencies, and corporations for the illustrations in this volume. Credits should read from top to bottom, left to right on their respective pages. All entries marked with an asterisk (*) denote illustrations created exclusively for *Science Year*. All maps, charts, and diagrams were prepared by the *Science Year* staff unless otherwise noted.

2	NASA; Sandia National Laboratories
3	NASA; Johan Reinhard, National Geographic Society; AP/Wide World
4	James R. Foster; Andy Sacks, Tony Stone Images
5	Didier Massonnet, French Space Agency; Karen Warkentin
10	© Jean-Marie Chauvet, Sygma
11	Galen Rowell; Glenn Randall, Natural Selection
12	© Jean-Marie Chauvet, Sygma
16	*Horse Heads* by an unknown artist. 32,000 to 30,000 B.C. Chauvet Cave near Vallon-Pont-D'Arc, France. (© Jean-Marie Chauvet, Sygma); Ancient Art & Architecture Collection
17	*Bison* by an unknown artist. 32,000 to 11,000 B.C. Altamira, Spain (SCALA/Art Resource); Logan Museum at Beloit College (Randall White); *Horse* by an unknown artist. About 15,000 B.C. Lascaux Cave. Dordogne, France. (Ancient Art & Architecture Collection)
18	Jan Wills*
20	*Venus with a Horn* by an unknown artist. 20,000 B.C. Musée d'Aquitaine, Bordeaux, France (Erich Lessing from Art Resource)
21	© Jean Vertut
24	Jan Wills*
28	NASA
32-34	Dan Swanson, Van Garde Imagery*
36-37	NASA
38	National Optical Astronomy Observatory
40	James R. Foster
42	W. Warren, Westlight
43	Barbara Cousins*
45	J. William Schopf, University of California at Los Angeles; Barbara Cousins*; CNRI/SPL from Photo Researchers
46	Barbara Cousins*
47	University of California at San Diego
48-50	Barbara Cousins*
51	Chip Clark
53	Barbara Cousins*
55	James A. Sugar
59	Alfred B. Thomas, Animals Animals; Glenn Randall, Natural Selection; David Charles, Gamma/Liaison; Charles Palek, Animals Animals
62	Jeff Lepore, Photo Researchers; Alfred B. Thomas, Animals Animals
63	C. C. Lockwood, Animals Animals; Robert Noonan, Photo Researchers
65	Glenn Randall, Natural Selection; Judd Cooney, Natural Selection; Renee Lynn, Photo Researchers
68	Melanie Lawson; Frans Lanting, Photo Researchers
69	Daniel J. Cox, Natural Selection; Michael H. Francis; Terry G. Murphy, Animals Animals
73	Robert E. Schwerzel
76	Estelle Carol, Carol-Simpson Productions; International Joint Commission, Toronto, Ontario
82	John & Ann Mahan; Detroit Edison Company
83	Robert Visser, Greenpeace
86	© Timothy Greenfield-Sanders
87	NASA
88	NASA; Dan Rest*; NASA
90	Ralph Morse/*Life* Magazine © Time Inc.
93	NASA; Dan Rest*; AP/Wide World
94	NASA; Dan Rest*; NASA
96	NASA; Dan Rest*
97	NASA; Dan Rest*; NASA
98	NASA; Dan Rest*
100-105	Galen Rowell
107	S. Klipper, National Science Foundation
108	A. Hawthorne, National Science Foundation; J. Lopez, National Science Foundation
109	A. Hawthorne, National Science Foundation
110	National Science Foundation; A. Hawthorne, National Science Foundation

112	Judd A. Case, Saint Mary's College of California; Michael Woods
114	ANSMET
116	J. Hester and P. Scowen, Arizona State University/NASA
118	P. James, University of Toledo and James Lee, University of Colorado/NASA
120	C.R. O'Dell, Rice University/NASA
121	H. Bond, Space Science Telescope Institute/NASA
122	J.P. Harrington and K.J. Borkowski, University of Maryland/NASA; C.R. O'Dell, Rice University/NASA
123	J. Hester, Arizona State University/NASA
124	D. Macchetto, European Space Agency/NASA
125	J.N. Bahcall, Institute for Advanced Study/NASA
126	R. Gilmozzi, Space Telescope European Coordinating Facility and S. Ewald, JPL/NASA
127	R. Williams and the Hubble Deep Field Team, Space Science Telescope Institute/NASA
128	*Espectador* from Gamma/Liaison
132	Michael Springer, Gamma/Liaison; Epix From Sygma
133	Bob Jackson, Gamma/Liaison
136	National Transportation Safety Board
137	Spooner, Gamma/Liaison
140	Dan Moore, Flight Safety International
142	Andy Sacks, Tony Stone Images
143	David Young Wolff, Tony Stone Images; Intel Corporation
144	UPI/Bettmann
146	University of Pennsylvania School of Engineering and Applied Science; IBM Corporation; David Hanover, Tony Stone Images
147	Carnegie Mellon University
148	Sony Electronics, Inc.
151	Advanced Recognition Technologies, Inc.
152-156	John Lambert*
157	VITA, Inc.
159	AP/Wide World
160	General Electric Company
162	Lamont-Doherty Earth Observatory
163	Johns Hopkins University; Technology Recognition Systems; M. L. J. Crawford, Sensory Sciences Center
164	Scott Bauer, USDA
165	Silsoe Research Institute
167	AP/Wide World
168	Phillip V. Tobias, University of Witwatersand, Johannesburg, South Africa
170	Johan Reinhard, National Geographic Society
171	SJS Archaeological Services
172	University of Pennsylvania Museum
173	Aaron Levin, Combined Caesarea Expeditions
174	Jean-Claude Aunos, Gamma/Liaison; WORLD BOOK illustration by Birney Lettrick
176	NASA; David Malin, Anglo-Australian Observatory, Reuters/Archive Photos
177-180	NASA
181	Gerald Cecil, University of North Carolina
183	Geoffrey W. Marcy, San Francisco State University
187	Benjamin Santer, Lawrence Livermore National Laboratories; NOAA
189	Reuters/Archive Photos
190	AP/Wide World; Max Planck Institut from Sipa Press; Reuters/Archive Photos
192	Westinghouse Foundation
195	Michel Peissel; George B. Schaller, Wildlife Conservation Society
196	David Grimaldi, American Museum of Natural History
200	R. Michael Garavito, Michigan State University
201	Richard P. Pharis, University of Calgary
202	Scott Oliver, et. al., University of Toronto
205	Thomson Consumer Electronics
207	Central Research Laboratories; Technology Recognition Systems; Technology Recognition Systems; Central

351

World Book Encyclopedia, Inc., provides high-quality educational and reference products for the family and school. They include THE WORLD BOOK MEDICAL ENCYCLOPEDIA, a 1,040-page, fully illustrated family health reference; THE WORLD BOOK OF MATH POWER, a two-volume set that helps students and adults build math skills; THE WORLD BOOK OF WORD POWER, a two-volume set that is designed to help your entire family write and speak more successfully; and the HOW TO STUDY video, a presentation of key study skills with information students need to succeed in school. For further information, write to WORLD BOOK ENCYCLOPEDIA, INC., 525 W. Monroe St., Chicago, IL 60661.